Disclaimer: The opinions presented herein are solely those of the author except where specifically noted. Nothing in the book should be construed as investment advice or guidance, as it is not intended as investment advice or guidance, nor is it offered as such. It is solely the opinion of the writer, who is not an investment professional. The strategies presented in the book may be unsuitable for you, and you should consult a professional where such consultation is appropriate. The publisher/ author disclaims any implied warranty or applicability of the contents for any particular purpose. The publisher/author shall not be liable for any commercial or incidental damages of any kind or nature.

First edition published October 2009
Second edition published January 2010

Oftwominds.com
P.O. Box 4727
Berkeley, California 94704

www.oftwominds.com

Survival+:
Structuring Prosperity for Yourself and the Nation

Charles Hugh Smith

This book is dedicated to the readers and contributors of the oftwominds.com weblog, who have taught me so much in the past four years.

A special thank-you to Unix Ronin for (perhaps imprudently) suggesting that I turn the "Survival+" series of weblog entries into a book, and to the following for contributing to the content of the book: Zeus Yiamouyiannis, Harun Ibrahim, Cheryl Adelman, Richard Metzger, Kevin Dodson, Steven Rodriguez, Pam and Pat, Don England, Eric Hoyle, Gary Baker, Matt Skerbitz, Noah Cicero and U. Doran.

The following readers were kind enough to help correct and edit the text: thank you, Judy Thorpe, Wesley McCollough, Ioan Vlad, William Blair, Ludovic Viger, Steve Allen, Kevin Abbey and Richard Pauli.

Of the hundreds of readers who have been kind enough to share ideas and experiences with me, I will mention a few and beg the forgiveness of the many who are not named here (list is random): Michael Goodfellow, Kevin Mercadante, Alberto Rodriquez, Eric Andrews. Chuck Davey, Craig McCarty, John Brennan, Protagoras, B.C., Dale Edgar, Chris Sullins, Jed Hirota, Albert T., John Branch, Fred Roper, Jim Strong, Gene McCreary, Joe Hecksel, Elaine Douglass, Jim Twamley, Rhone, Ernesto M., Ian Lind, Jim Erler, Fred Roster, Steve Toma, Riley Thorpe, Peter N., Scott Cole, Brendan O'Connell, Chris Hudson, Janet M., Dan Kolton, Bart Dessart, Maggie Risk, Eugenio Minoli, Mike Dixon, Grant Palmer, Ken K., Miriam Jannol, Phillip Hext, Rainer Hauer, Tony Tsai, Jaanus Leoste, Steve Reynolds, Subuddh Parekh, Michael Surkan, James DePrisco, Trey Standish, Jeff Ray, Robert Zenith, John Shone, M.D. Creekmore, Brian Hopkins, Maclean, Rich Hollabaugh, Mark Dickson, Nina (ArtLifeWest), Tom Spartz, Lee Bentley, Edward Dinovo, David Arth, Mark Arthur, Michael Setty, Paula Hay, Michael Schweisguth, Patrick Killelea, Ruthann, Scott Detrick, R. Stephen Dorsey, Tom Peifer, Dennis Feucht, Walter Howard, Michael Hamilton, Megamike, Allen Jirikowic, David Cazin, Brian, Chad Woolley, John Foster M.D., Charley Fleetham, David Binkowski, David Vaughn, Dennis Gaudet, John Uhlir, Doug Walden, Joseph B., Kevin Kelley, Marinite, Strawgold, Terence Parker, Darrell Clarke, Cindy Furukawa, and Bill Murath, for the sounds that calm my cluttered office and mind.

Table of Contents

Section Two   **239**

Introduction

Since launching my blog www.oftwominds.com in May 2005, nothing seemed more important than warning readers that the unsustainably leveraged credit-mad global financial system was poised to break down. Once the system finally crashed in late 2008, my goal switched to writing a practical guide for not just surviving the coming Great Transformation but prospering: a concept I called **Survival+** (Plus). This requires liberating ourselves from failed models of credit expansion, resource depletion, financial looting and a counterfeit prosperity built entirely on debt.

I immediately ran into several great difficulties. Many others had foreseen the same calamity, and their focus narrowed on individual survival: relocating to a remote/sustainable spot and preparing for societal collapse by stockpiling self-defense and food.

While prudent and practical on a short-term timeline, this response struck me as incomplete on several levels. Most importantly, stockpiling six months' supplies would not sustain anyone through a 20-year Crisis and Transformation; their own Crisis was simply being delayed a relatively short time. In other words: "what happens in month seven"?

Secondly, many "survivalist" proponents focus on individual preparation, as if a single person or household can prosper without a stable, caring community for reciprocal support. This notion ran counter not just to my own experience but to all of human history. While I understood the desire to "opt out" and become an Isolationist--a solution to general turmoil which has roots going back to the dissolution of the Roman Empire and the Warring States era in ancient China--I felt a more practical, longer-term option to Isolationism should also be presented.

The second great difficulty is that individuals, households and communities exist in larger units: city-states, counties, nations and continents. Even if nation-states were to break apart, the world would remain tightly interconnected. Events, weather, shortages and surpluses in distant places would continue to impact us all. States (by which I mean all forms of government) will continue to extend control over resources and wealth.

Trade has been a key component of security and prosperity since the dawn of civilization. Long before fossil fuels dominated the global economy, land and sea trade in both goods and innovations bound Asia, the Mideast and Europe. Thus a retreat to isolated islands of self-sufficiency, while understandable and practical on one level, does not align with what history teaches us about prosperity. Prosperity ultimately depends on stable communities, surplus production and trade. These essentials have been largely ignored in analyses of the coming Great Transformation.

Thus our individual survival and prosperity are inextricably bound up in larger contexts: we cannot just ignore community, State and trade forces as if they will cease to exist. Viewing ourselves in isolation is ultimately misleading.

That is why I subtitled this book "Structuring Prosperity for Yourself and the Nation." To believe that we can prosper individually without regard for the actions of our fellow citizens and the State (government) is simply not practical. Yes, a handful of very rugged people have the experience required to live in the deepest remains of wilderness; but the wilderness cannot support more than a handful of people, and most of us do not have the requisite skills or ruggedness to survive that splendid isolation.

This, then, is a practical book for the rest of us.

As I organized the book, another great difficulty quickly arose. I realized that the way a problem is phrased implicitly stakes out the eventual solution. As a result, the greatest challenge in understanding our plight, both as individuals and communities, is essentially conceptual. The forces which benefit most from the status quo are pouring all their prodigious resources into framing the "problems" in such a way that the "obvious solutions" leave their own power, influence and wealth intact.

Lest you wonder how this works, recall that all through the initial phase of the financial crisis in 2008, the mainstream media and standard-issue financial punditry (SIFP) blamed the entire crisis on foolish low-income homebuyers who had chosen to finance their purchases with subprime mortgages.

Framed in this way, the "problem" appeared to be caused by credulous citizens in the lower socio-economic levels. The "solution" was thus to eliminate these people from the pool of potential homebuyers, and auction off their foreclosed homes to worthier buyers.

But subsequent events revealed this framing of the problem to be highly selective: the "problem" extended far beyond feckless subprime borrowers into the top rungs of American Capitalism: the money-center and investment banks, and a politically driven absence of oversight by the very governmental agencies tasked with protecting the public.

The status quo's convenient "framing of the problem" insured that any "solutions" would leave their power, wealth and influence entirely intact; only the impoverished subprimers would suffer, not those who profited so immensely from the housing/credit bubble.

It was thus clear that a practical analysis of the crisis and coming Transformation requires a deep understanding of how "solutions" are set in the framing of the "problem." Indeed, what is "obvious" must be questioned on the deepest levels, for what is "obvious" has two powerful characteristics: it can be managed/manipulated via the mass media, and it directs "solutions" which leave the rentier-financial Power Elite (what I call *the Plutocracy*) intact. (Key concepts are italicized when introduced.)

The nature of propaganda in a so-called free State must then be explored in depth as well.

The last great difficulty is also conceptual. It is relatively straightforward to present the causes of the coming global crisis: resource depletion, disintegration of the credit bubble, demographics, etc. Many books do a fine job of outlining the nature of these interlocking crises.

The books attempting to present solutions typically focus on either individuals (along the lines of "get rich as the world falls apart") or idealized policy "fixes" based on narrow academic understandings of large-scale structures (recommendations on G-20 trade policies, etc). The flaw in both approaches is that neither flows from what I call an *integrated understanding* of the actual problems. Practical solutions must follow from this integrated understanding. Without such a comprehensive conceptual framework, then all proposed solutions will be ungrounded and thus dangerously misleading.

Any "solution" which ignores key elements of the problem is doomed to solve nothing. As in our example of the so-called "subprime crisis," the "solution" of limiting uncreditworthy borrowers did nothing to address the actual problems: highly profitable fraudulent practices riddling every level of the mortgage/rating/securities industries, perverse incentives that created unprecedented opportunities for *windfall exploitation, over-reach* and looting.

I cannot claim that reaching such an integrated understanding will be easy. Many of the concepts presented here may be unfamiliar and thus difficult to grasp at first. Many are so alien to status quo "explanations" that they may well strike you as the opposite of "obvious." But since I have thought about these concepts and forces for years, they seem "obvious" to me. In the language of our Declaration of Independence: I hold these truths to be self-evident.

So let us begin.

We stand on the threshold of a Great Transformation that will unfold over the next 20 years--a generation. The exact turn and sequence of events is unknown, but a clear-eyed appraisal of the forces, trends and cycles already at work will help us, collectively and as individuals, weather the challenges and turn what could be a catastrophe into a positive transformation.

To the status quo understanding of how our world works, this appraisal will be anything but "obvious." (Sorting out what is "obvious" is a big part of the analysis that follows.)

A number of other writers have addressed preparing for the Depression that has just begun. These books are, within their limited scope, practical and useful. Other books, most notably The Upside of Down: Catastrophe, Creativity, and the Renewal of Civilization, address the positive potential for collapse.

(All books referenced in the text are listed in "Further Reading.")

This book, imperfect as it is, aims at a different, far more comprehensive goal: once we understand all the complex forces at work, then we can structure a response on all three levels: household/family, community and nation. For if there is anything we can confidently predict, it's that the nation's crumbling finances will drastically affect every individual, every family and every community.

Attempting to combine a structural/historical analysis with an abstract conceptual analysis and a practical framework of response is risky and perhaps even foolhardy; the typical approach would be to undertake only one narrow piece of such a comprehensive project. But then the opportunity for an integrated understanding would be lost, and hence my gamble to integrate not just history and the tangible world but also the political and internal/experiential realms.

Just as I will integrate the responses on three levels--individual, community and nation--I present the analysis on three levels-- conceptual, tangible and internal (experiential/psychological/spiritual).

As if this wasn't enough to get me in trouble, I am also incorporating essays previously posted on www.oftwominds.com which include personal stories from readers and occasionally from my own experiences. I realize it may be jarring for you the reader to move from the highly conceptual to the personal, but I see no other way to combine the analytical and the practical in one volume.

Perhaps this anachronistic structure reflects my own anachronistic experience: while earning a degree in Comparative Philosophy (the study of both Eastern and Western traditions) I was also learning the construction trades. I became a builder for seven years and then *opted out* some 20 years ago for the same reasons I describe in this book.

Readers of my blog occasionally accuse me of possessing a puritanical streak, that is, a preference for sacrifice, frugality, physical skills, prudent planning and a contrarian emphasis on inner spiritual strengths rather than conspicuous wealth/personal aggrandizement. I plead guilty on all counts and turn to my family's religious roots for my defense. My grandparents forbade the reading of the Sunday newspaper comics as frivolous and served as lay missionaries in Central America.

While I personally don't find anything in Jesus' words or deeds which forbid the small honest pleasures of life, I do find plenty which condemns the lies, cheating, misrepresentation, fraud and willful obfuscation at the heart of our financial and political system's *simulacrum* of democracy and prosperity.

The notion that morality has anything to do with the coming collapse of the U.S. economy and political Elite has been entirely marginalized; ethics has no role or value in a system which only recognizes GDP, higher spending, bank profits, etc. and which only cheers "growth" as measured by these (easily manipulated) metrics.

To include morality and ethics in an analysis of our financial system is not just anachronistic but subversive in the sense that all such ideas have been driven out of the public sphere. That the concepts of sin and just desserts (in a Buddhistic term, karma) might have some purchase on our situation has been safely marginalized. This is indeed strange in a nation that has long welcomed freedom of worship and religious expression.

One does not even need to be a believer in any particular faith to sense the spiritual/ethical rot at the center of American finance and the politics which it controls. Nor does it require faith to recognize that this spiritual/ethical rot has consequences in the real world. Even those with no religious leanings whatsoever can detect the status quo's intense desire to suppress any moral/ethical lines of inquiry into the sources of their power and wealth.

Perhaps my worldview has made me overly skeptical of the rewards offered by the "American Dream" of debt-based consumption. I sense not limitless joy but a powerful divergence between the promised fulfillment and the reality of a society plagued by insecurity, declining integrity and loss of meaning, an over-medicated culture suffering from poor health and rampant drug abuse (legal and illegal), and a society harboring a peculiar penchant for resentful denial and adolescent fits of pique, rage, entitlement and self-destruction.

As an alternative to this highly profitable but doomed-to-disappoint definition of "prosperity" and "happiness," the goal presented here is what I term *full spectrum prosperity*. Simply put, much of true prosperity cannot be measured by rising GDP or other financial statistics. In this sense, it lies beyond the understanding and reach of the status quo and indeed of economics.

Since I hold no rung in the status quo other than moderate-income taxpayer, I am not beholden to any academic, State or corporate powers. I am self-employed and need not meet with any academic approval, assuage any political authority or satisfy any corporate publisher. I do not expect a lucrative publishing contract and am not seeking one. I don't expect anyone will buy the "pay the author fair value" version of this work though I do hope the free version gains wide distribution. I have no interest in appearing on TV or radio or in the mainstream media. The ideas speak for themselves and thus have no need for a spokesperson.

As a final note, I want you to know this book is not "dumbed down" in any fashion. Highly abstract, difficult-to-describe concepts are presented full-strength; no punches are pulled for the sake of increasing the audience or easing the challenges such a comprehensive book presents.

My goal is to provide an *integrated understanding* of why the devolution and insolvency of the U.S. economy is not just a possibility but an inevitability. But rather than feel the despair experienced by the status quo at this prospect, I am energized by a new understanding of prosperity and security based on the founding principles of our nation. This understanding is beyond the tired boundaries of "liberal" and "conservative" or indeed, of any ideological labels.

Much of this analysis might be familiar to you, or it might be entirely alien. In either case, I hope to change your understanding of our nation and our world's potential for sustainable prosperity.

I do not claim to provide solutions or answers per se, but I do present a framework which arises from this analysis like water from a spring. If this book furthers our collective discussion on the coming transformation, I will consider it a success.

Key concepts in this Introduction:
Plutocracy (rentier-financial Power Elite)
Integrated understanding
Windfall exploitation
Over-reach
Simulacrum (synonyms: sham, facsimile, counterfeit)
Full spectrum prosperity

Chapter One: An Overview

A great clash between what we are told is unfolding and what is actually unfolding lies just ahead.

The status quo "Powers That Be" and its mainstream media repeatedly insist that:

- We have abundant cheap energy for a long time to come; shortages or permanently costly energy is decades away. We have plenty of time for technological wonders to arise and replace petroleum.

- The Social Security and Medicare entitlements promised to all Americans, though totaling some $50 trillion in excess of projected tax revenues, will be paid; all that is needed are modest policy adjustments.

- The current financial meltdown was unexpected and could not have been foreseen; it is a temporary "bad patch" which has already been fixed by government intervention and modest policy/regulatory adjustments.

- Public and private credit and debt can continue expanding three times faster than GDP indefinitely; rising credit and debt are the essential lifeblood of permanent growth.

- Environmental issues such as the stripping of the world's fisheries, dead zones in the Chesapeake Bay, dwindling fresh water aquifers, etc. can all be fixed with modest policy adjustments.

- The consumerist culture that has evolved over the past 60 years is a natural and highly successful perfection of capitalism, prosperity and American values; Americans are the happiest, most prosperous people on the planet.

- The fast-growing epidemic of obesity and related chronic diseases in the U.S. are puzzling and worrisome, but we have the finest healthcare system in the world.

Yet all of the above is demonstrably false.

In reality, the decline of abundant cheap oil (oil under pressure in supergiant fields) has already begun. The iron laws of demographics dictate the promised entitlements cannot be paid and that Medicare is only a few short years away from insolvency. The current financial meltdown was not only easily predictable, it was inevitable, as the consequences of systemic fraud, deception, embezzlement, misrepresentation, collusion, debauchery of credit, exponential expansions of risk, debt and speculative leverage could not be held off forever.

The reduction of American culture and values to a one-dimensional "consumerism is the highest good" was not natural, and rather than produce the perfection of capitalism, it has produced the perfection of crony capitalism, monopoly capital and an ever-expanding State beholden to an Elite which owns or controls the vast majority of the productive assets, wealth, income and lawmaking machinery of the U.S.

Rather than being the happiest people on the planet, Americans are visibly unhappy, anxious, angry, depressed, distracted and all too often heavily sedated with powerful psychotropic medications.

This is not to question the positive contributions made by psychiatric medications to those suffering from psychiatric disorders; but we should question the idea that tens of millions of our citizenry (including children) are suffering from serious psychiatric disorders. We should wonder if the overzealous dispensation of such drugs masks cultural rather than psychiatric disorders, and an unspoken desire to "treat" these cultural disorders in a relatively low-cost fashion by numbing the patients' awareness of their own alienation, anxiety and unhappiness.

Rather than having the finest healthcare system in the world, we have the most perniciously incentivized system in the industrialized world, a system which consumes a staggering 16% of the nation's entire output but which provides little to no healthcare for tens of millions of citizens and which supplies incredibly costly but largely ineffective care to the elderly covered by an increasingly unaffordable Medicare.

Up to 40% of the entire sum spent on healthcare is paper shuffling, fraud and useless/harmful "care." Despite this vast outpouring of the nation's wealth, the health of its citizenry continues to decline in measurable ways; this vast expenditure has done nothing to stop the astonishing rise in obesity and related chronic diseases, arguably the most pressing public health issue facing the nation.

In effect, the U.S. healthcare system is bankrupting the nation even as it fails to improve the health of the citizenry at large. It is thus a stupendous failure, creating ever-smaller marginal gains with ever-greater expenditures for costly tests, drugs and treatments.

Rather than look to an increasingly unhealthy diet and lifestyle, the nation's "sick-care" system seeks ever more costly "treatments" and pharmaceutical "fixes" for complex chronic diseases which are simply not curable by "magic bullet" drugs.

Contrary to the constantly repeated assurances of The Powers That Be, modest policy and regulatory modifications are not replenishing the nation's fisheries or ground water, nor is tweaking the parameters of various systems reversing environmental and economic decline.

You may think these assessments are sensationalist, harsh or even offensive. That is not my intention. I believe the evidence is overwhelming that all these soothing contentions pressed upon us by the Powers That Be on a daily basis are in fact false.

If this assertion is true, the vast majority of what is "reported" and "consumed" as "news" and "commentary" is essentially propaganda, either conscious or subconscious.

If the status quo's intellectual justification for their dominance is fundamentally false, then we can anticipate the wholesale destruction of that justification as events undermine all the self-serving propaganda.

As a result, we will have to construct an alternative understanding of our world which aligns far more closely to reality than the current status quo's complacent faith in a decaying, failing system.

If this is true, then we have no time left for distracting little debates about policy tweaks, economic hairsplitting and modest adjustments; the time such modifications could have any measurable impact are long gone. We have run out of time for trivializing conversations along ginned-up ideological lines, "I'm a conservative and you're a liberal" and the mass media's entertainment-passed-off-as-analysis. We have also run out of time for the easy distractions of complexity itself, the unspoken idea that things are now too complex to modify in any meaningful way.

Reality, in contrast, has no problem adjusting complexity downward.

If all the fundamental contentions of the Powers That Be are demonstrably false, we are forced to ask why they press them so mightily and persuasively on us.

The answer to this critical question can be found by asking *cui bono*: to whose benefit? Although we are constantly told the system benefits all of us, that it is the very perfection of prosperity, free market capitalism and thus of happiness itself, this is also demonstrably false.

This leads to the conclusion that the entire intellectual structure which supports and enables the U.S. economy, government and culture is nonsense, and those pushing it so mightily and perseverently are doing so out of a highly refined self-interest--a self-interest which does not magically better the nation or those not fortunate enough to belong to the Elite (the Plutocracy) or to its *high-caste* technocratic workforce.

These are troubling assertions, and they require careful analysis.

Before you decide this is merely sensationalist, please read the following analysis and look into the sourced books. Compare your own lived experience and intuitions with the mass media's "happy story" that everything is just fine, minor financial perturbations have been resolved and a consumerist Utopia is still firmly in place.

It is my contention that the global meltdown has exposed the Plutocracy's *over-reach* via ever-larger bets, ever-riskier leverage and ever-larger redistributions of national income to its own coffers. To protect its interests and dominance, it must defend at all costs the intellectual framework that enables its dominance.

Thus there is a whiff of desperation in its campaign to convince the world that this is not at heart a global crisis which threatens to bring down the entire structure but a "normal" if slightly deeper recession which has already been repaired by the usual "fix" of State manipulation of interest rates and money supply.

We must be alert to the concentrated ownership/control of the mass media, and to the overwhelming need of the global Elites to reassure their restive, anxious populaces that the structure of Elite dominance and wealth is robust, secure, and in the populace's self-interest.

We must also be alert to the irony that the Elite's first task is to convince the underclasses that there is no Elite, no Powers That Be and no Plutocracy. While there is no "membership" card in the Plutocracy, the simple facts of concentrated ownership, influence and income roughly define that class. Conflicts between various segments of the Elite does not mean there is no Plutocracy--it only means that greed and over-reach naturally set up some shuffling and pushing to head the line.

In actuality, the structure is not in the populace's self interest, and it is increasingly insecure, brittle, and vulnerable to decay and/or disruption on numerous levels. Much of the vulnerability stems not from Elite over-reach but from the fact that we as a species have reached the carrying capacity of the planet in terms of a high-energy consumption dependency on cheap abundant petroleum for food, transport, water, "growth," etc.

Nonetheless those who control the vast majority of assets, wealth, and tools of persuasion have the most to gain from a continuing belief in the system's stability. Thus their defense of the system which serves their interests above all else will be fierce and unremitting.

The human mind harbors a bias for what I call *independent agencies*, a bias which finds full flower in conspiracies both real and imagined. Ancient humans saw an independent agency of fickle gods who punished or rewarded human supplication with drought or rain.

All human groups form loose confederacies, alliances and "secret societies" (such as cliques in high school) which outsiders rightly identify as conspiracies formed for the benefit of the members.

This bias to perceive independent agencies has a selective advantage: the ability to discern causal agents offers substantial advantages over a passive perception of chaos/randomness.

Why bring this up now? Only to note that The Plutocracy is not a conspiracy in the formal sense of a membership which gathers like the Bohemian Club or even an informal assemblage such as the Bilderberg Group. "Membership" is granted solely by great wealth and control of productive assets; political influence flows from that.

People who control, say, $100 million or more (via family ownership or managerial position) tend to meet one another socially or to do business, and while they jockey for advantage within a group like the rest of us, they form a small class of citizens possessing virtually unimpaired political influence.

Thus in describing a Plutocracy I am not positing a semi-formal conspiracy but simply a financial elite which controls some 2/3 of the productive wealth of the U.S. This is simply a statement of fact. Their collective self-interest is in maintaining the conceptual, legal and financial systems which enable their continued dominance of wealth and influence.

It is important to note this bias for independent agencies is founded both in our minds and in the real world. People with similar self-interests naturally band together in *self-organizing networks* and groups to protect those interests, and since information is power then the inner workings of various *self-organizing groups* are confidential as part of that self-protection.

Thus when I speak of The Plutocracy I refer not to a formal conspiracy with meetings and officers but to a self-organized Elite based on protecting their ownership of 2/3 of the productive wealth of the nation. As each acts to protect his/her wealth at the highest reaches of influence (tax shelters, tax breaks, legislative exclusions, legal rulings, etc.) then they are also acting to defend their class.

The notion that a rentier-financial power Elite wields largely hidden sway over much of the U.S. wealth, political process and media is not new.

Indeed, the evidence describing this Elite is widely available in books such as: How The World Really Works, The Rich and the Super-Rich (out of print, but used copies are available), Tragedy & Hope: A History of the World in Our Time, Wealth and Democracy: A Political History of the American Rich, The Power Elite and This Land Is Their Land: Reports from a Divided Nation.

What I term the Plutocracy has been fully researched and documented. To question its existence and power is not a matter of opinion but of misinformation.

Why would intelligent middle class people consciously or unconsciously defend and support a conceptual system which so heavily favors an Elite over the common good? Certainly self-interest plays a major role. If you are reporting events and trends that undermine your employers' wealth and power, you may well conclude that favoring the status quo in all matters will protect your career, income and status far more effectively than announcing the Emperor has no clothes.

As a free-lance writer in the mainstream media, I witnessed how such mechanisms work in the real world. Media organizations depend on large advertisers for their income, and even though "editorial" (news and commentary) is separated from "advertising/marketing," everyone is aware that negative reporting could influence income and thus eventually detract from each individual's ability to pay their child's tuition, make the car payment, etc.

Thus stories which reflect poorly on major advertisers like realtors and builders are not killed outright--they are merely strangled by demands for more evidence, more documentation, etc., or watered down in the name of "fairness" and placed in little-seen areas of the media outlet's offerings.

In some cases, otherwise independent-minded people have never encountered a serious critique of the status quo's conceptual foundation and thus they believe that understanding of the world is "obvious." Without a skeptical accounting of *cui bono* (to whose benefit?) then what is "obvious" will naturally tend to defend and support a status quo which has labored to construct and defend an "obviousness" which protects its own wealth, ownership and influence.

As its own interests diverge from those of the society at large, the Plutocracy has an irresistible incentive to foster the illusion that policies which benefit the Elites also benefit the middle class. Thus while the Plutocracy and its mass media minions trumpet the benefits of the free market, these same Elites work with unremitting zeal to exempt themselves and their State factotums from these very same free market forces.

Lastly, the status quo understanding of the world is that any problem is inherently "fixable" with minor policy adjustments. Thus even as the global financial pyramid of highly leveraged bets and debts unravels, the status quo response is bureaucratic shuffling of oversight duties, minor tweaking of regulatory rules trumpeted as "major fixes" and behind the scenes, trillion-dollar bailouts of the Plutocracy funded by the non-Elite taxpayers.

When the non-Elite citizen comes to understand this, a new mechanism takes hold that I call *when belief in the system fades*.

This is how empires fall: complacency joins hands with self-aggrandizement.

There are four other subtle processes at work in the dissolution/erosion of the system's intellectual foundation:

1. As we shall see in the following chapters, Elites and underclass alike respond to the visible crumbling of the empire with a sublime complacency grounded in vague appeals to some mythical past spirit which will magically arise to enthuse a torpid, self-absorbed Elite and populace. In the U.S., appeals are made to "the can-do spirit" which powered America's past confidence and resolve.

Unfortunately for both the Elite and the underclass (both of whom depend on State largesse and a vibrant middle class paying high taxes), rousing but ultimately empty incantations are no substitute for difficult choices, tradeoffs and sacrifices.

2. Even as interconnected crises afflict the empire, the Elite moves deeper into an increasingly visible self-aggrandizement marked by pervasive over-reaching. Having mastered its influence over the State, the Plutocracy finds few limits or obstacles to its over-reach.

This over-reach has the characteristics of a positive feedback loop: the more wealth the Elite controls, the greater its influence, which then enables even more wealth acquisition and ever greater influence, and so on.

3. As a result, the interests of the Plutocracy and thus the State diverge from the common interests of the citizenry as a whole. This widening structural imbalance of power creates cynicism and a *profound political disunity* that cripples any attempt at structural solutions.

Given that any real solution would reduce the Plutocracy and State's share of the national income, both the Plutocracy and the State (including all those dependent on its various fiefdoms) resist all structural change, preferring stagnation to any reduction in their income and power.

One of the single most powerful mechanisms at play is windfall exploitation.

Windfalls in Nature are rare, and thus all organisms are selected to exploit them as fully as possible--gorging, so to speak, on any newfound riches. The Plutocracy's influence enables it to suppress or weaken counterforces (such as regulatory systems) and thus open up windfalls which it can then exploit.

For example: having dispensed with troublesome barriers between finance and banking and nettlesome limitations on securities ratings and off-balance sheet assets, investment bankers opened up new windfalls: mortgage-backed securities, bogus "low-risk" ratings, CDOs and other derivatives, and so on.

A second related mechanism is over-reach.

As barriers to Plutocratic expansion topple and the Elites' share of national income rises, then a positive feedback loop forms: the more the Plutocracy expands, the greater the profits, which then fuels greater political influence, and so on. At a critical (and largely invisible) juncture the Plutocracy inevitably over-reaches.

Over-reach takes many forms. It might be an unparalleled expansion into highly risky derivatives, or a domestic Plutocracy reaching into international speculations. The key point is that over-reach pushes the Elites' financial speculations beyond a level of known, controllable risk into uncharted territory, a territory which promises stupendous profits along with equally stupendous but purposefully obscured risk.

Over-reach inevitably pushes a stable system into instability.

Once the Plutocracy's income, power and influence are threatened by the rising instability caused by over-reach, then the Elite resorts to propaganda and other mechanisms to mask the structural instability from the populace. The hope is that the system which so greatly benefits the Plutocracy can be restored to health, but the mechanisms of "recovery" are essentially inauthentic: *simulacra* of reform, propagandistic manipulations of financial and economic data to mask the structural instability, and outright fraud/looting of State resources (bailouts, loans, etc.)--that is, publicly-funded exemptions from risk and free market forces that would otherwise require the Plutocracy to absorb the catastrophic consequences of its over-reaching leveraged gambles.

This failure to address the underlying causes--systemic over-reach and Plutocratic domination of the economy and political system--insures the instability will only worsen. As ever-more frantic attempts to protect the interests of the Plutocracy fail, then another feedback loop forms: the more sham reforms and State bailouts fail to restore stability, the more desperate the Plutocracy's attempts to retain power.

It is worth recalling that the average compensation for the 10 top hedge fund managers during the go-go years of the 2000s was $600 million each. That is not a typo. This is an excellent (if extreme) example of over-reach and windfall exploitation.

As it enriches itself via semi-legal or simply officially sanctioned looting, fraud, deception, embezzlement, collusion, "sweetheart" State contracts, tax avoidance, environmental loopholes and a hundred other mechanisms of over-reach and windfall exploitation, the Elite inadvertently provides the lower classes with a compelling example of increasing wealth via fraud and manipulation rather than production.

Both the *high-caste* technocrats (who keep the State and economy running smoothly for their Plutocratic overlords) and the underclass sense their shares of the national income and wealth are diminishing as the Plutocracy diverts a greater share to their own pockets; quite naturally they seek some way to maintain or grow their own declining purchasing power/wealth.

As they watch the Plutocrats in action, they learn the most effective ways to increase one's share of the income/wealth are looting ("gaming the system" of pensions, benefits, State entitlements, etc.), deception, fraud and embezzlement (accounting trickery, collusion, sweetheart contracts, etc.) and influence-peddling, known in the Third World as corruption, baksheesh, etc.

As the middle class increasingly runs afoul of the byzantine,

Kafkaesque regulations imposed by an ever-expanding State, they find that financial leverage and legerdemain is far more lucrative than actually producing goods and services.

Unsurprisingly, the Plutocracy finds ways to gain exemptions, loopholes and special dispensations that greatly reduce the reach of troublesome regulations and taxes that burden middle class entrepreneurs.

As the middle class abandons thrift and production for financial speculation and highly leveraged debt (following the example of their Plutocratic overlords), tax revenues soar as leveraged speculation pyramids into bubbles, enabling vast expansions of a State which is inherently seeking constant expansion of its income and powers.

When these financial bubbles eventually deflate, then tax revenues plummet as productive work and investment have declined. Why bother working hard when the big, easy money is made via leveraged speculation? Only fools would tolerate all the regulatory costs and high taxes imposed on producing goods and services; far easier to speculate in bubbling assets like housing, stocks, energy, etc.

The State responds to this drop in tax revenues by raising taxes on the remaining productive middle class, creating a positive feedback loop which reinforces the incentives to either drop out, move to speculation or game the system.

Though heavily marginalized, the underclass also copies the Plutocrats' lead by gaming whatever entitlements the State offers to buy the underclasses' silence, passivity and compliance. Thus petty corruption and fraud increases in all State entitlement programs as every sector of society seeks to suck off the maximum benefits while contributing the least possible to the public coffers.

Thus does a nation or empire built on the sacrifices and communal spirit of its citizenry degrade into a doomed culture of self-aggrandizement in which sacrifice is for suckers and looting, manipulation, fraud, embezzlement, exploitation of influence, debauchery of credit, maximization of leverage and the pursuit of speculative riches are the order of the day from the Plutocracy on down through the technocratic upper caste to the underclass.

4. In a society with what we might term an *adult understanding* of the world, it is understood that difficult trade-offs are a necessary part of life. One cannot pursue every path at once, acquire every desired object at

once or learn every skill at once. Priorities must be established via vigorous, open-minded debate (either within oneself for one's own decisions or within the nation-State for larger issues) and a painful triage laid down in which some wants are set aside in favor of actual needs.

Broadly speaking, this is the result of a cost-benefit analysis. Items with increasingly higher marginal costs and increasingly lower marginal returns (a topic covered later) are sacrificed in favor of projects with low costs and high returns. This is, after all, mere common sense.

This painful "adult" process has been replaced in the U.S. by a *permanent adolescence* in which accountability, integrity and trade-offs have been banished by stupendous borrowing. Infantile tantrums and various states of psychological denial have crowded out open-minded discussion; every want has been funded by breathtakingly massive borrowing by the State, private enterprise and households alike.

Once the thick shield of denial is finally pierced by events, it is replaced by the search for an external force or agency to blame for self-destructive indulgences. Personal responsibility, integrity and accountability are set aside in favor of an adolescent sputtering rage.

A pernicious, largely unexamined legal system creates tremendous incentives for unnecessary actions designed to ward off lawsuits, feeding vast armies of high-caste technocratic parasites who produce nothing in the way of wealth-producing goods and services even as they burden the remaining productive sector with make-work rules and costly strategies to avoid potentially ruinous lawsuits.

In true Orwellian fashion, much of this parasitism is described by its practitioners as protecting the "little guy" from the oppressive Elite and State. But as the Plutocracy and State increase their share of the national wealth at the expense of the citizenry, this claim rings increasingly hollow.

Thus we have seniors covered by Medicare receiving multiple costly (and often useless) tests designed less to identify the active causes of disease than to shield the practitioners from lawsuits and to enrich those administering the tests.

Meanwhile, millions of non-elderly citizens cannot obtain even a single test as they lack the benefits provided to the upper-caste State and corporate technocrats.

Rather than face the impossibility of funding such a morally and fiscally bankrupt system of parasitism and profiteering, we as a nation have simply borrowed trillions of dollars to stave off any painful prioritizing.

Very few weapons systems are ever cancelled for the same reasons; the profiteering by a few enterprises and the contributions they make to lawmakers insure that every weapons system will receive funding, even if that requires borrowing gargantuan sums year after year.

This evasion of hard choices (and free market forces) via endlessly rising debt will eventually bring down the nation's currency and its debt-ridden State. The irony is that this carefree self-indulgent adolescent avoidance of cost-benefit analysis guarantees systemic collapse.

Let's begin our search for an integrated understanding with a look at how over-reach, windfall exploitation and the divergence of Elite/State and middle-class interests illuminate the disintegration of post-World War II America into the present Depression.

1. The great postwar income convergence (i.e. the rise of the great middle class, the reduction of poverty and the relative reduction of the Plutocracy's share of national income) reverses in the early 1970s as the "true prosperity" of the postwar era ends and is replaced by income flowing increasingly to the top as stagflation, globalization and the decline of the dollar gut the purchasing power of the middle class.

2. The rising productivity of the 50s and 60s slips to the flatline through the 70s and early 80s, only picking up again as computers revolutionize the back office, sales, manufacturing, just-in-time shipping/production, etc.

3. Concurrent with this gradual return to increasing productivity is the rise of finance as the key profit-center of corporate America. As income skews ever more heavily to the top 1%/5%, then capital (productive assets) become ever more heavily concentrated in the hands of the rentier-financial Plutocracy. The top 1% now owns some 2/3 of the nation's entire productive wealth.

4. As profits rise (from rising productivity) then the profits flow not to wages (which remain flat to down 1975-2009 for all but the top 10% upper-caste professional class) but to those who own the capital.

5. As the middle class experiences a decline in their income and purchasing power (for reasons cited above: declining dollar, rising income disparity, and wages falling due to global wage arbitrage) then they take on ever-larger debts to fund what they have been brainwashed by the media to believe is "the American dream" of imported luxury

goods, expansive homes, overseas cruises, etc.

The only other mechanism available to the middle class to increase household income is for Mom/Aunt/Grandma to enter the workforce, which she does in the tens of millions, with sociological consequences which are still unfolding.

6. This advertising/media-driven desire to borrow to fund the "good life" is hugely profitable to the money-center and investment banks, which expand rapidly into mortgage securitization, derivatives and consumer credit to the point that they come to dominate corporate profits.

7. The financial Plutocracy, observing that actually producing goods is not very profitable unless you can fix prices as per ADM (Archer Daniels Midland) or gain government subsidies and tax giveaways (oil lease depreciation, etc.) sinks its capital into the FIRE economy (finance, insurance and real estate), eschewing real-world investments as comparatively unprofitable.

Though rarely noted, this is a longstanding trait of capitalism stretching back to 1400-era Venice. When trade became less profitable than mainland farming, the Venetian Elite stopped funding trade and bought farms on the mainland. As a side effect, Venice ceased to be a military and trading power. But the Elite remained immensely wealthy.

8. As the tech bubble expands, middle-class investors see the Plutocracy (those with enough capital to qualify as angel investors and vulture, oops, I mean venture capitalists) reaping huge gains, and they enter the dot-com stock bubble buildup with a vengeance.

9. In a happy accident, the Soviet Empire collapses just as productivity begins its computer-fueled rise in the U.S. In a so-called Unipolar World in which U.S. military, political and financial influence is unrivaled, non-U.S. investors seek the relative safety and high returns (based on appreciation of the dollar) of U.S. financial instruments.

10. The dot-com bubble implodes in a speculative meltdown, and retail investors (a.k.a. the middle class 401K investors) are devastated. The ephemeral wealth they once possessed, however briefly, fuels their speculative desire to get into the next get-rich-quick game, which just so happens to be "something everyone understands:" real estate.

11. Having exhausted the dot-com play, Plutocratic capital is seeking a new high-profit home. The miracles of derivatives (CDOs, credit default swaps, etc.) and securitized debt (mortgage tranches, etc.) open up vast

new opportunities for leverage, off-balance sheet shenanigans and outright fraud. As chip wafer plants disappear from Silicon Valley (too dirty, costly, etc.) then they're replaced with paper: mortgage-backed securities. (Over-reach and windfall exploitation writ large.)

12. Sniffing gold in them thar exurban hills, the under-capitalized and over-indebted U.S. working class and middle class reach for the chalice of easy-money gold: leveraged real estate. (Over-reach and windfall exploitation writ small.)

13. With the Federal financial regulatory agencies in a Republican/Democrat-enforced somnambulance, the coast is clear for brigands, shysters, fraudsters, con artists, liars, cheats, and assorted riff-raff in the realty, mortgage and appraisal businesses, who all feed the ravenous maw of the money-center banks' apparently limitless appetite for real estate assets to securitize and leverage in exotic and stupendously profitable ways.

14. For a wonderful five years circa 2002-2006, the game is afoot and no-down-payment Jill and $100 million-bonus Jack are immensely enriched. Meanwhile, the underlying real economy is becoming ever more imbalanced and ever more fragile as real production and real productivity plummet as everyone rushes to the speculative riches of exurban McMansions and malls.

15. Elite and middle-class interests seem to converge during this speculative mania: everyone is benefiting from the real estate bubble except the poor, who are bought off with minimal social welfare programs and endless entertainment (via TV) then safely ignored, as they don't vote or spend.

But this convergence was illusory; while the Plutocracy and State functionaries benefited (via stupendous capital gains for the former and vastly richer pension promises for the latter), the private-sector middle class is in essence the bag-holder: when the newfound "wealth" in housing and stock market gains vanish, it is the middle class wealth which is destroyed en masse.

16. This last best speculative leveraged credit bubble pops (alas, exponential expansion of credit cannot go on forever), gutting the stock market which had grown utterly dependent on leverage, debt, gamed/fraudulent accounting and asset bubbles for its rising profits.

17. Doubly devastated by the implosion of housing and their stock investments (mostly in 401K and IRA retirement funds), the middle class

faces the terrible consequences of its 26-year stupor of ever-rising debt and leverage. Alas, the Emperor's clothes are revealed as remarkably transparent.

18. Having borrowed and squandered trillions of dollars since 1981 on unaffordable entitlements, military misadventures and assorted bridges-to-nowhere pork spending, the Federal government (The Fed and the Treasury) finds its ability to borrow its way out of its current debt hole annoyingly limited. The rest of the world has finally caught on to the con, and Chinese university students are openly mocking the Treasury Secretary's Orwellian claim of "we support a strong dollar." The rest of the world shuns Treasury debt and works to create an alternative reserve currency, shutting down the "dollar con" (we take your tangible goods and give you paper in return.)

19. With the global media concentrated in a scant few corporate hands (less than 10), this pulling away of the curtain is deleted/excised from media coverage in a ruthless campaign of pure propaganda.

20. As the wheels fall off the U.S. economy and the bubbles cannot be re-inflated, fruitless attempts at holding back the tide with incantations (stop, tide, I speak for the U.S. Treasury!) and loopy sand castles (the bottom is in, buy now!) abound. Unresponsive to propaganda, the real world grinds down into a global Depression without visible end.

If we do nothing, we will be swept along in the Great Descent. Alternatively, if we want to prosper, then we must first gain an integrated understanding of all the interlocking crises we face.

Key concepts in Chapter One:

Cui bono (to whose benefit?)
Independent agencies
Self-organizing networks and groups
High-caste, upper-caste (technocrat/government employee class)
When belief in the system fades
Profound political disunity
Adult understanding
Permanent adolescence

A note on underclass and unproductive/productive classes:

I use two terms which partially overlap: underclass and unproductive class, and it's important to distinguish the two.

I have used productive/unproductive classes to differentiate citizens earning income and paying substantial income taxes, property taxes, capital gains taxes, etc., to the State and those who are dependent on the State: retirees, disabled, unemployed, etc. This distinction is critical because the vast majority of entitlements and pensions funded by the State are "pay as you go"--that is, the current productive workforce pays the taxes which fund retirees, the disabled, Medicare, Veterans benefits, etc.

Even public pensions that are paid out of trust funds are partially "pay as you go" because shortfalls due to pension fund losses must be paid out of current tax revenues.

Simply put, 120 million productive citizens (working class and the middle class are essentially equal in my analysis because both are productively paying taxes) are supporting 180 million dependent (that is, not paying significant taxes) citizens as well as millions of non-citizens. As employment, wealth and taxes plummet, this imbalance between the State's gargantuan obligations and its plummeting revenues will lead to insolvency. As millions of taxpayers lose their income, the State will not have enough revenue to fund the promised entitlements and pensions.

We also need to distinguish between unproductive in the sense of not paying substantial taxes and unproductive in the sense of producing little value. By underclass I mean the class of citizens who are capable of producing value, unpaid or paid, but for a variety of reasons do not; they are dependent on the State for their livelihood (i.e. "welfare"). It is this class which receives the modern equivalent of "bread and circuses" to give them a reason to be complicit (silent and passive) in the status quo of Elite dominance and looting.

Alternatively, citizens can be very productive but having "opted out" they no longer belong to the high-income/high-taxpaying class. They are productive in their own household and community but are no longer supporting the State with high taxes.

Chapter Two: Contexts and Causes

Any guide claiming to be practical must first present all the contexts and causes of the interlocking challenges we now face. Without such an integrated understanding, all response planning is like building a house on shifting sand.

If we are indeed entering a multi-decade Great Transformation, then as prudent as it is to stockpile a few months of food and supplies, that will obviously not get us through the Transformation, either as individuals or as communities. We need a thoroughly integrated understanding before we can fashion a response that will make the Transformation a positive one. Our goal is a sustainable, productive economy and a full appreciation of the fundamental rights to life, liberty and the pursuit of happiness.

I know it is tempting to skip ahead to the list of proposed responses, but they won't make sense unless we ground ourselves in the contexts of our planet, era, society and economy.

First, we must identify the fundamental contexts; second, critique the status quo understanding of the "problems" and "solutions," and then third, present solutions which flow directly from our critique.

Our goal is a critique so incisive that the solutions become "obvious," that is, they are implicit in the critique itself. Not all critiques manage this; the grandfather of cul-de-sac critiques was Marx, whose profound critique of capitalism did not produce any coherent alternative system.

It is also important to understand that every "solution" benefits someone, and the key to establishing that "solution" is to frame the "problem" in such a manner that the self-serving "solution" becomes essentially inevitable. This is why we constantly ask: *cui bono*, to whose benefit?, and why we take such care in analyzing how "problems" are framed by the status quo.

It is my thesis that the standard (status quo) understanding of our "problems" is heavily promoted precisely because it benefits an Elite at the top of the income/asset pyramid.

This carefully designed and marketed understanding of the "problem" is presented in ways which can only be described as artful propaganda. The chief goal of this relentless marketing is to convince you that the "solutions" being presented are in your self-interest; that is, that they will benefit the entire nation (if not the entire planet, too), including you.

The possibility that these "solutions" exclusively serve the interests of a small Elite is rarely considered, for the obvious reason that the question itself threatens the entire understanding of what constitutes our "problems" and the Elite's "solutions."

A key feature of the current era of interlocking crises is that the interests of the Plutocracy are increasingly diverging from the interests of the society as a whole. This divergence must be masked by simulacra and propaganda, lest the citizenry become aware of the widening split and start demanding that the Plutocracy and the State relinquish some of their ever-growing share of the national income.

By way of example of such divergence, consider globalization as a catch phrase. We are constantly bombarded with shrill warnings that any limits on globalization will cause a worldwide Depression akin to the 1930s. Yet this is disingenuous for a number of reasons.

To the degree that trade is globalization, then the world has been globalized for thousands of years; Imperial Rome, India and China were trading partners. But "globalization" covers not just wealth-creating trade but also the most one-sided exploitation of materials and labor. The one catch phrase conveniently covers both beneficial commerce of the sort which has gone on for thousands of years and exploitative looting of local resources by global forces.

So when hardwood forests are leveled and the seas poisoned, do the local people really benefit as much as promoters of "globalization" insist? Do all the workers displaced --not just in advanced industrial economies but in Africa as well--really benefit? Or is the entire intellectual framework of "globalization" essentially a front to provide cover for the enrichment of the few at the expense of the many?

The intellectual framework which supports the Elite's dominance and makes it apparently "natural" or "beneficial" is the Plutocracy's key defense; and the limits of human language and thought make it relatively easy to undermine reasoned skepticism.

Thus a defense of "capitalism" turns out not to be an appeal for open markets but the exact opposite, an enabling of crony capitalism. The defense of globalization is not a promotion of the exchange-of-surplus-production that characterized trade for millennia but of a targeted grab-and-run exploitation of vulnerable resources and peoples. A defense of "financial stability" is actually a defense of the illusion of stability.

Regulations to curb the Plutocracy's over-reach are undermined by the Plutocracy persuading the State that "these are the regulations we want," that is, a simulacrum of regulation that imposes virtually no limits on Elites but effectively strangles the middle class and keeps it "in its place."

Given the enormous benefits to be gained by this relentless obfuscation, mystification and superficially appealing framing of contexts and problems, we must prepare ourselves for a difficult analysis.

Our first step is to ask *cui bono*, to whose benefit? Our second step is to tease apart the intellectual defenses of over-reach and income redistribution, and consider how the status quo dismisses our actual "problems" as mere bumps in the technocratically maintained road to consumerist Nirvana, i.e. "prosperity."

One often effective technique deployed to quell questions about Elites' dominance or self-interest is reduction: that is, reduce the situation to an "all or nothing" conflict, or frame it as an extension of a current situation which can be addressed by modest policy tweaks.

Thus Peak Oil is not a problem as we have 400 years of coal, etc. Those in charge of the machinery have a huge stake in technocratic "solutions" which leave power, profit and consumption structures firmly in place.

Identity itself can be reduced; thus a once-active citizenry is reduced to "consumers." As long as "consumers" benefit in any way, then what might be lost to workers, voters, citizens, etc. can be cast aside as meaningless.

Since profits are made by selling something to consumers, it's extremely handy for all other roles and identities to be extinguished, diminished or marginalized.

The key point here is that dominance flows directly from an intellectual framework which constructs and justifies that dominance as natural and beneficial to all believers.

In this sense consumerism is in effect the de facto state religion of the U.S.A., and it directly benefits the Elites who own or control the vast majority of the nation's financial wealth, income, law-making machinery and productive assets.

The second point is that it is impossible to make a clear-eyed assessment of the actual challenges we face when our understanding of those realities is constantly being massaged, manipulated and "framed" out of existence by an elite-dominated media. (A few global companies control most of the world's broadcast, Web and print media.)

It is important to understand that the low-level conflict and anxiety created by the media (entertainment such as Rush Limbaugh being passed off as political commentary, for instance) are directly in the interests of the Plutocracy.

Anything that undermines a coherent understanding of the Plutocracy's over-reach and the inherent brittleness of the status quo's illusory "stability" works to the advantage of the Elites.

The third point is that many people who consider themselves smart realists nonetheless end up defending an oppressive and manipulative status quo because they have been persuaded by their salary and other benefits (such as enhanced personal status) to defend a self-serving Elite--or more precisely, the intellectual framework which justifies the Elites' dominance.

This leads to the fourth point, which is that the Elites have already won the key battle once their high-caste technocratic "army" of academics, managers, captains, et al. identify this intellectual framework as being in their own self-interest. These technocrats are members of a loyal upper "caste" which defends and enforces the Elites' dominance over the rest of the citizenry.

Even as the economy slips into a *Plantation-like structure* populated by *debt-serfs* laboring under the illusion they are free spirits pursuing their own self-interest, the upper caste technocrats labor to maintain a façade of "entertaining" staged "news" that masks the "theft by other means" (looting, embezzlement, fraud, collusion, etc.) that is the modus operandi of an unaccountable Plutocracy.

As on a Plantation, the power and wealth owned by a small Elite indentures the majority of wage earners via the mechanism of crushing debt (debt-serfdom). Debt-serfs are managed and policed by a managerial caste of overseers (*lunas* in the terminology of the Hawaiian plantation where I worked in the late 1960s).

The fifth point is that this process of gaining compliance is not a conspiracy; it is a complex mixture of conscious and subconscious realignments of incentives and disincentives to maximize attractive risk-return opportunities (i.e. windfall exploitation and exemptions from market forces) for the Plutocracy and its upper-caste workforce.

Thus the incentives for public employees to game the system to boost their retirement pay (effectively looting the public treasury in the process) are high while the penalties, thanks in part to union protection, are minimal.

In a similar way, the chicken farm which dumps its waste directly into the bay has a large incentive (profits) to avoid regulations which would require treatment of its vast waste. If it only costs $1 million in campaign donations to persuade lawmakers to exempt the farm from environmental regulations while the treatment plant would cost $10 million, the cost-benefit analysis is clear: buy the legislative loopholes and continue killing the bay.

With elections becoming ever costlier, the lawmakers have incentives to garner large contributions from enterprises that need "to present our perspective." It isn't corruption per se but simply the "rational response" to incentives and cost-benefit ratios embedded in the very structure of the system.

Once the entire system is riddled with gamesmanship, looting, loopholes and exemptions for the Elite and secret dispensation of public funds, then belief in the supporting intellectual framework and the fairness of the system fades. The middle class outside the "caste" of State technocrats is squeezed by Plutocratic and State over-reach; as they drop out then the taxes they paid to support the ever-growing State decline, eventually leading to the State's insolvency.

The sixth point is that empires and States collapse when the costs far outweigh the marginal gains; in effect the cost of maintaining the over-reaching State and Plutocracy far exceeds the increasingly marginal benefits provided by the State and "belief in the system." Marginal benefits are low, marginal costs are high.

One example of this is medicinal. Antibiotics provide enormous benefits for low marginal costs. In contrast to this tremendous leverage-- low costs produce enormous gains--modern pharmaceuticals are often staggeringly costly even as their benefits are minimal. Adding a costly medication to a senior's already long list of drugs is extremely costly (high marginal costs) even as it offers scant or even negative benefits (low marginal benefit).

The seventh point is that structures (both political and intellectual) which once made sense are extended to absurdity as the State and Plutocracy over-reach (over-borrow, over-leverage, take increasingly large risks to sustain the status quo, increase taxation and looting, etc.)

Thus regulatory systems which once limited the Elites' excesses now smother the middle class while the Plutocracy operates beyond any accountability.

The eighth point is that a terribly ironic mechanism gathers force: since free markets are inherently risky (that is, ontologically based on risk and return and shifting supply and demand), the Plutocracy and State functionaries/parasites both have compelling incentives to escape exposure to market forces via exemptions.

Thus State functionaries buy political support for public-sector wages which are two or three times higher than market wages, and healthcare/pension benefits which are unmatched by private enterprise. Parasitic firms such as defense and healthcare contractors gain "guaranteed contracts" or other exemptions from market forces, while the Plutocracy gains exemptions via public guarantees (backstops, bailouts and low-cost loans) of risk-laden private banking bets.

The irony is that Neoliberal Capitalism supposedly reveres free markets: but that is mere propaganda. A counterfeit free market is erected for middle class consumption but behind the veils of obscure tax laws, sweetheart deals and the like, the Plutocracy and State functionaries both avoid any exposure to actual market forces which might limit their share of the national income.

The ninth point is that reality does not respect the intellectual constructs of the Elite (let's call this dominant ideology *Neoliberal Capitalist Democracy* for want of a more accurate term). As a result, as reality increasingly conflicts with this understanding of "how our world works," then that intellectual framework must increasingly substitute carefully designed simulacra for authentic structures (for example, elections in which 98% of all incumbents win re-election) and work to *derealize* any direct experience which runs counter to the Plutocracy's narrative.

This process of bridging the widening gap between what we experience and what we're told we should be experiencing via the substitution of simulacra for authentic structures is central to this entire analysis.

Why are the State and the Plutocracy (two sides of the same coin) substituting simulacra for authentic structures and truthful accounts? Let's answer by asking: what would a truthful accounting of *cui bono*-- to whose benefit?--reveal?

A truthful accounting would reveal that the status quo benefits the rentier-financial Elite and high-caste technocrats at the expense of the rest of us. (For a detailed account, please read It Takes a Pillage: Behind the Bailouts, Bonuses, and Backroom Deals from Washington to Wall Street by Wall Street insider Nomi Prins.)

That is, the 99% who do not own 2/3 of the productive assets of the nation and the 75% who do not belong to the State/technocrat upper-caste which serves the system for its own self-aggrandizement.

In sum: a truthful accounting of *cui bono* would result in the exposure of the over-reach, exploitation, deception, fraud, mismanagement, malinvestment, manipulation and self-aggrandizement of the Plutocracy and its high-caste State/corporate technocracy (two "masters," one system). A truthful accounting would result in the shattering of the illusion that supporting the status quo is in your self-interest.

Maintaining this illusion is the key to maintaining the Plutocracy and the State's share of the national income. This explains why the Plutocracy and the State (two sides of one coin) are obsessed with creating sham structures and narratives designed to lull the citizenry into the comforting illusion that they are the beneficiaries of:

- Democracy (when 98% of incumbents win re-election, can that be authentic democracy?)
- Free press (when a handful of corporations own the vast majority of the print/broadcast/radio/web media and the State manipulates statistics without media challenge, can that be an authentic "free press"?)
- Higher education (a factory for producing high-caste overseers /enforcers for the State/Plutocracy Plantation)
- Healthcare (a quarter of the citizenry have no healthcare, another quarter have sham "coverage")
- "Ownership" (of debt and rapidly declining collateral--the perfect setup for debt-serfdom)
- Low-tax (low tax for the Plutocracy and unproductive class, high tax for the dwindling productive class) "free enterprise" (crony Capitalism).

To maintain their share of the dwindling national income, it is essential that the Plutocracy and State mask the devolution and insolvency of the State. The primary prop of non-elite *belief in the system* is the faith that the *Savior State* will fund everyone's retirement, healthcare and security as promised--a promise that cannot be fulfilled. (A *Savior State* promises to save everyone from personal responsibility via entitlements funded by demographic and financial fraud.)

As a result of this pervasive substitution of sham structures and narratives, truthfulness evaporates, replaced by clever deception and propaganda.

Transparency is replaced by obscurity and staged entertainments are presented as "news" or "democracy in action."

Facts are replaced by massaged statistics; accounting is replaced by trickery.

Common purpose is replaced by self-aggrandizement and game-the-system looting.

The Elites' interests diverge from those of the society as a whole, and the result is a *profound political disunity* of hardened, embittered camps warring over the remaining spoils of a decaying State.

Regulations are replaced by protection schemes and layers of purposefully impenetrable obfuscation which exempts the Elites from market forces (risk and subsequent losses).

Healthcare is replaced by a highly profitable facsimile in which 25% of the citizenry receive no care and another 25% pay for sham "healthcare coverage" which offers little to no actual care. The high-caste class of State and corporate technocrats is rewarded for their services to the State/Plutocracy with full coverage. (Observe the parallels to State employees' coveted positions in Third World kleptocracies.)

The free press is replaced with a corporate media tasked with protecting the interests of the State and Plutocracy that owns it lock, stock and barrel.

Truthfulness is replaced by lies, deception, trickery and a pervasive, willful obscurity in every level of society and the economy.

Simulacra of capital are passed off as assets. A sham prosperity based on exponential growth of credit/debt is presented as sustainable "capitalism." Misallocation of capital and looting are masked as "market forces."

Incomplete, misleading, and romanticized information is presented as "fact" while truthful accountings are suppressed, belittled and undermined.

Lived experience is derealized by ever-present media fantasies ("we have the finest healthcare system in the world," "the banking sector is free enterprise at its finest," etc.) and the schizophrenic gap between experience and media fantasy is papered over with drugs (prescribed, illegal and legal) and distractions (celebrity worship, entertainment/sports, narcissistic indulgences, shopping, etc.)

Dissent is filtered into distracting, meaningless "ideological conflicts" of no substance, "debates" which leave the Power Elite and State in control of the national income.

Obesity, passivity and addiction are incentivized as poor nutrition and chronic illnesses are the highest-return "profit centers" for the agribusiness/packaged/fast-food industry and the "healthcare" (actually sick-care) industry.

The destructive consequences of the status quo are systematically internalized as personal failings: lack of will power, poor judgment, etc.; a simulacrum of "personal responsibility" masks the internalization of master narratives which leave the Plutocracy and State safely unaccountable.

From the perspective of a media sustained by marketing, the ideal internal state is a deep, unresolvable insecurity which can be temporarily soothed by shopping/entertainment.

A simulacrum of citizenship reduces a self-directed populace to passive "consumers."

This process is so subtle and subconscious that it is difficult to discern. But once you understand this substitution mechanism, a type of enlightenment occurs; you no longer accept simulacrum for "the real thing," and the State/Plutocracy has lost your compliance, that is, your belief in the system's fair accounting of your self-interest.

This conflict between direct, lived experience of our ever-worsening problems and the State/Elites' "ignore reality, keep believing in our system" machinery causes a pervasive cultural and individual schizophrenia which causes participants to feel adrift, depressed, alienated, isolated and misunderstood.

The Elites' intellectual framework has a ready response to this ever-widening divide between their increasingly rickety narrative and reality: the metaphors of illness and medicine. Thus the "solution" to the deep misgivings of those who sense the divide between a false narrative and their own experience is prescription medications in quantity.

This growing gulf between lived experience and the Elites' heavily hyped narrative of how our world works eventually causes an enlightenment in some of the managerial/technocrat caste: their belief in the system fades and they drop out.

Once they realize the institutions they have given their lives to will fail, they either withdraw or begin work on an alternative framework of understanding based on their own experience. In seeking experience-based ways to understand our challenges and potential solutions which don't simply serve and enrich Elites, they become part of The Remnant, a self-selected assembly of citizenry who lead by example, not exhortation--in other words, the advance guard of a sustainable economy and free society.

The Remnant is a diverse and self-organizing group of people who are skeptical of overly simplistic contexts and solutions, and skeptical of the Elites' authority structures (the prison/drug gulag, taxation of everything and everyone but the sheltered Elites, recruitment of the poor to military service so the Elites' offspring need not serve, a food and "healthcare" system which encourages illness and chronic ill-health as the most profitable possible conditions, etc.)

The Remnant has learned that the Power Elite has essentially rendered itself unaccountable and thus the consequences of its vast over-reach will fall not on its own small membership but the ill-prepared citizenry below.

The entrenched high-caste bureaucrats and other technocrats are busy looting the coffers of the State on behalf of themselves and their Plutocrat Masters, and this large caste will only wither when the State becomes insolvent--the end-game of the current borrow-and-spend debt orgy which has sustained the American economy, Plutocracy and State for decades.

Thus the Remnant is preparing for life without State largesse, because the State will no longer be able to borrow or print enough money to support its increasingly burdensome castes, entitlements and fiefdoms. In my terminology, the Remnant's goal is radical self-reliance.

Lastly, The Remnant is acutely aware that the environmental, financial and FEW (food, energy, water) dilemmas facing the planet are not ones of interpretation; they are very real and cannot be explained away or "framed" out of existence with appeals to soothingly vague future technocratic wonders.

This book is an attempt to strip away the obfuscatory intellectual framework which has cloaked and protected the Elites' self-serving over-reach. It is an attempt to speak directly to the real problems we face. Once we understand our own experience and the world directly then the messy, conflicting realities of various solutions and trade-offs will become clearer.

Then we will have to choose which trade-offs have the best chances for long-term success. The goal is to construct a sustainable, productive economy and a political culture based not on self-serving game-the-system looting but on *the radical self-reliant* appreciation of the fundamental rights to life, liberty and the pursuit of happiness.

End note: I know this must strike some readers as lunacy; there are no simulacra, and the State cannot possibly dissolve in insolvency. Others will be tempted to enter the merry-go-round "debate" as to whether the State should or should not be a "Savior." It doesn't matter; the State cannot print up $100 trillion without reducing the value of the dollar to zero, nor can it fund the military/finance Empire, its own domestic fiefdoms and the Savior State entitlements now promised to 300 million citizens without borrowing/printing $100 trillion. So however you care to calculate the end-state, it remains the same: insolvency and the complete devolution of the Empire/Savior State.

Key concepts in this chapter:
Plantation-like structures
debt-serfs
Derealize/derealization
Neoliberal Capitalist Democracy (the dominant ideology)
Profound political disunity
Savior State
When belief in the system fades
The Remnant
Radical self-reliance

Chapter Three: Toward an Integrated Understanding

The first task is replacing the crumbling intellectual framework of the present status quo system with one grounded in reality.

There are five distinct issues to sort out:

1. The elements of human nature which lend themselves to cycles and manipulation

2. The nature of the energy, financial and environmental trends/crises which are heralding the Great Transformation

3. The nature of the *negative and positive feedback loops* which determine the system's stability and direction

4. The responses which have a high probability of making the Transformation positive

5. The nature of future work and the principles best suited to prospering during the Great Transformation

If we mischaracterize the nature of the crises and fail to grasp the forces powering these trends, then we will select inappropriate responses that will not prepare us to prosper. If we fail to understand how the status quo benefits various Elites, then we will inaccurately frame the "problems" and reach guaranteed-to-fail "solutions."

You may well disagree with much or perhaps most of this book; that's fine, because the primary goal of the book is to spark a reappraisal of our situation and generate practical responses. I don't claim to have "the answer;" what I hope to present is a way of thinking about the challenges which is more productive than the status quo.

You may also find some of the ideas presented here difficult to accept. None of us like to think of ourselves as debt-serfs (yes, I have a mortgage, too), yet how can we move forward if we cannot be honest about our responsibilities and dilemmas? We are all vulnerable to groupthink, propaganda and marketing at various times; there is no shame in simply being human.

Some of you may find parts of the analysis smacking of warmed-over Marxism, while an equal number may find certain sections "right-wing." This urge to categorize any idea or analysis ideologically is part of the *simulacrum of thinking* we accept as "obvious"-- the largely unconscious *politics of experience*. That much of what we accept as "obvious" might be wrong is deeply unsettling.

Context One: Human Nature

The first context we must understand is human nature. Regardless of the era or challenge, humans remain "wired" to respond to crisis in the same basic ways. Unfortunately for us, our responses in "default mode" (our first emotional responses) and the solutions we find highly compelling in default mode (inertia/complacency, fear/panic, casting our lot with a "Big Man"/leader or fatalism/giving up) are often not constructive, and may well be highly destructive.

Even more pernicious, our default mode is extremely short-term. As small groups of hunter-gatherers, we simply walked away when we'd depleted the environment of resources; there were always other lands (or islands) available. In this fashion, ancient humans wandered the entire planet long before the first tilled crop was ever planted.

Our default ability to foresee the consequences of our actions is poor; thus time and again human societies have added population and "overhead costs" during prosperous times of ample rainfall and grain yields, only to collapse in catastrophic decline when a string of lean years inevitably came along.

In abundance, we freely spend what's "cheap" and in shortage we mourn what is now "dear." It's not difficult to see the same pattern repeating today.

While it is possible for humans to fashion long-term plans out of self-interest, we are peculiarly ill-equipped to make the critical distinction between relative scarcity and absolute scarcity. Thus we will hunt a species to extinction without regards to the long-term negative consequences for own diet.

To a mind selected for hunting and gathering, the local scarcity (that is, relative scarcity) of any one critical food or energy source is remedied by simply moving on to a new hunting ground with relative abundance.

Where humans have hunted a species to extinction, such as the woolly mammoth, then the human solution remains the same: move on.

In the event some other tribe already occupies a territory of relative abundance, the human response is to begin hunting their own species of the "other tribe." In terms of straight kilocalorie analysis, this is entirely rational: the "cost" of war in terms of lives lost and calories expended is well worth the long-lasting benefits of conquering new fertile territories and eliminating competitors.

Thus it is not at all specious to suggest that *monopoly capital* and conquest by whatever means offer the most attractive cost/benefit ratio have long been a human strategy to maximize gains. Marking off another human group as the "enemy" is a highly useful tool to gain support of one's own tribe for conquest/looting.

Monopoly capital finds eliminating competition to be far more profitable than competing in a free market. Thus mature industries with high barriers to entry by new competitors (often these barriers are political or regulatory, purchased by the Plutocracy for modest sums) end up being dominated by a mere handful of enterprises. The global mass media is but one example.

A similar mechanism is the exempting of capital and high-caste Elites from risk--that is, from the risks inherent in free markets. Just as monopoly capital strives to eliminate "uncertainties" (i.e. losses) by eliminating competition, capital and high-caste Elites (public employees, technocrats, etc.) strive to exempt themselves from risk by constructing fiefdoms protected by the State.

Risk is not a characteristic of capitalism or free markets; it is a characteristic of life which markets simply reflect.

In both cases, the goal is to lock in returns without being exposed to risk. The returns are funneled to the Elites while the risks are spread to the middle class via public bailouts and guarantees. This is called privatizing profits and socializing risks.

The advent of language gave humanity tremendous powers of knowledge acquisition, and the storage and transfer of information. It also provided methods whereby our interpretations of experience could be influenced and managed.

For example, it has become culturally correct to support "taking care of the elderly;" this now automatic public support has enabled a relatively small group of enterprises to reap enormous profits. They play on an induced consensus without ever quite defining what it means. Medicare, costly new medications and treatments, care given without appreciation of the consequences of reduced quality of life – all of this can increase suffering in the elderly and diminish them.

But it is profitable to the sloganeers. Spending on such programs now increases at twice the rate of the overall economy, year after year, despite dubious results. The formulary of drugs increases because it is profitable to those who manipulate our expectations. The same can be said of the manufacturers of costly new diagnostics and cutting edge equipment. Expense be damned, say those who eat from the plate of a profit-induced shibboleth of great momentum: "health care."

The tool, language, easily becomes a weapon in skilled hands, and the strongest group will do all in its power to protect its own interests.

The compelling catch phrases which are deployed to mask looting and profiteering are legion: "defending our nation," "restoring the health of our banks," etc. Thus we must be especially alert to how Elites deploy these powerful emotional attractors to cloak their monopolies.

Lastly, the mind is remarkably easy to hijack via emotional reward receptors. Former FDA head David Kessler recently described how the food industry designs its products to activate these reward centers with faux-foods loaded with sugar, fat and salt (from his book The End of Overeating: Taking Control of the Insatiable American Appetite):

"They aren't selling just any commodity. They've designed highly stimulating products, and consumers come back for more. Nothing sells as much as something that stimulates the rewards-circuitry of the brain. It's all about selling product."

Unfortunately, humans are prone to a formidably long and varied List of cognitive biases. Those tasked with manipulating public opinion for political or financial gain are of course well versed in these biases, which I would characterize as *cognitive traps*, and highly attuned to the most productive times and places to deploy them.

Despite the many traps in our default modes of thinking and our pernicious tropism toward short-term contexts, when we have no choice left then we are capable of making short-term sacrifices to further long-term gains. This is the response we need to foster to survive the Great Transformation just ahead.

Context Two: Cycles and Patterns of History

While every era of crisis is unique, authors such as David Fischer (The Great Wave: Price Revolutions and the Rhythm of History), Jared Diamond (Collapse: How Societies Choose to Fail or Succeed) and Joseph Tainter (The Collapse of Complex Societies) have carefully researched how cycles of price, conflict and resource depletion tend to repeat as human populations rise beyond the carrying capacity of their environment.

I address these cycles in *Food Shortages, Rising Prices, Stagnant Wages: Welcome to the 13th Century* (reprinted in a later chapter).

As we seek to understand long-wave cycles, we must also recognize that the crises of our era are unique even as they are manifesting within historical cycles.

A number of recent books have described the unique set of challenges we face: for instance The Long Emergency: Surviving the End of Oil, Climate Change, and Other Converging Catastrophes of the Twenty-First Century by James Howard Kunstler and Financial Armageddon: Protecting Your Future from Four Impending Catastrophes by Michael Panzner. Other books have addressed critical environmental, energy and demographic issues: The Future of Life, Beyond Oil: The View from Hubbert's Peak, Fewer: How the New Demography of Depopulation Will Shape Our Future, The Coming Generational Storm: What You Need to Know about America's Economic Future, The Rhythm of War and The Fourth Turning.

Given this wealth of material, I hesitate to even attempt a short summary of all the interwoven structural challenges of our era. But the key context is this: financial and resource crises are not new; they are recurring features of human civilization. But many aspects of our era's crises are unique in all of human history: never before have we faced depletion of fossil fuels and the population pressures of over 6.5 billion humans to feed, house, clothe, transport, heal and care for in their old age. Never before have we as a species been so dependent on fragile supply chains and fast-depleting global resources.

Consider the overfishing of the world's oceans; what once seemed inexhaustible—the supply of fish—is now heading to near-zero.

Ironically, this cyclical nature of crisis lends itself to complacency: if we managed to get through those crises, then we can do it again, the power of human innovation will save us, etc. Unfortunately, there have been many times when the human populace did not "get through" the crisis; populations collapsed to mere shadows of their levels reached in the years of rising abundance.

Current structural challenges include:

1. demographics (promised retirement benefits are unaffordable)
2. global financial deleveraging (renunciation/write-off of debt)

3. high-cost advanced economies, "Planet of Slums" developing economies

4. rising interest rates (shortage of surplus capital)

5. de-scaling/disruption of entrenched fiefdoms by the Web

6. scalability traps/structural job losses in all economies

7. crippling regulation and overhead burdens on small entrepreneurs

8. fossil fuel depletion (Peak Oil)

9. "head-fake" drop in energy costs removes incentives for alternative energy

10. political disunity; elites' interests diverge from those of the society as a whole

11. rising income disparity

12. depletion of fresh water, ocean and soil resources

13. climate change (weather extremes, rising sea levels, etc.)

14. increasingly drug-resistant bacteria and viruses

15. rising chemical and industrial pollution levels (air, water, soil)

16. increasing availability of bioweapons and nuclear weapons

I summarize the four primary cycles in my book Weblogs & New Media: Marketing in Crisis:

1. Peak oil, or the depletion cycle/end-game of the global economy's complete dependence on inexpensive, readily available fossil fuels.

2. The cycle of credit expansion and contraction (approximately 60-70 years), which is now beginning the transition from unsustainable credit expansion (bubble) to renunciation of debt (credit collapse) and global depression.

3. The generational cycle (4 generations or approximately 80 years) of American history which leads to nation-changing social, political and economic upheaval. (The American Revolution: 1781 +80 years = Civil War, 1861 +80 years = 1941, World War II + 80 years = 2021)

4. The 100+ year cycle of price inflation and stagnation of wages' purchasing power which began around 1901 is now reaching the final stage of widespread turmoil, shortages, famine, war, conflict and crisis.

Without a firm understanding of the cyclical nature of human history and the unique challenges of our era, we are hard-pressed to escape the comforting illusions of complacency and fatalism.

A key point is that the above crises (or potential crises) are not discrete phenomena which can be solved in piecemeal fashion but rather interlocking, overlapping and in some cases reinforcing problems which range from long-term depletions to volatile geopolitical tensions which could burst into conflict. Over an intermediate time scale, a weather crisis such as extended drought could cause a food shortage which might then put a match to a smoldering geopolitical tinderbox.

The complacency and misplaced confidence of the status quo render these unpredictable interactions all the more combustible because so little has been done to anticipate the potential domino effect of these global crises.

Context Three: Interlocking Crises, Time Scales and Globalization

One of the factors which renders the intersecting crises of the next 15-25 years so difficult to predict is the multiple time scales at work. A global petroleum shortage, for example, could stagger the developed world in a very short timespan as hoarding and governmental rationing would quickly magnify the disruptions.

Food shortages might develop over a longer period of months as drought, energy shortages and geopolitical issues caused a sharp decline in grain production and/or shipping.

A nuclear war between two long-standing adversaries such as India and Pakistan could erupt in a matter of weeks should internal crises trigger border tensions. China might suddenly deem the moment ripe to conquer Taiwan with military force, loosing a cascading crisis which could lead to limited or even nuclear war between the U.S. and China.

Any war involving the Mideast, East Asia or the U.S. might dramatically effect oil, currencies and trade which would quickly impact economies, food supplies and the psychology of instability/fear/hoarding.

Ironically, the great benefits of globalization--long oil-dependent supply chains leading from distant factories to free-spending Western consumers--can reverse with extraordinary speed as these very same fragile supply chains degrade or shatter in moments of energy, financial or geopolitical crisis.

Long-wave erosions are only visible to historians and those willing to root around obscure data. Thus the slow, steady redistribution of national wealth away from the middle class into the pockets of the State and Plutocracy is barely discernable. Yet just because this movement of wealth, capital and income appears glacial does not mean the effects are insignificant. On the contrary, over-reach by the State and Plutocracy at the expense of the tax-paying productive class has undermined the stability of the status quo to the point that a crisis which might have been contained in the past will spread in positive-feedback fashion, toppling other teetering dominoes in ever-widening circles.

That crises unfolding in different time scales will overlap is easily predictable, but the precise intersection or overlay of various crises is entirely unpredictable. Some geopolitical tension might close the Straits of Hormuz or Malacca, and the resulting restriction of sea lanes and oil tankers might trip some other related and highly unstable situation from brewing crisis to full-blown crisis.

It is also easily predictable that any one nation and its citizenry will have limited control or influence over a truly global crisis (though the one global Empire will have more sway than other nations). We can also safely predict the complacent nations and citizens will suffer more than those who proactively anticipated the likelihood of interlocking, reinforcing crises occurring within the next decade or two.

Ideally, such proactive anticipation should involve households, communities and the nation at large. But if the State (government at all levels) is in denial or deadlock, or crippled by debt or otherwise insolvent, then households and communities will also have to prepare themselves for dwindling State aid.

Even if the State does set aside prudent reserves, these are designed to smooth short-term crises, not semi-permanent declines in the FEW essentials (food, energy, water). For instance, the 600-million barrel U.S. Strategic Petroleum Reserve holds about one month's supply of oil (20 million barrels a day consumed in the U.S. X 30 days). While this is certainly a reassuring number in a short-term crisis, it would be foolhardy to think a one-month's supply will prove to be anything more than a stopgap should oil imports plummet over the long-term.

As we shall see later, various feedback loops (both positive and negative) are at work as each crisis erupts; in some scenarios negative feedback might stem the crisis; in others, a domino effect could transpire, toppling vulnerabilities which encircle the globe.

This is why time-sensitive predictions are foolhardy, both those predicting "the end of the world as we know it" and those spouting the "it will all work out just fine" complacency favored by the mass media and Plutocracy.

What we can predict is that fragile systems without redundancy are vulnerable to disruptions which could then freeze up or degrade the entire network of finance and trade. If these impact the critical FEW resources (food, energy, water) then the disruption can quickly spill over to other systems that were previously considered secure.

System prone to *positive feedback* (runaway self-reinforcing crisis) are inherently more vulnerable to collapse than those with multiple *negative feedbacks*--forces which counteract the trend.

The problem for the complacent is that time scales and vulnerabilities overlap and interactions differ for each crisis. Thus a fast-moving crisis with slow negative feedback (correctives) could race beyond the reach of corrective action, triggering other fast-spreading crises in its wake.

In a world so deeply dependent on cheap, abundant liquid/gas fossil fuels for everything from transportation to food, the vulnerability of all energy-dependent systems to shortage or disruption is acute and works across all time scales.

Context Four: Oil and Empire

There is one commodity unlike any other: oil.

Standard-issue economists tend to treat oil/fossil fuels as a commodity like any other; when demand rises, new or alternative supplies will emerge once they become profitable. But this model is utterly misleading, for liquid hydrocarbons are special in three distinctive ways: they contain very high energy densities, they are stable at normal temperatures and they are readily transportable via pipeline, ship or vehicle. No other energy source possesses all these traits, and those that get close (lithium ion batteries, for instance) are very costly to manufacture and are dependent on dwindling ores (in this case, lithium).

Supposedly "renewable" sources like biofuels and "unlimited" sources like shale oil require so much energy to produce, process and transport (when calculated in equivalent energy densities) that the net energy (useful energy produced minus energy used in production) is actually rather paltry.

Until very recently, oil had the distinct advantage of being cheap to extract. Super-giant fields under pressure produced oil for as little as $1 per barrel in raw costs. But the super-giant fields which supply much of the world's oil now require costly extraction technologies such as water or gas pressurization. New production has been located offshore, in deep water or in extreme climates like the Arctic Circle. It is no longer cheap to locate, extract or process oil or oil equivalents like shale oil.

Oil's most unique characteristic is that every other industry in the global economy depends on oil or oil equivalents: transportation, military, agriculture, tourism, and on and on. Thus a global shortage or disruption will quickly cascade into every corner of the global economy, for new supplies of oil cannot be brought on line quickly (five years would be quick, ten years would be average). Even worse, new production is not even replacing fields in decline; that is the essence of Peak Oil.

As for alternatives: currently, all alternative energy production, including both "old technology" like hydropower and new wind, solar, biofuels and tidal technologies, account for about 3% of the world's energy consumption. Thus a ten-fold increase in alternative energy--a scaling up which is not yet even technologically feasible, and one that in any event would cost trillions of dollars to accomplish--would leave the global economy dependent on petroleum for 2/3 of energy consumption.

Various standard-issue pundits (and always those outside the energy complex, I note) promote the easy-to-swallow notion that gasifying coal "cleanly" and transforming "unlimited" tar sands and shale oil is the "answer." But turning mountains of low-energy coal into gasoline and jet fuel is not clean, cheap or easy, especially when we are talking about stupendous quantities of liquid fuel: the U.S. consumes roughly 500 million gallons a day of liquid fuels (gasoline, diesel and jet fuel).

Thus any model which views energy/petroleum/fossil fuels as subject to the same forces as other commodities such as copper is fatally flawed. Every industry and financial sector ultimately rests on cheap, abundant petroleum. Once petroleum is no longer cheap or available in sufficient quantity to meet demand, then the energy domino will topple all the rest in rapid succession.

The unique commodity petroleum is thus the very foundation of interlocking crises on a global scale.

For more on these topics, please read John Michael Greer's two books, The Long Descent: A User's Guide to the End of the Industrial Age and The Ecotechnic Future: Envisioning a Post-Peak World.

The American Empire

I use the word "Empire" because to avoid it would be artifice. What word other than Empire describes a nation with a commercial, diplomatic and military presence in most of the planet's nations?

I use the term without ideological spin. For the purposes of this analysis, it is not a structure to deny, deplore or glorify but one which must be carefully described as a unique context of all global issues, even those which may appear to have little connection to military matters.

It is important to preface any discussion of Empire by noting that those serving their nation honorably in the U.S. Armed Forces are not always well served by their civilian leadership. The reason citizens serve is to defend the nation, which is the Constitutionally mandated, legitimate purpose of the Armed Forces.

Yet we must not blind ourselves to the reality that the military can also be deployed to serve illegitimate purposes which are presented ("sold") as legitimate to the American public and service members. The citizens who take the oath of service are sworn to uphold the Constitution and to obey their civilian leadership's orders. If the civilian leadership is pursuing agendas other than true national defense--for instance, a commercial and diplomatic Empire--then the U.S. military can be ordered to pursue missions which have little or nothing to do with national defense and everything to do with protecting and extending the interests of the Power Elites which dominate the civilian leadership of the nation.

Those who serve in the U.S. Armed Forces at mid-rank levels of responsibility are aware of the U.S. military's global reach. The average citizen might not know that the U.S. maintains bases in 63 countries and has personnel stationed in approximately 150 nations.

The entire world has been divided into six military zones (Africa was recently set up with its own command), with separate U.S. commands which each control extensive communications, intelligence, war-gaming and planning resources.

"These facilities include a total of 845,441 different buildings and equipments. The underlying land surface is of the order of 30 million acres. According to Gelman, who examined 2005 official Pentagon data, the US is thought to own a total of 737 bases in foreign lands. Adding to the bases inside U.S. territory, the total land area occupied by US military bases domestically within the US and internationally is of the order of 2,202,735 hectares, which makes the Pentagon one of the largest landowners worldwide (Gelman, J., 2007)."

Approximately 369,000 active duty personnel out of a total of 1.4 million serve overseas. Many U.S. military postings are small (a few hundred personnel) and are not combat missions but peacekeeping, medical/logistics, intelligence, support of alliances such as NATO, etc.

The U.S. also maintains Reserve forces (National Guard, etc.) of which about 145,000 are on active duty, and employs an unknown but substantial number of civilian employees (contractors) overseas as well.

Though the Intelligence Community (CIA, NSA, NRO-National Reconnaissance Office, etc.) and the Pentagon (Defense Intelligence Agency, Naval Intelligence, etc.) have some overlapping functions and hence some rivalries, in the larger context the Armed Forces and the Intelligence Community should be viewed as pieces of a truly global Empire which is under the control of the civilian government of the U.S.

No other nation or even alliance has an equivalent global reach. In effect, every nation in the world is a "point of interest," as the U.S. has interests-- commercial, diplomatic and "soft power"--in every nation larger than a small city.

If the U.S. influence were limited to a global military system, it would not be much of an Empire. But the Pentagon and Intelligence forces are merely one branch of a much larger structure which includes a vast diplomatic network--equally as impressive as the military reach--and pervasive commercial interests, of which Coca-Cola, McDonalds and Kentucky Fried Chicken are simply the most visible.

Many American commercial interests are hidden from view behind limited partnerships, wholly owned local corporations, joint ventures and the like; financial and banking interests are similarly cloaked. There is also some overlap of military and corporate interests, as U.S. weapons systems are sold to foreign governments for commercial, diplomatic and military gain.

U.S.-based global corporations receive the majority of their profits from overseas operations; thus the commercial importance of maintaining a Neoliberal capitalist-centric world of open trade and finance--the U.S. Empire--should not be underestimated.

One mechanism of influence and control used by corporations

worldwide is interlocking directorships, in which certain influential people serve on numerous corporate boards, in effect knitting various interests and strategies into a network.

The U.S. Empire can profitably be viewed in this same light. American interests need not own operations outright; the Empire's structure is not one of coercion (except when persuasion and subterfuge fail) but of interlocking interests.

Although it tends to raise ideological hackles, it would be remiss not to observe that the U.S. Intelligence Community is not entirely a passive network; on occasion it has engineered coups, uprisings, protests, etc. and retains the capability to do so--at the command of the civilian government of the U.S.

Why did I include oil and empire as one context? Both are global, and both are intertwined. What's the point of constructing an empire if it cannot secure global energy supplies for the home nation? If all wealth is in effect stored energy, as I contend, then the only real wealth other than food and water is energy.

To the degree a crisis anywhere on the planet affects oil, or any other critical interest of the U.S., then the U.S. Empire will act as a potentially decisive negative or positive feedback, regardless of the location.

Context Five: Ontological Forces Which Power Trends, Reversals and History

Within each context, various forces are at work to resist and accelerate trends. These forces include feedback loops (both positive and negative) and marginal returns. Models which apply equally to the natural world and human society are useful tools to map how ontological forces play out.

Negative feedback can be understood as forces which act as built-in stabilizers, while *positive feedback* can be understood as self-reinforcing trends which lead to runaway expansion and *disequilibrium* (the state of disharmony; out of equilibrium, unstable).

One theme which will re-occur throughout this analysis is that the over-reach of Elites and the State are manifestations of positive feedback: the more powerful they become, the more power they can appropriate. This self-reinforcing dynamic eventually consumes all the surplus of the society, an over-extension (extreme disequilibrium) that ends in collapse.

Forces may arise to counter the self-reinforcing trends--this is negative feedback which tends to stabilize systems around an equilibrium.

Distribution probabilities provide another useful model. In Chapter Six we will discuss the Pareto distribution power law--the *Pareto Principle* or the "80-20 rule" which predicts that 20% of any group has an outsized influence on the "trivial many" (the 80% majority). Though not a physical law like gravity, the Pareto distribution works remarkably well in mapping distributions of income, population, and other large-scale phenomena.

The Pareto Principle is one model within a larger family of mathematical models known as *power laws*, which model the relationship between the frequency of events and the size of those events. The frequencies decrease very slowly as the sizes of the event increase. The classic example is an earthquake twice as large is four times as rare. This model helps us understand why history and Nature do not maintain an "average" or "typical" balance but are ceaselessly moving above and below the equilibrium point.

This model also helps us understand why large disruptive events are infrequent and difficult to predict; the stable and linear suddenly gives way to volatile instability.

Another aspect of power laws is *scale invariance*. A map of a jagged coastline provides a good example: the rough irregularity looks about the same up close as it does from afar. (This is also called self-similarity.) For our purposes, the point is key concepts of this analysis--feedback, over-reach, windfall exploitation, etc.--are scale invariant, working equally within households, enterprises and nations.

Non-equilibrium systems--what we find in nature, economics and history--are dynamic systems which can exhibit what is known as *self-organized criticality* (SOC). (These ideas also find expression in fractals and chaos theory.) The classic example is a sand pile. As sand is slowly added to the top of the pile, small "sand slides" occur as the sand piles up into unstable formations. Every once in awhile, a large sand slide occurs, completely reshaping the entire pile.

This model helps explain why stock markets can suddenly crash after months or years of near-equilibrium and why large forest fires occur far less frequently than small fires, even as their proximate cause (a lightning strike, for example) is essentially identical.

Within the SOC concept lies an even more powerful analytic tool, the *Stick/Slip hypothesis*. During the long "stick" phase (when the sand adheres to the pile) things appear stable. But the longer this phase lasts (the pile growing without disruption), the more likely it becomes that the forces building within the pile will be released suddenly and violently. This dynamic is the explanation for how shifting tectonic plates build up energy which is unpredictably released in many small tremors and rare but massive earthquakes.

I am indebted to oftwominds.com contributor Harun Ibrahim for his introduction to these profoundly practical (if initially abstract) concepts.

Together, these concepts explain how decades of relative equilibrium can suddenly give way to instability, volatility and collapse once unseen forces build to threshold levels.

I will cover these ontological forces and analytic tools in more detail in Chapters Seven and Eleven.

Context Six: The Environment

It is tempting to hope that all the structural environmental challenges will "sort themselves out" or be solved by some new technology that magically scales from the lab to global ubiquity. But the realities do not lend themselves to either benign neglect (that is, just leave everything alone and it will rebalance itself naturally) or technological "fixes."

The human population has exploded in a geological eyeblink from several hundred million to 6.5 billion. In terms of energy and resource consumption, each resident of the First World (Europe, North America, Japan) has an environmental impact up to 100 times larger than that of a Third World person. As 2 billion people in China, India and elsewhere aspire to an energy-intensive consumerist First World lifestyle, that the planet does not have the resources to support 3 billion middle-class consumers is readily visible.

The list of global environmental ills is well known. Overfishing driven by insatiable demand and politically popular subsidies of national fishing industries has driven the world's fisheries to the point of collapse. The technological "fix" is aquaculture, but artificial fisheries spawn another entire host of their own challenges to long-term sustainability.

Fresh water aquifers are being drained everywhere from the American southwest to China, and there are no sustainable ways to compensate for this drawdown of irreplaceable fresh-water resources.

Schemes to desalinate vast quantities of seawater requires stupendous amounts of energy; a recent plan by Saudi Arabia would burn fully 1 million barrels of oil a day--1 million barrels that could no longer be exported to the U.S.

Regardless of what we believe the causes might be, glaciers are melting at increasing rates. Once the Himalayan and Andean glaciers vanish or recede to mere patches of ice, the rivers 2 billion people rely on for irrigation water will become seasonal.

Add in massive soil erosion in China and elsewhere, extended droughts in Australia, etc., and you get a picture of global resources stretched to the breaking point.

The more you know about the technical details of supposedly miraculous technological "fixes" like desalination, tidal energy, algae-based fuels, etc., the more you understand that very few if any of these emerging technologies may "scale up" to global applications.

In other words, algae-based fuels can work just fine on the rooftop of a university lab, but the hard part is scaling it up to produce 1.7 billion gallons of gasoline-equivalent liquid fuel a day—which is only half of the world's current consumption of oil. (Total global consumption of oil, 80 million barrels a day, so 40 million barrels a day X 42 gallons/barrel.)

Add these realities up and the context is a potential crash of global food and fresh water supplies, exacerbated by energy shortages. As authors such as Jared Diamond have explained, eras of resource depletion often trigger war/conflict between competing groups/nations.

In essence there are four interlocking crises: environmental, energy, financial and geopolitical. Excellent sources abound on these topics: The Future of Life, Beyond Oil: The View from Hubbert's Peak, and The Long Emergency: Surviving the End of Oil, Climate Change, and Other Converging Catastrophes of the Twenty-First Century come to mind of the many useful texts in print.

Context Seven: The End of Debt-Based "Prosperity"

The "prosperity" of the past two decades was based not on savings, investment and productivity, as the mainstream financial media and think-tank punditry maintain, but by extremes of speculative credit, leverage, debt and risk-taking, all enabled by a financial system based on obfuscation, deception, embezzlement, fraud, abuse of credit and grossly inflated asset valuations, a.k.a. bubbles.

This debt binge was fed by a marketing-based consumerist culture in which shopping and acquisition became recreation, therapy, self-fulfillment and status all in one profit-driven package.

Compounding the collapse of this debt-based "prosperity" are two long-term trends: the end of cheap, abundant fossil fuels which enabled inexpensive global supply chains and tourism, and the "end of work," a global contraction of paid labor.

Context Eight: Squeezing the Middle Class

The intersection of various long-term political and financial trends is effectively squeezing the middle class, which the State (government) depends on to pay most of the taxes. Caught between the over-reach of both the state and its elites (the Plutocracy) and the end of debt-based, cheap-oil "prosperity" which enabled it to maintain an illusion of wealth, the middle class is being squeezed to the breaking point. I address this topic in a later chapter.

Context Nine: The Nature of Prosperity and Happiness

The U.S. Declaration of Independence recognizes the inalienable rights to "life, liberty and the pursuit of happiness." Oddly enough, happiness turns out to be a slippery concept, and much of what Americans spend their lives pursuing does not actually increase their happiness. Indeed, it is self-evident that the stress levels, medication usage and miseries of the "American lifestyle" even in times of prosperity are far higher than one would expect were happiness as abundant as cheap consumer goods.

And even prosperity itself turns out to be rather more slippery than rising GDP or other metrics would suggest. It seems that much of what passes for "essential accoutrements of prosperity" such as large suburban homes, multiple vehicles and closets crammed with clothing do not bring happiness to their owners. Rather, they are largely the mirage-like results of marketing propaganda conjured up to generate profits, not life satisfaction or happiness.

Indeed, were we to travel back in time to 1870s San Francisco, for example, we would find people feeling quite prosperous even though they lived in what we would now consider relatively primitive poverty: no electricity, no vehicles except public streetcars, (On August 2, 1873, the inventor of the San Francisco cable car, Andrew Hallidie, was the system's first passenger), trains and horse-drawn wagons, primitive healthcare, costly consumer goods, etc.

Thus the entire notions of prosperity and happiness must be examined objectively before we can even say with any reliability what the words actually mean.

Context Ten: The Framework of Our Response

Our responses to these interwoven, reinforcing challenges of our era can be organized into three inter-related levels:

--family/household

--community/networks

--nation

Each level requires different skills, resources, inputs and solutions. I will cover these topics in the second section.

Key concepts in this chapter:

Simulacrum of thinking

Monopoly capital

Politics of experience

Positive feedback

Negative feedback

Disequilibrium

Pareto Principle

Power law

Scale invariance

Self-organized criticality (SOC)

Stick/Slip hypothesis

Chapter Four: Complacency and Fatalism

Let's begin by considering *Context One: Human Nature* in more depth. Entire libraries have been written on the subject of human nature, but for our practical purposes those which probe humanity's "default settings" such as Jared Diamond's The Third Chimpanzee: The Evolution and Future of the Human Animal and E.O. Wilson's Sociobiology: The New Synthesis are the most useful.

Although we can slice and dice complex human responses in hundreds of ways (for instance, Who am I? The 16 Basic Desires that Motivate Our Actions and Define Our Personalities), for the purposes of a stripped-down practical analysis we can group our "default responses" into four basic categories: inertia, fear/panic, casting our lot with a "Big Man"/leader or fatalism/giving up.

While we can collectively sacrifice short-term gain for long-term security, as Jared Diamond describes in his book Collapse: How Societies Choose to Fail or Succeed, it is equally likely that a society will continue down the path to complete collapse. One of the key conditions Diamond identifies is a society's understanding of its primary challenges and dilemmas. Those that did not grasp their limitations and restricted options failed. So our first step must be to adequately understand the limitations and options we face while avoiding the denial and complacency that will doom our economy to collapse.

The emotionally charged state of fear/panic ("fight or flight") requires a quick reaction, but decisions made in this instinctive mode tend to be rash, hasty, impulsive and poorly planned. Thus the key is to recognize this mode and consciously avoid making decisions with long-term consequences while in the grip of this "instant response" survival-mode.

Humans, like our relatives the chimpanzees, are social animals. Like chimps, we are "wired" to form groups and select/follow leaders who reach their high status by offering something back to the community: protection, "potlatch" type sharing of wealth, etc. We will examine this political/social response to crisis in a later section.

But humans also have the capacity to be alone, like our other primate relatives the orangutans. Thus withdrawing from the community has deep roots in human nature and history.

Being creatures of habit—and habits are a survival mechanism, for why change anything when "everything's working"?-- humans prefer the status quo until crisis forces us to change. This inertia/attachment to the status quo is complacency, which acts as a *cognitive trap* or *emotional attractor*, as does fatalism/withdrawal.

Complacency and Fatalism

Complacency and fatalism are both seductive cognitive traps and emotional attractors which we have to avoid if we are to think clearly. Each is an attractor because each is highly appealing for several fundamental reasons.

1. Human nature veers between these basic social/anti-social emotions: complacency/status quo (inertia) and fatalism/resignation (withdrawal).

2. History reveals these attractors (complacency and fatalism) were active in previous great declines/collapses, such as the Roman Empire circa 400-576 C.E. (see below)

3. Humans prefer simplistic "answers" to challenges/problems, and a blind faith in the status quo or resignation both fit the bill.

Complacency is best understood as what's expressed in the phrase, "Don't worry, it will sort itself out on its own." In stable "normal" times, this complacency is usually rewarded; various corrective feedback loops within complex systems kick in and problems are met with countermeasures that act to restabilize the system.

But in very dynamic eras, destabilizing factors overwhelm the usual corrective feedback mechanisms, and things do not sort themselves out. Dramatic, even radical action must be taken. In these times, complacency is not a practical or helpful strategy: it is a soothing but dangerous cognitive trap which guarantees the believer will be unprepared for the challenges just ahead.

In the cognitive trap of fatalism, we recognize the risks/dangers of the situation but feel helpless to correct or solve the problems. In this trap, we remove ourselves from action and give up, dooming ourselves to being swept up by whatever passing winds arise.

The goal here is to avoid these traps, analyze the challenges we face clearly, and then plan out a simple but interconnected three-part strategy for not just survival but prosperity and security.

Complacency can take many forms. For instance, people who have prepared themselves for a doomsday collapse of civilization, i.e. "The end of the world as we know it" (TEOTWAWKI) may well find themselves ill-prepared for an equally probable slow decline in social cohesion and living standards. That is, living conditions in highly developed nations may descend not to a Collapse of Civilization into Chaos but to Third World levels of stable impoverishment.

Stable impoverishment describes a system which produces little national surplus but which produces the necessities of life in enough abundance that the instabilities of famine are generally stayed. Radios and TVs are in sufficient supply to offer the populace modest entertainment, and the State is neither burdensome nor repressive, as taxation cannot exceed what little surplus remains after minimally feeding, clothing and transporting the populace.

The key feature of stable impoverishment is the lack of incentives to any class to disrupt the status quo. The Elites dare not risk insurrection and the citizenry below dare not risk turmoil which might lead to famine. Another way of describing stable impoverishment is that the ruling Elites do not over-reach but maintain a stable division of national income.

These divergent but equally undesirable options, TEOTWAWKI and stable impoverishment, highlight the need to ground our analyses and expectations in history-- not because it repeats, but because it rhymes. No one can know the future, so we must be cautious about putting all our eggs in one basket/scenario. Prudence suggests always maintaining a skeptical point of view: what if we're wrong? What's our Plan B/ alternative strategy?

Fatalism is similarly devious. People who withdraw from society are certainly taking action, but they have surrendered the opportunity to influence the outcome positively: that is fatalism of the first order.

If you're reading this, then you have already advanced beyond the naïve complacency of "don't worry, everything will work itself out" which is mesmerizing large segments of our citizenry. You may well be a member of The Remnant—more on that later.

The Politics of Complacency and Fatalism

In Greek mythology, two sea monsters Scylla and Charybdis forced sailors into an unsavory choice of facing one or the other when navigating the Strait of Messina. In modern vernacular, we might say the sailors were "between a rock and a hard place."

Our "default mode" responses were selected for a hunting-gathering lifestyle; humanity has pursued agriculture for perhaps 5% of its long history as *homo sapiens sapiens* and dealt with advanced technology for perhaps 1% of its history.

The consequences of these unconstructive responses can be seen in the advanced civilizations (Mayans, Rome, etc.) that collapsed despite a wealth of experience and knowledge.

As a result, even as we work at devising rational, long-range solutions, we will be fending off the "monsters" of complacency and fatalism every inch of the way.

Analyzing challenges and then plotting out practical solutions is arduous, precarious work, as the answers are rarely clear and painful trial-and-error attempts are often the only way forward. Rather than engage in this difficult process, many find doing nothing (complacency) or withdrawing (fatalism) much less risky and demanding. This inaction feeds on itself, setting up a point-of-no-return that could have been avoided by bold action when the problems were first visible.

Humans cannot remain in the high-stress "fight or flight" status for long; we seek a resolution or equilibrium, both intellectual and social. Thus the most constructive approach is to assess the challenges in a clear-eyed fashion, hashing out the strengths and weaknesses of each major strategy. Then make a decision, and commit the time, resources and unity the strategy needs to succeed—or fail conclusively, perhaps, at which point make a reassessment based on what's been learned from the experience.

At each point in this process, two new temptations arise: to either leap erratically from strategy to strategy as a short-term desire ("fight or flight" mode) for instant results sabotages any long-term effort, or to tire of the process of negotiation and analysis and give up sustained effort.

Many who do engage the challenges will base their solutions on inflexible ideological (political and/or religious) worldviews that are too rigid to be practical/realistic. Rather than face the problems with an eye on actual solutions, these players seek to protect their own fiefdoms, privileges and benefits under the guise of emotionally appealing ideologies. Faced with the loss of their sacrosanct (to them) privileges and benefits, they view the battle for diminishing resources as a "fight to the death." In a real sense, their status and advantages are definitely at risk; but ironically, by focusing on their ideological opponents instead of the actual problems, they seal their own destruction by insuring the collapse of the entire system.

Both ends of the political spectrum are prone to this frantic defense of the failing status quo: the plutocracy/holders of wealth and those drawing benefits/welfare. This too mirrors the experience of the Roman Empire's decline, which saw massive expansion of wealth disparity (those at the top gained ever more wealth at the expense of the middle class) even as an ever-growing army of unproductive recipients at the bottom received the infamous "bread and circuses" of free bread and public entertainments.

As a consequence of this rabidly self-serving political battle over diminishing resources and surpluses, those championing flexible, practical solutions are crowded out by the shrill, desperate voices of those protecting their fiefdoms and privileges. The result is a profound disunity in the body politic in which compromise is abandoned and common ground vanishes. As external and internal threats increase and resources shrink, the culture and economy are frozen into warring camps, each of which seeks to undermine the other rather than actually address the severe problems facing the entire body politic and economy.

All these forces—complacency, fatalism, fanatic self-interest, ideological rigidity at each end of the political spectrum and political disunity—pose enormous challenges to those seeking long-term solutions to critical problems.

If we seek historical examples of the immense power of complacency, we need look no further than the Western Roman Empire.

For an explication of just how destructive such deep complacency can be, I turn to the excellent account of the causes of the Roman Empire's collapse by Michael Grant, <u>The Fall of the Roman Empire</u>.

"Enmeshed in classical history, all he can do is lapse into vague sermonizing, telling the Romans, as many a moralist had told them throughout the centuries, that they must undergo an ethical regeneration and return to the simplicities and self-sacrifices of their ancestors.

There was no room at all, in these ways of thinking, for the novel, apocalyptic situation which had now arisen, a situation which needed solutions as radical as itself. His whole attitude is a complacent acceptance of things as they are, without a single new idea.

This acceptance was accompanied by greatly excessive optimism about the present and future. Even when the end was only sixty years away, and the Empire was already crumbling fast, Rutilius continued to address the spirit of Rome with the same supreme assurance.

This blind adherence to the ideas of the past ranks high among the principal causes of the downfall of Rome. If you were sufficiently lulled by these traditional fictions, there was no call to take any practical first-aid measures at all."

But fatalism, often expressed by opting out/withdrawing from society, can be just as destructive as complacency. As Grant noted elsewhere in The Fall of the Roman Empire:

"Considerable sections of the population of the later Roman Empire decided to opt out altogether. In the first place, a large number of people, finding the social system intolerable, went underground and became its enemies. But a second movement consisted of numerous men and women who merely abandoned the company of their fellow human beings and divorced themselves from the community.

And so as the final political and military reckoning rapidly approached, this substantial number of men and women was no longer available to contribute either to the actual defense of the Empire or to the revenue needed to pay for the defenders."

Grant traces much of the intellectual justification for what might be termed "a fatal fatalism" to Christian thinkers like Augustine:

"And so Augustine preached, as other had before him, that 'we do not want to have dealings with the powers that be.' That is frank: a call to withhold service from the government. Equally frank is his reminder that the Empire is bound to collapse anyway.

Augustine shifted the center of gravity so that the state is now a good deal less that half of what matters: far from helping his own country to survive, his attitude contributed to its downfall. But his suggestion that, since it was up to Providence whether the Roman world should collapse or not, human endeavor could do nothing about it in any case, met with the strong disapproval of thinkers such as Pelagius.

Pelagius' reaction to the sacking of Rome in 410 by Alaric was by no means limited to fatalistic gloom and despair. Both before and after the capture of the city, he found himself deeply dissatisfied with the moral sluggishness of many prosperous people of Rome. He insisted on a strenuous individual effort to attain salvation: we sin by a voluntary imitation of Adam, and an equally voluntary decision can cast our sins behind us.

His doctrine of the will at least wanted people to try. Augustine's philosophy, on the other hand, led to fatalism."

Given the stupendous inertia of complacency, the fierce defense of the status quo from those contributing little but reaping plenty and the intellectual and emotional charms of fatalist withdrawal, those seeking practical solutions and strategies may well see the battle as essentially hopeless.

As tempting as that fatalism might be, there is hope offered by the Pareto principle: the influential few (The Remnant) can indeed lead the trivial many.

Opting Out/Opting In

The desire to withdraw from a corrupted, declining society, or indeed, from the imperfect company of humans, stretches back to the dawn of civilization. In many cultures, a spiritual quest for Oneness with God/Enlightenment encourages withdrawal and rejection of worldly goods and goals.

We have seen in the example of Rome how eras of crisis encourage many to opt out of society. But opting out of society can mean either a withdrawal to what we might call splendid isolation or an opting in to an alternative social structure.

Thus the yogi, spiritual seeker, or Transcendentalist might well seek complete isolation in a wilderness, while others opting out of a failing state might join a religious commune or monastery. Such communities are largely self-sustaining, even as they retain ties to various parts of the greater society and economy.

Both of these methods of opting out have deep roots in American culture and history. The noble desire to seek Oneness with God and fulfillment via oneness with Nature was championed by Henry David Thoreau in Walden, while various faith-based communes and communities have found fertile ground in every century.

Splendid Isolation also ties directly into a key American Myth: the Rugged Individual. This is a tangled web of fantasy, reality and hidden dependence on a functioning economy beyond the wilderness. Thus even Thoreau walked back to town on numerous occasions, for food and social contact, and the Buddhist mendicant monks of Southeast Asia rely on the alms of productive people for their sustenance. In other words, Splendid Isolation still relies in most cases on "the outside world" to grow the grain, etc. which the "one alone" ultimately relies upon.

It is exceedingly difficult to grow, nourish and sustain all that life requires alone. That is the fundamental reason why most primates, including humans, form groups: a group is simply a far more productive, robust survival structure than a single individual.

Thus, rugged individuals who could survive on their own form communities to reap the advantages of such mutually beneficial networks.

A few years ago the U.S. Army ran an advertising slogan "An Army of One." But this was a misnomer, for the single most important combat asset is unit cohesion. Even the supreme Rugged Individual survives best in a circle of others willing to fight together for a common cause.

Another enduring myth of American culture is "living off the land." Many of my correspondents who hunt and fish report that when discussions of financial hardship arise, many of their acquaintances say they will simply bag some deer and go fishing to feed their families.

Sadly, what was possible in the remote, largely unpopulated America of the distant past is not possible for a nation of dwindling wilderness and 300 millions mouths to feed.

The more one has actually walked remote areas of the nation like the Rockies, High Sierra, great deserts and untilled plains, the more one comes to understand just how little food for humans exists in the wild.

This is why hunter-gatherers require vast tracts of land: Nature is indeed bountiful, but rarely for humans.

It is easy to over-estimate the number of wildfowl, fish and large mammals available for human consumption in the "wild," and even easier to overestimate the calories available to be reaped from the wild before the land is stripped of game and other edibles.

The hunter who bags several dozen pheasant, for instance, ends up with a pitifully small bag of dried meat at the end of the process. As for the plentiful fish—let's not forget they were stocked by an advanced-technology, oil-fueled, well-funded state agency. Once the fish are no longer stocked, the illusory bounty disappears.

To the unknowing eye, the Hawaiian rain forest looks like it must be a veritable cornucopia of edibles suitable for human consumption. In fact, the truly native rain forest offers very little to hungry humans. If you come across a mango or banana tree, that was planted by other humans.

You would also find that the "wild" mango tree is remarkably stingy with its bounty. Growing high above the ground, most of the fruit is unreachable, even with ladders, and the fruit is small and mostly seed; the actual pulp is stringy and meager compared to the farm-coddled mangoes we find in markets.

Thus a small intensive garden may well contain more human-suitable food than a square kilometer or square mile of wilderness. Many bounteous wild crops like acorns require a backbreaking amount of work before they can be rendered suitable for human consumption— and they require copious amounts of fuel for cooking.

It is sobering to recall that tiny bands of primitively armed humans hunted the wooly mammoth to extinction in a matter of a few decades, and a relative handful of better-armed Americans shot millions of bison in a few short years, driving the herds which once blackened the plains to the precipice of extinction.

We should be very wary of all such complacency traps: there is simply no way to feed 300 million people by foraging a mostly calorie-barren landscape and fish-stripped sea. Such a stupendous population requires a large-scale, heavily mechanized intensive production of grain.

Conclusion #1: everyone who opts out of a given social circumstance opts into some other circumstance. There can be no "opting out" without a corresponding opting in to something else.

Conclusion #2: Opting into a myth is not a sustainable option;

humans developed social networks /communities and agriculture precisely because the alternative options of Splendid Isolation and foraging were perilously less successful survival strategies.

Conclusion #3: The key difference between opting for isolation and opting into alternative communities/networks is the sustainability and productivity of the community. Very few who live in isolation are truly independent of a larger productive society. This simple truth is the engine behind agriculture and urban centers.

Thus the skeptic gazes at the latter-day isolationists who stockpile six months of advanced-economy, advanced technology consumables in a remote cabin and asks:

What happens in Month Seven when the stockpile is gone?

Or make it Month 13 or Month 25; the point is withdrawing without creating a productive sustainable source of food, energy and other critical necessities is not a survival strategy at all, it's simply pushing the day of reckoning forward a bit.

Creating an integrated, independent, sustainable productivity by oneself or as a couple is akin to raising a child in isolation: it looks fun until you really give it a try. A baby may well be adorable to a teen for an hour or so, but give the teen the baby for 48 hours straight and his/her reaction will be quite different.

Haul water in five-gallon buckets from a stream for a few weeks, cut wood by hand, carry a 5-gallon propane tank by bicycle down to the refilling station, sharpen a chisel by hand, fix a balky gas-powered refrigerator—the list of skills and energies required are far longer than a myth-based culture can imagine.

While it is possible to envision a technology-rich "splendid isolation" fueled by solar panels, water pumps, satellite Internet links, geothermal-exchange heating, triple-pane windows, all protected by elaborate security technology, there are two difficulties with this scenario: few can afford to set it up, and those few who do have created a high-value, very vulnerable target in the middle of an existing population with whom they have no social or economic ties. One need look no farther than luxury vehicles being smashed and burned in the streets to foresee the possible responses such wealth disparity causes.

There is a model for barricading oneself and one's wealth behind high walls of security: all "planet of slums" cities in the Third World contain small heavily defended islands of wealth in a vast sea of poverty.

If this lifestyle appeals to you, there are ample opportunities to try it out today in any Third World mega-city.

The skeptic wonders if the Isolationist expects others to have constructed a large-scale productive sustainable economy in their absence, and to welcome those who opted out of contributing to the arduous construction of this sustainable future with open arms.

Just because the grasshopper squirreled away a stash to last the winter does not mean the productive colony of ants will welcome his future freeloading come spring.

Thus the goal must be a truly sustainable productivity, not a temporary opting out dependent on a stockpile of unsustainably produced consumer goods.

In some societies, the religious mendicant can freeload off the productive society because the productive members believe feeding the mendicant provides them with religious merit. But the U.S. is not such a society; its historical religious principles are expressed in the line, "The Lord helps those who help themselves," and stockpiling high-tech supplies to last a few months is not actually helping oneself or others in any long-term, sustainable fashion.

Manifestations of Political Complacency/Fatalism

The great danger of complacency is that a misplaced trust in the Powers That Be and their supposedly robust economic and political structures of control and distribution will lull us into the placid fantasy that the State will somehow rescue us from whatever crises befall the nation.

Ultimately, the belief in the almost godlike powers of the State breed a dangerous complacency. The writings left behind by citizens of the late Roman Empire speak with the utmost faith of Rome's everlasting power and its eternal glory. Yet a few decades hence the once-mighty global empire collapsed in a heap--a sharp reminder that no State is all-powerful or immune to financial ruin.

This faith in the powers of the Savior State manifests in several ways.

1. The State can provide us all with the FEW essentials (food, energy, water) in emergencies and extended crises.

In actuality, all the FEW systems are fragile and have low levels of redundancy. Most cities (and most of the populace in developed nations live in urban centers) have a week or so of food on hand and are dependent on long rail, trucking and shipping lines of supply which are themselves largely dependent on liquid petroleum.

While some nations possess enough nuclear generation capacity to provide electricity for their citizenry should petroleum supplied be disrupted, electricity will not fuel the tractors, trucks, petrochemical industries, etc. which are integral to agriculture and the global oil system.

Though the mainstream media marginalizes the "survivalist movement," the media itself rarely offers any realistic assessment of the FEW system's great vulnerabilities and dependency on cheap, abundant fossil fuels.

2. The State will provide the entitlements it has promised to us in our retirement years.

Is there any more pernicious misrepresentation than the endless assurances spewed by the Federal government and the mass media that the insolvent carcasses of Medicare and Social Security will continue to send out tens of millions of checks to the citizenry and its "healthcare providers" even as the entire government slides toward an inevitable insolvency?

The gap between projected tax revenues (and these estimates were made before the current Depression took hold) and projected entitlement spending in the next two decades is around $56 trillion--equivalent to the entire value of the U.S. and four times the nation's GDP.

Add in the costs of maintaining a global Empire and bailing out the banking industries for a generation and it is simply not within the realm of possibility that the U.S. will be able to borrow $100 trillion on top of its already unsustainable "normal" deficit spending. It is misleading to the point of pure deception to claim that if the U.S. prints $100 trillion the resulting dollar will have any purchasing power whatsoever.

If your Social Security check bears a number around $1,000 but has the purchasing power of $5 today, will that fulfill the government's entitlement promises?

3. The State will act to protect private property.

There are numerous ways the State can fail to protect private property, or in essence steal it from its citizenry.

The most visible way the State can fail to protect private property is to be unable to stop or discourage outright "street crime" theft via burglary, robbery, etc. The reason why this is a plausible scenario is financial; as police officers now cost well over $100,000 each per year in salaries, benefits and pension costs, cities and counties may simply be unable to pay peace officers at these pay scales as their tax revenues plummet and their unsustainably generous pension plans require ever-larger sums.

A second more pernicious way the State can fail to protect property is to increase taxes in order to pay what are essentially confiscatory public employee wages and pension benefits, and "gaming the system" looting by local government officials, contractors, and various other State parasites.

Though this may seem farfetched, we have not seen the end of the cycle in which the State (Federal, state, county, city and municipal agencies) gradually increase the tax burdens on the remaining productive elements of the economy in order to fund their own employees (the protected, upper-caste technocracy), the Plutocracy's perquisites (loopholes, exemptions, etc.) and the underclass whose compliance the State must purchase.

As Rome crumbled, the remaining middle class fled to the Plutocracy's estates to willingly become serfs, as the Imperial taxes had become so onerous that freedom was no longer a viable option.

The third way the State can fail to protect private property is via its abject failure to constrain or punish "theft by other means" in which financial players such as investment banks loot public funds. The money lost to financial thievery, corruption, fraud, etc. must be paid by the remaining productive members of the economy and their children and grandchildren--presuming the State remains solvent that long, a highly unlikely possibility.

The fourth way the State can fail to protect private property is by outright confiscation of private property such as gold, or the confiscation of private real estate via eminent domain which is then turned over to other private hands (the Plutocracy) for their enjoyment and gain.

The fifth way the State can fail to protect private property is to actively encourage (or fail to limit) inflation of the nation's currency, the dollar. Inflation is in effect theft from all holders of the dollar, most of whom are U.S. citizens.

The State benefits from inflation, which is essentially a hidden tax on all wealth holders and earners, for inflation enables the State to pay off its stupendous past borrowings with depreciated currency and to continue the illusion of paying entitlements at full value.

While some observers claim inflation also benefits private citizens, as they too can pay off debt with depreciated dollars, the citizenry who hold dollars or financial assets such as savings accounts and bonds are also losers, as these assets are severely reduced in purchasing power by inflation.

Traditional hedges against inflation such as real estate and collectibles, i.e. tangible goods, may not provide a durable hedge as oversupply and other factors may cause even tangibles to lose value when measured in gold or oil.

Equally as crippling as a complacent faith in the State is a fatalistic assumption that the State cannot be saved and thus we should stand aside and let it fall. It may well fall of its own weight, regardless of our actions, but to assume we citizens are powerless to force the State to adapt to reality is just as foolhardy as trusting it to save us from wave after wave of global crises.

The king of France, Louis VIX is purported to have said, "L'etat, c'est moi": the state, it is me. In that sense we the citizenry are the State, should we wrest control of it from the Plutocracy and other parasitic classes that feed off it.

If we fall into either complacency or fatalism, then the State and its dependent classes will act in their own self-interest rather than in the interests of the citizenry at large.

The Complacency of "This is the only way the system can work"

In addition to a baseless faith that yesterday's prosperity will magically reappear on its own, there is another kind of complacency: "This is the only way the system can work."

To help us grasp just how deep complacency runs in the U.S., I turn to correspondent K.D., who recently filed this report:

"I visited a friend of mine who lives in Fountain Hills Arizona. Nice 5,000 sq ft house with a huge pool in back, and if you walk outside his house you can see the fountain in the middle of town shoot water about 500 ft. in the air. I think the rainfall in the area is abut 9 inches a year (qualifies it as a desert) with a summer temp of 105 or so.

I visited him a few years ago and there were many 5000+ sq. ft. houses under construction. At that time, he mentioned his house had doubled in value in just two years and people couldn't buy lots fast enough. This visit, as I went for a morning jog around the area, I couldn't help but notice that every other house or lot was for sale.

He had a Superbowl party and many of his neighbors came over. These were all highly educated, affluent people, ages from 45-65ish (hard to tell the upper limit, plenty of nip/tuck work). I made it a point to ask a few of them about:
1. general state of the economy
2. housing bubble
3. energy/peak oil and
4. water resources

The unanimous responses (in order above): 1. just a blip, things will start looking up once the stimulus hits, 2. no way prices will drop much more, it is a great time to buy, 3. there is plenty of oil, the recent price spike was do to speculators ("saw the same thing in the 70's..."), and if it does start to get expensive, we can run off of solar, 4. we have plenty of water - no way we can run out.

I won't bother with an analysis of the above - good times ahead for Fountain Hills, no doubt...."

This complacency/denial on all levels is slowly being eroded by reality. The 500-foot useless fountains are about to be turned off because the water and money have run out. We will belatedly discover that the systems we believed could only work one way are collapsing. There is an alternative to working one way: they can stop working altogether.

Key concepts in this chapter:
Cognitive traps
Emotional attractors
Splendid Isolation
Stable impoverishment
Opting in/opting out

Chapter Five: The Art of Survival, Taoism and the Warring States

In addition to the near-impossibility of long-term sustainability, Splendid Isolation has another drawback: an insurmountably intrinsic insecurity. (A version of this chapter was published on www.oftwominds.com in June, 2008.)

I'm not trying to be difficult, but I can't help cutting against the grain on topics like surviving the coming bad times when my experience runs counter to the standard received wisdom.

A common thread within most discussions of surviving bad times-- especially really bad times--runs more or less like this: stockpile a bunch of canned/dried food and other valuable accoutrements of civilized life (generators, tools, canned goods, firearms, etc.) in a remote area far from urban centers, and then wait out the bad times, all the while protecting your stash with an array of weaponry and technology (night vision binoculars, etc.)

Now while I respect and admire the goal, I must respectfully disagree with just about every assumption behind this strategy. Once again, this isn't because I enjoy being ornery (please don't check on that with my wife) but because everything in this strategy runs counter to my own experience in rural, remote settings.

You see, when I was a young teen my family lived in the mountains. To the urban sophisticates who came up as tourists, we were "hicks" (or worse), and to us they were "flatlanders" (derisive snort).

Now the first thing you have to realize is that we know the flatlanders, but they don't know us. They come up to their cabin, and since we live here year round, we soon recognize their vehicles and know about how often they come up, what they look like, if they own a boat, how many in their family, and just about everything else which can be learned by simple observation.

The second thing you have to consider is that after school and chores (remember there are lots of kids who are too young to have a legal job, and many older teens with no jobs, which are scarce), boys and girls have a lot of time on their hands. We're not taking piano lessons and all that urban busywork. And while there are plenty of pudgy kids spending all afternoon or summer in front of the TV or videogame console, not every kid is like that.

So we're out riding around. On a scooter or motorcycle if we have one, (and if there's gasoline, of course), but if not then on bicycles, or we're hoofing it. Since we have time, and we're wandering all over this valley or mountain or plain, one way or another, then somebody will spot that trail of dust rising behind your pickup when you go to your remote hideaway. Or we'll run across the new road or driveway you cut, and wander up to see what's going on. Not when you're around, of course, but after you've gone back down to wherever you live. There's plenty of time; since you picked a remote spot, nobody's around.

Your hideaway isn't remote to us; this is our valley, mountain, desert, etc., all 20 miles of it, or what have you. We've hiked around all the peaks, because there's no reason not to and we have a lot of energy. Fences and gates are no big deal, (if you triple-padlock your gate, then we'll just climb over it) and any dirt road, no matter how rough, is just an open invitation to see what's up there. Remember, if you can drive to your hideaway, so can we. Even a small pickup truck can easily drive right through most gates (don't ask how, but I can assure you this is true). If nobody's around, we have all the time in the world to lift up or snip your barbed wire and sneak into your haven. Its remoteness makes it easy for us to poke around and explore without fear of being seen.

What flatlanders think of as remote, we think of as home. If you packed in everything on your back, and there was no road, then you'd have a very small hideaway--more a tent than a cabin. You'd think it was safely hidden, but we'd eventually find it anyway, because we wander all over this area, maybe hunting rabbits, or climbing rocks, or doing a little fishing if there are any creeks or lakes in the area. Or we'd spot the wisp of smoke rising from your fire one crisp morning, or hear your generator, and wonder who's up there. We don't need much of a reason to walk miles over rough country, or ride miles on our bikes.

When we were 13, my buddy J.E. and I tied sleeping bags and a few provisions on our bikes--mine was an old 3-speed, his a Schwinn 10-speed--and rode off into the next valley over bone-jarring dirt roads. We didn't have fancy bikes with shocks, and we certainly didn't have camp chairs, radios, big ice chests and all the other stuff people think is necessary to go camping; we had some matches, cans of beans and apple sauce and some smashed bread. (It didn't start out smashed, but the roads were rough. Note: if you ever suffer from constipation, I recommend beans and applesauce.)

We camped where others had camped before us, not in a campground but just off the road in a pretty little meadow with a ring of fire-blackened rocks and a flat spot among the pine needles. We didn't have a tent, or air mattress, or any of those luxuries; but we had the smashed bread and the beans, and we made a little fire and ate and then went to sleep under the stars glittering in the dark sky.

There were a few bears in the area, but we weren't afraid; we didn't need a gun to feel safe. We weren't dumb enough to sleep with our food; if some bear wandered by and wanted the smashed bread, he could take it without bothering us. The only animal that could bother us was the human kind, and since few people walk 10 or more miles over rough ground in the heat and dust, then we'd hear their truck or motorbike approaching long before they ever spotted us.

We explored old mines and anything else we spotted, and then we rode home, a long loop over rutted, dusty roads. In summer, we took countless hikes over the mountainous wilderness behind his family cabin.

All of which is to say that the locals will know where your hideaway is because they have lots of time to poke around. Any road, no matter how rough, might as well be lit with neon lights which read, "Come on up and check this out!" If a teen doesn't spot your road, then somebody will: a county or utility employee out doing his/her job, a hunter, somebody. As I said, the only slim chance you have of being undetected is if you hump every item in your stash on your pack through trailess, roadless wilderness. But if you ever start a fire, or make much noise, then you're sending a beacon somebody will eventually notice.

The Taoists developed their philosophy during an extended era of turmoil known as the Warring States period of Chinese history.

One of their main principles runs something like this: if you're tall and stout and strong, then you'll call attention to yourself. And because you're rigid--that is, what looks like strength at first glance--then when the wind rises, it snaps you right in half.

If you're thin and ordinary and flexible, like a willow reed, then you'll bend in the wind, and nobody will notice you. You'll survive while the "strong" will be broken, either by unwanted attention or by being brittle.

Another thing to ponder is that the human animal is a much better predator than it is an elusive prey. Goats and wild turkeys and other animals have very keen senses of smell and hearing, and it's tough to get close without them smelling you or hearing you. They're well camouflaged, and since human sight is selected to detect movement and color, if they stay quite still we have a hard time spotting them.

In comparison, the human is a clumsy prey. It can't smell or hear very well, and it's large and not well camouflaged. Plus it's usually distracted and unaware of its surroundings. It doesn't take much to kill a human, either; a single-shot rifle and a single round of .22 long is plenty enough.

If the chips are down, and push comes to shove, then what we're discussing is a sort of war, isn't it? And if we're talking about war, then we should think about the principles laid down in The Art Of War by Sun Tzu quite some time ago.

The flatlander protecting his valuable depot is on the defensive, and anyone seeking to take it away (by negotiation, threat or force) is on the offensive. The defense can select the site for proximity to water, clear fields of fire, or what have you, but one or two defenders have numerous disadvantages. Perhaps most importantly, they need to sleep. Secondly, just about anyone who's plinked cans with a rifle and who's done a little hunting can sneak up and put away an unwary human. Unless you remain in an underground bunker 24/7, at some point you'll be vulnerable. And that's really not much of a life--especially when your food supplies finally run out, which they eventually will. Or you run out of water, or your sewage system overflows, or some other situation requires you to emerge.

So let's line it all up. Isn't a flatlander who piles up a high-value stash in a remote area with no neighbors within earshot or line of sight kind of like a big, tall brittle tree? All those chains and locks and barbed-wire fencing and bolted doors just shout out that the flatlander has something valuable inside that cabin/bunker/RV.

Now if he doesn't know any better, then the flatlander reckons his stash is safe. But what he's not realizing is that we know about his stash and his vehicle and whatever else can be observed. If some locals want that stash, then they'll wait for the flatlander to leave and then they'll tow the RV off or break into the cabin, or if it's small enough, disassemble it and haul it clean off. There's plenty of time, and nobody's around. That's pretty much the ideal setting for leisurely thieving: a high-value stash of goodies in a remote area accessible by road is just about perfect.

Let's say things have gotten bad, and the flatlander is burrowed into his cabin. Eventually some locals will come up to visit; in a truck if there's gas, on foot if there isn't. We won't be armed; we're not interested in taking the flatlander's life or goodies. We just want to know what kind of person he is. So maybe we'll ask to borrow his generator for a town dance, or tell him about the church food drive, or maybe ask if he's seen so-and-so around.

Now what's the flatlander going to do when several unarmed men approach? Gun them down? Once he's faced with unarmed guys, he can't very well conclude they're a threat and warn them off. But if he does, then we'll know he's just another selfish flatlander. He won't get any help later when he needs it; or it will be minimal and grudging. He just counted himself out.

Suppose some bad guys hear about the flatlander's hideaway and stash. All it takes to stalk any prey is patience and observation; and no matter how heavily armed the flatlander is, he'll become vulnerable at some point to a long-range shot. (Even body armor can't stop a headshot or a hit to the femoral artery in the thigh.) Maybe he stays indoors for 6 days, or even 60. But at some point the windmill breaks or the dog needs walking or what have you, and he emerges--and then he's vulnerable. The more visible and stringent the security, the more he's advertising the high value of his depot.

And of course guarding a high-value stash alone is problematic for the simple reason that humans need to sleep.

So creating a high-value horde in a remote setting is looking like just about the worst possible strategy in the sense that the flatlander has provided a huge incentive to theft/robbery and also provided a setting advantageous to the thief or hunter.

If someone were to ask this "hick" for a less risky survival strategy, I would suggest moving into town and start showing a little generosity rather than a lot of hoarding. If not in town, then on the edge of town, where you can be seen and heard.

I'd suggest attending church, if you've a mind to, even if your faith isn't as strong as others. Or join the Lions Club, Kiwanis or Rotary International, if you can get an invitation. I'd volunteer to help with the pancake breakfast fundraiser, and buy a couple tickets to other fundraisers in town. I'd mow the old lady's lawn next door for free, and pony up a dollar if the elderly gentleman in line ahead of me at the grocery store finds himself a dollar light on his purchase.

If I had a parcel outside town that was suitable for an orchard or other crop, I'd plant it, and spend plenty of time in the local hardware store and farm supply, asking questions and spreading a little money around the local merchants. I'd invite my neighbors into my little plain house so they could see I don't own diddly-squat except some second-hand furniture and a crappy old TV. And I'd leave my door open so anyone could see for themselves I've got very little worth taking.

I'd have my tools, of course; but they're scattered around and old and battered by use; they're not shiny and new and expensive-looking, and they're not stored all nice and clean in a box some thief could lift. They're hung on old nails, or in the closet, and in the shed; a thief would have to spend a lot of time searching the entire place, and with my neighbors looking out for me, the thief is short of the most important advantage he has, which is time.

If somebody's desperate enough or dumb enough to steal my old handsaw, I'll buy another old one at a local swap meet. (Since I own three anyway, it's unlikely anyone would steal all three because they're not kept together.)

My valuable things, like the water filter, are kept hidden amidst all the low-value junk I keep around to send the message that there's nothing worth looking at. The safest things to own are those which are visibly low-value, surrounded by lots of other mostly worthless stuff.

I'd claim a spot in the community garden, or hire a neighbor to till up my backyard, and I'd plant chard and beans and whatever else my neighbors suggested grew well locally. I'd give away most of what I grew, or barter it, or maybe sell some at the farmer's market. It wouldn't matter how little I had to sell, or how much I sold; what mattered was meeting other like-minded souls and swapping tips and edibles.

If I didn't have a practical skill, I'd devote myself to learning one. If anyone asked me, I'd suggest saw sharpening and beer-making. You're legally entitled to make quite a bit of beer for yourself, and a decent homebrew is always welcome by those who drink beer. It's tricky, and your first batches may blow up or go flat, but when you finally get a good batch you'll be very popular and well-appreciated if you're of the mind to share.

Saw-sharpening just takes patience and a simple jig; you don't need to learn a lot, like a craftsman, but you'll have a skill you can swap with craftsmen/women. As a carpenter, I need sharp saws, and while I can do it myself, I find it tedious and would rather rebuild your front porch handrail or a chicken coop in exchange for the saw-sharpening.

Pickles are always welcome in winter, or when rations get boring; the Germans and Japanese of old lived on black bread or brown rice and pickled vegetables, with an occasional piece of dried meat or fish. Learning how to pickle is a useful and easy-to-learn craft. There are many others. If you're a techie, then volunteer to keep the network up at the local school; do it for free, and do a good job. Show you care.

Because the best protection isn't owning 30 guns; it's having 30 people who care about you. Since those 30 have other people who care about them, you actually have 300 people who are looking out for each other, including you. The second best protection isn't a big stash of stuff others want to steal; it's sharing what you have and owning little of value. That's being flexible, and common, the very opposite of creating a big fat highly visible, high-value target and trying to defend it yourself in a remote setting.

I know this runs counter to just about everything that's being recommended by others, but if you're a "hick" like me, then you know it rings true. The flatlanders are scared because they're alone and isolated; we're not scared. We've endured bad times before, and we don't need much to get by. We're not saints, but we will reciprocate to those who extend their good spirit and generosity to the community in which they live and in which they produce something of value.

The best way to look out for Number One is to start looking out for Numbers Two through Twenty.

The alternative to a vulnerable Isolation and living-off-the-land mythology is to join The Remnant and lead by example, building a productive, sustainable future for one's family, community and nation.

Chapter Six: The Remnant, the Pareto Principle and You

Leading by example can be a far more powerful force for positive change than is commonly understood. (A version of this chapter was originally published on www.oftwominds.com on June 25, 2008.)

Frequent oftwominds.com contributor U. Doran sent in a link to this fascinating essay, which was published in the depths (Year 7) of the Great Depression: *Isaiah's Job* by Albert Jay Nock (from *The Atlantic Monthly*, 1936)

> In the year of Uzziah's death, the Lord commissioned the prophet (Isaiah) to go out and warn the people of the wrath to come. "Tell them what a worthless lot they are." He said, "Tell them what is wrong, and why and what is going to happen unless they have a change of heart and straighten up. Don't mince matters. Make it clear that they are positively down to their last chance. Give it to them good and strong and keep on giving it to them."
>
> "I suppose I ought to tell you," He added, "that it won't do any good. The official class and their intelligentsia will turn up their noses at you and the masses will not even listen. They will all keep on in their own ways until they carry everything down to destruction, and you will probably be lucky if you get out with your life."
>
> Isaiah had been very willing to take on the job — in fact, he had asked for it — but the prospect put a new face on the situation. It raised the obvious question: Why, if all that were so — if the enterprise were to be a failure from the start — was there any sense in starting it?
>
> "Ah," the Lord said, "you do not get the point. There is a Remnant there that you know nothing about. They are obscure, unorganized, inarticulate, each one rubbing along as best he can. They need to be encouraged and braced up because when everything has gone completely to the dogs, they are the ones who will come back and build up a new society; and meanwhile, your preaching will reassure them and keep them hanging on. Your job is to take care of the Remnant, so be off now and set about it."

Let's follow up on this notion of "Remnant" by invoking the Pareto Principle.

If the parameters in the Pareto distribution are suitably chosen, then one would have not only 80% of effects coming from 20% of causes, but also 80% of that top 80% of effects coming from 20% of that top 20% of causes, and so on (80% of 80% is 64%; 20% of 20% is 4%, so this implies a "64-4 law").

This suggests that a mere 4% of the 300 million Americans could influence 192 million of their fellow citizens. Since children and the very elderly generally wield less influence than those adults of working and child-bearing age, let's subtract the 60 million Americans under 14 years of age and the 18 million over 75 years of age (*Annual Estimates of the Population by Sex and Five-Year Age Groups for the United States: April 1, 2000 to July 1, 2007*, U.S. Census Bureau).

That leaves about 220 million Americans between 14 and 75 years of age. 4% of that number is 8.8 million. So the critical number for the Remnant in the U.S. appears to be about 9 million people.

When 9 million people start leading (4%), then 140 million (64%) will follow. Once those 150 million are moving in the same direction, then they will collectively be an irresistible force for positive change.

As the essay so brilliantly describes, members of the Remnant are not on the pulpit or writing for the Mainstream Media; they are unpublicized, unnoticed, perhaps viewed as outsiders by those around them, perhaps not. But their influence is generated by action and example, not by preaching, pontificating or cajoling.

I believe most of you are in the Remnant simply by virtue of being part of this little (unpublicized, zero-marketing budget) online community of www.oftwominds.com readers, contributors and correspondents.

Many of you are doing real work in the real world. Don E. raises chickens in Maine, David V. has Yukon gold potatoes in the ground up north, and Noah Cicero is pursuing permaculture in Ohio. (Note on gender: many other readers doing similar work happen to be female, for instance, Freeacre, who we'll hear from in a moment.)

On the financial front, frequent contributor Harun I. has written about how to hedge yourself against various financial risks, and about becoming a more successful investor.

If you glance through the www.oftwominds.com *Readers Journal* archives, you will find dozens of amazing essays by readers who to the best of my knowledge do not occupy positions of influence in government or the media.

Given the government's abysmal non-response to the growing financial and energy crises, then I conclude the 9 million will have to lead government, not vice versa.

Note that the Remnant is not engaged in any one pursuit; smart people are just doing what they think is right and good, which includes being skeptical of the received "wisdom" of the media and government pronouncements/propaganda, trying to avoid the financial vortex which is pulling down the non-elites (and maybe a few elites, too), living lighter, cheaper, better lifestyles away from the stomping masses of the Consumption Is Our True God mainstream, working to improve the soil of a patch of earth, and a thousand other projects and interests.

If anything characterizes the Remnant, it is skepticism, a disdain for aggrandizement, and an awareness that doing with less is actually a happier, more fulfilling life than Always Chasing More in the Public Eye.

For one example of how this works--first at the local level, which then influences the region, then the state and eventually the nation--let's turn to Freeacre in Oregon:

"It's nice to read your essay on permaculture and community gardening. I forwarded it to our city manager. Last week I attended a town meeting where we were to pick some goals and prioritize them, etc. I wrote down that I'd like to see our community gear up for economic collapse by localizing our food supply and ride sharing, etc, to help people on their commutes to work. I suggested community gardens, a tool bank, etc. Surprisingly, a bunch of people agreed with me and put me on a committee to hire the next city planner! So, something must be changing in the popular consciousness...

We live in Central Oregon at 4,200 ft. altitude. Our garden is situated on 30 ft. of volcanic ash. We have almost no organic stuff in the "soil" except pine needles, which are acidic. No worms - they would starve to death. And, you can only count on 30 nights a year that don't freeze. To say the least, it is tough to grow stuff here. We have to heat our greenhouse and cover our garden with thermal blankets at night. And, water frequently because it is also a desert.

But, despite that, we grew almost all of the vegetables that we ate last fall and winter. We have great luck with snow peas, Chinese peas, snap peas, carrots, beets, lettuce, onions, garlic, kale, and

Swiss Chard outside, and tomatoes, summer squash, pole beans, cucumbers, and green peppers in a little greenhouse.

What is also a great help is chickens. We love our chickens. They give us great eggs and are very fun and relaxing to observe and live with. I would never have believed that I could look forward to my edition of "Backyard Poultry" as much as I used to like to read *Newsweek*. What a laugh.

When the trucks stop rolling, we will probably start to keep rabbits, too, for protein. I can't eat a lot of carbs. Bad for me. Maybe even guinea pigs to feed to the dog. Sounds horrible, doesn't it? But, we've got a half St. Bernard/half Tibetan Mastiff. They can't eat dandelions.

We need to re-think so much. Right now, I'm looking into where the hand pumps went that the state parks used to have, since they've been replaced with electric ones. There must be a pile of them somewhere. If (when) the electricity fails, it's going to be hell getting water from the well without a hand pump - in the winter."

Don E. recently checked in with this report from Maine:

"I have looked about me here in Maine and wondered what my tribe will be. I agree that they will emerge. We joined MOFGA, the oldest organization in the country for organic living, and in surveying what their network looks like Maine comes off as a very sane place. Redneck to a large part, but also a lot of industrious hippie-types raising goats and crops. A very interesting place. The watchword seems to be 'lisa'; low impact sustainable agriculture. It really is amazing how big the movement to grow local food without chemicals is in this state. My hope, slightly tongue in cheek, is that new hampster, Vermont and Maine will break off into a new nation with a regional gov't that looks more toward Canada than south."

Though these accounts are local, these same members of The Remnant are also acting on a national level—not in an organized fashion, but in a Remnant fashion, by example.

Chapter Seven: Ontological Forces and Analytic Tools

The ideas presented in this chapter are abstract and difficult, but without an understanding of these concepts our analysis would be superficial.

We cannot hope to understand the forces which will shape the Great Transformation unless we examine what might be called *ontological forces*: structures of Nature which work not just in organisms but in human societies and history, and ontological states which can be characterized as the *politics of experience*. By ontological I mean these forces are not limited to certain eras or cultures; they act upon human societies in all era and locales.

How do we make sense out of the vast, interlocking complexity of the modern world? We started with an accounting of key contexts: human nature, the environment, waves and cycles of history, etc., and then proceeded to explore human nature within the context of complacency and fatalism. We concluded by exploring the Pareto Principle and the way a relatively small group can end up influencing the majority of much larger population.

Though not a strictly predictable law of nature like gravity, the Pareto Principle nonetheless reflects patterns which are not just cultural constructs of the human mind: it can be observed in Nature, not just human behavior.

The same can be said of feedback loops. All biological systems contain feedback loops that strengthen or counter other feedbacks. Thus one way to understand any system is to identify the various inputs and feedbacks present. Again, feedback systems are not simply cultural constructs; they are observable ontological forces.

These ontological forces are powerful analytic tools. A superficial explanation of the subprime crisis would be: human greed overwhelmed common sense. While this may well be true, it does not explain the mechanisms of the crisis or explain why the subprime crisis occurred in this time and place. It also offers no predictive value, as human greed has always been present and will always be present: what I call windfall exploitation is a beneficial trait in Nature.

Various ideological explanations are also superficial: it was all the Democrats/Republicans' fault, etc. The way to avoid ending up in worthless superficiality is to seek out the ontological forces and states at play in any context or situation.

Thus an analysis of the subprime crisis would have to tease out the various feedbacks in play: the Federal Reserve's easy-money/low interest rate policy, the changes made to the way rating agencies were paid and issued their ratings on securities, the windfall exploitation of derivatives based on mortgages by the investment banks, and so on.

This approach can be characterized as "systems analysis," but we have to be very careful to note that "systems analysis" is itself an ontological state with limitations imposed by the values and tools of the practitioners.

Thus the systems analyst will reject cycles of human history as invalid: the cycles are too open to interpretation, insufficiently rigorous, etc. Trapped within the confines of this one ontological state, we would then miss the profound insights offered by an understanding of patterns within human history.

The dangers of being trapped within an exceedingly limited ontological state are best illustrated by the field of economics, which seeks a global understanding via a small set of analytic tools and a worldview so limited that it can be characterized as a state of psychotic disassociation from the real world.

If we were to limit our reading to academic economics papers, either traditional or of the "freakonomics" variety, we would come to believe that Foreign Direct Investment and various other metrics were the right and proper context for understanding our world.

But entirely missing from the vast majority of professional economics is any hint that an economy is based on a real world of dirt, evaporating rivers, smog-choked air and people responding to viral pandemics, religion and long-term ontological forces which cannot be described or measured by the tools available to the professional economist.

The utter failure of economics as a predictive "science" is well-known; and given this failure, we might wonder what value metrics such as GDP, M2 and all the rest actually possess in terms of understanding the Great Transformation ahead.

The answer seems rather clear: precious little.

One reason is that an ontological state I term the *politics of experience* is always in play. By way of example, consider a typical academic economist or Wall Street financial analyst. Both are seeking to understand China by way of the yuan-dollar exchange rate, foreign direct investment, electricity consumption, official unemployment and various other quantitative measurements, as if those numbers are meaningful reflections of realities such as a dried-up river and an angry mob of disenfranchised peasants.

Within the confines of the academic politics of experience, all that really matters is that the paper is accepted by a prestigious journal and that it bolsters the economist's chances for the golden ring of tenure. Anything which upsets the academic status quo (presenting dry papers filled with equations, making nuanced "improvements" to accepted gospel, etc.) would introduce a troubling uncertainty into the career prospects of the practitioner.

By way of contrast, the public health practitioner examining the diseased lungs of the disenfranchised peasantry has an entirely different politics of experience: an indifferent and potentially hostile government, personal danger, outrage at the human cost of all that "growth" so tidily represented in the economists' columns of numbers, despair at the impossibility of changing the forces of corruption and wealth extraction which dooms the peasantry to the margins, and so on.

The word "globalization" will mean entirely different things to these two people. Indeed, what is "obvious" to each person will be radically different. This is why I will spend considerable time exploring the ontological state of "what is obvious."

By coupling all our methods of understanding (*cui bono*--to whose benefit?, over-reach and depletion as cycles of history, simulacrum/propaganda as defenses against erosion of the status quo, etc.) with an understanding of the politics of experience, we can then assemble a fully integrated understanding of our world's interlocking crises.

Much more could be said about ontological forces and states, and I can only hope this brief chapter will be enough to render the concepts comprehensible.

Feedback Loops, Phase Shifts/Reversals and the Politics of Experience

The human mind seeks patterns and trends as a key survival strategy: if we can anticipate a problem before it overwhelms us, or discern a pattern or cycle in the world around us, we can make a timely and very beneficial corrective adaptation.

Trends may be profitably understood as vectors: a predictable direction influenced by measurable forces. Once we identify a trend/vector, we quickly anticipate it will continue in the same direction.

Thus in the early 1960s, oil seemed so abundant and the promise of nuclear power so bright that the envisioned future included flying vehicles for every suburban home, plastic pod homes and a leisure founded on endless prosperity.

Now, a few scant decades later, the future vector to many has darkened to a collapse that will return advanced economies to the 18th century in the best-case scenario and to a violent AK-47-ridden Dark Age in worst-case scenarios.

Neither of these extremes seem likely, in my view, because neither one is grounded in an analysis of culture, history or feedback systems.

Feedback is built into Nature, including us. A bacterial infection triggers an immune response; without such a feedback loop, we would never survive past a few hours of life.

All of life, from bacteria to the largest organisms and systems, responds to its environment with feedback; there are no vectors or trends that do not meet with positive (self-reinforcing) and/or negative (built-in stabilizers) feedback. Thus the bacteria responds to anti-bacterial medications by developing resistance, companies respond to changing market conditions, etc.

Positive feedback reinforces itself; the classic example is nuclear fission, in which decaying uranium atoms trigger a cascade of radiation that becomes a nuclear explosion. Doomsday scenarios assume that such positive feedback loops will overwhelm any negative feedback loops that would act to slow or reverse the trend.

Thus the Doomsday scenario assumes all civilizations fall in a great heap; some have, some haven't. The ever-popular "technology-will-save-us" scenario downplays or denies the full measure of positive feedbacks and assumes negative (counter-trend) loops will correct or reverse any downward trajectory. We cannot arbitrarily assume either alternative: that would be joining complacency with fatalism.

The outcome depends on our understanding of the crises and our responses (feedback) to those challenges: as families, communities and as nation-states.

We can be fairly certain of one thing: the likelihood of everything remaining like it is today is near-zero. All trends are merely temporary vectors influenced by positive and negative feedback loops which can drop away, strengthen or interact in unforeseen ways.

Those who assume runaway feedback will trigger complete collapse may also be anticipating a phase shift--a sudden jump from one state to another. This concept has been popularized as a "tipping point" in the book The Tipping Point: How Little Things Can Make a Big Difference. In the stock market, such a shift takes the form of a reversal of trend; this is also visible in elections, when the electorate seeks to reverse polarities, so to speak, and place the other party in power.

But a system has to be near a tipping point or *phase shift* for little things to matter. This ties directly into our exploration of The Remnant and the Pareto Principle: seemingly small percentages of people leading by example can have an outsized influence on the "trivial many," slowly building a trend for change which can "phase shift" at certain points, changing the entire cultural milieu and mindset in a short period of time.

That is, phase shifts do not have to be collapses; they can also be relatively sudden "awakenings" or positive transformations wrought by the informal leadership of The Remnant or by a technological innovation which rapidly replaces a less efficient technology. The messy, lengthy revolution launched by the printing press is a good example of the latter; the Web/Internet is an example of a new technology that enables entirely new distributions of knowledge and levels of interactions.

Power Laws, Pareto Distribution, Self-Organized Criticalities (SOC) and the Stick/Slip Hypothesis

Phase shifts are an integral feature of the ontological models we first discussed in Chapter Three. We should be skeptical of any "natural laws" which are being applied to human culture and history, as history is littered with models derived from a specific time and society which claimed to be universal but which failed to map unfolding events.

The question for those applying power laws to human behavior and history is simple: what dynamic causes human history to follow power laws (distribution, SOC, etc.)? The answer is two-fold: one, humans are organisms and thus their large-scale behavior can be tracked statistically like that of other organisms. Two, the positive feedback loops of windfall exploitation and over-reach are causal mechanisms which explain how a minority can control most of the wealth and influence the "trivial many."

The power laws briefly described in Chapter Three provide large-scale models for the build-up of forces which then lead to sudden instability.

As an example, consider a broad, fertile valley and its human population. The first human inhabitants have stumbled on a windfall: a lush valley with good soil and water. They promptly proceed to exploit that windfall, and like all other organisms they proliferate rapidly in the presence of surplus food.

As the surplus and population grows, the surplus wealth accretes along Pareto distributions and some sort of governance, be it religious or secular, arises to protect the windfall from outsiders and to siphon off surplus for capital-intensive structures--defensive forts, palaces, temples, burial mounds, etc. Whatever form of governance gains the upper hand finds itself in a positive feedback: having vanquished its rivals (negative feedback forces) and shed restraints, it is now free to gather an ever larger share of the valley's surplus.

The productive land in the valley floor is quickly plowed in another positive feedback: the more land put into production, the more surplus is generated which spurs more productive labor, and so on.

As the population rises beyond what the valley's surplus can feed, then farmers move up to marginal land on the hillsides. But the soil is poorer and the labor required to irrigate and terrace the land is higher, so the surplus generated by tilling more soil diminishes as ever more marginal areas are brought into production. At a certain elevation, surplus drops to near-zero: the output (crops/food) only sustains the work required to plant, irrigate, nurture and harvest the crop.

Though on the surface the valley's prosperity appears stable, the forces generated by over-reach are gathering beneath the surface--the stick/slip hypothesis in action. The governing elite has over-reached, burdening the productive class with high taxes to support temple/fort building, lavish palaces, conquests of surrounding valleys, and similar projects of over-reach.

At the same time, the soil in the valley floor is becoming exhausted by over-exploitation, and the higher-elevation marginal lands are slipping into net liabilities as agricultural over-reach reaps what has been sown.

As fewer farmers generates large surpluses, the productive populace slips into widening inequality: more households slip into subsistence poverty while a handful of the elite class increase their wealth and power at the expense of the remaining productive farmers.

The easy lumber, wood, soil and water have all been exploited, and as the costs rise the marginal resources have also been depleted.

In the positive feedback of over-reach, the elite class has grown in size, reach and complexity; as inequality rises, whatever marginal negative feedback loops existed in prosperity (craft and trade associations, etc.) fade along with prosperity. The elite's diversion of the valley's surplus (income) runs into the physical obstacle of declining surplus.

In response, the elites raise taxes on the declining class of productive farmers and begins poaching off the weaker elements of the elite class: what I term *Internecine Conflict Between Protected Fiefdoms*. If neighboring regimes or trading blocs have surplus capital stored (as money, grain, fuel, etc.) then the valley's elite borrows this capital to fund the shortfall between its expenses and income or attempts to appropriate the surplus via military conquest.

The valley also attempts to offset its depletion of local resources by extending its supply routes to ever-more distant sources of wood, grain, metals, water, etc.

As windfall exploitation returned ever-more marginal returns on capital and labor invested, perturbations begin cropping up: incursions from neighboring valleys increase, harvests fall, religious cults arise, drawdown of stored reserves is not replaced, some religious/cultural rituals are abandoned, etc.

This devolution follows the Pareto Principle: negative changes in as little as 4% of the market/populace wield outsized effects on 64% of the group. Once 20% are affected, then that "vital few" influence the remaining 80% of the "trivial many."

Devolution marked by occasional small crises fits the power law model: frequent events are modest in size while infrequent events are much larger and more significant.

If we were to plot out the increasingly marginal returns, the rising borrowing and interest payments, the higher costs of maintaining the elites, the capital buildings, military defense, etc., we would discern Self-Organized Criticalities (SOC).

In physical phenomena, a critical point is the threshold at which a system radically changes its behavior or structure--for example, when

H2O (water) melts from solid to liquid. In standard systems, a parameter controls the rate of change. In the case of ice melting, the parameter is temperature.

Self-organized criticalities, in contrast (recall our previous example of the sand pile), reach a critical state via the action of their intrinsic dynamics. Adjusting the rate of sand falling on the pile does not change the fact that sand avalanches will occur along a power law chart (small frequent sand slides interrupted at longer intervals by large sand slides).

In our valley example, depleting the remaining wood and soil at slightly faster or slower rates (changing the parameters of depletion) will not change the eventual "landslide": the valley can no longer feed or sustain itself, despite the borrowing, conquests, longer supply chains, etc. which were instituted to overcome local depletion.

Lastly, we note that the depletion/over-reach/devolution is scale-invariant; the small plot of land offers up diminishing yields, the lower valley's yields also diminish, and the entire valley ecosystem has lower yields as well. The villager walks two hours now to gather firewood, the elite harvests lumber from mountains a hundred kilometers away, etc.

We now see how one critical-point "landslide" can topple interlocking systems which are barely clinging to the "stick" phase to the "slip" phase: collapse.

Beneath the surface, the depletion, heavy borrowing, rising burden of interest, ever-more marginal returns on ever-greater investments of capital and labor, rising costs of military defense and conquest, widening inequality and all the other pressures are building from ontological (intrinsic) dynamics which cannot be released by adjusting the parameters (changing the palace guard, burning twigs instead of sticks, etc.).

As each system devolves, feedback (getting wood from distant sources, etc.) maintains the surface trend even as the strain to do so grows ever larger. At some unpredictable point, what might have been a small landslide/point of instability becomes a major dislocation that topples all the now-vulnerable, over-extended systems like dominoes.

The end-state is the valley crashes in output, population, wealth and stability.

Oftwominds.com contributor Harun Ibrahim offered this explanation of how systems can be viewed as oscillating above and below a level of equilibrium.

"In reference to the Power Law, which separates system into subcritical, critical and supercritical states, I submit that the critical state is a transient zone or an equilibrium around which the system oscillates. Therefore, systems will spend much of their time in either the subcritical or supercritical state. Because we spend so much time in these zones we tend to accept them as normal. Moves to the critical state (equilibrium) are seen as anomalies.

Clearly our economy has been in a supercritical state for decades and there is no doubt that this has become what we perceive as normal. Government, in attempting to stimulate a recovery, is in reality trying to return to the supercritical state.

If we apply the Stick/Slip hypothesis to the global economy then we understand that during the Stick phase things appear stable while in actuality the longer the time spent in this phase, the more likely it has gone from a marginal critical state to a supercritical state. Tremendous forces may be building that when released, 'we observe a power-law region with a Gaussian surplus of large events.' Is this an accurate description of what we are experiencing?

But with government at perfect MQ (perfect incompetence), which is also a supercritical state, no sustainable or effective solutions can be found for just about any system. The problem with this setup is that as problems mass and compress in time and space (energy, food, water, population growth, etc.) the competency to deal with these problems at a policy level declines.

If any of this is remotely correct then Mr. Kunstler (The Long Emergency: Surviving the End of Oil, Climate Change, and Other Converging Catastrophes of the Twenty-First Century). is proven correct that we must manage ourselves down to the critical state and learn to remain there. If history or the Peter Principle is any guide we will not do this consciously or voluntarily because we are incapable due to incompetence. Therefore an overshoot to the marginal subcritical state is almost assured."

This is why the insolvency and subsequent implosion of the State and its Elites is inevitable.

Sociological "End of History" Theories

Grand theories of history and ontological forces held great appeal to several generations of German thinkers in the 19th and 20th centuries, and as a result we have various "end of history" schemata from Hegel, Marx and Spengler.

Distilled to their essence, each theory posits internal forces within history and/or human society which will culminate in some version of "the end of history," that is, an inevitable end-point: the end of capitalism, decay of civilization, an illuminated state, etc.

Though these theories are essentially sociological in nature, they are described by their originators as ontological--that is, inherent and thus inevitable. This is the source of their great insights and also their fundamental weakness. Thus while Marx claimed the mantle of "scientific socialism," he provided no evidence for his "end of history" stateless "dictatorship of the proletariat." This was in essence an idealized fantasy of the sort which Marx had vehemently criticized in others' conceptions of socialism.

Ironically, the ideals propounded by Pierre-Joseph Proudhon and others (worker co-ops, credit unions for the non-elites, income taxes on the wealthy, etc.) whom Marx criticized were far more practical and "scientific" (that is, backed by experience) than his own vague, generalized descriptions of a worker-ruled post-capitalist Utopia.

Marx's chief accomplishment was his economic analysis of capitalism's internally contradictory forces--a critique which continues to provide insight. As I have described in this analysis, capitalism requires competition and transparency to function yet the highest, lowest-risk profits are gained from secrecy, collusion, fraud, monopoly and cartels and a partnership between the financial-rentier private-sector Elites and the parasitic Elites which control the State: the precise stage of Capitalism we find dominates the present era.

Marx also identified the *scalability trap* of industrial production in which factories displace labor, creating poverty, and the ontological nature of capitalist over-production (windfall exploitation of new markets) and the resultant collapse which leads to Monopoly/Cartel Capitalism. In this mature stage of capitalism, the means of production and vertical-market, integrated, scalable benefits end up concentrated in the hands of one dominant corporation or a cartel.

These insights continue to play out in our own era, as I show in Chapter Sixteen, The Crisis of Neoliberal Capitalism.

Max Weber codified many sociological insights in his analysis of capitalism, religion, the State and bureaucracies; his book Economy and Society: An Outline of Interpretive Sociology is generally held to be the best summary of his work.

Weber identified three basic types of social authority--charismatic, traditional, and rational-legal--which can be characterized thusly: charismatic--what I term the "Big Man" form of leadership and authority; traditional--value-oriented organization (obey your tribal leader, your parents, your church, etc.), and rational-legal--goal-oriented bureaucracy.

Weber traced the development of capitalism from traditionalist Feudalism and Christian Protestantism (which some later revised to the more neutral "work ethic") to a fully rationalized economy which Weber described as a "polar night of icy darkness." In his view, an over-bureaucratized, rules-based capitalism essentially imprisons individuals in what he termed "an iron cage."

Weber showed that capitalism cannot be adequately described by Marx's purely materialist view of history, as it grew out of specific religious and cultural ideals which extend beyond ownership, technological advances and other metrics (what I term the *quantification trap*--see Chapter Fifteen, Interlocking Traps.) His analysis of why medieval China, despite its great technological advantages and bureaucratic expertise, failed to develop capitalism, is a masterful display of integrating history, anthropology, economics and sociology.

Advancing Marx's critique of "free-market" capitalism to socialist capitalism, Weber saw that when socialism appropriates privately owned means of production (productive land, factories, labs, etc.), it *necessarily* abolishes market calculations of cost and profit, thus leaving any "centrally planned economy" with no experiential (supply-demand) basis for setting production, prices, wages, etc. The *ontological consequence* (i.e. the inevitable result) is the gross inefficiency, corruption and mispricing of labor and assets which led to the demise of the Soviet and Maoist-era Chinese economies.

While Weber saw some value in democracy as a market-like mechanism for competition between leaders and parties, he did not view it in a romantic, idealized light. Even as the general public legitimizes government with elections, the policies are essentially those of the Elites; the participatory role for citizens is proscribed.

Thus the end-state of capitalism as foreseen by Weber closely maps our present reality: elections legitimize Elite control of the economy and Empire while the citizenry are powerless cogs in a highly rationalized and bureaucratic "iron cage." The "inner cage" within the "iron cage" which Weber could not foresee was debt-serfdom, the indenturing of the citizenry via exponentially rising debt.

Oswald Spengler, who wrote <u>The Decline of the West</u> in the early 20th century, extended this flinty-eyed view of democracy's limitations.

Spengler elaborated the causal connections between money, influence and elections best summarized by H.L. Mencken's acerbic observation: "Every election is a sort of advance auction sale of stolen goods."

In Spengler's analysis, once voters are organized into groups funded by wealthy Elites (that is, into voting blocs, parties and interest groups) then the election is nothing but a recorded legitimization of a government immune to non-Elite citizen influence.

As wealth becomes increasingly concentrated in Elite hands, the struggle for political power is dominated by money. From Spengler's ontological perspective, this reduction of elections to a battle for influence by concentrated wealth is not corrupt, it is the necessary end of capitalist democracy.

The reason is simple: "The private powers of the economy want free paths for their acquisition ... No legislation must stand in their way. They want to make the laws themselves, in their interests."

Recognizing its role as the propaganda conduit of concentrated wealth and power, Spengler scathingly characterizes the mass media thusly: "Electrical news-service keep the waking-consciousness of whole people and continents under a deafening drum-fire of theses, catchwords, standpoints, scenes, feelings, day by day and year by year."

Thus democracy and Plutocracy are one in the same in Spengler's view.

Spengler predicted the rise of what he termed Caesarism, political leaders wielding Weber's Charisma as a social authority powerful enough to overcome the forces (negative feedbacks) limiting the concentration of power into one person or Executive office.

Caesarism marks the death of the ideals that originally informed the State and its institutions. The classic ideals have expired even as the institutions are conserved (see Preservation of Institutions Trap in Chapter Fifteen, Interlocking Traps) and maintained as simulacrum masking the reality that all authority now rests with the Caesar executive. This transition from democracy to an Imperial Age parallels that of Rome.

In an uncanny foreshadowing of the collapse of the Soviet Union and the subsequent emergence of the U.S. as sole global Empire, Spengler anticipated the rise of idealistic imperialism in the aftermath of a major geopolitical enemy's demise.

Spengler also foresaw a devolution of participatory democracy. Though the citizenry once fought to establish fundamental civil liberty rights, in the late Plutocracy- dominated stage of democracy the citizenry has little interest in exercising those rights. Participation in elections drops, and the most qualified candidates opt out of the political process.

This entire process--the growing domination of political power by concentrated wealth and the devolution of participatory democracy and institutions into simulacrum of their former authenticity--perfectly captures the essential character of the present era.

Despite their illuminating, groundbreaking analyses, I am unpersuaded by these three thinkers' "end of history" projections. Marx's muddled "dictatorship of the proletariat" ran aground on humanity's innate self-interest (people turned out not to want to work hard on the commune for everyone else's benefit), while Weber's "iron cage" of rigid rationalized social/economic authority seems particularly vulnerable to devolution and collapse. Spengler's extension of Roman history--the emergence of a "Big Man" Caesar-type leader to herald in an Imperial Age--seems more like a reflection of his own culture and era than an inviolate ontology of history.

Thus it seems that Feedback Loops, Phase Shifts/Reversals, Power Laws, Pareto Distribution, Self-Organized Criticalities (SOC), the Stick/Slip Hypothesis and the Politics of Experience provide better models for understanding the coming Great Transformations than "end of history" ontologies.

Having briefly described the natural-law models of change, it's important to understand the structure of "the politics of experience."

Defining the Problem Defines the Solution

Some ideas are easier to express and understand than others. This stems from language being an ontological force in itself; language carries with it vast powers and equally vast difficulties of interpretation and ambiguity.

For instance, if I were to say the solution to all the problems listed above is to buy gold and a ton of rice, we can all understand the idea of not trusting paper money and a fragile supply chain of grain.

But if I say that how we identify a "problem" defines the "solution" we will accept, that is more difficult to grasp. The reason is that most of the assumptions we make in framing a "problem" are subconscious or deeply embedded in our cultural/intellectual worldview.

R.D. Laing, author of Politics of Experience, penned this prescient lecture in 1972, *The Obvious*, explained the inherent difficulty of understanding "the obviousness" of any "problem":

"To a considerable extent what follows is an essay in stating what I take to be obvious. It is obvious that the social world situation is endangering the future of all life on this planet. To state the obvious is to share with you what (in your view) my misconceptions might be. **The obvious can be dangerous.** The deluded man frequently finds his delusions so obvious that he can hardly credit the good faith of those who do not share them.

What is obvious to Lyndon Johnson is not at all obvious to Ho Chi Minh. What is obvious to me might not be obvious to anyone else. The obvious is literally that which stands in one's way, in front of or over against oneself. One has to begin by recognizing that it exists for oneself.

The study of social events presents an almost insurmountable difficulty, in that their visibility, as one might say, is very low. In social space one's direct immediate capacity to see what is happening does not extend any further than one's own senses extend. Beyond that one has to make inferences based on hearsay evidence, reports of one kind or another of what other human beings are able to see within their equally limited field of observation. As in space, so in time.

Even in the most detailed investigations of small fragments of micro-history, in studies of families, one finds it difficult to get past two or three generations. Beyond that, how things have come to be as they are disappears into mist."

By way of example: Many of us recognize that paper money (i.e. fiat money) has declined precipitously in value when priced in gold. Rather than watch our wealth (as measured in currency or gold) vanish, then we seek to find a store of value which will not fall to zero: gold.

But this "solution" assumes the "problem" is limited to paper (fiat) money. If we understand that "money" as a store of wealth is simply stored energy, then we reach another understanding of "the problem" and thus of the "solution."

Let's say that the fragile supply chain of remaining oil breaks down in a complex interaction of positive feedback loops. Oil would not just be costly; it would be unavailable to individuals. The government would undoubtedly ration what was left for essential services like agriculture, food distribution, police and hospitals, etc.

Let's say we anticipated this and responded not by hoarding gold but by buying a 4 kilowatt solar power array, productive land in a mild climate, a store of fertilizer and a few electric vehicles to share with our family/community. We own zero gold but we own a power supply, the means to grow food and transportation that does not require petroleum.

Now would we sell these productive assets for gold? At what price, if they were essentially irreplaceable? What would we do with our pile of gold if we can't go anywhere, can't grow food and have no power source?

The holder of gold assumes that all goods can be purchased with a means of exchange holding a tangible value, i.e. gold or an equivalent commodity. But this may not be entirely true. Yes, we will sell some of our power/energy **output** for gold, but we will not sell our "wealth," i.e. the power plant for gold, which may or may not be able to buy a replacement. As a store of wealth, gold is no match for a productive source of energy.

The reason is "money" as a store of wealth is simply stored energy.

From this point of view, fertilizer is stored energy. You may or may not be able to exchange "money" in any form for stored energy, for "wealth" is either stored energy or the capacity to generate energy sustainably. Everything else is merely a means of exchange.

Will gold hold more value as a means of exchange than paper money? If history is any guide, yes—but that's a different "problem" than building or storing wealth.

There are many other examples of "problems" whose solutions may well completely fail to address the structural challenges we face. Once again we must explore complacency, not just as an emotional haven, but as a cognitive attractor.

If we define the "problem" incorrectly, that is a way of selecting a "solution" which may only turn into a positive feedback loop, i.e. make the real problem worse.

Here is another example: consider these two questions and what each implies about the politics of experience and goal (i.e., who benefits from the implied outcome) of the person posing the question (that is, framing the context):

Since we have 400 years' supply of coal in the U.S., why not build "clean coal" plants to generate electricity?

How many owners/executives of "clean coal" plants live downwind of one of their own plants?

The context and politics of experience reflected in each question is radically different; the response implied by each question is thus also radically different. The first question implies that it is "obvious" we should construct "clean coal" plants in volume, while the second question implies that it is equally "obvious" that "clean coal" may be a propagandistic fabrication of a self-serving industry controlled by members of the Plutocracy who have no intention of risking their own health with exposure to the airborne results of "clean coal."

To assemble an integrated understanding of "clean coal," we would have to begin by asking "to whose benefit?" and examining the politics of experience of each participant/commentator. Those who do in fact live downwind of "clean coal" plants trump the well-paid analysts and academics who are members of the high-caste technocracy tasked with supporting the State and Plutocracy. Everything they claim as fact must be viewed with rigorous skepticism, starting with basic questions such as: how many "clean coal" plants are currently operating? By what metric is a coal-burning plant declared "clean"? Where is the long-term data to support this claim of "cleanliness"? and so on.

Those who stand to profit immensely from the construction and operation of such plants have a tremendous incentive (windfall exploitation) to create simulacrums of environmental cleanliness and statistical justifications for their windfall exploitation. As for "consumers" and residents surrounding the proposed plants and coal mines: a rigorously transparent cost-benefit analysis might conclude the benefits of the new plants outweigh the environmental costs--or it might not.

For we must be aware from the outset that the analysis presented on behalf of the Plutocracy and its well-paid servantry in the State will be intrinsically self-serving; thus care must to be taken to analyze exactly how the "problems" are framed and posed, for the "solutions" have already been carefully planted within the language defining the "problems."

Key concepts in this chapter:
Ontological forces
Politics of experience
Feedback Loops
Phase Shifts/Reversals ("tipping points")
Internecine Conflict between Protected Fiefdoms
Quantification trap

Chapter Eight: The Politics of Experience

The human mind makes sense of the chaotic jumble of sensory experiences and internal mental states by assembling *explanatory narratives*—what we also call "stories." To the believer, the "story" "explains" how things work. In pre-scientific cultures, many such stories were not simply wrong but injurious. Thus we have cultures in which it is believed that pregnant women shouldn't eat much. While we in advanced economies like to think of ourselves as above this sort of "superstition-passing-as-causal explanation," we also have cultures today in which living animals are considered "things" more or less equivalent to inanimate rocks and economies which believe "the market" is always efficient and rational.

What if those narratives also contain hefty doses of injurious superstition? To those who see living animals as commodities, then extirpating them for financial gain is "obvious" and indeed "natural." To those who believe in the ontological (i.e. inherent or a priori) efficacy and rationality of "the market," then the pricing of the last ten wild tuna on Earth via the auction block is entirely "obvious" and "natural." The notion that the eradication of a species might have some value not calculated by "the market" is sacrilege and suppressed with the same fanatic fervor as any interfaith challenge to religious authority.

Politics is consent, persuasion and power.

Humans are social animals because banding together by consent and bloodlines provides significant survival benefits over "going it alone." In its essence, politics is the granting of power to leaders for some benefit to those consenting to be led. The leaders must persuade consent or compliance, either by touting a persuasive narrative or creating a coercive system of punishment/terror.

The ultimate summary of politics is power.

In lower animals, this boils down to power over reproduction (i.e. being able to improve one's chances of passing along one's genes via choice or coercion) and food. In humans, reproduction remains key (hence every despot acquires a harem and every official a mistress) but power also includes the various fruits of civilization such as wealth and wide-ranging political powers expressed through institutions such as religion, the state, etc.

In financial terms, imposing one's will via coercion/terror is a costly affair. Maintaining a vast gulag of prisons, secret police, domestic armies, etc., drains off a tremendous share of the national wealth, and the coercive state/Empire has a nasty habit of destroying or driving away many if not most of its most productive citizenry.

Thus the "natural selection" process of the coercive state (be it monarchy, oligarchy, state or Empire) weeds out the rebellious, the skeptical and the most productive, leaving the cowed unproductive or the sullen, willfully unproductive and a huge class of dependent drones ruled by a class of overlords with few limits on what they can skim from what remains of their economy.

The better choice is to persuade the people you wish to skim from to freely offer their consent and their compliance. This is best accomplished by creating a series of narratives in which your power (and the power of your class) is "obvious," "natural" and "beneficial." Thus we have cultures of caste in which the "high-borns'" privileges and power have been accepted as the "natural order of things." All the Powers That Be need do is maintain this narrative via whatever mediums are available (the pulpit, the media, etc.) and suppress or marginalize any challenging narratives as irrational, unnatural, representing the forces of Evil, counter to our sacred way of life, etc.

As an example in the U.S., we might consider the entire narrative of debt/credit. The idea of credit has been sold as a "benefit" for the average citizen; with credit, one needn't save up for five years to buy an auto, one can drive a new car out of the lot today and enjoy it for the five years it takes to pay it off in installments (debt/credit).

All narratives with political and thus economic consequences can be best untangled by this simple question: *cui bono,* **to whose benefit?**

While credit "obviously" has some visible benefits to the borrower, the line between a borrower and a debt-serf can be thin indeed.

If we examine the profits generated by auto sales, we find that the profits generated by the credit/debt used to purchase the vehicle far exceed the profits made by manufacturing the vehicle. The same is true of housing and virtually all other goods.

So who benefits from an economy based on credit? Everyone, we are told; but it seems some benefit more than others.

Is there any more ideal system than one in which the vast majority of citizens are so heavily indebted that they have little time or energy left to question the system that has essentially enslaved them? Their high indebtedness generates a constant stream of heavy profits while their overworked, anxiety-ridden lifestyle ensures that political challenges to the Powers That Be will be stillborn or easily shunted aside as the ravings of cranks and doomsayers.

For one of the most powerful narratives in America is that we must always be positive and upbeat. One of the easiest ways to dismiss a critic in any setting is to label him or her a "doomsayer." "Just get with the program": that is, put your nose to the grindstone, make your debt payments and shut up.

Another powerful narrative with immense political consequences is the casting of 24/7 "entertainment" as a positive benefit to the masses. To be offered a cornucopia of distraction at any hour—what could be better? What could be better, indeed, for keeping a populace too distracted to question the "obvious" narratives which shape their compliance to debt-serf servitude?

This is the Politics of Experience: the presentation of a narrative, a context and a "problem" framed such that the "solution" richly benefits a self-serving Elite.

For instance: as public transit agencies and school districts face insolvency, the "problem" as presented by the public employee unions is that the stingy taxpayers are not providing these essential public services with sufficient funds to operate. The "solution" is "we need more money, so raise taxes."

If this is the only "problem," then why are requests for overtime pay, directors' salaries, the average monthly pensions of retirees, the length of service required to retire, explanations for why 80% of firefighters retire on "disability," etc., met with stony silence or angry resistance? Why are analyses comparing the labor costs of operating the systems today and 30 years ago suppressed or dismissed? Because the labor costs have shot up far faster than ridership, number of students, or the underlying economy; the Elite, in this case, the "high-caste" of public employees, has enriched themselves at the expense of the no-real-wage-increase-in-30-years public.

Any and all attempts to question the "obvious solution is we need more money" are suppressed, marginalized or attacked because revealing the actual causes of the insolvency--over-reach by public/State employees--would topple the narrative which supports the Elites' control and power.

In a similar way, "the market" has achieved a quasi-religious status as the perfect arbiter of efficiency and rationality. Thus the last ten wild tuna on the planet will be priced on the auction block based on their scarcity. The value of that species to humanity as a whole and the ecology of the seas is not factored by "the market's" flawless efficiency and rationality.

Or consider a small tree frog that will be extirpated by the logging of its habitat. The small frog has zero market value; as a commodity, it has no value since nobody wants to eat it or turn it into a marketable product.

But what if the skin of this frog produces a film with anti-bacteriological characteristics that might be highly valuable to humanity? "The market" has no mechanism to assess this potential or future value.

Rather than being an "efficient" or "rational" machine, the market in these cases is a blind, irrational machine that reduces all planetary inputs to a type of *scarcity-value* gravel. If you happen to profit from the trade in that gravel, it's may well appear rational and efficient. But if you recognize all that the market failed to value, not just rationally, but in any way at all, then you might see "the market" as not just irrational but so out of touch with reality as to be psychotic.

Try getting that perspective into the mass media, and you'll discover that you're the one considered psychotic and out of touch with reality. That's "the politics of experience:" narratives which support Elites' power and privileges as "obvious" and "natural" are sustained, as are "entertainments" which distract and dilute questions like cui bono; all else is marginalized, dismissed, refused or rejected as a form of sacrilege.

R.D. Laing was a psychiatrist by training, and his understanding of the politics of experience flowed from his analysis of troubled families with "psychotic" or "insane" members. He found that in some cases, the family's "leaders" (the adults) had subconsciously selected one member of the family to bear the blame for the family's troubles and conflicts. This child was then labeled "rebellious," "uncooperative," "a troublemaker," etc., and as the child's resistance grew then they were viewed as a psychiatric case.

Laing found (along with Gregory Bateson) that when humans are given a narrative which runs counter to their own experience this disconnect forms a double-bind--an internal state of "no way out." At this point the human can slip into passivity or other states which are categorized as psychiatric "problems" to be treated with drugs.

This is not to say that all madness is essentially political, only that the resistance to irrational narratives is easily cast by those intent on preserving their own power as some sort of psychiatric "illness." The dominant narrative which supports the power structure cannot be allowed to be recognized as the "problem;" thus the beauty of a system in which rebellion, resistance or *cui bono* questioning can be cast as an "obviously" psychiatric "problem" to be "treated."

Those unable to be "processed" medically can be dismissed as "fringe" people unworthy of comment. Those who experience a double-bind between the supposedly "obvious" narratives they're expected to accept and their own internal experiences are given prescription drugs to ease their anxiety and depression.

Again, this is not to say that some of us do not suffer from chemical imbalances in the brain; many of us do, and for those, these psychiatric drugs are a godsend. But we must also be careful about what "problems" end up being "treated" by "solutions" which happen to be drug-based.

Thus we have evidence that children diagnosed as hyperactive responded positively to a lifestyle stripped of sugar, junk food, TV and video games. Imagine the immense reduction in profits if drugs, sugary snacks, junk food, TV and video games were no longer "consumed" by American children. *Cui bono* indeed.

The narratives that operate beneath the surface compress all of experience into a limited number of hammers; so when a nail resists, guess what happens? It gets pounded down. When you hold the hammer, that "solution" is "obvious."

Key concepts in this chapter:
Explanatory narratives (intellectual frameworks)
Scarcity-value

Chapter Nine: Simulacrum and the Politics of Experience

Just as our "solutions" are shaped by how we frame "the problem," our understanding of our world is shaped by a "politics of experience" created by our cultural milieu, education, mass media and government.

As noted in the excerpt from R.D. Laing above, *the key feature of "the obvious" is its elusiveness.* Thus we don't consciously formulate the notion that what we buy and own defines our "true self;" that notion is like air, everywhere around us and thus not in our conscious awareness.

Our politics of experience is by definition not selected or consciously chosen; it is precisely the invisible assumptions we live by which are so unconscious that we cannot even recognize them as anything but "obvious" without great effort.

As an example, consider the work of author Douglas Rushkoff. Rushkoff's reply to an interview question on the consequences of ubiquitous marketing reveals how media/marketing has created an unquestioned politics of experience in which one's identity and sense of self is constructed almost entirely by what one buys:

"Children are being adultified because our economy is depending on them to make purchasing decisions. So they're essentially the victims of a marketing and capitalist machine gone awry. You know, we need to expand, expand, expand. There is no such thing as enough in our current economic model and kids are bearing the brunt of that.... So they're isolated, they're alone, they're desperate. It's a sad and lonely feeling....

The net effect of all of this marketing, all of this disorienting marketing, all of the shock media, all of this programming designed to untether us from a sense of self, is a loss of autonomy. You know, we no longer are the active source of our own experience or our own choices. Instead, we succumb to the notion that life is a series of product purchases that have been laid out and whose qualities and parameters have been pre-established."

As Laing also described, the past's *politics of experience* is largely inaccessible to us for the same reason we cannot discern how unobvious our own "obvious" truly is: the assumptions were so deep and elusive that contemporary accounts never even mention them, and thus histories are blind as well except by extrapolation of what was considered worthy of comment.

An excellent analogy to this problem can be found in the common Mississippi river barge of the 19th century. So common was this mode of river transport that no one bothered to fashion a drawing of one or count them. They literally vanished without a trace simply because they were too ubiquitous to elicit notice. Recently a few representatives have been exhumed from the mud; these forgotten artifacts are our only evidence of what was once unremarkable but vitally important.

Thus is it difficult for us to register how drastically our experience has changed over time. What seem "normal" and "obvious" to us—the constant bombardment of marketing, the financial stress of over-indebtedness, the insecurity of employment, the reliance on powerful psychotropic prescription medications to "get through life"-- are actually artifacts of an obviously destructive set of assumptions and values.

Individuals pursue their livelihoods in this peculiar state of unawareness in which they are unaware of what they are unaware of, and unaware of the consequences of the "obvious" incentives and assumptions that underpin their sense of identity and seemingly "conscious" choices.

Consider a mortgage broker or salesperson. In the real world, their compensation depends on persuading a "consumer" (a word loaded with subtle assumptions and incentives) to take on more debt to acquire a good or service.

This individual is not consciously seeking to overburden another individual with too much debt, but this is the net result of what's "normal" and "obvious" in the salesperson "doing their job" and the "consumer" setting out to achieve what he/she has internalized as "happiness" or "success:" a bigger house, a nicer car, a faster computer, a trendier outfit, a top-notch personal trainer, etc.

As we explore the elusive qualities of our common "obvious" experience, we must differentiate between the mostly unconscious actions of most of us and the carefully plotted conscious actions of those seeking to influence our experience for specific gain.

For instance, most elected officials do not set out to be evil or to acquire wealth and power at the expense of others; most are well-meaning people who are attracted to the power of office but also to the notion of doing some good or serving their community.

Since running for office requires vast sums of money, they find that listening to those willing to donate large sums to their campaign makes sense. Once these lobbyists and representatives of the Plutocracy have aired their concerns and interests in various specifics, it only makes sense for the elected official to pay attention to their concerns.

And since the long-term consequences of satisfying the donors-- national insolvency--is safely in the future, then it "obviously" makes sense to tend to the business at hand, which is getting re-elected and juggling all the competing demands of various well-funded interest groups.

The average voter--and how many citizens actually cast a ballot? Some 40% on average?-- has little interest in most of the complexities of governance, and so the elected official need not trouble themselves with their views other than auto-responses to the usual "noise" of "fringe" issues: cruelty to pets, some foreign policy imbroglio, etc.

Thus "just doing my job" and pursuing "what's obvious" can lead to the reinforcing crises we now face. In the politics of our collective experience, we're all simply doing what is "obvious" as officials, employees, consumers and voters.

But there is another class of citizenry for whom "the obvious" is an invitation to conscious manipulation.

For example: the first project of "the Powers That Be" is to deny the existence of The Powers That Be via a sustained propaganda campaign touting the great opportunities, justice and equality of our society and economy. The goal is to shape our interpretation of our experience into a politically pliable complacency which leaves the powers and influence of the Plutocracy safely accepted as "natural" and thus unquestioned.

The "politics of experience" which operates at a very subconscious level includes all the myths, incentives and assumptions which form our worldview.

Here is another example: "the rugged individual" myth that is core to American society has many positive elements--for instance, the ideal of individual responsibility for one's life and actions--but it also works to mask political and financial overreach by the plutocracy/Powers That Be by cloaking large-scale movements of vast profits and power as the disconnected workings of unrelated individuals.

Recall how the "politics of experience" of the subprime mortgage meltdown was presented by the Mainstream Media as the fault of irresponsible subprime borrowers. Then, as the U.S. government funneled hundreds of billions of dollars in bailout funds to save the Plutocracy from losses, the full extent of the corruption, greed, recklessness and fraud within the investment banking/mortgage/finance complex was revealed.

The "politics" behind that interpretation was revealed as a clever masking of the true cause: a Plutocracy operating without regard for laws or regulations and unhindered by political oversight. Please read Fiasco: The Inside Story of a Wall Street Trader and Greed, Fraud & Ignorance: A Subprime Insider's Look at the Mortgage Collapse for fuller accounts of the chicanery, greed and blatant disregard for law and risk.

The Mainstream Media (MSM), a highly centralized, corporate-owned structure, is a key player in shaping the politics of experience, as described in Manufacturing Consent: The Political Economy of the Mass Media.

One key concept/mechanism in the politics of experience that we need to understand is how simulacra are consciously presented as the "real thing" to protect the Elites' power and privileges.

Simulacrum is defined as "an insubstantial form or semblance of something."

Consider how the word "capitalism," with its powerful invocations of free markets, capital freely risked, transparency, entrepreneurship, etc., is constantly deployed to mask crony capitalism, which fundamentally undermines all the key elements of true capitalism.

Thus the crony capitalism on display when stupendous government bailouts are sunk into a handful of Plutocracy strongholds is masked by explanations that "we're doing this to save capitalism."

Capitalism does not require the State to borrow a trillion dollars and throw it into the coffers of the Plutocracy. What is being presented as "capitalism" by the Plutocracy and its MSM minions is in fact only a simulacrum of capitalism, a sham representation decorated with just enough shreds of resemblance to the real thing to fool the unwary.

Another key job of the mass media is to distract the populace from the political realities with endless entertainments, just as the Roman Empire provided the citizens of Rome with free bread and fully 175 days a year of free public entertainment.

So our national "politics of experience" serves three explicit goals:

1. Provide a superficially plausible simulacrum of justice, opportunity, equality, capitalism, good governance, etc., so the unskeptical/credulous will comply with the wishes of The Powers That Be and blame themselves (or a carefully designated "other group") for whatever is awry in their communities.

2. Offer up a cornucopia of compelling distractions via mindless "entertainments" and a broadcast media presenting a nonstop diet of "crimes, cops and docs" and a simulacrum of meaning and authenticity via social networks. (Please see my book Weblogs & New Media: Marketing in Crisis for more on the superficiality of social networking.)

This includes a politically potent entertainment of divisive finger-pointing and rancor which works to create superficially appealing "us and them" ideologies.

3. Construct a simulacrum of authenticity bound and defined by consuming, buying and presenting an attractive avatar in the media, i.e. a simulacrum of authority, "coolness" or celebrity which creates a sham *Infrastructure of Self* in a politics of experience dominated by hollow social networks, consuming/shopping and celebrity worship.

Since the key goal of the marketing/mass-media complex is to instill a pervasive, ubiquitous sense of insecurity in each "consumer" (how else to render someone susceptible to buying some needless item or service than make them feel unworthy without it?), then it is predictable that the consumer responds by constructing an Infrastructure of Self of various brands and symbols of identity (tattoos, certain bands/brands of music, etc.) which is an absurd simulacrum of authentic identity.

An authentic identity can only be formed by actions and deeds based on coherent internal beliefs--what was once known as strength of character--and internal states (faith, rules of conduct, self-discipline, etc.) which are inaccessible to marketing.

The Web's potential for propagating knowledge, innovations and practical solutions via *self-organizing networks* is visible to all. (I mentioned self-organizing networks in Chapter One in describing how the Plutocracy was not a conspiracy or secret club as much as a group bound by the same self interests.) That the Web enables people to self-organize in ways which were simply not possible in a world limited to telephones, centralized print and broadcast media and physical travel is self-evident.

But such ephemeral self-organizing networks vary in utility and duration. Lacking the bonds created by meetings and organizations in the real world, most such collections have very limited lifespans and results.

Nonetheless the political leverage offered by networking technologies (the Web, SMS-mobile phone texting, wikis, blogs, etc.) is already so powerful that repressive central States quickly disrupt, jam or shut down these networks when their power is threatened by popular insurrection.

The profitability and reach of such networks has not been lost on the global media empires, which have quickly taken control of the commercial social networks. But their dreams of windfall exploitation/untold profits may be misplaced, as these commercial social networks are largely Potemkin Villages, simulacra of authentic networks largely inhabited by zombie "members" who have long since dropped out of active membership for the simple reason that the networks create little meaningful content or community.

The "meaning" derived from these corporate social networks is achieved by online avatars which project a simulation of "self-worth" via popularity (how many "friends" do you have?), coolness (more "valuable" than character or accomplishment in a media organized to sell something 24/7), authority (how many university degrees do you have?) and sham "authenticity" (what do you own or project which is in scarcity or which has yet to be co-opted by marketers?)

In a peculiar distortion of friendship and shared interests, these corporate social networks are perceived by their members and owners alike as marketing vehicles: one ceaselessly promotes one's band or "brand" and uses one's page to organize marketing campaigns.

The "value" of one's contacts is in the commercial "networking" they enable; those with large numbers of "friends" (the ultimate inauthentic simulacrum) can push more "product" and therefore they have more "value" than someone with actual authentic friends in the real world, who as a consequence has neither the time nor desire to construct a counterfeit "self" in a counterfeit "community" of counterfeit "friends."

These facsimiles of community and friendship appeal to the population most vulnerable to the pervasive insecurity implicit in all marketing: teens. But as anyone who is a teen or knows teens knows, the inauthenticity and artifice of these social networks soon reveals itself and the teens slip into zombie membership, visible on corporate records but no longer engaged in the attempt to satisfy authentic longings with artificial constructs. (Yes, teens do use these networks to communicate with their real-world friends, but this is an extension of texting and the phone, a reflection of their existing network rather than some new community.)

If we examine social networks' politics of experience, we might conclude they are akin to South Seas Cargo Cults which sprouted up after World War Two ended and the nearly supernatural technology and wealth brought by the Americans to remote islands stopped coming.

In a painfully impossible hope of communicating with the vanished Aliens, Cargo Cult members painted rocks to look like radios (simulacrum radios) and called for the ships to return. Social networks designed for profitable marketing are the equivalent of stone radios; true friendship and community cannot be "called forth" by simulacrums and avatars. The social and spiritual poverty of such counterfeit social structures starkly reveals the internal poverty of our collective experience.

I will address the positive possibilities of the Web in Section Two.

Propaganda as Conscious Manipulation of the Politics of Experience

Though "propaganda" does not fully cover all that I mean by the politics of experience (which includes assumptions which are largely subconscious and subliminal, i.e. "the obvious"), it is nonetheless extremely important to understand how education actually makes one more vulnerable to carefully crafted marketing/propaganda. A classic text on the subject is Propaganda: The Formation of Men's Attitudes by Jacques Ellul.

The book Age of Propaganda: The Everyday Use and Abuse of Persuasion offers these principles of propaganda.

--Our data-processing capabilities are limited and so we are unable to critically review all the information we receive. As a result, we resort to so-called heuristics, simple rules for solving the problem. Heuristics are distilled from our previous experience in similar situations.

--Although relying on heuristics is a useful way of dealing with a decision-rich environment, basing our decisions primarily on heuristics is problematic. First, our heuristic cues may be false. Furthermore, a rule may be appropriate in certain situations but be misapplied in others. Another problem is that heuristics can be easily faked and manipulated. Knowledge of heuristics enables control our politics of experience.

--Shaping a favorable climate for the message is called pre-persuasion. If we establish the agenda and context then we shape the results. One technique is to use statements as axioms such as "what everyone takes for granted" and "what everyone knows." Another is to attach black-or-white labels (positive or negative) to topics which cannot be easily disputed.

--Establish a "source credibility" of "experts" and/or attractive communicators to activate the audience's own self-persuasion.

-Create a simple message that focuses the audience's attention on the specific "problem" which will define their "solution."

Mental shortcuts (heuristics) are most likely to be used when the audience is under time pressure and so overwhelmed with information that it becomes impossible to process it adequately. If the audience has little other knowledge or information, then they will base their decision on whatever heuristics come quickly to mind within the context already established in the pre-persuasion stage.

--Evoke an emotion that will effectively channel the audience toward the desired conclusion. Fear is often effective, as is guilt; feelings of obligation and indebtedness invoke reciprocity, so we acquiesce. Appeals to universal values we hold trigger the desire to agree, for we all want to be self-consistent.

--Recruit the audience to a small role in the larger "play." Individuals then feel committed to the Cause, setting the stage for their agreement to future actions.

--Define group parameters so that the audience feels "we are all on the same side." Once they feel "membership" then they will feel obliged to "follow the group."

Note how the concepts of "what's obvious" and "framing the problem defines the solution" seamlessly fit into propaganda's mechanisms.

An early pioneer of full-spectrum marketing/propaganda was Edward Bernays, who formalized his systemic approach in his book Propaganda. Bernays justified marketing as an essential element of democracy, even as he summarized his work as *engineering consent*: "The engineering of consent is the very essence of the democratic process, the freedom to persuade and suggest."

Given that a handful of Elite interests own the vast majority of mass media outlets, we conclude that what Bernays presented as the authentic "democratic process" was in fact merely a simulacrum, designed to lull the unwary into believing marketing is the core of a democracy shorn of participation other than as a consumer of packaged ideas. When we ask cui bono of his scheme, the answer is himself and his corporate/Elite clientele, not the citizenry.

Another essential text on the media's subjugation to marketing and Elites' interests is Manufacturing Consent: The Political Economy of the Mass Media.

Simulacrum: From Con Game to Full Spectrum Defense of the Status Quo

Let's begin by repeating this definition of simulacrum: an insubstantial form or semblance of something. The reason why someone would construct and deploy a simulacrum is (shall we risk this word?) obvious:

A simulacrum is used to mask or distort a reality that, once revealed, would cause the target audience to act in ways that would not serve the interests of those deploying the simulacrum.

The spectrum of simulacra runs from simple sidewalk confidence games to highly elaborate global propaganda campaigns.

In a simple con game, the facsimile of a "fair game of chance" (or "open market") is presented to the target audience to persuade them to put their money into what is the opposite of fair and open: a setup carefully rigged to transfer the target's wealth to the purveyor. In other words, the sham offers the illusion that the game/market might benefit the target, while the reality is the game has only one end-state: it only benefits the con-man/"house" at the expense of the targets/"marks."

A con game is a willful distortion of an authentic game of chance which masks the reality that the game serves only the interests of its owners. A simulated fair game of chance coupled with slick marketing ("See that guy? He just won a hundred bucks!") is an effective strategy to gain the trust of the target. ("Con" comes from confidence, as the con game's main challenge is to win the confidence of a skeptical mark).

For a context larger than the sidewalk con game, consider the stock market and its elaborate simulacrum of "open markets," "sound ratings" and "expert investment advice." The target audience--the tens of millions of citizens with money in retirement accounts and similar funds--have suffered stupendous losses in the past decade by trusting the ratings promising low risk and the "expert investment advisors" who counseled "stay fully invested for the long-term" and "buy on the dips."

Every one of these actions required the confidence and trust of the marks, and every one served the interests of Wall Street rather than the interests of the marks. Every one enabled Wall Street to maximize its profits and transaction fees using the marks' own money, and every one provided Wall Street with maximum opportunity to sell losing positions to the marks and transfer the marks' wealth to Wall Street.

Many of the exotic mortgages (during the housing bubble, these were known as "exotic;" now that reality has broken through the distortions, they're known as "toxic") were also first-order cons: a simulacrum of a legitimate mortgage was presented, along with simulacrum of supporting documents, in order to fleece the unwary mortgage holder/ home buyer into a transfer of wealth from the mark (both the holder of the mortgage and its eventual buyer in the global mortgage-backed securities market) to the con owners.

(That a few of the marks managed to dump their piece of the con onto "greater fools" before the game folded only enhanced the illusion of easy wealth.)

A persuasive facsimile offers many advantages, hence the great number of examples. Consider seduction: the male offering a simulacrum of love and enduring affection (tender attention, flowers, etc.) gains sexual gratification should the female find his artifice persuasive and perhaps even passes on his genes should the female mark become pregnant.

The crooked construction contractor creates a plausible veneer of legitimacy--business cards, well-worn tools, perhaps even phony references provided by confederates--in order to persuade the homeowners to sign a contract and put money down for a job which will never be started.

A worthy simulation of productive work can enable an artfully lazy worker to gain the same benefits enjoyed by his/her truly productive colleagues.

The simulacrum of prestige offered by a counterfeit Rolex watch is solidly in the self-interest of the person buying it, hence its appeal to marks. The buyer of a counterfeit pharmaceutical, on the other hand, may be paying full price for a worthless simulacrum counterfeit medication; the replacement of a legitimate label and product with facsimiles offers huge rewards to the purveyors and nothing to the unwary buyer.

In each of these cases--the con, the seduction, the counterfeit--the potential gains far outweigh the nominal cost of creating and presenting the simulacrum. This hugely imbalanced cost-benefit ratio explains the ubiquity and prevalence of cons, counterfeits and seductions in all cultures and eras.

The key defenses against simulacra are knowledge and experience. Thus the 30-year old woman with painful personal experience of being seduced will be far more difficult to con/seduce than an inexperienced, insecure 20-year old woman. What Wall Street fears is not regulation (which can be watered down with subsequent lobbying) but a dearth of new credulous marks willing to believe that Wall Street works to their benefit in a fair and open market.

But simulacra offer a much broader spectrum of deception beyond seductions, counterfeits and con games; the great power of the concept lies in its unification of a tremendous range of distortions, deflections, deceptions, illusions, masks, obfuscations and inauthenticities presented as authentic.

Within our analysis of the politics of experience, the fundamental mechanism simulacra provide is what I term *full spectrum defense of the Status Quo*. Such simulacra can be found in all time scales and settings, from marriages to nations.

Thus we find simulacrum not just in willfully conceived confidence games but in good-faith efforts to sustain or "reform" failing institutions.

A partner who is fundamentally indifferent to the marriage will consent to counseling--in the case of those who have already given up, a simulacrum of the process of saving the marriage--not just to appear willing to save the status quo, but perhaps to sustain their own self-image as one who "tried."

Managers and politicians will go through the process of "reforming" failed, corrupted institutions, not with the intention to deceive so much as to "play the part" they feel is demanded of them, even if they know the reforms are superficial and will not resolve structural problems.

Thus simulacra are designed and supported for a number of reasons beyond outright deception; their key feature is that they protect the self-interest of the participant and deflect challenges to that self-interest. Simulacra can be designed to deflect criticism ("see, we are trying"), distort an attempt to replace the status quo with something much less beneficial to those controlling the market ("beware, socialized medicine is evil"), or even further an ultimately self-destructive self-delusion ("serving this Master is furthering my own interests").

Politicians and marketers, of course, depend entirely on simulacra of "value" and persuasion to further their own interests, but the same can be said of the entire status quo. Thus we find media pandering to their target audiences via simulacrum "issues" to serve their own interests (selling advertisements and subscriptions) while prudently avoiding any penetrating critiques of their audience or advertisers.

The greatest simulacra are designed to foster the illusion that a system which benefits an Elite over the common good is actually serving the common good. This is the primary tool of persuasion of the State (all government at all levels) and entrenched Elites like the medical and legal establishments.

Stated another way: as the Elites' interests diverge from those of the society as a whole, they construct elaborate simulacrums to win the society's compliance and complicity (that is, the self-aggrandizement of "I don't care, I got mine").

For example, though the actual design and contracts for the construction of a massive State project will have already been decided behind closed doors, a simulacrum of "public participation" will be presented to foster the illusion that the process was transparent and in the public interest. A series of superficial "town hall" meetings is generally enough to mask the reality--an inside job all the way--with a soothing simulacrum of "democracy in action."

The same can be said of corporate annual meetings, show trials, and other simulacrum of participation, fairness, and decisions supposedly made for the common good.

A key goal of all systemic simulacra is the disruption of common-sense assessment and decisionmaking: what is called *the OODA loop:* (observation, orientation--what I would term identifying contexts--decision, action.) If every step can be confused, obscured, distracted, distorted and deflected via disinformation, propaganda, deceptive framing of the problem, etc., then the process of change itself will be crippled. This is a key goal of all State/Plutocracy simulacra: *by crippling all adaptation and transformation, the status quo is defended.*

The great irony, of course, is that every organism and system must adapt to changing circumstances if it is to survive, much less prosper; and so the rigid defense of the status quo against all challenges renders it brittle and increasingly unstable to unstoppable devolution/phase shift/collapse.

This irony is perhaps best reflected in the Elites' self-reinforcing mechanism of exempting themselves (both the private capital-Plutocracy and the State functionary/public union Elite) from the very market forces which impose adaptation, creative destruction and evolution. The irony is deepened by the Plutocracy and State's alleged worship of "the free market"--the very market each exempts itself from at every turn.

Thus our first step in parsing the politics of experience will always be to ask cui bono of all participants, and to dig through the simulacrum (both the illusions of authenticity and the disruptions of OODA loops) to the underlying realities.

The second step will always be to realize that complacency and complicity with the status quo will almost always be self-serving for participants, even those with little to gain from supporting the status quo. Why is this so? Losing whatever crumbs one does receive by challenging the owners of the cake will always be riskier than remaining passively compliant and complicit.

Put another way: maintaining the security of the known (status quo) is inherently less risky than embarking on a new path because the outcome is unknown; while change might bring improvements, it might also result in catastrophe: losing even a very limited security would be far worse than passively accepting the status quo. We might even posit that risk aversion is a naturally selected trait.

Risk-aversion certainly explains why people stay in jobs and marriages they loathe--the risks of change are perceived as more dangerous than the suffering of staying put. This mechanism works on individual and societal levels alike.

If this is so, then transformation/change becomes inevitable only when the supposed security of the status quo gives way--when, for instance, the State becomes insolvent and its "security" is revealed as illusory. At that point it will become obvious that change is coming one way or the other and so the "low-risk" option of passive complicity is no longer available.

Thus open insurrection only occurs when the crumbs have been swept away, and there is no reason left to support the status quo. This is why the State's greatest power is distributing crumbs widely enough that few will be served by challenging the State's growing share of national income and its steadfast protection of the Power Elites. The ideal situation for the State (and thus the Plutocracy) is every family in the nation receives a payment from the State and abundant free entertainment (bread and circuses).

The State will only devolve when it can no longer fund this universal largesse or the largesse is paid in a currency that has lost all value.

Both circumstances were present in the devolution of the Roman Empire, and so let us examine the forces at work in the patterns, waves and cycles of human history.

Key concepts in this chapter:
Infrastructure of Self
Self-organizing networks
Engineering consent
Full spectrum defense of the Status Quo
OODA loop

Chapter Ten: Legitimizing the Illegitimate

One of the key goals of the status quo's propaganda is to convince the target audience (the U.S. citizenry) that institutionalized deception, fraud, obfuscation and looting have always been "business as usual" and thus protests are specious.

The key technique employed to accomplish this goal is to *derealize* U.S. history, depriving the target audience of any context that does not support the soothing contention that "everybody has always cheated, politicians have always been crooks," etc.

Any history which suggests that the present era of fraud, debauchery of credit, State over-reach and Plutocratic excess is unprecedented or parallels moments in U.S. history which were immediately followed by financial collapse, strife and war is dismissed or expunged from the mass media.

This derealization of history has several moving parts:

1. Emphasize the present unceasingly and ignore the past as irrelevant. The "news cycle" shortens into soundbites and video snippets, eliminating any moment of relative calm for analysis or context. This could be termed *induced amnesia.*

2. Present a frenzy of images and emotional content that confuse and numb the audience via sensory and verbal overload.

3. Delegitimize skeptical inquiry and demands for transparency by dismissing our era's ubiquitous fraud and over-reach as standard practice that has always been the norm in U.S. history.

This approach is effective because there is a kernel of truth in every admonishment that greed in inherent in human nature. But this appeal to greed as normal (if not "good") masks the reality that previous eras of American history were characterized by robust negative feedbacks that limited financial fraud, deception and embezzlement.

4. *Decontextualize* scale. If the rentier-financial Elite pillaged $10 million in a previous period of unlimited financial looting and debauchery of credit (to grab a number from the air), then claim today's looting of hundreds of billions of dollars--adjusted for inflation, an amount a 100-fold larger than the past sum--is "no different than the past, it's just business as usual."

The goal is to mask the truth that today's over-reach and embezzlement is very different as it is two orders of magnitude greater and has reached its larcenous claws past the usual "den of thieves" on Wall Street into the heart of middle class wealth, housing and retirement savings.

This technique also effectively masks the very different scale of the U.S. military and its global reach. Prior to World War II, the U.S. military quickly shrank back to its prewar modest scale after the cessation of hostilities. The U.S. Navy was significant enough to defend sea-lanes for commerce and enforce the Monroe Doctrine (domination of Central America and the Caribbean) but other navies were larger. The Great White Fleet (14 ships) of 1908 which sailed around the world in a display of American seapower depended on friendly ports of call to refuel; now the U.S. maintains global fleets homeported in its own bases around the world.

(As a footnote, the "Splendid Little War" of 1901--the Spanish-American War--certainly opened up new bases for the U.S. in the Philippines and elsewhere; the annexation of Hawaii in 1898 also secured a key strategic Pacific base.)

Once again, the fact that the U.S. possessed a Navy and Army in 1908 can be used to mask the scale of the present military: "we've always had a Navy," which sounds much like " banks have always been greedy," etc. This language is designed to distract us from the realization that today's financial fraud and today's American Empire are unprecedented in their scale and reach.

5. *Decontextualize* history. By downplaying comparisons with legitimately prosperous eras in U.S. history, propaganda masks key differences between the past and present. Thus when banks were tightly regulated after the fraud and debauchery of the 1920s led to the crash of 1929, financial profits were a modest slice of total U.S. corporate profits. In the past decade of deregulated "financial innovation," financial sector profits have come to dominate corporate earnings. This is extraordinarily different from the prosperity of the 1950s and 60s in which profits flowed from producing goods and services, not financial legerdemain.

In the same manner, the fact that inequality has leaped since the early 1970s has been derealized to protect those who have benefited from this trend (i.e. the top 5%).

6. Confuse the taxonomy of profit and wealth generation. This can also be termed "purposefully confusing apples with oranges." Thus the neutral word "profit" is used to describe the legitimate profits earned by

innovative enterprises such as Apple which earns money by providing greater value than the competition, and illegitimate profits reaped by fraudulent mortgage-mill lenders who sold "toxic" mortgages to unqualified borrowers.

Despite the visible difference in type and category of these "earnings," the mainstream financial media (a key arm of the propaganda/marketing machine) compares the numbers as if they deserve the same standing in the taxonomy profit and wealth generation. Yet one is clearly illegitimate as it ceases to function without deception, fraud, embezzlement, distortion, misrepresentation, malfeasance and collusion. And indeed, once questions were raised, these firms vanished overnight.

7. Obscure the institutionalization of mispriced risk and assets. Bluntly stated, mispricing risk and assets is lying. If I sell you a car which is worth $1,000 (after spray-painting the old battery, filling the engine with heavy oil to mask the knock and hiding the rust beneath a quick coat of cheap paint) for $5,000, I have intentionally "mispriced" the "asset"--in simple moral terms, I have lied to you for my own gain. The sellers of derivatives, mortgage-backed securities, stocks inflated by bogus earnings, etc. have in effect sold high-risk junk as low-risk valuable assets.

The key point is they did so with the collusion of the State agencies tasked with oversight.

With the active collusion of the U.S. Treasury, Federal Reserve and the alphabet-soup agencies (SEC, FDIC, etc.), highly leveraged and thus highly risky banks are presented as "solvent" when in fact if their assets were priced by the market ("marked to market") they would be revealed as insolvent.

Derivatives which in an unregulated and thus "buyer beware" market might be forced to be marked to market are, with State collusion and facsimile "oversight," sold as "safe" risk management instruments.

8. Present simulacrum oversight as genuine regulation. By referencing the regulatory agencies created after the Great Depression to restrain the excesses of debt and fraud which enabled the Great Crash, the mass media explicitly implies that these same agencies are still authentic forces of oversight. But the reality is they have been reduced via Power Elite capture and co-option to mere facsimiles of regulation riddled with loopholes and incapacitated by gutted staffs and

weakened mandates.

9. Confuse the taxonomy of capitalism and ownership. In another derealization of scale, two-thirds of the "tax cut for the middle class" flows to the top 1% of taxpayers. In a similar way, small business which actually faces a free-market competitive environment is purposefully confused with crony capitalism, oligarchy, cartels and monopoly.

Thus "save the family farm" legislation and regulation ends up benefiting corporate agribusiness and the Power Elites' ownership of vast tracts of forest, grazing and farmland.

10. Mask the reality that the political Elite has been effectively "captured" by a "financial Mafia" --a process and structure akin to kleptocracy States controlled by organized-crime syndicates or oligarchies. Regulators attempting to enforce restrictions on the rentier-financial Power Elite (financial Mafia) are effectively neutralized by interference from the political class (elected officials and high-caste technocrats) who are beholden to Power Elite interests for their own wealth and power.

This "capture" is not necessarily the brute-force "ownership" enforced by bribery, threats (of non-support) and mutual profiteering--though these are the money/power pathways--it is also the capture of the State Elites' politics of experience.

That is, elected officials and high-caste State apparatchiks may actually believe the nation will collapse if Power Elite banks and other rentier/debt-serf structures are allowed to fail, i.e. be declared insolvent. Thus the State Elites are so enthralled, seduced, beholden and manipulated that they are blind to the fact that the exact opposite is true: the nation would be freed from the shackles of enslavement by the destruction of the rentier-financial Elites' investment banks and other *concentrations of power.*

Once again I call your attention to the fundamental power of the politics of experience; enslavement, capture and surrender all become inevitable once the Power Elites' intellectual framework is accepted as "true." Once "belief in the system fades," then a non-Power-Elite frame of reference becomes possible.

The goal of Plutocratic and State propaganda is thus to legitimize the illegitimate.

Consider, for example, complex derivatives. Although these financial instruments are presented as "risk management tools" akin to futures contracts and options (which have been in place for hundreds of years), they are mere simulacra of these time-tested risk-management tools.

Where a futures contract or option has simple, transparent features--the contract gives the owner the right to buy shares of stocks or a specified commodities--a complex derivative is designed to be obscure and opaque, offering a facsimile of risk management that actually masks inordinate hidden risk.

Such instruments might include currency swaps and credit default swaps which only those originating the derivative truly understand. This purposeful complexity provided a rationalization for the derivatives to remain unpriced, unlike options and futures contracts which are "marked to market" every trading day on transparent exchanges. Masking their true value, complex derivatives are marked not to market but to fantasy: whatever the holder claims the value to be.

Since no one outside the underwriter can assess the value, the underwriter enters a "game the system" collusion with a ratings firm which then issues a AAA "safe investment" rating on the deceptively risky derivative.

And since there is no market to set the value, such instruments can be claimed as assets even as they approach zero valuation.

By any measure, such instruments are not legitimate risk-management tools; they are purposefully fraudulent from inception and by design, and immensely profitable to the underwriting firm. Thus it is no surprise that some $600 trillion in notational value derivatives have been written and are floating around the global financial system, carrying illusory valuations and endemic risk.

The net result is immense profits for the insiders perpetrating the fraud and the eventual undermining of legitimate credit and risk-assessment and management systems.

Legitimizing the illegitimate necessarily ends up delegitimizing the authentic foundation that the illegitimacy preyed upon. Claiming financial fraud is legitimate delegitimizes capitalism, the U.S. financial system and the U.S. as a nation. It's as if a serial adulterer announced that now that his wife is having an affair then his own adultery is thus legitimized. But this justification fools no one; the adulterer has delegitimized his own fraudulent, debauched marriage and himself.

That is precisely the situation of the U.S. financial sector and Empire, which has employed legitimate military forces in illegitimate "preemptory" wars and other uses of force which are purposefully kept as State secrets lest the American citizenry question their legitimacy and necessity.

This process of legitimizing the illegitimate and thus delegitimizing what was once trustworthy and authentic can be seen in all the mechanisms and structures described in this analysis, financial, intellectual and political. It is a pattern that is repeated again and again in the substitution of simulacrum for authentic systems and the masking of this substitution with delusions, deceptions and misrepresentations actively promoted and disseminated by a sophisticated mass media marketing/propaganda machine.

Here are examples of "business as usual" which were not "business as usual" a relatively short time ago:

• Advertising medications directly to consumers was banned until only a few years ago. Pharmaceutical firms could advertise only to doctors in professional journals. Compare the advertising pages of mass-distribution magazines such as *National Geographic* in 1979, 1989, 1999 and 2009--the present dominance of pharmaceutical marketing is a recent phenomenon.

• Investment banks were not allowed to perform commercial banking until 1999.

• Banks' profits flowed from conventional lending and constituted a relatively modest percentage of overall corporate earnings until the last decade when they became the dominant profit-center, reaping fully 40% of U.S. corporate profits.

All of these fundamental changes have been legitimized and sold as "business as usual" via propaganda and *induced amnesia*.

It is critical to note that the State enables the legitimizing of the illegitimate in three fundamental ways:

1. It sanctions fraud and embezzlement as "business as usual"

2. It sponsors risk-taking via guarantees, backstops, bailouts, loans and limitless liquidity to the financial industry

3. It creates an illusion of financial stability which masks both the systemic fraud and embezzlement and the extreme vulnerability of the entire financial edifice.

Parallel Shadow Structures of Privilege

One technique for legitimizing the illegitimate is to present a formal, visible structure that is carefully legitimized for public consumption. Examples include bank earnings statements, state university admissions policies and job openings at institutions such as universities, corporations and state agencies.

Behind a carefully nurtured facade of legitimacy, however, lies a well-cloaked parallel shadow structure of privilege, also formalized with its own rules and procedures but opaque to public scrutiny or even awareness.

In this sense, the "legitimate" structure is an artifice constructed for the express purpose of presenting enough transparent transactions to convince the public that it is the "one, true system" rather than a facade to cloak the real action: a shadow system operated for the benefit of the few at the expense of the many.

The "shadow" system of governance is comprised of elected officials who demand backdoor loopholes and favors, "fox hired to guard the chicken coop" technocrats who move fluidly (the infamous revolving-door) between corporate headquarters, the State and lobbying firms, where cartel lobbyists write the regulations that are duly passed into law.

The "shadow banking system" is an entire parallel universe of assets, credit, risk and liabilities which are completely invisible to anyone studying the "transparent" financial statements of the banks.

These shadow assets are "off-balance-sheet," meaning an examination of the bank's public balance sheet will not disclose them. Various credit instruments and derivatives can also be held off-balance sheet, rendering the task of actually measuring the bank's risk and total credit outstanding essentially impossible.

Insiders--the privileged few--can then skim the gains from shadow assets purchased with shareholder funds for themselves and their cronies via various accounting and tax schemes.

Even non-financial corporations maintain off-balance-sheet derivatives and accounts.

Behind the facade of an apparently transparent admissions policy, insiders within a prestigious state university system may maintain a shadow system of admissions available to political favorites, major donors and other cronies. In this manner the accomplished non-privileged student can be rejected for opaque reasons and the mediocre offspring of a well-connected crony admitted under ambiguously defined "special circumstances."

Job openings at institutions are duly made public in compliance with transparency rules, but behind this facade the job description and process have been rigged to insure the hiring of cronies.

These are but three of countless examples of apparently legitimate processes and institutions being mere facades to mask the illegitimate distribution of privileges to various Elites.

When this corruption is revealed, then the defense is bashfully schoolyard: everybody does this, it's standard practice; my only mistake was getting caught. The excuses are cold comfort indeed for the non-privileged many deceived for the benefit of the few.

In what might be considered a grand irony, the tables of "shadow systems" within institutions can be turned on the Elites. Transparent non-privileged parallel structures can be established which bypass the corrupted Elite-run institution entirely.

As the State and its institutions devolve, opportunities to set up alternative self-organizing, transparent formal organizations which completely bypass the Elites' concentrations of power and privilege will arise.

I will address these further in Chapter Twenty-Six: Structuring the New American State.

Key concepts in this chapter:
Induced amnesia
Decontextualize (scale, history)
Delegitimize the authentic foundation
Concentrations of power
Parallel Shadow Structures of Privilege
Transparent non-privileged parallel structures

Chapter Eleven: The Forces Behind Cycles of History

It seems self-evident that like Nature (sunspot cycles, the seasons, etc.) history would lend itself to cycles, but there are two basic critiques of historical cycles:

1. Cycles are essentially arbitrary, an order extracted from random data to support a *priori* claims (i.e. finding data to support pre-selected positions)

2. Without an explanation of the causal mechanisms which power the cycles, cycles cannot be predictive

The first argument has the strength of skepticism but the weakness of forced obscurity. Anyone looking at displays of prices over time notices patterns; the question is whether they are regular enough to suggest underlying causes are at work.

For example, if we discern cycles of crop prices, we might look first at crop yields and population growth, that is, supply and demand. We might next profitably look for regular variations in weather (rain/drought, warm/cool, etc.) which might explain why crop yields rose or fell in what appear to be cycles.

Taking the investigation one step further, we might look at the sun's energy output and the orbital variations in the planet's rotation around the sun. And indeed, we would find an imperfect but discernable cycle of sunspot activity that correlates to weather and crop yields.

The more inputs/feedback loops there are in a system, then naturally the more complex the interactions between all the "moving parts" will be. Nonetheless, within the "noise" of weather data various long-term patterns do emerge.

So if we are positing cycles in human history which we claim predictably repeat, what are the causal mechanisms for these cycles?

1. Environmental/demographic over-reach. Like all other organisms, humans tend to fill every available niche to the maximum carrying capacity of that environment. This cause is explored in The Great Wave: Price Revolutions and the Rhythm of History. In essence, humans expand their population and resource extraction right up to the high-tide line. Then, when the tide recedes--as it inevitably does in droughts and other weather patterns, resource depletion, etc.—humans are suddenly faced with starvation/pandemics and endless conflicts over remaining diminishing resources.

2. State over-reach. States tend to expand whenever the opportunity presents itself as the spoils of conquest (not necessarily of territory but of markets) outweigh the costs. States also relentlessly expand their share of the national income via higher taxation.

3. Plutocracy over-reach. As the state expands, the Plutocracy leverages its growing wealth into greater power over state functions. With no natural limits on its power or share of the national income, the Plutocracy inevitably over-reaches, taking so much of the national income and wealth that the middle class, the backbone of the state's tax revenues and support, breaks down.

4. The four-generation cycle of forgetfulness. As individuals, we tend to truly trust only what we have experienced directly or heard directly from parents and grandparents. As a result, the follies of excess and over-reach that caused declines or collapses in previous generations are forgotten in the passage of four generations, or roughly 80 years. Even cultures with written histories exhibit this pattern. Please read The Fourth Turning for more on this topic.

5. Marginal returns. Expansions run out steam for many reasons, but exhaustion of resources and increasingly marginal returns on investment are proximate causes.

6. Illusion of incremental change. As trends run out steam and reverse course, the State and Plutocracy respond with incremental changes (simulacrum of fundamental change) which they hope will reverse the decline without affecting their power, wealth and privilege. Alas, merely adjusting the parameters in a failing system is not enough to rescue it from collapse.

Once the costs of Empire/expansion rise above the value of the spoils gained, the state is caught between the demands of its ever-growing army of dependents for higher tax revenues and the demands of the Plutocracy for greater tax relief.

As individual leaders within the state are inevitably beholden to sponsors in the Plutocracy, such appeals cannot be denied. Given the inevitable rise of state powers and taxation, the leaders are loath to cut either their powers or their power base--the bureaucracies and dependent citizenry that both feed on rising tax revenues.

As a result, the relatively powerless but productive middle class is squeezed for more taxes to spare the Plutocracy and those dependent on state largesse from any pain. This is the inevitable result of state and

Plutocracy over-reach.

In an effort to forestall the collapse of its middle class while still increasing revenues, the state inevitably turns to two mechanisms: borrowing vast sums from foreign lenders and debasing the currency to create the illusion of increasing revenues/money supply.

Just as inevitably, the State eventually defaults on its foreign debt, and the currency collapses in value and is replaced with a new "good money" currency. In the decline/collapse phase, the impoverished middle class, a powerless underclass and a recalcitrant Plutocracy do battle for the diminished resources and State powers.

In cases such as the French Revolution, the Plutocracy is overthrown, however briefly, and replaced with a "revolutionary" ascendant class of political plutocrats. In cases such as the American Revolution, the middle class joins with enlightened segments of the Plutocracy to achieve a more balanced state structure. The Plutocracy agrees to these limits not out of selfless noblesse oblige but out of a long-range understanding that political and financial stability serves its own interests.

Increasingly Marginal Returns Lead to Collapse

One of the structural impediments to fashioning a true prosperity from the ashes of the bogus prosperity now imploding is marginal returns and the illusion of incremental change, two key topics I have covered many times on www.oftwominds.com.

Author Jeremy Rifkin describes this mechanism extremely well in his fascinating book The Hydrogen Economy. He illustrates the concept on a global scale by using the Roman Empire as an example.

Rome's early conquests yielded huge returns on "investment": large tracts of fertile cropland, significant treasure, productive populaces, etc. But as time progressed, more and more of the Empires' wealth flowed to the citizenry of Rome, and conquests of distant lands such as Britain yielded less and less return; garrisoning these distant territories began costing more than they produced.

Eventually even holding onto the now-exhausted croplands and restive populations exceeded Rome's dwindling wealth, and the Empire collapsed. There are many ways of accounting for empire-collapse, be it Roman or Mayan, but certainly "marginal returns" describes one element.

Here is how Rifkin applies the concept to U.S. farming practices:

"The pesticides also destroy the remaining soil. The soil contains millions of microscopic bacteria, fungi, algae, and protozoa, as well as worms and anthropods. These organisms maintain the fertility and structure of the soil. Pesticides destroy these organisms and their complex habitats, hastening the process of soil depletion and erosion.

American farms lose more than four billion tons of topsoil annually, much of it because of the high-tech farming practices introduced over the past half century. By the 1970s, the U.S. had lost more than one-third of its agricultural topsoil. The depletion and erosion, in turn, have required the use of ever-increasing amounts of petrochemical fertilizers to maintain agricultural output. Marginal returns have set in. More and more energy inputs are required to produce smaller gains in net energy yield..."

The Seductive Illusion of Incremental Change

An apt summary of the principle can be found in the ancient Chinese saying, "the journey of a thousand *li* starts with a single step." We all know small changes can eventually make profound changes in a system or person's life. For instance, lose a pound a week and in a year one has lost 50 pounds. As a society, increasing the efficiency of buildings and homes, one at a time, can add up to stupendous savings of energy and money.

The illusion is in the happy story that incremental changes will fix a fundamentally broken system. If a person doesn't profoundly change their understanding of self, diet, nutrition, self-image, identity, marketing, exercise and discipline, then the likelihood of incremental changes in their lifestyle producing profound long-term results is unfortunately low. The same can be said for a wastrel, profligate economy that wastes energy on a vast scale or an economy addicted to cheap, abundant credit.

In systems analysis, incremental change is likened to adjusting the parameters of a system. But as Donella Meadows outlined in her seminal paper, <u>Leverage Points: Places to Intervene in a System</u> (Sustainability

Institute), adjusting the parameters of a system has limited effects. What this means is that fiddling around with "reforms" like increasing the fee paid by Medicare recipients by $10 will never make Medicare financially sustainable.

As an example of how the forces discussed above work in the real world, we turn to an essay first published on www.oftwominds.com in June 2008.

Food Shortages, Rising Prices, Stagnant Wages:
Welcome to the 13th Century

Human history is not just a chaotic cacophony; if we pay attention, we observe rhythms and structures. The reason is as obvious as it is profound. Like all species of life on earth, humanity has been structured/selected via complex adaptations to survive and reproduce within various ecological niches. That our social structures and our histories share certain characteristics over historical time is common sense.

History, like an individual, is unique even as it shares characteristics with previous eras. Without studying history, we are prone to both arrogance and insecurity. Unaware of the past, we proudly reckon we've gone beyond the reach of cyclical history; and then, when the cycle turns and we are adrift and fearful, then we feel inadequate to the task of righting the sinking ship.

History properly studied renders s humble about our ability to control nature and events, and confident that we too can survive bad times.

Which brings me once again to The Great Wave: Price Revolutions and the Rhythm of History by historian David Hackett Fischer (recommended by reader Cheryl A., who kindly sent me a copy of the book.)

In Fischer's well-documented view, there is a grand cycle of prices and wages that turn on the simple but profound law of supply and demand; all else is detail.

As a people prosper and multiply, the demand for goods like food and energy outstrips supply, causing eras of rising prices. Long periods of stable prices (supply increases along with demand) beget rising wages and widespread prosperity. Once population and financial demand outstrip supply of food and energy--a situation often triggered by a series of catastrophically poor harvests--then the stability decays into instability as shortages develop and prices spike.

These junctures of great poverty, insecurity and unrest set the stage for wars, revolutions and pandemics.

It is remarkable indeed that the very conditions so troubling us now were also present in the price rises of the 13th, 16th and 18th centuries. Unfortunately, those cycles did not have Disney endings: the turmoil of the 13th century brought war and a series of plagues which killed 40% of Europe's population; the 16th century's era of rising prices tilled fertile ground for war, and the 18th century's violent revolutions and resultant wars can be traced directly to the unrest caused by spiking prices.

(The very day that prices for bread reached their peak in Paris, an angry mob tore down the Bastille prison, launching the French Revolution.)

After a gloriously long run of stable prices in the 19th century--prices were essentially unchanged in Britain between 1820 and 1900--The 20th century was one of steadily increasing prices. Fischer takes great pains to demolish the ideologically appealing notion that all inflation is monetary; the supply of money (gold and silver) rose spectacularly in the 19th century but prices barely budged. In a similar fashion, eras of rising prices have seen stable money supplies. Yes, monetary expansion can play a part, but Fischer has done his homework, and population growth is a far stronger correlation than money supply.

Monetary inflation can lead to hyperinflation, of course, but there are always mitigating factors in those circumstances.

The long wave is not one of hyperinflation but of supply and demand imbalances undoing the social order.

Americans are inherently suspicious of anything that seems to threaten constraint of the American Dream; thus it is not surprising that cycles of history are largely unknown in the U.S. As Fischer explains:

"This collective amnesia is partly the consequence of an attitude widely shared among decision-makers in America, that history is more or less irrelevant to the urgent problems before them."

Fischer notes that he describes not cycles but waves, which are more variable and less predictable. (Surfers know to count waves, as they tend to arrive in sets.)

Is the sudden rise in the price of oil unique? Not at all. Energy in 1300 was firewood, and as Fischer relates, the cost of energy skyrocketed then, too:

"In England from 1261 to 1320, the price of firewood and charcoal rose faster and farther than any other commodity. Close behind the soaring cost of energy came price-rises for food-stuffs of various kinds--particularly for grain, meat and dairy products."

Talk about being ripped from the headlines: this describes our current situation remarkably well.

In response to this great rise in prices of essentials, both commoners and governments debased the currency. In their day, this meant shaving the edges of coins, or debasing new coins with non-precious metals. The debasement was an attempt to increase money to counteract the rise in prices, but it failed (of course). Every few decades, a new undebased coinage was released, and then the cycle of debasement began anew.

Just as insidiously, wages fell:

"But as inflation continued in the mid-13th century, money wages began to lag behind. By the late 13th and early 14th centuries real wages were dropping at a rapid rate."

Hmm--sound familiar? Now guess what happened next:

"At the same time that wages fell, rents and interest rose sharply. Returns to landowners generally kept pace with inflation or exceeded it.

This growing gap between returns to labor and capital was typical of price-revolutions in modern history. So also was its social result: a rapid growth of inequality that appeared in the late stages of every long inflation."

And what happened to government expenditures? It's *deja vu* all over again--deficits:

"Yet another set of cultural responses to inflation created disparities of a different kind: fiscal imbalances between public income and expenditures. Governments fell deep into debt during the middle and later years of the 13th century."

Oh, and crime and illegitimacy also rose. Fischer summarizes the end game of the price-rise wave thusly:

"In the late 13th century, the medieval price-revolution entered another stage, marked by growing instability. Prices rose and fell in wild swings of increasing amplitude. Inequality increased at a rapid rate. Public deficits surged ever higher. The economy of Western Europe became dangerously vulnerable to stresses it might have managed more easily in other eras."

And there you have our future, writ large in the 13th, 16th and 18th century price-revolution waves that preceded ours. It is hubris in the extreme to think we have somehow morphed into some new kind of humanity far different from those people who tore down the Bastille in a great frustrated rage at prices for energy and bread they could no longer afford.

It is foolish to blame "speculators" for the rise in food and energy, when the human population has doubled in 40 years and the consumption of energy and food has exploded as a result. Yes, technology in the form of the Green Revolution enabled vastly greater yields per acre; and yields in many places can still be increased with fertilizers, improved seeds and so on.

But all of this was the result of cheap, easy-to-pump, readily available oil. All the miracles resulted from cheap oil, and now that it's gone--yes, yes, there is more, but it's not cheap or easy to pump--then we have to replace it with some other energy source.

Petroleum and natural gas are wonderfully adaptable energy sources, handy for making fertilizer, plastics, and other chemicals as well as for fuel. Both are readily stored and possess very high energy densities. Yes, Lithium-ion batteries also have a high energy density, but it isn't a matter of drilling a hole and complex lithium-ion batteries gush out. It takes tremendous energy and technology to fashion lithium-ion batteries, and as a result they're expensive.

If the market responds to the oil price-revolution with sufficient verve, capital and innovation, perhaps a rich brew of petroleum replacements will appear in mass production. But there is a peculiar feedback loop at work; there has to be enough energy on hand to build this new infrastructure of solar-cell factories, algae-to-biofuels plants and all the rest. If we consume all the cheap oil in a vain attempt to maintain the status quo, then the replacement becomes ever more costly. And then we have a price-revolution on our hands which looks eerily like the ones which swept Europe in the 13th, 16th and 18th centuries.

So where does this leave us?

The intersection of four long-term cycles suggests that the era from the present (2009) to 2021 will be troubled indeed, and may result in a war, revolution or equivalent re-ordering of U.S. society and perhaps the world.

It doesn't take much thought to anticipate the post-cheap-petroleum era might be fraught with risk and turmoil as the transition--messy and unpredictable in some ways, but predictably messy in any event--takes place. Based on the history so painstakingly assembled by Fischer, we can anticipate:

- Ever higher prices for what I call the FEW Essentials: food, energy and water.
- Ever larger government deficits which end in bankruptcy/ repudiation of debts/new issue of currency.
- Rising property/violent crime and illegitimacy.
- Rising interest rates (by a lot, not a little).
- Rising income inequality in favor of capital over labor.
- Continued debasement of the currency.
- Rising volatility of prices.
- Rising political unrest and turmoil.

Chapter Twelve: Squeezing the Middle Class

As noted above, the Roman Empire's decline can be traced to a variety of causes. But we can summarize them collectively as the middle class being squeezed to death by the over-reach of the state and its Plutocracy/Elite managers.

Stated another way: as the Elites' interests diverge from those of the society as a whole, the middle class is caught in a financial and political vice between the State and Plutocracy and the large underclass dependent on the largesse of the State. As each class (the Plutocracy and the class of unproductive citizenry) become ever more dependent on the State's power and revenues for their privileges and entitlements, they demand the State's share of national income expand at the expense of the middle class.

Since the Plutocracy and the underclass both need the State's power (to exclude the Elites from service and taxes) and revenues (to fund entitlements), they will fight ferociously and ceaselessly for their share of the dwindling national income. The middle class, distracted by the pressures to remain productive in a declining economy, have neither the time, will, capital or organization to match the upper and lower classes' desperate lobbying.

As a result, the middle class loses the political battle and either opts out (what I call *Voluntary Poverty* or simply collapses into penury, joining the underclass.

It is important to refute one of the state's primary emotional points of leverage in demanding an ever-larger proportion of national income: we need this to help the poor. A close examination of the roughly $3 trillion Federal budget and the $1.5 trillion budgets of local government reveals that programs which directly alleviate the direct consequences of poverty such as hunger and lack of shelter (food stamps, now called SNAP and Section 8 housing vouchers, for example) are essentially trivial percentages of all government outlays.

For instance, the entire food stamp program (SNAP) serves approximately 30 million people at a cost of just over $30 billion—a mere 1% of Federal outlays. Section 8 Housing Vouchers costs about $16 billion—less than one-half percent of Federal outlays. The entire Housing and Urban Development department which also serves the homeless is about 1% of Federal outlays.

Add in programs with successful track records like Head Start and at most perhaps 5% of all tax revenues and government borrowing actually directly aid the poverty-stricken. So where does the rest of it go? To behemoth programs like Medicare ($600 billion and rising at double-digit rates year after year), of which private analysis suggest 50% is waste and fraud, and a huge percentage of the balance either harms or does not improve patient health.

It is, however, very profitable for pharmaceutical companies and other vendors. Consider that approximately 1% of the citizenry control 2/3 of the productive assets of the U.S., and the question cui bono--to whose benefit are $4.5 trillion in taxes levied? Is quickly answered: not the poor. Sadly, the poverty-stricken are the "moral justification" simulacrum marketed by various Elites to justify their own stupendous take of ever-rising state revenues and debt issues.

The Artifice of Political Ideologies

From this long-range cyclical perspective, the artificial nature of political ideology is starkly revealed. The Right focuses all its attention and ire on the insatiable appetite of the State for more power and revenue, while the Left focuses all its attention and ire on the insatiable appetite of the Plutocracy for increased privilege and wealth. Unknown to the ideological adherents, each is one side of a single coin.

While the Left focuses on the plight of an underclass distracted by the "bread" provided by the State and the "circuses" provided by the Mainstream Corporate Media, the Right focuses on the diminishment of rights and income which results from the State's ever-increasing taxes and regulatory powers.

Neither side sees that the insatiable appetite of the State and Plutocracy for larger shares of the national income are one in the same. As both are blind to the causal structures, each seeks to defend its chosen champion (the Left--the State, the Right--the Plutocracy) from the slings and arrows cast by the ideological "opponents."

A handful of Revolutionaries fantasize about the underclass grabbing power from both the State and the Plutocracy, but since the underclass is by definition not productive enough to tax, there is little to entice the middle class to join their revolution. For they foresee they will have to pay for the costs of the "revolution" just as they carried most of the weight of the old State/Plutocracy. This is the classic "meet the new boss, same as the old boss" situation in which a new Plutocracy simply replaces the old one.

Libertarians, in their haste to focus on the rights of the individual to unfettered political and economic liberties, fail to notice that the Plutocracy is delighted to encourage their focus. For a nation of subservient debt-serfs can exist quite peaceably in a low-tax State dominated and controlled by a Plutocracy.

Indeed, a semi-feudal State founded on debt-serfdom has the luxury of offering generous political and economic liberties to its indentured citizenry--as long as they don't join together to challenge the perquisites, privileges and wealth of the Plutocracy.

In this analysis, the Plutocracy is well-served by a politics of experience which neatly dices the political ideological spectrum into various non-threatening and mutually distracting slices of rancor and illusion.

Democracy, Empire, Socialism and the Fantasy of Self-Regulating Markets

Since the middle class is the foundation of the State (by paying the taxes and providing political support for the status quo), then questions of democracy, markets and empire directly affect the squeezing of the middle class.

While this discussion may seem far afield from practical responses to the intersecting crises we face, it is actually of paramount importance. For if the American State/Empire over-reaches globally, and the Plutocracy over-reaches domestically, then the middle class must either respond in its own defense or collapse beneath rising taxes.

The State and ruling Elites will defend the status quo very robustly and perseverently, overriding or simply ignoring middle class attempts to limit its power.

We should pause here to remind ourselves that the politics of experience, the "obvious" incentives and assumptions which we do not even notice such is their "naturalness," masks the actual mechanics of this destruction of the middle class.

Thus the State will argue that regulation protects everyone (even if it doesn't, and is riddled with profitable loopholes that served Elites' interests behind a sham transparency), the "underprivileged" "need" various services and benefits (even if the supposedly "necessary" benefits like bilingual classes fail in their stated objective) and an ever-increasing public payroll is needed to "serve the public."

The question of who pays for all this is left uneasily unsaid; the Elites will pay a much smaller percentage of their income than the middle class, and as a result their share of the national income continues to rise as the middle class founders.

The Elites will quietly voice their needs in the hushed halls of power, confident that the media (recall that they own or control the mainstream media) will provide a simulacrum of transparency, a facsimile to satisfy an easily distracted public.

Thus it is not at all clear that democracy and Empire, that is, geopolitical hegemony, are compatible. Nor is it clear that centralized State planning (socialism) and democracy are compatible, either (please see The Road to Serfdom by F. A. Hayek).

Why? Socialism always contains the potential for "the tyranny of the many" which concerned many of the United States' Founding Fathers. If 51% of the citizenry are receiving benefits or "free" services from the government, they can essentially dominate the minority productive class via the ballot box.

Put another way: the percentage of people who will gladly accept free money or services is virtually 100%, while the percentage of those willing to risk their time and capital for productive enterprise is considerably less than 100%. Thus the less-productive benefactors of government largesse can extract ever-higher taxes from the remaining productive members of the society, until the productive members either collapse into penury as in the late Roman Empire, or they opt out of the burdens imposed on them by the tyranny of the State's more numerous benefactors.

In his book Capitalism, Socialism, and Democracy, economist Joseph Schumpeter argued that capitalism collapses from within as democratic majorities vote for the creation of a welfare state. This so burdens entrepreneurship that the capitalist infrastructure which supports the State and its dependents collapse.

Ironically, perhaps, the structure of Empire remains the same regardless of the ruling ideology: Neoliberal Capitalist or Socialist (democratic or autocratic) or totalitarian: a small ruling Elite benefits enormously from the Empire, and bestows sufficient benefits on the home nation's citizenry to buy their passive complicity.

In all cases, the Empire is managed by a centralized-State Elite which is untouched by any feedback/influence instigated by the citizenry.

Democracy is thus ontologically at odds with Empire; democracy can exist in the home nation of the Empire but the citizenry do not control the Empire managed in their name. Secrecy, subterfuge and propaganda are thus essential elements in legitimizing the Empire in the eyes of the domestic citizenry and in gaining their compliance/support.

The forces drawing outsized benefits from the Empire have the wealth and influence (concentrations of power) to dictate the State's global decisions. In any Empire, the citizenry effectively have no say over the policies of their State; propaganda is deployed to stir up patriotism when the rubber-stamp of popular approval is deemed necessary.

Congress no longer declares war, as dictated by the U.S. Constitution; it empowers an Imperial Executive branch with open-ended "resolutions" while the citizenry are pummeled into submission with endless propaganda.

Another way of understanding this dynamic is to analyze the cost-benefit of Empire. U.S.-based global corporations receive the majority of their profits from overseas operations. In recent years, U.S. corporate profits were about $1.4 trillion, so we can estimate that close to $1 trillion of that profit was generated overseas. (Note that overseas production greatly increases corporate profits on goods sold in the domestic market.)

Given that the U.S. Empire works to keep cheap oil, commodities, manufactured goods and labor flowing to the domestic economy, we might also estimate that the Empire funnels at least $1 trillion in direct financial benefits to the domestic economy.

The Pentagon budget is approximately $650 billion a year, or roughly equal to the Social Security budget. The core Defense budget is about $515 billion for fiscal 2009, with another $70 billion for the Global War on Terror (GWOT) and additional funds for Veterans and active wars in Iraq and Afghanistan.

According to the U.S. Department of Defense, these funds include providing world-class health care for 9.2 million eligible Service members, families, and retirees and maintaining 545,000 facilities at 5,300 sites in the U.S. and around the globe.

(Source:www.defenselink.mil/releases/release.aspx?releaseid=11663)

Other highlights include $389 million to establish the U.S. Africa Command, and $184 billion for weapons systems procurement, research and development. That is a staggering sum which is divided up amongst a handful of large defense contractors, all of whom have facilities spread over the U.S. so the largesse can benefit all 535 members of Congress. These elected officials view the Defense budget as a stupendous opportunity to bring jobs to their district even if the Services do not want the weapons being procured.

Given the large number of citizens benefiting from this spending (9 million active and retired personnel and their families, millions more working in weapons R&D and manufacture, the Veterans Administration, the civilian Pentagon workforce, etc.) and the enormous profits to be made from supplying the Pentagon, we can safely state that the Elites controlling these sums have *asymmetric stakes in the game* (a topic to be covered in depth later) and thus tremendous incentives to support the Empire's status quo.

From the point of view of those benefiting from the Empire's direct maintenance costs, then $650 billion appears to be returning $2 trillion in direct benefits: a healthy return on investment.

Critics ask what else might be funded if the Pentagon budget was slashed from Empire levels to nuclear deterrence and self-defense levels (say, $300 billion less than the current $650 billion). But social spending (or deficit reduction) would not benefit the State and corporate Elites extracting huge benefits from the Empire. Thus they will defend their Imperial share of the national income at all costs.

Democracy has little role in the Empire's spending or policies until such time as the cost-benefit falls to the point that the Empire costs more to maintain than it reaps for the Elites and brings home to the domestic populace. Until then, the populace has significant incentives (defense jobs, cheap oil, commodities and manufactured goods) to remain passive and those Elites and dependents benefiting from the Empire have every incentive to actively support the status quo.

Here is the dynamic between the productive middle class, democracy, the State and its global Empire:

1. Democracy offers the middle-class some modicum of power. If democracy is undermined, the middle class has essentially no power. The fall of Rome provides an excellent template.

2. Empire costs a great deal of money that must be raised by taxes, mostly on the middle class. Thus Imperial over-reach in the form of costly wars in defense of the Empire's reach/control (a classic example of marginal returns) end up overburdening the middle class. While over-reach reaps huge profits for the Imperial Elites, the productive domestic middle class receives rapidly diminishing returns on their "investment" (taxes paid) in the Empire. This is precisely what occurred in the decline and fall of Rome.

3. Central planning/government control of assets and revenues favors the politically influential Plutocracy over the middle class, as government ends up serving the Plutocracy's interests under the cover of expanding benefits to the less productive.

4. Government (State) regulations intended to rein in global corporations end up strangling middle-class entrepreneurs as the Plutocracy arranges for loopholes and exclusions which the middle-class cannot exploit.

5. State over-reach domestically (within the U.S.) insures that multiple agencies and regulatory bodies create conflicting, overlapping layers of authority and decision-making, crippling middle-class entrepreneurship with bureaucratic sclerosis.

One example of too many governmental stakeholders resulting in bureaucratic sclerosis is the astonishingly time-consuming and arduous process of adding a new railway station in California. Everyone agreed that "smart growth" and common-sense transportation planning required an additional railway stop to serve commuters living in a new medium-density community on an existing rail line.

Despite the obvious need and the will of the people as expressed by a general plan voted into law, the process is now in Year Nine with no resolution in sight due to the staggering number of state and private "stakeholders" /agencies with some say over the rail lines and station.

It is amazing that anything at all gets accomplished in the U.S. when situations such as this are examined in detail. As always, the proper context is the high cost to the middle class when political approval by various overlapping governmental stakeholders and Elites is required. Democracy has in effect been undermined by an ever-expanding government of overlapping authorities and ever-higher fees and taxes and a Plutocracy that gains exclusions and loopholes via political influence.

The Fantasy of Self-Regulated Markets

The fantasy that markets can be effectively self-regulated is encouraged by the self-serving Plutocracy and its "free market" enthusiasts in the MSM, as unregulated markets enable the fullest expression of greed, fraud, legerdemain and chicanery. No better proof of this can be found than the insiders' exploitation of the mortgage/housing/credit bubble's excesses of lies and leverage. Please read Fiasco: The Inside Story of a Wall Street Trader, Greed, Fraud & Ignorance: A Subprime Insider's Look at the Mortgage Collapse and It Takes a Pillage: Behind the Bailouts, Bonuses, and Backroom Deals from Washington to Wall Street for more on these topics.

Put another way: "free" markets require transparency of inputs, competitors, pricing, value, ingredients, etc. Without transparency, then customers/participants' decisions cannot be sound. Yet transparency offers no competitive advantage, while secrecy and obfuscation offer tremendous competitive advantages. For example, an arcane and duplicitous property appraisal is a simulacrum of transparency, manipulating data to support a bogus valuation in order to qualify for a mortgage. A transparently false appraisal would not support the fraudulent mortgage or the immense profit it generated for everyone involved.

The mortgage itself is written in such a fashion that its true costs are obscured-- the very opposite of transparency. Thus, the mortgage/leverage/derivative/ratings bubble of fraud and greed depended on obscurity and obfuscation, and indeed, market participants lost competitive advantage in terms of profit if they dared choose transparency.

This is why it is specious to claim an unregulated finance-based economy will regulate itself. Though the government is by nature attempting to expand at the expense of the citizenry, that doesn't mean there is no need for governmental regulation. It simply means the regulations must be strong yet simple: transparency in all matters, no exceptions.

The classic examination of how self-regulating markets turn everything and everyone into commodities ripe for exploitation is The Great Transformation by Karl Polanyi.

The big losers in the fantasy of self-regulating markets are the middle class; the Plutocracy buys itself exclusions. The costs of dysfunctional markets eventually end up on the backs of the middle class while the outsized profits end up in the pockets of the Elites. Profits are privatized and losses are socialized, i.e. borne by the middle class taxpayers. Like the Roman citizens granted free bread and endless public entertainments, the less productive citizens are pleased to support the status quo (simply by remaining passive) as the status quo has effectively bought them off with "bread and circuses."

Markets, The Commons and Lifecycle Costs

Just as we must be careful of government because of its inherent self-interest and vulnerability to influence/control by the Plutocracy, we must be careful not to assume that markets are effective at establishing prices in all settings just because they work in limited, short-term contexts. The reason for our caution: markets are incapable of pricing the full social, medical and environmental costs of a product's entire lifecycle. Thus coal is priced by its demand as fuel and the cost to extract it from the earth. But if coal is burned in great quantities, as in China, then the air quality becomes adverse to human health.

People breathing such particulate-polluted air are far more likely to die from respiratory diseases than those who don't breathe such toxin-laden air. So shouldn't the cost of treating millions of people and the loss of millions of man-years of productive labor be priced into the cost of mining and burning coal?

And suppose the cost of restoring strip-mined areas to some semblance of its pre-mined natural state was built into the cost of mining surface coal. What would the price per ton be then?

Markets will never price in the full lifecycle and social/environmental costs on their own; self-regulated markets are about reaping maximum short-term profits, not seeking out long-term costs which competitors might be able to shirk. Further, the full lifecycle costs of any product are often ambiguous; how do we price in the cost of restoring a landscape when we don't yet know the cost of doing so?

In both socialist/Communist nations like China and "free market" capitalist nations like the U.S., the market effectively shunts all these "common area" costs of doing business onto private individuals who had no choice in the matter (of the air they breathe or the power source they purchase electricity from) or onto the government which must then shoulder the healthcare and environmental costs via taxes on productive citizens.

Following our precept that all markets require transparency above all else, we find that the Plutocracy engineers obscure tax credits and subsidies for its industries, masking the true cost behind these government tax breaks. Thus the citizenry will find the task of sorting out the real benefits of transparent solar subsidies and obscure nuclear power/gas-oil subsidies quite difficult. This is of course quite purposeful; transparency may create a well-oiled marketplace but obscurity and obfuscation generate much larger profits.

The analog to this is monopoly.

If one enterprise (or a handful in collusion) gains near-total control of a market, then the profits to be gained are immensely greater than those earned in a highly competitive market. This is why Marx posited that the drive to monopoly is inherent to capitalism. And of course a monopoly on information also generates far more handsome profits than transparency. This is why we find both government and its hidden masters, the Plutocracy, are constantly seeking to bury the truth at every turn, and why each fights transparency so fiercely.

To expect the State not to seek expansion as its self-interest, to expect wealthy citizens not to seek to influence the State to align policy with their own interests, to expect capitalism not to trend to monopoly, to expect markets not to shun transparency in favor of obfuscation and secrecy--these are all akin to expecting gravity to cease pulling us to earth. These are what we might call ontological forces, forces which are built into the very nature of the state, capitalism, markets and thus into human nature itself.

This is why we have to be careful not to fall for the seductive artifice of ideology as we choose responses to the multiple challenges ahead. Neither the market nor the State is an answer; each is as much a part of the problem as it is a part of the solution.

Political Disunity Squeezes the Middle Class

Political disunity ends up crushing the middle class's wealth and political influence.

In The Fall of the Roman Empire, author Michael Grant identified political disunity as one the one key causes of the fall of the Western Roman Empire (Rome).

One engine of such disunity and squabbling, of course, is a deep-denial complacency: if a large percentage of the ruling class/citizenry sees nothing wrong, or counts on feeble "reforms" to resolve mounting global challenges, then they will hobble those seeking systemic, sweeping changes required to survive the challenges.

Another key reason for this crippling disunity is the resistance of the Plutocracy/underclass recipients to any change in the status quo.

It may strike some as ironic that the two ends of the political spectrum are united in one goal: fiercely resisting any shifting of largesse/benefits. At the top, the "fortunate 400" in Roman society paid less and less tax as the crises mounted, while 300,000 fortunates at the bottom rung continued to draw free bread and 170 days of free public entertainment in Rome even as the Empire imploded.

We see plentiful evidence of both trends around us. The number of recent political appointees who felt paying taxes was for plebeians is not just embarrassing, it's indicative of a broad cultural trend; and it seems many of the riots we read about in western Europe stem from proposed cuts in what are essentially "bread and circuses" welfare benefits which the Empire can no longer afford to shower on its unproductive (non-tax paying) residents.

As the plutocracy contributes less and less to the finances of a heavily burdened central government, wealth disparity rises.

This trend has been firmly in place for years. As documented by *The Wall Street Journal* and other sources, tax rates for the top 1% have been tumbling for years.

As in fast-declining Rome, the plutocracy is pleased to wield its wealth and influence to insure it pays 17% tax rate (much, much less when tax-free municipal bonds are counted as income) while the productive elements of the economy are saddled with 40%-50% tax burdens.

Also as in headed-to-oblivion Rome, the plutocracy no longer contributes its sons and daughters to military service; that is left to the poor.

Lastly, rigid ideological camps are creating disunity as the middle (and the middle class) are eroded.

Thus we have a Congress which united under pressure to give $700 billion in borrowed money to the banks under a Republican administration, and now under a Democratic administration the Republicans in Congress have belatedly discovered a deep desire for fiscal prudence--a desire which they mysteriously lacked for the 8 years of the borrow-and-spend Bush administration.

Though it is impossible to summarize the wealth of information in Jared Diamond's monumental Collapse: How Societies Choose to Fail or Succeed, it seems that the inability to see the underlying fragility of the environmental base of the economy was a key factor in the collapse of the cultures Diamond examines.

In an eerily similar way, the Plutocracy in the U.S. is essentially blind to the extreme fragility of the global energy complex, global fresh water supply, global soil reserves and the global public health system. As many authors have detailed, a global economy without abundant cheap fossil fuels will be unable to feed and maintain 6.5 billion humans.

Though neither Grant nor Diamond mentions this specifically, I note that the Roman central leadership obviously hoped that additional regulations and edicts would somehow turn the tide.

The same over-reliance on legal mechanisms, edicts and minor policy adjustments are abundantly visible in the U.S. today.

A Congress of attorneys rather unsurprisingly is enamored of legalisms and policy tweaks, and a plutocracy and welfare class wary of any reduction in benefits and tax breaks is pleased to hope tweaks and tucks will somehow maintain a crumbling status quo.

But as Donella Meadows outlined in her seminal paper, Leverage Points: Places to Intervene in a System (Sustainability Institute), adjusting the parameters of a system has limited effects. Tweaking the gas mileage of the U.S. fleet by a mile or two, and 99.9% of all the other "reforms" proposed and fought over, will effect no fundamental change.

What we have in essence is an over-regulated, overly complex, cost-heavy structure which we attempt to "fix" by adding further layers of complexity and overhead costs. The idea that these incremental approaches can change the fundamental structural flaws is simply false; their net effect will be to hasten the collapse of the systems they seek to repair.

This is what I call *the illusion of incremental change*.

As noted before, Tainter's The Collapse of Complex Societies suggests that at some point the citizenry of failing societies more or less choose to let their unsustainable systems topple rather than continue the draining attempt to support the burden.

Disunity, complacency, growing wealth disparity, rising military and taxation burdens, fragile environmental foundations--all these need only a sustained drought or energy shortage to tumble like dominoes.

Key concepts in this chapter:

Voluntary Poverty

Asymmetric stakes in the game

Chapter Thirteen: When Belief in the System Fades

In March 2008, six months before the collapse of the global financial dominoes, I posted the essay <u>When Belief in the System Fades</u>, which likened the faith of those pouring their lives into sustaining the status quo to religious belief.

The essay drew a mixed reaction ranging from "you nailed it" to dismissal. Now that the global financial structure has succumbed to gravity, I wonder how many readers who dismissed it then would now modify their reaction. Certainly those receiving pink slips might ponder how suddenly faith in the system can be lost.

The entire *Survival+* analysis centers on trying to understand the multilayered ways the middle class is being squeezed to insolvency.

My good friend G.F.B. (also a small business owner, as you might have guessed) likened the tax and fee-for-services system to a parasite and host. The parasite is careful not to extract too much, lest the host die.

But sometimes parasites become so numerous and greedy that they end up killing the host and thus themselves. Perhaps the single key task of the Plutocracy/State (two sides of a single coin) is to convince the host (the middle class) to keep laboring despite the ever-increasing extraction of their earnings and wealth.

The task requires an actively supported mythology (you too can be Bill Gates!) and a subtle cultivation of interlocking beliefs in the fairness and rightness of the system. The overriding faith that hard work and individual greed will both be rewarded as long as the middle class believer "keeps his nose clean," i.e. plays along with the set rules, is carefully nourished.

If we withdraw from the 24/7 propaganda of the Mainstream Media, the absurdity of these constantly repeated themes becomes painfully clear. For example, "Socialism is bad and evil because it redistributes wealth." Well, now that's interesting, because Crony Capitalism does the same thing, gathering heavy taxes from the productive class and funneling it into the hands of a Plutocrat class who shoulder relatively modest tax burdens while reaping vast rewards via government contracts, bailouts, tax loopholes, special legislation, etc.

In other words, the key difference between Euro-style Socialism and

Crony Capitalism as perfected in the U.S. is the middle class receives few benefits from their onerous tax burdens. In much of Europe, college and medical care are mostly paid by taxes; here in the U.S. productive citizens pay stupendous taxes and yet they also pay tens of thousands of dollars for a university education and huge, wealth-destroying co-payments for medical care--if they even have insurance.

This is truly Orwellian: the middle class is conned into supporting income redistribution which favors the super-rich and those paying no tax whatsoever (for instance, undocumented laborers).

Nice gig if you can get it: reap the rewards, pay no taxes. Unfortunately, middle class wage earners don't get that option.

Here's another howler: "The U.S. healthcare system is the finest in the world." Ooh, I have to be careful not to laugh too hard--I can't afford to hurt myself. Just today my dermatologist prescribed a "been around for 20 years" topical cream to burn off the sun-damaged spots on my hands and arms. I've used this cream for a decade: Efudex is the brand name, and it's not some "new miracle drug" which cost billions to develop as per the pharmaceutical industry propaganda.

Some years ago a small tube of the stuff cost an absurdly high $79. Then it jumped to an even more insane $120 for a few ounces of cream. Even though the patent has long expired, it jumped to $218 per tube a few years back. Guess the current price: $272 per small tube.

How can any system justify a four-fold jump in the cost of a cream that was developed decades ago, other than rampant, uncontrolled greed and avarice? (Needless to say my own self-paid bare-bones medical insurance has no drug, dental or eyewear coverage.)

The pharmacist, herself a recent immigrant judging from her accent (I leave her ethnicity out other than to note she was non-Caucasian) shook her head and noted that in this country, you either have to be poor or rich. She added that undocumented workers get Medicaid (i.e. they pay nothing in taxes or fees) while people who have worked for decades get nothing. (Unless they hang on long enough to qualify for Medicare, of course, at 65.)

Those fortunate enough to have excellent medical insurance would co-pay $5 or $15 for this $272 tube of cream, and never know how much it cost the insurer/employer. Far from being "the best system in the world," the exact opposite is true: *without any doubt, the U.S. has the worst medical/sick-care system of all industrialized nations.*

If you think it's great, that's because your costs are being paid by someone else; try asking for the "real cost" of the medications and services you've received, or better yet, paying for them cash. Your faith in just how wonderful the system is will dissipate with truly amazing alacrity.

The middle class citizens now losing their jobs are receiving just this "lesson" in how fast faith in the "best in the world" system can vanish as they face paying COBRA fees of $1,000 or more per month for stripped-down healthcare insurance, or find themselves without any healthcare at all.

When Belief in the System Fades

At some point--perhaps a "tipping point" or just an erosion--the middle class bails out of the increasingly burdensome task of propping up the State and the Plutocracy. I call this phenomenon "When Belief in the System Fades."

There are elites in every human culture (and in the social apes as well). But unlike a troop of chimps ruled by an alpha male, today's elites cannot operate the vast complex structure of the U.S. economy, government and society themselves. They need hundreds of thousands of well-educated, hard-working people to believe in the system of meritocracy, justice, opportunity, etc., people who will choose to invest their entire productive lives in sustaining the structure which the elites influence/control.

The corollary to this structural need for highly motivated, dedicated people to work the gears is that if their belief in the machine fades, then the machine grinds to a halt.

In the Armed Forces, the key layer of staffing is in the middle: lieutenants, captains, chief petty officers, etc. If those non-coms and junior officers leave the service, the Force is essentially gutted, regardless of the generals and admirals and high-tech weaponry and the valor of the recruits.

There is some evidence that just such a migration is occurring.

In a large law firm, the essential layer is the hungry-to-be-partner attorneys who labor insane hours for years, enriching their bosses as they pursue the carrot of "partner."

In the retail world, it is the store managers and assistant managers who keep the store running smoothly.

In construction, it is the foremen/women and onsite supervisors who get the building built.

In every case, the person takes on the burdens in the belief that their career will be enhanced and they will make more money/gain more prestige. Yes, we all understand this. But they also must believe in the structural fairness, justice, opportunity, security, meritocracy, etc. of the machine they willingly serve—even if their belief is subconscious or rarely in their conscious thoughts.

This belief is far more vulnerable than the Powers That Be seem to understand. You see the alienation, the bitterness, the disbelief, in factory workers when the factory shuts down, and their livelihoods are gone—and all too often, so too are the pension and benefits they were promised.

You see it in the face of an academic who worked long hours for years "on the tenure track," carrying much of the department's teaching load, when she/he is ultimately denied tenure. Thank you for working for $40,000 a year for years alongside people doing the same work for twice the salary; good night and good luck.

When the most dedicated servants of the system awaken to the realization that they are not benefiting from their service as they'd once believed, that their near-religious faith in the System has been bruised by the grim knowledge that the few are benefiting from the lives and sacrifices of the many, then they simply quit, or move down the chain to an undemanding position.

You can still work in law without having to bill 80 hours a week. You can resign your commission at 20 years and go live on a farm and leave all the headaches behind. You can resign from the commissions and boards and "career-enhancing" stuff you've crammed in after your regular hours. You can refuse the offer of the position of supervisor, or manager, or head of sales, because you now see the extra pay and phony prestige isn't worth it.

In a way, a belief in the value, transparency, trust and reciprocity of the System is like a religious belief.

The converts, the true believers, are the ones who work like crazy for the company, or the Force or the firm. And when the veil of illusion is tugged from their eyes, then the Believer does a reversal, and becomes a devout non-believer in the System. He or she drops out, moves to a lower position, or "retires" to some lower level of employment.

One trigger of such destruction of belief in the worth of the System is the loss of a job or house—an event I unfortunately anticipate will become very common. "But don't these people have to work to support their lifestyles?" Yes they do, until they realize they can live on half the money they thought they needed as an absolute minimum.

Not that most people choose this—they find out via bankruptcy or being laid off, or by watching their buddies and friends getting laid off (or killed/wounded) around them. Their belief in the goodness and reciprocity of the System—that if you work hard and keep your nose clean, we're gonna take good care of you—fades and then dies.

Immigrants are by self-selection believers, and the rise from poverty to relative wealth they see around them offers visible proof that sacrificing one's productive life for the System is rewarding.

But once you've reached the plateau of relative wealth, then the proposition becomes contingent on exactly what happens to you and your family. If your kids all get advanced degrees and they can't find a decent job in their chosen profession, then you start wondering. If you get laid off, despite your decades of selfless service, then you start wondering. If you get passed over in favor of some brown-noser, you start wondering.

And then you realize you don't have to work 60 hours a week, or live in a big house. An apartment works just fine, and 30 hours a week is enough. Let somebody else step up and take all the heat and the guff and the never-catch-up endlessness of the work.

At that point—a point I anticipate will come to pass in the next 5-10 years--then the Elites' machine grinds to a crawl. People don't have to throw their bodies on the gears of the machine—they just have to stop believing, stop taking that promotion, and stop wanting to trade their entire lives for a thin slice of more more more.

If that day comes, then the social contract will have to be rewritten, or an entirely new set of Elites will have to emerge with a new social contract which people are willing to believe and trust.

Another way of stating "when belief in the system fades" is this: when the Plutocracy over-reaches.

As noted above, societies collapse not just from foreign invasion or drought or environmental implosion but when the productive citizenry realize it's easier to let the increasingly burdensome structure collapse of its own weight than continue to support it.

Once the productive class removes its political and economic will to preserve the institutions via taxes, the institutions will fall. In our current situation, we can say that once the middle class opts out of the system, the burdens of Empire and entitlements will bring the Federal government to insolvency.

The social contract between the government/State and the middle class in advanced post-industrial democracies is fundamentally this: we pay substantial taxes, and you the State will handle the infrastructure of our society via various bureaucracies which don't require our input or oversight: Department of Defense, the judiciary, highway maintenance, etc.

But as the State over-reaches—and by that I mean the both the State over-extending its powers and its functionaries claiming ever-higher shares of the national income-- **then the social contract breaks down.** The middle class is dealt ever-higher taxes and fees, yet it receives less and less benefit as the less productive class and the Elites (including the "upper caste" of public employees) leverage their patronage of the status quo at the expense of the middle class.

The middle class sees their income as measured by purchasing power declining, even as the roads fall into juddering disrepair, the public education they counted on to educate their children falls under the sway of ideological fads and every State fiefdom indulges in grandiose self-serving spending.

The upper middle class which pays the majority of the taxes then finds itself in an unfamiliar and increasingly unsustainable bind. The unspoken social contract with the state not only guaranteed working roads and a responsive, efficient bureaucracy for the high taxes paid; the status quo was supposed to offer its citizenry free expression. The ideals of personal liberty translated into leisure to pursue individual interests and to indulge in personal expression via music, the arts, sports, etc.

Now the middle class finds itself in an ever-tightening vise. To maintain its lifestyle and pay the higher taxes demanded by the state, it finds that leisure and the opportunity for free individual expression have diminished. Instead of expression, the middle class experiences the stress of financial insecurity and overwork.

With growing resentment, it looks at the entitlements granted the less productive classes in exchange for their passive acceptance of the status quo, and the increasing share of national income and wealth garnered by the self-serving Plutocracy.

In nations where the citizenry are still struggling for basic survival, free expression is not a key value; traditional restrictive "glues" of the social order like arranged marriage and unquestioned gender inequality hold firm sway.

In terms of human nature, we might surmise that these traditional societies are perched so close to the edge of survival that innovation is simply too risky; the potential gains do not outweigh the potential disruptions to a fragile, precarious order.

In advanced post-industrial societies, on the other hand, innovation and transformation of the economy and institutions are seen as essential adaptations; failure to compete globally via innovation is recognized as a sure path to national poverty.

There is a certain irony in the political and economic decline of the middle class.

The very success of the middle class in becoming productive enough to gain leisure and the opportunity for individual expression was won at the cost of relinquishing involvement and oversight of the State.

Freed of the restraint of oversight, the State was free to extend its powers, and its functionaries were free to feed on the rising taxes paid by the productive class. Now that the middle class finds itself squeezed on all sides, it has only three choices, none positive:

1. Attempt to preserve the institutions of the status quo by working harder and paying more taxes, surrendering meaningful individual expression

2. Opt out ("when belief in the system fades"), quit the high-paying, high-pressure, high-tax jobs and slip into the low-tax informal economy

3. Challenge the self-serving Elite and state by demanding oversight and democratic limits on "bread and circuses," the state's powers and the wealth being siphoned off by the state's parasitic "high-caste" functionaries.

Unfortunately for the middle class, today's "democracy" has been reduced to a sad simulacrum. When 97% of the incumbents win re-election via gerrymandering and propaganda (the remaining 3% either resigning in disgrace or dying in office) then exactly what is this "democracy"?

Any middle class attempt to build a meaningful political voice will be fiercely resisted by the state and its employees and dependents. "Class warfare" will be invoked, not between the Plutocracy and the middle class, which would at least reflect reality. No, the State and the Plutocracy will task the propaganda machine of the Mainstream Corporate Media to place the conflict between the middle class and the less-productive class (those not productive enough to pay much taxes). Any claim to lessen the burden on an increasingly overwhelmed middle class will be shaped into an attack on the inalienable rights to various entitlements at the state's expense.

It is in the self-interests of the Plutocracy and State to gin up a phony "class war" to distract the middle class from their true opponents: the State and its masters in the Plutocracy.

We need only look at the millions of prescriptions for anti-anxiety and anti-depressant medications to measure the toll this ever-increasing burden is taking on the middle class.

For each productive individual, opting out is far easier than trying to engage in a long, exhausting political battle. After all, the Plutocracy has immense resources and a huge stake in the outcome, as do those protected by State fiefdoms and those receiving benefits without paying taxes.

Each of these constituencies recognizes the fight to maintain the status quo (i.e. to keep the middle class productive and paying the lion's share of the taxes) is a fight to the death. Thus the Plutocracy will pull out all stops to defend its influence, just as the public unions and beneficiaries of State largesse will throw their entire forces into maintaining the status quo.

This is what I term an *asymmetric stake in the game*, which I cover in Section Two.

Meanwhile, the middle class productive taxpayer has far less at stake; just another junk fee to pay, just another 10% surtax, etc. Pressed by the demands of commute, career, debt, family, etc., the productive citizen has little or no time or energy for a protracted political battle. So the Elite, the state and its beneficiaries will always win.

But what neither the State, nor its public employees or its beneficiaries of government largesse understand is that by denying the middle class some respite and some stake in the political division of the tax revenues, they are insuring the middle class will eventually opt out and let the system collapse. It will simply not be worth the cost or the effort to maintain these top-heavy, high-cost institutions.

Another irony is that the Plutocracy and the State will attempt to define the battle as "preserving our institutions" and "our middle class entitlements."

Sadly, truthfulness plays little role in this structural political battle.

We might ask: if the middle class was garnering such stupendous entitlements and benefits, then why are they so stressed, so unhappy, so burdened and so alienated, not just from their State but from themselves? Having been promised free expression and individual liberty, they find instead that they are essentially debt-serfs, working either to pay off debt owed to the Manor Houses of the Plutocracy or crushing taxes and junk fees owed to the State.

Some of this can be attributed to structural changes in the very nature of post-industrial work (see Chapter Fourteen), but much can be laid on the divergence of the interests of the State and the Plutocracy from the interests of the middle class which supports them.

So deep is the alienation and confusion that the middle class citizen, anxiety-ridden, staggering beneath worrisome debt and an ever-rising workload, popping countless bottles of psychotropic prescription drugs to maintain a semblance of "normalcy," blames their own inadequacies for their deep unhappiness and inability to bear the burdens imposed by the broken social contract.

Indeed, opting out isn't just the best choice for many; it may be the only choice that enables sanity and a return to free individual expression. Once you're distracted by debt and overwork, you lose track of what's been lost.

As always, we must ask: *cui bono*? To whose benefit?

Certainly not the unhappy debt-serf. Yet so powerful are the simulacrum of democracy, prosperity, etc., many believe they are indeed working for their own goals and glory. But if this were true, why are they so unhappy, so burdened, so alienated and so perplexed by their own unhappiness? Would anyone choose this if they were truly acting on their own behalf?

Chapter Fourteen: The End of (Paying) Work

Many commentators refer back to the Great Depression as a historical guide or template to our present situation. But our current predicaments are far deeper, as commentators such as James Howard Kunstler have shown. To mention a few of Kunstler's observations:

- In 1929, the U.S. was the equivalent of Saudi Arabia today: the world's largest oil producer. Now we have to import fossil fuels on a gigantic scale.
- In 1929, the U.S. had a fully functioning rail system for passenger transportation. This has shrunk to a shadow of its former capacity.
- As extreme as debt loads were in 1929, our current level of indebtedness (as measured by GDP) is far higher for all sectors: government, business and households.
- In 1929, millions of jobless citizens could return to the family farm or a family home in the countryside or small town. Now that the U.S. is heavily urbanized, this "Plan B" is no longer available for most unemployed.
- In 1929, the U.S. was a major manufacturing/exporting power which actually ran trade surpluses for much of the previous 50 years.
- In 1929, the government sector extracted a much smaller percentage of national income than it does today.

Hidden beneath these visible material, financial and demographic changes is a deeper one: the end of (paying) work.

The drivers behind this long-term decline in paying work cannot be reversed:

1. The U.S. is a high-cost economy with high structural overhead costs which cannot be reduced by any mechanism short of bankruptcy/insolvency or political revolution.

These costs include:

A. High taxes on business and households

B. Absurdly high "healthcare" (a.k.a. "sick-care") costs which are inexorably climbing at twice the rate of growth of the underlying economy

C. High real estate valuations based on cheap, "no-risk" money which have raised the costs of commercial rents and housing to levels which are far beyond historical correlations of real estate to income

D. The growth of government and its employees who have won pension benefits and wages which are roughly twice the cost of average private-sector wages and pension benefits.

2. The Internet and digital information technology are creatively destroying entire industries and entire job classifications which will not be coming back. Examples include the music and publishing industries and administrative jobs such as clerks and customer service representatives.

Even the IT sector itself (information technology) is vulnerable to the automation of software and coding. In industries such as tax preparation, 90% of their high-priced labor can be replaced by $30 software.

The consequences of the Internet's ubiquity are far-reaching. Not only can vast swaths of digital work be automated, much of the remainder can be performed overseas at lower labor rates than in the U.S. (Recall that up to half of a U.S. employee's compensation costs are healthcare and other overhead costs, so a wage-to-wage comparison will be misleading.)

As the Internet enables telecommuting and home-based digital work then the need for millions of square feet of office space falls, further pressuring the demand for high-cost commercial real estate.

Internet-enabled retail trade (Amazon.com, eBay.com, etc.) is decimating high-rent brick-and-mortar retail outlets; as these close their doors then the demand for retail space falls precipitously, pressuring rents downward.

Just as craigslist has essentially wiped out print classified ads and Internet ticket sales have driven most travel agencies out of business, many other fields and industries will be reduced or eliminated by the efficiencies made possible by the Internet. Even fields like education may find the need for costly physical space may diminish as high-cost education migrates online.

Political control depends in large part on a quasi-monopolistic mass media amenable to the political goals of the State and Plutocracy. To the degree that the Web undermines that mass media's monopoly on "news" then it also undermines the political control of the State and its Plutocratic overlords.

The Internet/Web is thus the acme of creative destruction, for it is undermining all monopolies except that of capital and petroleum.

3. Globalization and a semi-open U.S. economy force global corporations and small businesses alike to make efficient cost-benefit

analyses of where to deploy capital and shift production. Economies of scale, flexible production and lower tax/labor costs spell the difference between profitability and insolvency.

Hopelessly expensive industries like healthcare which have been protected to date will find global competition for scarce healthcare and pharmaceutical dollars rising.

4. As cheap, abundant energy disappears, the cost of materials, transport and production rise, leaving less for labor. As cheap, abundant energy disappears, tourism and the "leisure industry" is priced beyond the reach of consumers facing declining real wealth and income, slashing service jobs in leisure/tourism.

5. The debt-based consumer economy was not a permanent new level of consumption but a one-time anomaly based on an imprudently engineered reduction in the cost and availability of credit combined with a (false) perception of near-zero risk. The entire FIRE economy (finance, real estate and insurance) will be permanently reduced by digital automation and the shrinking of these sectors as the global debt and real estate bubbles burst.

If history is any guide, then interest rates will rise for a generation, depressing real estate and other debt-dependent assets for a generation.

Though the Federal government is furiously borrowing and printing money, the ability to do so at no cost to the dollar (in terms of depreciating purchasing power) and at low interest rates is ending. Since Federal borrowing of trillions of dollars has effectively backstopped the U.S. GDP, the end of the government's "borrow and spend trillions" campaign will remove that backstop and cause spending and employment to further shrink.

Even worse, the rise in interest rates will divert billions from programs to service the Federal debt, further reducing expenditures on goods and services. Since so much of the debt is held by non-U.S. entities, a significant share of this interest paid will end up overseas. This feedback loop will further reduce Federal spending and employment.

If reckless Federal borrowing and money-creation ends up destroying the purchasing power of the U.S. dollar, then that will add yet another feedback loop as consumers pay more for imported oil and other goods and have less to spend domestically, further suppressing employment.

As collateral (bubble-era real estate valuations) and credit fall, so will consumer debt and the spending it enabled.

6. The demographics of a large cohort (the global Baby Boom) entering retirement coupled with longer lives and costlier "healthcare" options guarantee all government entitlement programs will face insolvency and collapse or greatly reduced benefits within a decade.

One of the consequences of this will be the reduction of currently "healthy" healthcare employment; another will be the diversion of vast sums of income away from consumption and into retirement savings.

7. ESSA (eliminate, simplify, standardize and automate) has barely touched much of the U.S. economy. Union rules, old habits and lush revenues have protected millions of processes, procedures and jobs from the scrutiny of plummeting revenues and taxes. As credit dries up and collateral falls in value, spending falls which reduces employment and taxes, which further erodes jobs in a self-reinforcing feedback loop of ever lower spending and ever falling employment.

For instance, buying a car or property no longer requires the expertise implied by a 6% transaction fee. In effect, the research and transaction could be done digitally.

8. Mechanization and automation form a "scalability trap;" once production can be scaled up then the necessity for human labor permanently declines. If I understand the concept correctly, it refers to the inevitability of new scalable technologies replacing human labor.

The Scalability Trap

To the best of my knowledge, the term "scalability trap" was coined by oftwominds.com correspondent Kevin Dodson who insightfully captured this powerful concept thusly:

"I think this 'scalability trap' that we find ourselves in (i.e. the more advanced we become, the more things scale, the fewer jobs we need) is like a hidden compounding tax on modernity - and we are about at the place where that tax is going to break the current model of tech innovation and entertainment consumption. A new model will surely replace it; let's just hope it is not some kind of Mad Max paradigm."

Or perhaps the scalability "tax" on modernity will combine with a reduction in credit, income and wealth and a rise in costs and taxes to form a combination of long-term factors which will be lethal to formal employment in the U.S. (Please see our later discussion of the rise of informal work.)

The example that first comes to mind is agriculture; once the scalability of fossil-fuel equipment and fossil-fuel fertilizers was in place via assembly-line production (of tractors, etc.) and industrial-scale chemical plants, then it became inevitable that farm/agricultural labor would fall from 20% of the U.S. workforce to 2%.

In a completely different model with the same results, the entertainment industry is being gutted by the scalability trap of the Web. It now costs almost nothing (to the end user, not the economy as a whole) to bypass the gatekeepers and oligopolies of the recording industry and eliminate the entire staff of the Capitol Records tower (the iconic round building in Los Angeles which calls to mind a stack of old 45 RPM vinyl records).

As one example of this, consider a recent *Wall Street Journal* piece: Musician Finds a Following Online: Word-of-Mouth on Blogs and Other Sites Attracts Fans -- and a Record Deal:

"In late 2006, Justin Vernon, a musician in Eau Claire, Wis., recorded nine songs while staying at his parents' hunting cabin in northern Wisconsin after a breakup with a girlfriend and his long-time band. He used just a desktop computer with recording software, a three-piece drum set and a guitar.

A few months later, Mr. Vernon posted the songs on his MySpace page, hoping to get some listeners and feedback. He also printed 500 copies of a CD with those songs to sell to friends and fans and send to music bloggers for review.

He got that and much more.

Thanks to the buzz his online tracks generated on music blogs and social-networking sites, Mr. Vernon has played at numerous venues and appeared on the "Late Show With David Letterman." He signed a record deal in October 2007, and his first album, "For Emma, Forever Ago," sold about 87,000 copies through mid-December, with about half of those downloaded online. With a band he formed early this year, called Bon Iver, Mr. Vernon is now playing sold-out concerts across the U.S. and abroad."

Was Justin's creative session in the cabin scalable? No; but his direct access to listeners and potential customers is not just scalable but even exponential. Furthermore, the tools he used to record are scalable; every PC is now a recording studio, with the addition of a decent microphone (which can be borrowed if need be).

Was his recording "work"? Of course it was, but not in the same sense as a paid A&R (Artist & Repertoire) employee in the Capitol Records Tower is "working": Justin wasn't paid, nor was he directed in his work toward some higher corporate function or goal.

And A&R is itself being taken out of the hands of record companies: for instance, Taxi: the world's leading independent A&R company.

I would agree with Kevin's brilliant assessment that "we are about at the place where that tax is going to break the current model of tech innovation and entertainment consumption." For really, what exactly is the zeitgeist of complacency based on but the twin ideas that tech innovations will "save" our lifestyle of 24/7 entertainment consumption?

Is all our economy's "work" necessary or even useful? Examples that spring to mind:

1. We might wonder why the number of generals and other staff officers exceeds the number of generals, admirals, etc. in World War II when the military had 10 times more enlisted personnel.

2. We might also inquire why the Navy's new DD(X) destroyer ship design slashes crew size by more than two-thirds: (source: DD(X) specifications, navy.com):

"Crew: Many of the functions performed by crews on conventional destroyers will be automated on the DD(X). That means a reduction in crew size – 330 fewer sailors than the Spruance class destroyers and 200 fewer sailors than the Oliver Hazard Perry class frigates. The crew will also be able to focus on fighting versus ship maintenance."

Why is reducing crew size critical to the future of the Navy? Here is the GAO's answer: Military Personnel: Navy Actions Needed to Optimize Ship Crew Size and Reduce Total Ownership Costs:

"The cost of a ship's crew is the single largest incurred over the ship's life cycle. The Navy's goal is to cut personnel on the DD(X) by about 70 percent from that of the previous destroyer class--a reduction GAO estimated could eventually save about $18 billion over the life of a 32-ship class."

The U.S. Navy cannot afford to overstaff its ships, period.

Now let's turn to two other "real world" examples. One of my correspondents is a senior police officer in a California city police department with a budget of around $46 million. His department is facing an $8 million reduction.

So where do you cut? Not cutting, i.e. the status quo, business as usual, is no longer an option. Every employee of the department, uniformed and support staff, could take a 20% pay cut; I doubt that would prove the most popular option.

Or the PD could look at what my correspondent noted: the department has more physical paper than ever before, and computers seem to have only added to the amassing of paper.

Does this situation seem ripe for some major ESSA--eliminate, simplify, standardize and automate, similar to what the Navy has managed with the DD(X) design? To deny the potential of ESSA to cut duplicate, inefficient or unnecessary "work" is denial of the first order.

This is complacency of the "this is the only way the system works" variety.

Here is another example from the real world. My sister works for a large healthcare non-profit. Her division of about 130 people recently went paperless, as in, no printing of files, period. As a result, 17 file clerks no longer have "work."

Roughly 15% of the entire division's staff has been eliminated by rather straightforward ESSA procedures which, while complicated on a software level, are extremely intuitive: leave digital files digital, eliminate procedures whose origins or purpose has been lost in the accretion of "prosperity," simplify, standardize and automate what is truly essential.

Prosperity enables all sorts of inefficiencies, redundancies, complexities and self-serving self-absorption (i.e. endless meetings in which little is actually decided or accomplished). We as a nation are entering a period in which a 10% reduction in income/revenues is not followed the next year by a 20% increase back to prosperity, but by another 10% cut in income/revenue. The third year requires another reduction, as do years four and five.

Is ESSA (eliminate, simplify, standardize and automate) scalable? Absolutely.

The End of Consumer-Based, Resource-Profligate, Debt-Dependent High-Overhead Work

In 2008, various analysts estimated the U.S. economy would shed about 2 million jobs in 2009. Given that as of December 2008 there were over 137 million jobs, that doesn't sound all that horrific. Here are the employment statistics by category from the Bureau of Labor Statistics:

Nonfarm employment: 137,331
Goods-producing: 21,351
    Construction 7,141
    Manufacturing 13,423
Service-providing: 115,980
    Retail trade 15,259
    Professional and business services 17,849
    Education and health services 18,975
    Leisure and hospitality 13,627
Government: 22,504

With job losses already exceeding 6.7 million as I write this in June, 2009, it seems the analysts were incredibly optimistic. (That is of course their job.)

Setting aside the absurdly low estimate of 2 million jobs lost, let's look at each category and make a rough estimate for how much paying work each category might support in, say, 18 to 24 months.

Construction. While bridges being repaired will certainly support heavy-construction employment, the far larger categories of residential building and remodeling and commercial construction (office towers, malls, warehouses, etc.) are completely overbuilt for years to come. So let's guesstimate that there will be 50% less demand for construction and a job loss of 3.5 million in this category.

Manufacturing. Unfortunately, a tremendous amount of manufacturing is dependent on construction (glass, appliances, steel, etc.) and transportation (rubber, steel, components, semiconductors, etc.) both of which are in freefalls. Exports are falling as fast as imports. Let's be charitable and only carve off 3.5 million jobs here, leaving 10 million intact.

Retail. Does anyone doubt that fully 1/3 of all retail outlets are now surplus?

We're talking about fulltime positions here; so cutting hours from everyone on the floor may actually save jobs (i.e. hours cut will not show up in the above statistics) but the equivalent fulltime positions (that is, 40 hours of paid work a week) may well have vanished.

Let's guesstimate that 5 million retail positions will no longer be supported by sales/profits.

Professional and Business Services. Legal and accounting services will suffer as businesses fold. Businesses will decide they need fewer contract workers, fewer consultants, fewer financial services and fewer software upgrades. Let's guesstimate that 2.5 million jobs will eventually be lost in this category.

Education and Health Services. These have been the growth industries, along with financial services, during the bogus "prosperity" of the past eight years. Once millions of jobs are shed, then millions of dollars of health insurance are no longer paid by employers, which means healthcare will get squeezed along with every other category.

Here is California, college enrollments are being capped as deficits soar; the inevitable next step is to leave jobs unfilled as people retire-- one way or another, a reduction in total education employment. Let's guesstimate 1 million of these jobs get cut--perhaps not by layoffs but by retiring workers not being replaced.

Leisure and hospitality. The sad fact is nobody needs to take a cruise or a vacation; both are the acme of discretionary expenditures. I would be shocked if the U.S. economy didn't shed 3.5 million jobs in this category.

Government. Local government (cities, counties, states and agencies) has added 12% more employees in the past eight years of bogus debt-based "prosperity," and the freefall in tax revenues means those 12% of "new" government jobs will vanish--and that's the best-case scenario. Let's guess that a total of 2.5 million jobs will disappear as tax revenues plummet and then keep plummeting.

The total: 21.5 million jobs--10 times the MSM-approved estimate of 2 million jobs lost.

Very few have the stomach to consider the reality that perhaps 20+ million jobs are no longer supportable by private industry revenues and profits and the tax revenues which depend on those profits and jobs. 21.5 million jobs lost works out to about 15.6% unemployment--a full 10% lower than the 25% unemployment rate reached in the Great Depression.

In other words, 21 million jobs lost is actually an optimistic guesstimate compared to what could transpire in the years ahead--a gradual evaporation of 30-35 million jobs. If Federal fiscal stimulus funds a couple million jobs--more likely retaining jobs in heavy construction and manufacturing that would otherwise be lost rather than adding jobs--then the total job loss might not be as severe until the "extra" Federal spending ends.

Just off the top of my head, here are industries which are sure to be hard-hit: media, advertising, cruise ships (many if not most will be mothballed), professional sports (how many people will be able to afford $45 tickets for lousy seats plus $10 for parking and $25 for a few beers and a hotdog?), spas, auto detailing, non-profits, pricey venues like museums which depend on wealthy donors (far fewer of those suddenly)--the list is long indeed.

Even worse, the deeper issue--the End of Work in a resource-profligate and consumer-based economy--isn't even being addressed yet.

Correspondent Matt S. recently recommended The End of Work by Jeremy Rifkin.

Rifkin's primary point is that the "full employment" of the bubble eras (dot-com asset bubble followed by credit-housing bubble) was a temporary aberration from the underlying trend caused solely by unsustainable credit-based (borrow and spend) consumerism. The long-term trend is this: productivity is raised by the replacement of human labor (jobs) with automation/machines/software.

As productivity rises, the number of jobs decreases.

This reality has long been visible in manufacturing. The reality of competitive global forces lead to factories of robots assembling robot-assembled components with a few hundred humans to maintain the machines. There are already auto factories like this in Japan. The entire world's auto industry will continue shedding workers even if the number of units produced increases.

Rifkin points to the U.S. steel industry as another example. Since 1981, the industry has boosted production by about a third while reducing the number of jobs from 384,000 to 74,000.

Many observers believe the answer is to pay all of us $25/hour for service work so we can all afford the high-priced services provided by each other. In other words, I prepare you a $5 coffee (plus $2 tax) and then spend my earnings on a haircut, downloading a song off iTunes, going to a club and buying a high-priced drink, playing golf, etc. etc.

While this is certainly appealing--a high-wage service economy that is entirely self-supporting-- the nations which most resemble this model (Japan, France, Germany and Scandinavia) all depend on exports and a trade surplus, and all live with structurally high unemployment.

In other words, their prosperity is still based on the old-fashioned model: make and sell more than you buy/consume from others.

The only nation which has run massive structural trade deficits during "prosperity" is the U.S., and now the painful reality is revealed: that deficit-borrow-spend model has essentially bankrupted the nation.

Here is how the U.S. has gotten away with it: we have arbitraged our currency, in essence creating a "surplus" of chimerical value via the U.S. dollar.

One way to think about this is: we have traded dollars for goods valued at X (in other currencies, in gold, whatever metric you want) and paid for them with currency worth X-$700 billion: the dollar. This is how we have been able to sustain trade deficits which have broken every other profligate nation's economy throughout recorded history.

Since the rest of the world depends entirely on the export/trade surplus model, they really have no choice: either accept the dollar arbitrage (in effect ceding $700 billion in excess value every year to the dollar) or face the end of the export/surplus model.

Since nobody has come up with a sustainable alternative to the export/surplus model, then the entire world accepted the dollar arbitrage: sell to the American consumer, pocket a surplus to support one's economy, and accept the dollar arbitrage.

The U.S. has "exported" two things in exchange for trillions of dollars of oil and other real goods: inflation via a depreciation of its own currency, and "financial instruments" based on the dollar arbitrage.

It continues to be a wonderful scam: we print/create with fractional lending as much paper money as we want (X), and everyone continues to accept it as an IOU worth X when in fact it is worth X-Y (with Y being the U.S. trade deficit).

Can this model of global prosperity continue essentially forever? It's hard to see how, but to date it has proven extremely durable because nobody has a Plan B. So it might last for years to come--as long as the dollar arbitrage doesn't become too onerous. At what point does it become too burdensome? Nobody knows.

The Dollar Crisis: Causes, Consequences, Cures argues that this currency arbitrage/structural deficit is indeed unsustainable.

When the scam breaks down, then the export/surplus model will break down, and global unemployment will skyrocket.

There is much being written now about the "race to the bottom" in currencies, in which every nation/trading bloc is trying to devalue their currency faster than their rivals in order to support their exports. What makes this so laughable is the one currency which is rising is--drum roll, please--the U.S. dollar. Why?

Because every other nation/trading bloc is still pursuing the export/surplus model: sell more than you buy. That requires they not only accept the dollar arbitrage, they must actively support it. Many observers are astounded by the dollar's strength: this profligate nation's currency should be plummeting like a stone, yet instead it rises!

Once you understand the global dollar arbitrage--we buy your goods to support your export/surplus model, and you accept a dollar intrinsically worth less than the goods sold, and everyone walks away happy--then this seeming impossibility makes sense.

Were the dollar to fall, as many expect, from 80 on the DXY (dollar index) to 45, the global export model of everyone selling their surplus production to the U.S. will no longer work. Since there is no Plan B, then it's in everyone's interest to keep the game going. It's a lot less painful to accept a "hidden" loss via dollar arbitrage than it is to face structural unemployment and civil unrest if the export model breaks down.

We also read how China is going to transition to a domestic economy, but a study of history finds virtually no examples of such a model. Wealth and thus prosperity has always been created by trade, and it precisely the point at which China turned away from global trade in the 16th century that its long decline began.

I recently toured a 40-acre biodynamic vineyard in Sonoma County, California. Biodynamic is basically one step beyond organic: not only are no pesticides or chemical fertilizers used, virtually no outside inputs are used: the land supports itself, as it were, by careful shepherding of insects, mulching, a few animals which graze off the ground cover, etc.

Yes, the vineyard has machinery which operates on oil: there is certainly an enormous energy input from outside the system. But other than the cost of shipping the product (wine) to market and transporting visitors to the site, most of the work is manual labor.

This model employs about a dozen people year-round. Most of the work is hard physical labor: pruning vines, spreading mulch, etc. This work cannot be entirely mechanized, and software can do little to add value/productivity. But then the question becomes: what is the tradable value of the resulting product? If the wine sells for $30+ a bottle, then the vineyard is a viable model in our high-cost economy. But if the tradable value of the product declines to say $10 a bottle, then the wages generated by the enterprise must likewise fall.

Rifkin is an optimist, as he sees the possibility of a new model in which "paying work" is replaced by "work" in a high-tech hydrogen-based economy.

The problem with this view is two-fold. First, hydrogen is not an energy source (except in fusion reactors which remain science fiction) but a method of storing energy generated by other means. Thus the replacement sources of energy as fossil fuels decline must be constructed before a hydrogen economy could arise.

Secondly, what would stop the hydrogen economy from scaling up (the Scalability Trap) to the point few workers were needed? Regardless of the future industry being touted (algae biofuels, nanotechnology, the hydrogen economy, etc.), each must be scalable to be important. And if they are scalable, then they will enter the Scalability Trap.

Thus the sustainability of the "full employment model" is questionable regardless of the specific nature of the "new industries" being hyped as "the foundation of the New Economy."

In Section Two, I propose that a model of *hybrid work* which combines some paid work with bartered/traded labor (unpaid work) may be better suited to the realities we face. In *hybrid work*, the focus is not on maximizing income but on being productive and generating surplus.

New concepts in this chapter:
Hybrid work

Chapter Fifteen: Interlocking Traps

In the course of this analysis I have attempted to identify cycles which illuminate our present circumstances and feedback loops which tend to counter (built-in stabilizers) or reinforce long-term trends.

But there is another class of forces called traps that are self-explanatory: once entered, traps are difficult or impossible to escape due to their inherent (ontological) nature. While all the traps have conceptual elements, each is very much grounded in the real world.

For instance, once a nation misallocates its capital into unneeded malls, office towers and exurban housing which now sit vacant and decaying, that capital can never be recovered.

1. Scalability Trap. This is a way of describing the inevitability of job losses in any industry as it scales up to technologically optimum (automated) production. Oftwominds.com correspondent K.D. (who coined the term Scalability Trap, as far as I can tell) termed this process a "modernity tax," or the cost of modern productivity.

It might be also be considered a "technology/trade tax on employment." That is, if an economy refused technological production then it could not trade such expensively produced products profitably. Even the lowest-cost labor is more expensive than machines because machinery does not get sick, does not need to be trained, does not spoil production with errors, does not riot when idled, etc.

Just as the agricultural workforce of the U.S. has fallen to 2% from 50% as mechanization scaled up, any work which can be largely automated (not just manufacturing, but software coding, tax preparation, etc.) will fall into a scalability trap once the technology is available to automate production.

2. Capital Trap. In my lexicon, there are three applications of this term:

• Banking/finance capital trap. As bank assets fall in value (mortgages on foreclosed homes and commercial real estate, credit-default derivatives, mortgage-backed securities, etc.) then banks' capital requirements increase dramatically.

Additional reserves are simply trapped capital as the capital constraint will lead to a downward spiral of higher interest rates for borrowers (as banks try to "earn their way out of insolvency"), a slowdown in borrowing (due to higher risk management/qualification standards), more loan defaults (as those who planned to roll over old debt find they no longer qualify to do so), and thus more erosion of bank capital as bad-debt/impaired loan losses keep mounting.

- National investment trap. The U.S. as a nation has poured staggering sums of its national wealth into speculatively built, rapidly depreciating real estate: malls nobody wants to rent or own, roads to weedy subdivisions, 20 million empty homes, office towers with 90% vacancy rates, empty storefronts, etc. The capital in all this unnecessary real estate is trapped because it cannot be sold--it is illiquid except at fire-sale prices, at which point the remaining shards of capital are finally freed but the owners have to book catastrophic losses in the capital. Rather than be declared insolvent, the owners (often the banks holding foreclosed properties) leave the capital trapped, hoping for some magical rescue via a new real estate bubble.

This misallocated capital hurts the owner and the nation in another way: trapped in impaired, unneeded real estate, it cannot be invested where it might earn a real return. Unfortunately, America's suburbs, malls and office parks are now "capital traps" of national savings.

- Homeowner's capital trap. The housing bubble attracted many buyers who either sought a low-down/no-down speculative investment (i.e. buy a super-leveraged house to "flip" for a quick profit) or who were unqualified by prudent pre-bubble standards but qualified via "liar loans" (no-document mortgages) and fraudulent appraisals and mortgages applications. As prices plummeted, the value of their houses soon fell far below the mortgage and these speculators exited via foreclosure, walking away, etc.

Since these speculators put up little or no capital, there is no capital to be trapped. But those who put down 20% cash or who already owned a home found themselves in a capital trap. When an asset starts depreciating rapidly, the smart investment decision is to sell it quickly and preserve whatever capital you still have--unless it's illiquid, in which case your capital is trapped.

That is the situation facing homeowners in markets where prices tumbled so far and fast that only fire-sale prices attract buyers--and for the vast majority of mortgage holders, that means they receive none of the capital back.

In the housing bubble glory days, these homeowners with capital (equity) could extract it via refinancing or HELOCs (home equity lines of credit). But those credit lines have all but dried up, leaving the capital well and truly trapped.

Though the cliche is that "housing always comes back," the owners of homes in Detroit and other depopulating, de-industrializing locales have found that to be misleading; in hard-hit cities and jobless, service-poor exurbs, house values are dropping toward zero. In these unfortunate situations, the homeowner's capital isn't just trapped; it has vanished entirely.

In many other locales, the capital in housing will remain trapped for years as sellers refuse to accept less than bubble-era valuations and buyers refuse to pay bubble-era prices. This illiquidity stasis requires either a loss of capital (selling at low prices) or trapping the capital (illiquid assets).

3. Value Trap. A value trap occurs when an asset such as a stock or house drops to a level which seems to offer a compelling value. But no sooner does the unwary buyer commit capital to the asset than it starts falling in value again.

The seemingly attractive value caused the buyer to step into the trap. Once snared, the unhappy new owner, drawn to the hope that values will rise again, refuses to sell. As asset values keep slipping, the owner falls into a capital trap: either sell for a stupendous loss of capital or leave the capital trapped in the depreciating asset.

4. Stranded Debt Trap. As assets fall in value, the debt (mortgages, etc.) cannot be repaid. The debt is stranded/trapped and cannot be sold except at fire-sale prices that require the owner to book stupendous losses. In the case of lenders/bankers, accepting/recognizing such losses would generally lead to a formal recognition of insolvency.

5. Saturation Trap. A saturation trap occurs when a product or service deemed essential and backed by a large sunk-cost (i.e. already paid for) infrastructure hits a saturated market: there is simply far too much supply and declining demand. Yet the pressure to keep providing the service or product is immense as so many jobs, enterprises and governmental agencies depend on the market's existence. Examples include homebuilding, mortgages, commercial space, retail, hospitality/leisure/travel, etc.

In a saturation trap, every attempt to create demand fails as the market is well and truly saturated; there are too many homes for sale, too many mortgages going begging, too many empty hotel rooms, too many garage sales, etc. and the cycle of cutting prices to attract the few remaining customers only extends the losses from weak participants to all participants.

On the supply side, production or capacity is relentlessly trimmed to no avail; the entire edifice must either be carried at a loss with no end or shuttered at a complete loss since there is no market for either the assets or skills.

Advanced capitalist economies are replete with over-indebtedness, overcapacity and thus with saturation traps.

6. Quantification Trap. In many cases, quantifying the situation leads to clarity and thus on to insights. Observation and the accurate logging of quantifiable data is the heart of science.

But economics, finance and human behavior are not always illuminated by choosing a quantifiable metric and then logging data. In some cases, quantification serves to obscure the actual forces and causal mechanisms at work. For instance, almost all economic activity in advanced economies stem from so-called "animal spirits" or the internal state of confidence which triggers some financial or economic decision.

If the economic field's massive data collection and quantification were actually useful, then economists would be empowered to make more accurate forecasts. As it stands, the overwhelming majority of financial downturns are "unexpected" by economists.

A quantification trap opens when data of questionable value is deployed as an "empirical metric" to support a policy or forecast which then serves to mislead policymakers, enterprises, buyers and sellers. Examples include costly public transport systems justified and constructed with borrowed money based on quantifications that mask the inherent unknowns and risks behind a falsely confident facade of data.

Another classic example is the data presented on the enormous profits to be gained by the purchase of a building, plant, etc.

In other cases, well-meaning researchers seek to quantify situations in which data is inherently incoherent, ambiguous or only marginally relevant. The State or other powerful enterprise may present ginned-up deceptively packaged quantifications which support its policies or propaganda: for instance, the birth-death model of job creation, which magically creates hundreds of thousands of jobs each month in the depths of the current Depression.

7. Skillset Trap. Similar to a saturation trap: the sunk costs of training and the awarding of degrees create a force akin to a mighty river behind skillsets for which there is no market. We may find that MBAs now classify as skillset traps as countless business schools seek to milk candidates for tuition even as the market for middle managers dries up. We might even find that the entire college degree industry is largely a skillset trap as the skills being taught have no analog in the job market.

At the lower end of the employment scale, "computer repair" training continues to attract funding even as it becomes ever cheaper to simply replace defective computers with new ones. Such functionally obsolete skills qualify as skillset traps.

8. Trend Extrapolation Trap. While it can be argued that this is merely a cognitive bias, not a trap, in cases such as the "accidental demographics" behind Social Security then I think it qualifies as a trap, as there is no way out of a policy based on a false trend extrapolation.

The Social Security system (and indeed, all "pay as you go" entitlements) was founded on a worker-retiree ratio of about 20-to-1 and an average lifespan of about 64 years. The trap was the extension of these demographic trends into the distant future.

Now the worker-recipient ratio has slipped to about 2.5-to-1 as the average lifespan has risen to 80+ years even as the retirement age has dropped to 63 and numerous other entitlements such as SSI have been added to the once barebones Social Security program.

Despite official assurances (which ring increasingly hollow), the reality is these programs will go broke far sooner than is politically convenient. Please read The Coming Generational Storm: What You Need to Know about America's Economic Future and Fewer: How the New Demography of Depopulation Will Shape Our Future.

Another trend extrapolation is "economic growth is only way to expand prosperity." While this trend has the appearance of a permanent "law," never before has humanity been so numerous or so dependent on a dwindling, easily portable high-energy resource, i.e. petroleum for that growth and its attendant prosperity.

As several billion people aspire to the high-energy consumption lifestyle enjoyed by the advanced economies, we can anticipate an end to the trendline of ever higher energy consumption and ever higher growth based on resource exploitation.

It is certainly possible that the world's population will enjoy a high-energy consumption lifestyle in 20 years (based on some "miracle technology" which is scaled up at enormous expense to planetary supply levels), but it certainly won't be enjoying cheap, abundant petroleum-based growth.

For it is also true that the world faces not just Peak Oil but Peak Coal (anthracite), Peak Uranium, and peak rare metals. Technocrat cheerleaders promise that new technologies will seamlessly arise to replace not just fossil fuels but every material facing depletion, but the more one knows about a specific field the more sustained one's skepticism. Thus it seems that lithium-ion batteries cannot be scaled due to materials limitations. Will some battery design emerge which is made from sand (silicon) or salt or some other abundant mineral? If not, then the reality is more sobering--we cannot evade one Peak by substitution because the Peaks are not just in oil but in minerals and metals as well.

Thus the idea that some new scalable technology will certainly emerge from some obscure lab to rescue the planet from peak Oil, peak uranium, peak iridium, etc., is, evidence to the contrary, a trend extrapolation trap.

9. Preservation of Institutions Trap. As the payoffs from ever-larger investments and borrowing continue to decline (marginal returns), those bureaucratic institutions which depend on "economic growth" find their own resources shrinking. In defense, each institution and the public unions and technocrats which thrive within its stout walls raise a clarion call that society and the economy will certainly collapse should their institution (or their salaries and benefits) suffer any diminishment.

Since such institutions, their dependent suppliers/contractors and their symbiotic unions wield tremendous lobbying powers, their cries of anger and despair will be heeded until the public coffers has been completely drained.

There are many pernicious reasons why "preservation of institutions" is such a trap. Consider the "early retirement buyouts" which are offered to reduce head count. The most competent will quickly accept the offers, knowing they can pocket the settlement and then find other work, while those with few other employment options will cling to the safety of the institution, leaving the organization weaker and more prone to marginalized returns on investment.

Those left behind will be even more strident and desperate in their demands to "save our vital institution" and will thus redouble their lobbying efforts to funnel more of the dwindling tax revenues to their fiefdom. As morale sinks and leadership weakens, the public grows ever more disgusted and dismayed that their taxes are producing such marginal returns.

Thus an unresolvable conflict arises: those left within the institutional fiefdom will fight for their entitlements with the zealousness of the resentful and desperate, while the taxpayers will rise up in rebellion against paying such high taxes which produce such poor returns.

There are other forces at work other than self-reservation and myopic entitlement. In many cases those bound up in the institution's bureaucracy suffer a failure of imagination: they literally cannot imagine the institution without endless staff meetings, layers of management, and all the other trappings of an enterprise which has lost its way but which remains viable because its source of income is no longer accountable to the market or to its output.

Rather than undertake the radical reform all sclerotic, overly complex institutions need, those employed by the fiefdom (or profiting from it indirectly via contracts) will fight to preserve not the institution's purpose but their own entitlements and perquisites. To attempt to preserve the institution in its present high-cost, marginal-returns decline is a trap that will result in complete insolvency/dissolution.

10. Growth Via Credit Trap. In a previous incarnation of capitalism, wage earners were encouraged to save money, thus creating pent-up demand for products and a pool of capital which could be lent to private enterprises.

In the current incarnation of Neoliberal capitalism, consumption requires ever-greater borrowing and debt to sustain ever more marginal growth. Due to Saturation Traps, basic needs are oversupplied in advanced economies, and thus ever more marginal demand must be manufactured via marketing and low-cost credit. "Growth" in GDP has thus become entirely dependent not on savings and organic demand but on marketing and debt-based consumption.

But as demand and sales rely to an ever-greater extent on ever-increasing borrowing and debt, the trap opens: any reduction in borrowing will cause a near-collapse as demand falls to organic levels--a level far below what is needed to sustain "growth" as measured in production and consumption.

This trap deepens with every State attempt to prod the over-indebted and over-indulged consumer (once a proud citizen, now nothing but a debt-serf "consumer") into further borrow-and-spend binges; like all addictive-type traps, this cycle of ever more extreme State stimulus-funded-by-debt campaigns has only one end-state: self-destruction.

11. Exemption from Free/Transparent Market Trap. As noted earlier, a key defense against erosion of the Plutocracy/State/high-castes' increasing shares of the national income is the Elites mechanism of "inoculating" themselves against disruptive market forces via the political construction of protected fiefdoms (public unions, no-bid contracts with parasite firms, etc.)

The trap is that as each Elite observes another Elites' success in dodging the market forces of change/risk/efficiency/productivity, then its own shrill lobbying efforts to strengthen its own protected fiefdom increase accordingly. The end-state of this process is the Elites' avoidance of market forces except as a facsimile promoted in officially sanctioned propaganda to persuade the middle class that the destruction of its own wealth and security was the result of "eternal laws" (the invisible hand, etc.) rather than from the transfer of risk from the Elites to the middle class taxpayers.

12. Derealization/Simulacrum Trap. I have attempted to describe the way in which authentic structures and systems are slowly replaced by simulacrum to protect an over-reaching Plutocracy from exposure and thus change. Coupled with derealization, the process of substituting simulacrum becomes more than a hollowing out: it becomes a trap.

In general, we can characterize the trap thusly: the more that citizens accept simulacra as authentic, the more their own internal experience of the world is derealized. As they try to repair the widening gap between what they experience intuitively and what the Plutocracy/Media/State project as what they should experience (what we call alienation), then the citizens will internalize this alienation as a result of their individual failings rather than the corruption of the power structures of our society and economy.

While *Wikipedia* defines derealization as a clinical term for a feeling of unreality, I am using it to describe the disconnect between what we experience and what the propaganda/marketing complex we live in tells us we should be experiencing.

One example of this is the explosion of obesity in the U.S. within the past 20 years. According to the Centers for Disease Control (CDC) data U.S. *Obesity Trends 1985-2007*, only 20 years ago a scant 8 states had obesity rates of 15% or more. As of 2007, only one state had obesity rates under 20%, and 30 states had rates of 25% or more. That is a dramatic, unprecedented demographic change in only one generation.

Here is a derealization/simulacrum trap. The unhealthy goods being marketed as "food" by the packaged food and fast-food industries are more accurately a simulacrum of nutrition wrapped around carefully engineered doses of powerful exciters of the deepest reward centers in our brains: fat, sugar and salt. In essence, the "food" being hyped and pitched 24/7 is the edible equivalent of crack cocaine.

For more on the science of obesity, please read <u>The End of Overeating: Taking Control of the Insatiable American Appetite</u> by Dr. David Kessler.

How has food been derealized by a supremely profitable industry? Try to eat a package of cold French fries. I don't mean lukewarm, I mean hours old cold French fries. Needless to say, the appeal of the "chips" is now limited.

Our actual experience of eating fast food delights is masked by what we expect to experience. The happy-happy adverts and the physical setting of the fast-food outlet (hard bright lighting, hard bright plastic, etc.) set up the expectation that we're not only going to enjoy the mouth-feel experience of chomping that hot greasy bundle of fries but that we're supposed to feel the warm happy sensation of sated appetite after the meal has been gobbled.

But what if instead of that happy feeling we actually experience a sense of nausea? That would be most unprofitable. So the entire worldview behind the marketing (including the government's collusion at many levels) is designed to derealize the actual experience of eating junk food.

Were it possible to break free of this carefully marketed mindset, you might find virtually all the foods you're supposed to crave are actually revolting.

I say this as someone who will eat ice cream or pizza or a fast-food hamburger a few times a year and enjoy it. But I am aware that it is not in my best interests to eat such "food" more than occasionally, and I am alive to the weird drugged-out sensations such meals cause.

Exercise has been derealized into a bizarre either/or world of extreme sports or TV-induced passive sloth/torpor as a spectator. Extreme risk and extreme conditioning are glorified (again, for the purposes of selling you a "sports drink" of sugar water and cheap vitamins or a costly bicycle, etc.) while a more normal pattern of enjoyable exercise has been positioned as "too time consuming" even as the average American household manages to watch almost eight hours of TV/Web per day.

Meanwhile, if you can escape this derealization, you will find that exercise, yes, even occasionally strenuous exercise, releases all sort of endorphins and mood enhancers--and not just extreme conditioning (which is often if not always destructive to overall health) but movement as simple as walking a few blocks here and there for 20 minutes.

The experience of walking, running, martial arts, digging, hunting, etc. has been derealized into a marketable "product," i.e. a gym which requires membership and familiarity with all sorts of costly machines or a "sport" which requires all sorts of costly classes, equipment, etc.

The "fitness gym" experience can also be derealizing. One mounts some contraption, puts on one's "my stuff, my world" iPod and then watches CNN or some other mindless loop of bogus "news" while maintaining a heart rate of X, as demanded by one's personal trainer as the "optimum" key metric of the whole experience. Never mind how you feel; keep it at 99, pal, or you "failed."

Personally, I'd rather dig a ditch (yes, I've dug plenty of ditches, so I know what's involved) than sit on some contraption lost in a cocoon of sensory override. I'd rather take a walk or get on my bike or do anything in the real world than go to a room of machines occupied by people ignoring each other. I know many of you feel the gym is a key element in your fitness program, and I understand it's practical; but I don't "get it" and would rather do *katas* or play around with my bamboo staff.

If this is what's pitched as required for "fitness" (and exactly what metric do we use to define that?), no wonder most people prefer lounging on the sofa watching cooking shows.

It seems to me a key cause of obesity, attention deficit disorder and a dull lethargy devoid of the fun and zest of exercise/physical motion is that our experience has been derealized in order to sell us some product.

A key element of the obesity epidemic derealization is that the obese citizen internalizes the responsibility for his/her weight gain as a personal failing--a lack of discipline, an unhealthy upbringing, etc.--anything other than the profitable cause, the relentless marketing of mouth-feel engineered food at stupendous profit margins, all enabled or approved by the State.

In terms of obesity, this spiral leads to endless dieting, classes, workshops, vitamin regimes, etc., none of which address the inner hungers of the frustrated and self-loathing consumer.

The Derealization/Simulacrum Trap appears throughout the economy. Thus "innovation" is often not so much innovation as its simulacrum; it may be warmed-over profiteering or false hopes presented to mollify/distract citizens from actual issues.

Simulacra are elusive by nature; much like quarks, they cannot be isolated but must be identified by their reflections or influences on other moving parts of a system.

13. Stability Trap. In a Stability Trap, brittleness and fragility are masked by apparent system stability. Examples include the global supply chain (apparently robust but actually quite vulnerable), the electrical power grid in the U.S. and many other systems.

One excellent overview of system vulnerabilities and brittleness can be found in the book The Upside of Down: Catastrophe, Creativity, and the Renewal of Civilization.

With the actual fragility thus masked, few feel the motivation to formulate a "Plan B" alternative should the system break down or be disrupted.

In some stability traps, the energy required to keep the system stable/in equilibrium increases, slowly but surely, to the point that the input costs exceed the output's worth. Those receiving the output do not notice the rising costs until the system breaks down, surprising everyone but those tasked with its maintenance.

14. Risk-Accountability Trap. In this trap, risk is disconnected from accountability. Thus investment bank employees are rewarded not for being accountable for the potential losses of the derivatives they originate and sell but for the profits generated.

Once someone can assume risks and avoid any responsibility or accountability for the consequences of creating those risks, then risk in the system grows exponentially to the point of collapse. Thus if I can purchase a house with no money down and extract 120% of the purchase price with no possible consequences to me other than walking away, then I can create that risk (of a mortgage which will default) with virtually no accountability.

15. Bull Market Trap. A bull trap is series of higher highs that lures investors back into the market, only to be followed by a resumption of a long-term market decline. A bull trap is baited by the classic investor emotions of hope, greed, and complacency, which of which lead investors to enter the market despite all fundamental warning signs to the contrary.

The optimistic bias of economists was revealed in a study of the consensus forecasts of economists made in advance of 60 recessions around the world in the 1990s. It showed that economists failed 97% of the time to predict the coming recession a year in advance. Many of the economists failed to foresee recessions that occurred as soon as two months later. Fully one-third of U.S. economists failed to recognize a recession that had already been underway at least nine months.

16. Stagnation Trap. As noted in Chapter One, a pernicious positive feedback loop is at work as the Plutocracy and State continually increase their share of the national income: their power and influence increase proportionately, which then enables even more wealth acquisition and ever greater influence.

The primary consequence of this widening gap between the ever-poorer middle class taxpayers and the ever wealthier State and Plutocracy is a structural divergence between the interests of the Plutocracy and the State and those of the middle class. This widening structural imbalance of power and share of the national wealth creates a deep cynicism and profound political disunity which is reflected in the blocking of any structural solution by the State and Plutocracy.

Since the structural problem is State and Plutocracy over-reach, any real solution will necessarily reduce their shares of the national income and limit their joint powers. Loathe to accept even the smallest reduction in their income and power, both the Plutocracy and the State (including those dependent on its various fiefdoms) resist all structural change with every force at their command.

The inevitable consequence is a profound *structural stagnation* in which real reform is betrayed in the name of compromise, the same simulacrum "solutions" which leave the powers and income of the State and Plutocracy fully intact are trotted out under new Orwellian names ("Save the American Homeowner Act," etc.) and all discussions of truly structural solutions are ruthlessly eliminated from the mass media or belittled/undermined in classic propaganda manner.

Thus the State and Plutocracy prefer stagnation to any present-day reduction in their income and power. This is the stagnation trap: in resisting structural change, the State and Plutocracy guarantee a stagnation which inevitably leads to collapse of the very system of privileges they seek to maintain.

17. Minimal Effort/Pain Trap. The ever-increasing reliance on short-term fixes and a "just-squeak-by" mentality can be summarized as the Minimal Effort/Pain Trap, a concept introduced by oftwominds.com reader Eric Hoyle who termed it the "shortcut/temporary fix trap:"

> "I see it regularly in my tutoring work: students develop a shortcut-riddled cursory knowledge that suffices to complete worksheets where all the problems follow the same format, or where you simply regurgitate facts. This is encouraged by the common methods of teaching and testing, especially in math. They don't cultivate understanding, they train for an animal response. But at some point this fails, or at least becomes much more laborious in comparison to the thinking and understanding method. For example, it's impossible to remember enough shortcuts and key words to get through Algebra 2 without understanding it, not to mention that it's drudgery. But the shortcut-dependent student is trapped, because it's too painful and time-consuming to go back and actually learn math, starting with division or fractions."

The attractor in this trap is compelling: rather than face the potentially sharp pain and sustained effort required by true understanding or meaningful structural changes, we expend the minimal possible effort to pass the test and keep the status quo functioning.

Like the stagnation trap, this is fundamentally a resistance-to-change trap that increases the brittleness and instability of the system until collapse/failure is inevitable.

If we combine the long wave cycles described in previous chapters with the multitude of traps outlined above, the difficulty of extracting ourselves from our overlapping complex crises without major disruption or collapse becomes abundantly visible.

Key concepts in this chapter:
Structural stagnation

Chapter Sixteen: The Crisis of Neoliberal Capitalism

It is both tempting and instructive to compare the current crisis of global Neoliberal capitalism with past crises such as the Great Depression of the 1930s or the long period of turmoil from the Panic of 1873 to 1894.

To the degree the current crisis is financial, then seeking echoes in past crises makes perfect sense. But to the degree we also face unprecedented energy and environmental crises, then these past periods of financial distress cannot be accurate models.

Several other factors make the current global crisis unique. Globalization has expanded to an unprecedented degree, and governments have responded to the collapse of credit by transferring unimaginable levels of risky debt onto the backs of taxpayers, all in the vain hope of reviving a model of "permanent growth" which has run its course: the Neoliberal iteration of advanced capitalism which depends on stupendous credit expansion and government intervention to ward off implosion.

We should also be mindful that the level of deception, obfuscation, fraud, securitization, misrepresentation and State collusion with private looting, debauchery of credit and excessive systemic risk-taking are beyond the reach of any previous private speculative frenzies. With truth debased, public faith in a self-serving State-Plutocracy media campaign to mask their overreach will collapse along with Neoliberal capitalism's promise of endless permanent prosperity.

This implosion of public trust might well find an echo or analog in the great transformations of the 1960s and early 1970s, when faith in the economy and State foundered under a barrage of government lies and economic decline.

As the state and its Plutocracy fail to reinflate the speculative credit-based asset bubbles which fueled advanced capitalism's last decade of bogus "prosperity," their relentless campaign to convince their citizenry that the system is sound and beneficial to all will be revealed as illusion. At that point values may suddenly shift and old loyalties and beliefs in the system will be jettisoned in favor of more sustainable value systems.

Globalization: Neoliberal Capitalism's Last "Fix"

In essence, globalization was Neoliberal Capitalism's attempt to save itself from the endgame of advanced capitalism foreseen by Marx: overcapacity which leads to a collapse in profits and thus a decline in capital and the overall economy.

Marx's insight was straightforward: the dynamic of capitalism is for production to rise to meet demand--and then keep rising. As demand is sated, capacity continues to grow because Capital is like a shark--it must move forward or it dies, and it moves toward what was immensely profitable in the recent past.

This is how we get overbuilding of office and retail space: as demand (and profits) soar, then everyone with capital rushes in to enjoy the profit spree. But ironically, this massive rush to the most profitable return guarantees overbuilding and overcapacity.

As Marx noted, supply soon overshoots demand and sales plummet, wiping out profits. The end result is a move to monopoly capital, in which a handful of the strongest players squeeze out or buy out all the weaker players who fold as the return on capital goes negative (losses). The last players standing then consolidate and shutter most of the capacity, setting up a monopoly which then lowers supply below demand to maintain outsized profits.

All the workers laid off as capacity is shuttered no longer have income so they stop spending, which lowers demand even further. This cycle of boom and bust was inherent to Capitalism and Marx expected them to steadily become ever more extreme.

But capitalism "solved" this cycle of overcapacity and crashing demand/income/profits by turning to new overseas markets. Those with a military-backed Empire (for instance, Great Britain) could simply force new markets for domestic goods into existence overseas: by requiring consumers in India to buy British cloth, for instance.

In other cases, advanced capitalist states opened new markets by forcing less developed economies to "offer" their low-cost manufactured goods, which quickly took market share from the more informally produced local goods.

The heyday of colonialism was driven by a simple "virtuous cycle" (virtuous for the advanced economy, not for the subjugated colony) in which the colony was forced to ship its raw materials to the colonial power at low cost while at the same time it was forced to pay a premium for the advanced economy's output/surplus goods.

Since the colonial power's domestic workforce benefited immensely from this "global trade" (low commodity prices thanks to the exploited colonies and plentiful jobs to make the goods forced onto the colonies) then the Colonial Power's Elites received great political support for the their one-sided "globalization" policies.

Apologists are quick to point out the supposedly stupendous benefits of this globalization for the "natives": high-quality advanced goods and paying work in an economy with little formal employment. Yet the reality is not so happy-happy: only economies with locally owned productive capacity such as Japan and Korea become wealthy economies. Those former colonies where foreign capital dominates the productive capacity and commodity extraction are in essence still exploited colonies.

Government ownership is also no panacea.

When less-developed economies' primary assets (including commodities like oil) are owned and operated by the government, then the nation actually becomes poorer, not wealthier, due to the perverse dynamic of the State (government) and capital.

As profits roll in, the State, unlike private capital, defers investment in favor of political patronage and the spoils of "leadership." The incentives to politicians and the State's technocrat managers is thus to eat their seed corn whenever possible, where private capital understands that surplus capital must be invested or deployed in search of high returns lest it dwindle to zero as all profits are extracted and spent.

This mechanism is called the *paradox of plenty* in which resource-rich nations such as Venezuela and Argentina grow progressively more impoverished under State control of the nation's assets.

A corollary of this mechanism is the impoverishment of oil-exporting nations who find redistributing the wealth created by fossil fuels much easier than creating a productive labor force and infrastructure. Thus as the income from oil gyrates (and as oil inevitably enters the depletion phase) then the nation has no cultural or economic Plan B to generate national income and wealth.

With these mechanisms in mind, we can see that the advanced economies attempted to save Capitalism by colonizing China for production and their own domestic populations for credit-based consumption.

Of the many misconceptions about China's spectacular economic growth, perhaps none is more misleading than the assumption that the capital and surplus profits being made in China will stay in China. Despite the much-touted public ownership of joint-venture companies, much of the profitable production in China is owned by non-PRC (People's Republic of China) companies based in Taiwan, Japan, Korea and the West.

From a more clear-eyed perspective, China has been colonized by advanced economies to lower the cost of production and to establish a dumping ground for environmentally unsound production that their domestic citizenry will no longer tolerate. As with all colonies, the profits are extracted and sent elsewhere while apologists are hired to tout the glories of employment for China's millions.

Until, of course, Marx's overcapacity cycle kicks in.

Now that China's stupendous production capacity exceeds the potential demand of the entire world, including its own mostly impoverished domestic populace, then capital is fleeing China in its usual pursuit of higher returns, leaving behind tens of millions of unemployed workers and a toxic landscape.

The Chinese State is now attempting to counter this cycle by spending its own capital on stimulus, but State spending is not a replacement for capital or organic demand. Even worse, the Chinese State saddled its own banks with hundreds of billions of dollars in uncollectible debt in a vain attempt to prop up thousands of State-owned enterprises which racked up gigantic losses even during the boom.

The Chinese State attempted to staunch this open wound by closing thousands of its factories but the uncollectible debts remain, buried by accounting tricks within the books of its four major banks and government finance ministries.

The bloom is off the rose now that the overcapacity in China is no longer profitable to global capital and in essence the Chinese State is left holding the bag: stupendous losses in its own financial system, horrendously costly environmental damage and an industrial infrastructure which is losing value as capital shifts elsewhere.

Meanwhile, advanced Capitalism expanded due to two key innovations: the colonization of its own domestic consumers and the exponential increase in speculative debt instruments.

The essence of colonization is the forcing opening of new markets for surplus production. Frustrated by the poverty of 80% of the Chinese and Indian populaces--people with almost no surplus income cannot consume much in the way of surplus production--global capitalism turned to its own domestic populaces.

By lowering the cost of money to near-zero and generating a gigantic asset bubble in the one asset every middle class consumer already owned--a house--then global capital in essence colonized its own domestic populaces by opening a heretofore limited market for surplus production: a consumerist blow-off of unprecedented scope fueled by limitless credit and a rising asset base (real estate) inflated by the same expansion of credit, all extended by a State propelled by the need for the sort of domestic economic growth which maintains political support for the State's leadership elites.

Now that game has expired as the advanced-economy consumers finally reached the limits of their ability to service their rapidly expanding debts. Even the U.S. government's massive meddling and the printing/borrowing of trillions of dollars is not re-inflating the real estate bubble, and thus there is no collateral left to support the limitless credit global capital now requires for growth.

Advanced Capitalism is thus facing a crisis of unprecedented scale and scope: the globalization/colonization "escape" from overcapacity has come to a dead end.

While some eternally hopeful capitalists look to the former colonies of Africa as the growth engine for global capitalism, a quick look at the capacity of China and Asia to produce goods quickly reveals that hope as baseless: if we add up the remaining production in the West and developed East Asia with China's monumental new capacity, we find that the global capacity outstrips all potential demand.

The world could easily ship 20 million new autos year to Africa, but unfortunately for the advanced capitalist nations, there isn't enough income in Africa to support 100 million autos and the vast infrastructure they require. The same can be said of the billion impoverished residents of China and India. Global capital would be delighted to sell them all its surplus production but for the sad fact they have no money or collateral on which to base consumer borrowing.

Now that the global real estate bubble has burst, global capital is facing a real dilemma: it has colonized and exploited virtually every populace available, and there is no one left to exploit. Their lackeys in the governments have eliminated moral hazard (that is, go ahead and speculate wildly, we'll save you all regardless of risk or the size of your losses) and expanded credit exponentially, but never-ending exponential growth is simply not possible.

And so now with the destruction of the bogus real estate bubble and speculative "wealth," global capital has screeched to a halt at the edge of an abyss it has avoided for a hundred years. Finally, there is no place left to sell overproduction, and the domestic populaces it depends on for political support are restive as they sense the ground beneath their "prosperity" has fallen away.

Thus global capital is desperately demanding the State print/borrow trillions of dollars in a futile effort to either inflate new bubbles or reinflate speculative bubbles which have popped. The reinflation will fail, even as they push governments into insolvency and fail to save Neoliberal capitalism.

Globalization also has a host of other pernicious features.

1. Concentration of resources and political power. Global capital, armed with virtually unlimited access to capital via the capital markets and various exotic instruments such as derivatives, can always outbid local owners/capitalists for resources. Once the forest, oil field, etc. is owned (or joint-ventured with local crony capitalists or Oligarch families) then it is promptly stripped/exploited/depleted.

2. Zero to minimal accountability for environmental damage. Any environmental damage that results is of no consequence because the local political Elite can be bought for relatively modest sums. There is no profit in cleaning up the site and so to do so would be "irrational" in a rational-market metric.

Perhaps this distance from the environmental consequences of resource/wealth extraction is globalization's most pernicious feature. Mine owners never live near the tailings, and the coal plant's owners never live downwind of the sooty plume, either.

The more distant the owner, the less accountable they are for local consequences.

In today's Internet-savvy world, global capital places some modest value on corporate image, and thus some sort of simulacrum of environmental concern is made and then hyped via company propaganda. In a handful of cases, wise stewardships is not just a propaganda talking point; but the circumstances behind these exceptions are not easily codified.

3. Redistribution of income to capital from labor or local ownership is "necessary" to encourage "investment." Even in Empire States like the U.S., foreign capital is given numerous tax loopholes and other redirections of income to capital. This is always explained as necessary to encourage "investment."

But this greater income did not appear out of thin air; it was redistributed from labor and local owners via tax loopholes and credits. But since global capital is driven to seek the highest returns possible, the income extracted from Locale A is rarely reinvested in Locale A. This justification for the income redistribution--to encourage "investment"--is thus a cover for resource/profit extraction.

In the U.S., global companies like General Motors have received taxpayer bailouts in the tens of billions, supposedly to keep their production and workforce in the U.S., when the demand of global capital for higher returns forces the company to expand in Brazil at the expense of domestic U.S. jobs.

In one sense, the company has no choice. It must deploy its remaining capital at the highest return or simply close down. In the Chinese model the State owns the factories and continues to operate them at a loss. But as China's own state-owned enterprises show, permanent losses are simply not sustainable, even for the government.

4. As middle class jobs are cut, demand falls, exacerbating overcapacity. Global capital shifts away from high cost production (except where that opportunity is limited by the State), replacing middle class employment in advanced economies with lower-cost labor in less-developed economies.

Ironically, this lowers demand for the global companies' goods even as their overseas capacity expands. The net result is that financial speculation becomes an increasingly attractive use for capital. Thus selling consumers credit with which to buy cars becomes more profitable than selling them cars. Additional profit is reaped by bundling these consumer loans into packages--securitization--and selling the newly minted securities to credulous investors around the world.

Thus speculative leveraged credit and securitization can vastly increase profits even as production falls.

5. As its own income falls, the middle class follows the lead of global capital by increasingly relying on credit-based speculation

rather than production for income. No one is more anxious to pursue speculative gains than someone whose income from labor is declining. Thus homeowners or prospective homeowners were delighted to follow global capital's forays into credit-based real estate speculation.

Unfortunately, speculation is no substitute in the long run for producing actual goods and services, and once the exponential blow-off was reached and the bubble popped, global capital simply sold off (or got bailed out) and moved on, while the middle class speculators were left with staggering losses in real wealth or capital traps (assets declining in value which could not be sold).

6. Due to its global nature, capital is no longer accountable for the consequences of its choices. Here's how it works: global capital gets huge tax credits (incentives that are basically nothing more than redistribution of income from labor and local entrepreneurs to global capital) for "investing" in the local economy. It then mines the local labor and/or resources of profits until overcapacity or depletion strikes. Then it shutters the factory or mine and moves its machinery elsewhere, leaving the local economy a shambles. Next it hypes the need for "investment" elsewhere, moving production to wherever offers the highest tax benefits, the least environmental restrictions and the lowest labor costs. Final step: repeat.

From the point of view of global capital, this is "obviously" the only model which "works." Local residents, workers and small-scale enterprise owners will disagree once their locale has been strip-mined of profits and wealth.

In sum: globalization is a key driver in the end of paying work and the impoverishment of local labor, resources and enterprise via the redistribution of profits and income to global capital.

The State's Vain Attempt to Distribute Systemic Risk to Taxpayers: The Yellowstone Analogy

The first task of those at the levers of Neoliberal global capitalism is to deny that global capitalism is in crisis.

"Neoliberal" refers to a model of State-managed capitalism which has been in vogue since the Great Depression and the Keynesian revolution: when capitalism's business cycle veers into discomfort (unemployment, slowing sales and borrowing, etc.) then the State (government) suppresses recession with monetary policy (making money cheap and abundant) and fiscal policy (quantitative easing, injections of liquidity, stimulus programs, etc.)

That sounds just ducky, but the Yellowstone Analogy reveals the flaw in this suppression strategy. Free market private sector capitalism's normal business cycle of over-investment and excessive risk-taking is naturally followed by a reduction in debt, the liquidation of bad loans and excess inventory, a trend to reduced risk, etc.--in other words, a fast-burning forest fire which incinerates all the deadwood, clearing space for the next generation of growth.

For decades, the operative theory of forestry management was that limited controlled burns-- mild reductions of dead underbrush and debris--would essentially reduce the possibility of a major fire to near-zero.

But the practice actually allowed a buildup of deadwood that then fueled the devastating forest fire which swept Yellowstone National Park in 1988. Various revisionist views sprouted up later, claiming the fire was not the result of misguided attempts to limit natural forces.

Now we're in a financial conflagration which is widely considered the result of failed risk-suppression policies. All the derivatives originated and sold were supposed to, along with "self-regulating markets" (smirk), limit the risks in the financial systems to near-zero.

In other words, even as dead branches piled ever higher, various complex hedges would insure no fire in the FIRE economy would ever spread.

Meanwhile, Mr. Greenspan and other officials made sure the slightest whiff of debt reduction or other signs of recession were instantly snuffed with super-low interest rates and abundant government stimulus.

But this private and public risk suppression not only failed to eradicate risk--it enabled risk to grow to unprecedented levels.

Globally, the State has responded to this failure to suppress risk by creating gigantic new risks and transferring them to taxpayers and buyers of government-issued debt.

The suppression technique being pursued by governments everywhere is simple: borrow and print staggering sums of money to bail out the private-sector banks which sparked the crisis, and then borrow and print even more money and throw it into the economy in an attempt to match the fiscal stimulus of World War Two spending.

Unfortunately, this stimulus is essentially adding more deadwood to an already vast pile that is already choking what's left of the economy's living forest. Rather than close down failed banks and businesses, various games are being played to negate the fires of creative destruction which real capitalism needs to thrive; without a write-off of bad debts and risky failed gambles and a closure of overcapacity, the new business cycle cannot take root.

Isn't it obvious that by trying to make forest fires a thing of the past, you're actually killing the forest?

The same mechanism is at work in the multi-trillion dollar attempts to make financial cycles of over-indebtedness and excessive risk a thing of the past.

The financial firestorm of 2008 burned off some of the deadwood, but it left no clearing. Thus the smoldering embers will set fire to all the new bad debt and deadwood blanketing the floor of our moribund, choked economy and a new round of monetary easing and fiscal stimulus will be attempted.

But policy makers will eventually find their borrowing desires will exceed the willingness of capital to flow into long-term low-interest government bonds. The zombie banks and businesses--the equivalent of dead but still-standing trees--will finally start toppling over.

You can't make people who are already over-indebted take on more debt, and you can't make people whose collateral is falling creditworthy. To shove more debt into the system is to pile more deadwood onto the already-dense pile of dry debris littering every inch of the economy.

The big conceit here is that borrowing trillions of dollars is risk-free as long as the government is doing the borrowing.

That is an illusion--there is always risk when you borrow or print or "backstop"/guarantee trillions of dollars of risky debt; the risk has simply been transferred to taxpayers, who will soon suffer the consequences.

For the crisis in capitalism is not just debt-based--it's also resource and demographic-based.

Here in the U.S., the Social Security system will reverse its long trend of generating a surplus in 2016 (or sooner as the Depression cuts tax revenues) and as a result it will start adding to a Federal budget deficit that's already running $2 trillion a year.

Medicare is even more fragile, and thus we can easily foresee a fiscal crisis looming in which the Federal government can no longer borrow enough trillions to fund these entitlements. And despite all the repeated soothing official assurances, the crisis is not in 2035--it will hit in 2015 or perhaps even earlier.

This is a classic example of the *Trend Extrapolation Trap*. Back when the Social Security system was designed, it was assumed there would always be 10 workers to "pay as you go" to support 1 retiree. The Baby Boom in the 1950s made that projection reassuringly long-term--or so it seemed.

Now that we're approaching a worker-retiree ratio of 2.5-to-1, the system cannot possibly pay the benefits promised without borrowing trillions of dollars each and every year--and from whom?

Meanwhile, oil has plummeted in a long-anticipated head-fake in which global recession cuts demand, masking the arrival of Peak Oil. Will there be enough oil to fuel 100 million new Tata minicars in India plus run the 600 million existing vehicles currently burning oil? And exactly where will the electricity come from to charge up 100 million plug-in hybrid cars made by China's BYD? (Not to mention the lithium-ion batteries.)

As for all the alternative fuels, well, maybe, but right now all alternative energy sources provide only a few percentage points of global energy.

Ramping up alternative energy from 3% to 30% of global energy production will be stupendously costly--and aren't governments vacuuming up much of the world's capital to squander it on their financial sectors and local government pork-barrel projects?

Neoliberal capitalism is in crisis for one fundamental reason: the State has played "the fixer" with monetary and fiscal policy in the belief that risk could be suppressed by spreading it over the entire taxpaying populace.

But the excesses of credit, risk, leverage and overcapacity are now gutting the very middle class which the State relies on to pay most of the taxes. And as tax revenues dry up, entitlement spending ramps ever higher and borrowing is no longer cheap or even possible, then the State and the "private sector capitalism" which depended on passing off its risks and gambles-gone-awry to the State will find the firestorm was not suppressed-- it was only delayed--and not for long.

The best explanation of systemic financial risk and why it cannot be "disappeared" is The (Mis)behavior of Markets: A Fractal View of Risk, Ruin, and Reward by Benoit Mandelbrot.

The demographics trends which are about to overwhelm entitlements programs are described in <u>Fewer: How the New Demography of Depopulation Will Shape Our Future</u> and <u>The Coming Generational Storm: What You Need to Know about America's Economic Future</u>.

Perverse Incentives, Rational Disincentives and the Substitution of Low-Risk Fantasy for Reality

The crisis of Neoliberal capitalism cannot be fully understood unless we grasp three mechanisms It's a classic example of the "Trend Extrapolation Trap." which have been deployed in the fierce defense of its ideology. When its myths, based on exploitation rather than production, spread to the common person (in the form of illusory home equity extraction, etc.), the system becomes overloaded and meltdown ensues. Everyone is trying to take someone else for a ride:

1. Perverse Incentives: Simulacra of value are substituted for real-world productivity making unproductive speculation, cronyism, deliberate fraud, and deception by design preferable because one can profit without any "skin in the game." Accountability becomes either an impediment or a sucker's proposition. This is reinforced by modes of thinking and plans of action which socialize losses and privatize gains, shifting of risk to taxpayers, and encouraging state-banker-dealer collusion.

2. Rational Disincentives: The gradual punishment (in relative terms) and destruction of support for production, integrity and accurate accounting places people who pursue these principles at a competitive disadvantage. When deployment of capital for speculation (i.e. unearned capital gains) is taxed at half the rate of production (i.e. earned income), then productivity is disincentivized. Unregulated "creative" accounting puts honest business at a disadvantage. Inflated earnings and hidden liabilities both make a company appear more profitable, and create competitive pressure toward collusion and deliberate fraud. The "rational" weight of various disincentives for honest and healthy commercial exchange buoys the market rationality for risky speculation.

3. The Substitution of Low-Risk Fantasy for Reality. These perverse incentives--propagated not just by financial and regulatory structures but by the mass media/marketing propaganda system described above--led the American citizenry to believe this simulacrum of value could be a low-risk, productive, "rich" way of life. Since simulacra require agreement (or at least passive complicity), we might ask why the motto of the age became "If it sounds to good to be true, it MUST be true."

Part of the answer lies in the apparently low-risk ease of profiting from real estate and financial speculation. Since organisms are selected to avoid undue risk (that is, investing significant assets and time in projects with unknown outcomes) and favor the security of the status quo, then the appeal of a seemingly secure, low-risk system which offered vast profits for modest investments of capital was overpoweringly "obvious." That it was all a fantasy based on lies was clearly visible, but the risks were so low and the rewards so high that the American people willingly substituted a fantasy for reality.

Any successful simulacrum rests on its ability to "make natural" (and thus rational) its assumptions and mechanisms. Thus what essayist Zeus Yiamouyiannis has described as the *Quadrillion Dollar Scam* has been constructed on the accounting conceit that debt is an asset.

Anatomy of a Quadrillion Dollar Scam: Assessing the Damage and Making Our Way in a Post-Gluttony Era

This essay was first published on www.oftwominds.com in June 2009, and is reprinted here by permission of the author, Zeus Yiamouyiannis, Ph.D.; copyright 2009, all rights reserved in all media.

Introduction:

Debts are never assets, yet debts have been defined as assets by banks, investment houses, credit card companies, and brokers. If these entities or persons loan you money, they call the resulting debt on your part an asset for them, because you will ostensibly pay them back the principal, with interest, creating profit for them. If you give them money, they must pay you interest (no matter how small), and hence they consider your money a liability. They offset that liability by loaning your money to others at higher interest and pocketing the difference. This used to be what banks did and how they made their money.

With the massive deregulation of financial markets, banks began to effectively merge with investment houses and insurance companies under a rubric of "complete financial services," leveraging and investing money in higher and higher interest ventures, with greater and greater risks, involving huge theoretical profits. These new ventures tended to involve something other than lending, i.e. providing "services" or "guarantees" in the form of default insurance and other promises.

None of these new ventures and products were or are necessary to the credit market, day-to-day business, or efficient economies. Some of these vehicles could, if managed correctly with adequate capital reserves, do some positive things like distribute risk. However, most appear to be simply a boondoggle-- siphoning real value, adding nothing, and substituting a promise of astronomical theoretical future riches for actual ability to pay out. Most have not been managed correctly and have neither had the necessary capital reserves nor prudent investment strategies to shore up those reserves. Predictably, the world financial market is now in free fall.

In this debacle, a profound metaphysical error has emerged--viewing debt itself as an asset. This has fateful and far-reaching practical consequences we are just now beginning to see and assess. Debt adds nothing. It does not produce anything or hold any value. Debt is not the asset but rather the lendee's ability to pay that debt, interest and principal, and, failing that, provide something of real value (collateral) that covers the full amount of the debt. Those are the assets, which the debt-extender holds claim to through a legal contract.

This error of debt-as-asset has spawned a series of wide-ranging and false assumptions about worth resulting in a massive financialization of markets, where derivative financial vehicles based in abstract and theoretical models for assigning value have gained an eerie and superseding reality over actual government managed money supply and concrete value production (stemming from labor, commodities, creativity, intelligence, property improvement, technological innovation, etc.)

Let me state this again: This financialization and its vehicles have no basis in actual, concrete assets. (Emphasis added: CHS) Their only power lies in their ability to trade theoretical, non-real value (what I call *counterfeit value*), for things of real value.

This financial "shadow market" is able to do this by deliberately infiltrating and integrating itself into a healthy economic system. Like a parasitic invader, it protects itself from detection by lobbying successfully to subvert government regulation, scrutiny, and enforcement, by claiming itself as "private" and thus immune from public transparency requirements, and by developing mechanisms that are so complex that no one knows exactly what they do or what they might be worth. It works just like any confidence game.

The more financial vehicles one could create, the more "innovative," abstract, and complex they could be, the more fees and profits one could take in, and the less people could question what these entities were selling, the more people had to trust institutional "experts" and their assertions of value, profit, etc. Financial institutions were essentially creating their own counterfeit money through these exotic vehicles as if they had the printing presses right there in their offices.

This is confirmed by widespread statements in the financial press that the value of these vehicles is not "unknown" but rather "unknowable". Many cannot even be traced back to the real assets they were meant to service or represent, including actual deeds to properties that were packaged into "complex" securities. Though the actual dollar value of complex so-called derivatives is not known, the amount in transactions on so-called "derivatives" has been estimated by some reports at over one quadrillion dollars, that is 1,000,000,000,000,000.00 dollars. If only a conservative 2% fee were charged on these transactions, that alone would amount to a 20+ trillion dollar skim job, and that is laying aside the profit-skimming and greater fees charged in many hedge fund arrangements (i.e. 20% of profits and 5% fees in one case).

The Macro View:

Oddly enough, given the fatal metaphysical error I have mentioned (debt = asset), almost all the concoctions stemming from that error have been "rationally consistent" with the irrational premise. Too bad logical consistency with false premises will virtually guarantee disastrous conclusions. Let us spell out in detail this "rational" behavior stemming from irrational assumptions.

First let us recast traditional debt in tune with the new, false assumptions mentioned above. In traditional economics, "good" debt would be a loan extended to someone with sterling credit, with a healthy income or revenue stream, and collateral that far exceeds the value of the loan. Collection is fairly simple. Risk is transparently low. The interest rate charged would be correspondingly relatively low. "Bad" debt would be someone with a low to middling credit rating, with borderline income or revenue, and with collateral that flirted with being equivalent to the loan. Risk is transparently higher. The interest rate charged would be correspondingly higher to offset the greater risk of default and failure to recoup the full value of the loan.

"Insane" debt would be someone with an incredibly low or no credit rating, whose income or revenue is well below what is necessary to pay off the loan, and whose collateral property has no, or even negative, equity in it (think of houses bought with liar loans, balloon loans, negative amortization loans).

In a traditional system, people with "insane credit" would never get a loan, because they have no way of paying it, and they do not have collateral worth anything near value of the loan. In the new system, debt is "equivalized" so that what I have called "insane" debtors actually become the most sought after market! Why? Think about it: No distinction is being made between debts that can be paid and those that cannot possibly be paid (at least without completely fantastical projections of increasing value in the property, commodity, stock, etc. upon which the loan is being drawn). All debt is seen as asset. Insane debt = bad debt = good debt = asset. This is confirmed empirically in Moody's rating of absolute junk as secure AAA investment.

The lousier and more untenable the loan, the greater the "risk", therefore the greater interest and fees one can charge on it, and therefore the greater the ostensible return and/or profit! Combine this with the ability to externalize or pass on the liability by selling the insane loan or insuring it against default, a lender or servicer has every incentive to hand out the worst possible loans because they generate the highest fees and interest rates. "But," you may protest, "there are no foundations or fundamentals underneath these deals. They are completely irrational." In this new system, there don't need to be fundamentals because mathematical models can now simply create and assign present value based on theoretical projections of future values accepted as if those future values were fact.

So all the incentive is toward expanding the market for heavy, pervasive debt that is impossible to pay, and then to further spawn lucrative financial derivatives (including servicing and guaranteeing loans) from that market. Add consumer industries to this balloon, like housing and automobile manufacturing that benefit from this false creation of equity based on future value, and you have a juggernaut. This house of cards is perpetuated by its own "new era" mythology ("values will always go up," "deficits don't matter") and the fact that everyone seems to be getting richer from the loan originator to the lendee/investor—the brokers, the servicers, the appraisers, the realtors, the county property tax assessments, the furniture store owner, the homeowner.

If this situation weren't bad enough, a new hyper-catalyst enters the picture--leveraging. Two major problems emerged here to magnify many thousand or millions fold the damage already levied by fraudulent and fantastical lending. First, unregulated private companies (equity firms, hedge funds, etc.) were able to fabricate wealth and inflate their holdings and net worth to either further invest or buy outright real companies, as Cerberus did with Chrysler. Their unregulated "money" was based in "equity" based on "marked to model" theoretical value.

Second, unregulated financial instruments like credit default swaps had no effectively no reserve requirement at all, because their reserve "money" was also based on "assets" based on "marked to model" theoretical value. Furthermore, this unregulated, self-assigned value could be, if they so desired, leveraged into investments in ratios that could defy infinity. As we know, zero multiplied by a million is still zero. Imagine if you or I could assign a 200 billion-dollar asset value to our dog's house, and use this assigned value to buy a major international conglomerate.

When people say that this is "unthinkable," what they are really saying is, "I don't want to think about it. I don't want to acknowledge this happened or can happen." However, just connect the dots. It's simple. Is there anything preventing this from happening. No. Applicable regulations have been removed, and those still on the books have not been enforced. Is there any reason not to do it given the incentives and principles at play? No. Therefore, it will happen.

What we have is essentially private, unregulated money creation prompting hyperinflation in certain markets. We have an intensely large, and at this time, unknown amount of counterfeit money and value mixed in with the real. Apparently we cannot tell real money apart from counterfeit money very easily, and/or we are trying to hide the counterfeit cash through deficit bailouts from the taxpayers.

We also know that we cannot keep these fraudulence-based markets (i.e. housing) artificially inflated because they are so out of line with reality-based fundamentals and facts. However, we also largely do not have the grit to face the consequences of this rip off. So our interim strategy appears to be to try to ease into austerity by hiding the deficits, allowing companies to continue to mark to model, holding foreclosed houses off the market, etc. It is a common and understandable (but not excusable) human response. It won't work, and it will both deepen and elongate the painful coming to terms.

Even money markets fell below 100% of principal. Think about that. That's unprecedented in its scale and severity. You don't need a canary to tell you what is going on. There has been a massive liquidity drain. Money has disappeared and been replaced with fraudulent substitutes of value. I've mentioned in other essays that this situation will eventually require massive debt forgiveness. Fraudulent or concocted wealth begets fraudulent debt. So we should come to terms with the necessity of debt erasure for larger swathes of the globe. The instigators have unfortunately, not only already been forgiven, but been rewarded with hundreds of billions of dollars of bailout money. Accountability, if it ever happens would demand these instigators go bankrupt, face criminal prosecution, and supply restitution, including returning their private, ill-gotten gains.

The Micro View:

How does this profoundly twisted macro mentality play itself out on the micro level? Let's look at some examples:

Credit card companies

Many people are aware that those consumers who pay off their credit cards every month are a liability to the credit card company. They get a short-term loan at no interest on a no-fee credit card (though the credit card company does charge a fee to the vendor). So credit card companies don't like those who pay off their cards. Furthermore by paying up, you, the borrower, have wiped out the credit company's "asset"—debt. They need someone who preferably misses a payment, so the effective interest rate can kick to 30 – 35%, someone who only makes the minimum payment, so the principal debt increases over time (enlarging the "asset"), and someone that will always pay the minimum payment even if they can never pay off the card.

Again the most desirable client is one who has the worst financial habits, not the one with the best. There is a reason that someone who carries a balance gets a higher credit score than someone who pays off the balance. All is swell at least until that underwater client defaults with thousand of others. Not even the industry written bankruptcy "reform" will hold the tide as that happens in increasing numbers.

Banks

Banks, in this "new era," expanded their traditional lending operations into broader "financial services." There was more money to be made and more market share to grab by creating a whole new host of products built around "servicing" loans (rather than just collecting them), providing financial advice, and establishing credit lines. Especially as money becomes cheaper and cheaper (i.e. the Federal Reserve sets effective bank lending rates near zero), the effective marginal profit from straight lending dwindles. Banks cannot pay anything lower than a quarter percent to savers, and competition forces the lending percentages down. Since traditional reserves are based on capital from savings (considered a liability), the pressure mounts to find a way to "capitalize" through debt.

So banks "branched out" in tune with "successful" lobbying and deregulation. This created both conflicts of interests and dangerous precedents, effectively merging banking with insurance and investment brokering. Maintaining capital reserves became a quaint notion because money lying around was so "unproductive." A myth arose that money would always be there and interest always low. This myth has proven, of course, false. Even with low interest, there is now a liquidity crisis, because real wealth was siphoned off by unproductive and no-value-added services, either stored as private wealth in opaque Swiss bank accounts, invested in worthless crap (like credit default swaps), or dumped into plunging markets (like housing).

Credit default swaps (CDS's)

I've already written many essays on this subject, so I will only summarize the transparent fraud perpetrated under these "vehicles."

CDS's are unregulated insurance against defaults on loans. Though the mechanisms have not been officially investigated and audited, it does not take a genius to conclude that AIG and others could "guarantee" loans and receives premiums for nothing, that is, without actually possessing any reserve capital or exchange service at all. Using their once respected reputation as collateral, and dubious investments conveniently and generously assigned value by their own accountants, these institutions could create cash flow without providing anything in return except assurances. No wonder these vehicles were so attractive.

This would be like you or me receiving nice batches of money from our neighbors to insure against their houses being destroyed by fire, using our own house as collateral, with all of us living in the middle of a tinder-dry pine forest. The fire simply is going happen sooner rather than later with these conditions (akin to the poor fundamentals in the economy), and you and I won't have anything left with which to pay others. However, we will have a huge private stash created by the fees and premiums we have charged and the bonuses we've given ourselves. This, at least, could help us rebuild our own mansions.

Housing

According to any kind of fundamental analysis, the transparent irrationality of house prices could not have been clearer. Real incomes have been flat or declining over the last decade, even though productivity rose substantially. Purchased houses in overheated markets required monthly payments three times what is would cost to rent the same house. Some people were paying as much as 10, even 20, times their salaries to buy a house. (I remember a newspaper report of a 750,000-dollar house bought on a 40,000-dollar/year salary.) Reporting and underwriting requirements simply disappeared on the false conviction that "housing prices will always go up in the new era." Of course this could not be sustained, any more than an actual house could be supported on a foundation of air.

Stocks

Stocks were bound to fall as well, since they were being inflated by a number of factors related to the outright greed and entitlement created by this "new era" thinking. First, many companies who once only manufactured products decided to financialize themselves, i.e. GM, which went from only manufacturing cars to providing GMAC financing. Second, chief executives found their huge bonuses tied to stock prices, so they found ways to manipulate demand/value, and thus stock prices, by buying up their own stock, or better yet by leveraging their assets 30 to 1 to expand business, merge with other companies in huge multi-billion dollar deals. Great paper profits mean great bonuses even when you are cannibalizing stability.

Third, housing and other irrationally inflated sectors provided stockpiles of illusory consumer equity and short-term job growth, encouraging a consumer spending orgy on a range of goods and services that buoyed the economy. Fourth, for eight years a presidential administration and its entire executive branch allowed industries to write environmental laws allowing for indiscriminant toxification of the environment, waste in energy, and pliant, absentee oversight in agencies like the Security and Exchange Commission. We are now coming to terms with the fact that environmental and economic limits are and will continue to force a decline in manufacturing and sales. Those cut GM dealerships and factories are not coming back.

Conclusion:

Believe it or not, the exposure of these falsehoods and a return to real economy should be the basis for optimism not pessimism. I, for one, am only too eager to leave behind the anxiety mixed with empty hedonism of a debt-driven economy. We now have a pressing need to commit to creativity, transparency, honesty, accountability, and real prosperity.

Our Greek tragedy lies not only in the economic hole our irrational bingeing has left us with, but the moral, physical, environmental, and character hole. It is no surprise to me that skyrocketing obesity, approval of torture, toxic products from China, the burying of a perfectly functioning electric car (GM's EV-1), and the out-of-control cost of sick profiteering (mistakenly called health care) all happened to attend this delusional phase of our economy.

Thank you, Zeus. I would like to end this chapter by noting that Zeus' explication of the Quadrillion Dollar Scam implicitly included several key features of the State/Plutocracy partnership which are covered in other chapters:

1. The existence of a parallel, formal "shadow system" of banking and finance which is essentially State-sanctioned fraud and looting.

2. State sponsorship of private Financial Elites' risk-taking via guarantees, backstopping and bailouts.

3. Information asymmetry: the State and Financial Elites have knowledge of the "shadow system" which is not available to citizens or non-Elite investors.

4. The "stability" of the State/Plutocracy financial system is entirely illusory.

As illusions of stability give way to devolution, we turn next to Models of Transformation.

New concepts in this chapter:
Paradox of plenty
Counterfeit value
Parallel, formal "shadow system" of banking and finance
Information asymmetry

Chapter Seventeen: Models of Transformation

Given the inevitability of some fundamental transition within the next decade or two, it is equally inevitable that the human mind seeks some pattern, model or cycle that will help predict the coming Transformation.

There is an inherent (ontological) uncertainty in the human future because our own choices and actions shape that future. Thus any attempt to model or predict the future is in essence predicting human behaviors--a highly uncertain enterprise.

Nonetheless it is instructive to outline several models of "system transformation" based on human history.

I have already presented an abridged case for intersecting waves/cycles as causal factors in major transformations and briefly referenced the decline of the Roman Empire as an example of the political and psychological processes which enable dissolution: complacency and fatalism.

I have also recommended authors such as David Fischer (<u>The Great Wave: Price Revolutions and the Rhythm of History</u>), Jared Diamond (<u>Collapse: How Societies Choose to Fail or Succeed</u>) and Joseph Tainter (<u>The Collapse of Complex Societies</u>) who have carefully researched how cycles of price, conflict and resource depletion/exhaustion tend to repeat as human populations rise beyond the carrying capacity of their environment.

While historical models and cycles help us reach an integrated understanding of our era's interlocking crises, their predictive value is limited: some societies collapse while others are positively transformed by crisis. In some cases, we might view partial collapse as the first essential step of the transformative process.

Model 1: Collapse/Die-Off

This model is commonly known as "the end of the world as we know it" (TEOTWAWKI) and is by all accounts the worst-case scenario. The model's basic premise is that all the fragile supply chains and negative feedback loops (built-in stabilizers) of the global economy will fall in domino fashion. History provides some "stock" examples:

1. An extended period of bad weather causes drought/hunger which then triggers geopolitical conflict; together the two forces cause massive

declines in population and/or outmigration.

2. A new disease (plague or equivalent) spreads to populations with little resistance to the new microbe. The resulting pandemic weakens food production, trade and social organization which undermines public health in a positive feedback loop.

The advent of weapons of mass destruction and a fossil fuel-based global economy offer up two "modern" scenarios:

3. A global nuclear/biological/WMD war decimates populations and triggers breakdown of food production and supply chains when then causes further suffering/death.

4. The depletion of cheap, abundant fossil fuels triggers geopolitical conflicts which undermine the global economy and eventually civil society.

5. If global warming is not primarily a natural cycle but one caused by greenhouse gases, then runaway burning of coal, etc. triggers a meltdown of the polar ice caps which raises sea levels, flooding much of coastal civilization.

There are many variations but the basic model remains: resource/soil depletion and population over-reach that leave the human population vulnerable to typical long-cycle weather fluctuations. Once food, energy and water become scarce (the FEW resources), then resolution is sought by conquest/conflict which triggers positive feedback loops which further erode supply chains, public health, State-imposed stabilizers, etc.

To claim the present human populace is not exposed to just this sort of risk would be folly. However, claims that TEOTWAWKI is also inevitable tend to ignore negative feedback loops which act to stabilize systems.

No one can know the future, but we can safely observe that societies with little redundancy, few robust negative feedback loops and a culture steeped in complacency are much more likely to suffer a runaway (positive feedback/domino effect) "doomsday" scenario than those societies which actively anticipate the consequences of over-reach/depletion and which refuse to heed the siren-song of complacency.

Collapse, Dissolution and Devolution

The dissolution of the Soviet Union in the early 1990s provides a compelling example of the collapse of a large-scale, complex political structure. Author Dimitry Orlov made a fascinating comparison of the relative strengths and weaknesses of the U.S. and the Soviet Union in his book, Reinventing Collapse: The Soviet Example and American Prospects. By his own account, "entertaining and thought-provoking" were his goals for the book, and he succeeded very admirably.

Before we begin an analysis of Orlov's work, we should note that the Soviet Union did not collapse in the same fashion as Rome, the Khmer (Angkor) Empire or the Mayan civilization. Yes, death and crime rates rose and there was much suffering and deprivation, but the population of Moscow did not crash from millions to 10,000. The nations formed (or reformed) after the dissolution of the Soviet Empire possessed significant soil, water and energy resources, and each nation-state retained a political/social structure. Thus the Soviet collapse was not a TEOTWAWKI event--a collapse--as much as a dissolution of a large-scale political structure which left pre-existing social and cultural structures intact.

In my analysis, the dissolution of the Soviet Empire was an example of *devolution* rather than collapse.

Devolution can be understood as a slide down the complexity scale: the piecemeal dissolution or erosion of highly complex systems to simpler structures and less energy-intensive states.

Devolution is thus the necessary and positive evolution of an unsustainable system into a less complex, less energy-intensive, more sustainable and thus more stable state of affairs.

The reason devolution gathers irresistible force is that all the people who are feeding at the trough of the complex, high-cost status quo (think of the 16% of the U.S. economy devoted to "healthcare") will resist any decline in their share of the national income.

Thus the system becomes ever more brittle and vulnerable as gradual adaptation to a lower-cost, less energy-intensive state is rejected in favor of holding a stagnating status quo together with accounting trickery (borrowing billions from future tax revenues, for example), propaganda exhortations and ever larger loans.

Having resisted meaningful adaptation as a way to resolve the overly complex, financially unsustainable status quo, those feeding at the trough guarantee its chaotic devolution: various subsystems break down in piecemeal fashion, in effect falling haphazardly down the stairs of complexity until it reaches a sustainable level.

We cannot predict the exact timing of this descent, but we can safely predict the final base of sustainability will be far below current status quo levels. Thus auto/truck sales reached 17 million vehicles a year in the U.S. during the credit-housing bubble boom times. Now that they've fallen down the staircase to 9 million units a year, two of the Big Three U.S.-based auto companies (high-cost, requiring huge energy inputs to manage the pensions, union negotiations, administration, marketing, etc., not to mention actually manufacture vehicles) have been driven into bankruptcy. Sustainable North American vehicle sales might even be less than 9 million a year.

Those feeding at the trough of each industry/State fiefdom will find the reduction in complexity, jobs and revenue painful, but "unsustainable" means just that. Change of some sort cannot be denied, and so the choice is adaptation/evolution, devolution or collapse.

Model 2: Dissolution of the Soviet Union

Orlov makes the case that the U.S. is actually less prepared and thus more vulnerable to social disorder/collapse than the old Soviet Union. This comparison is an excellent way to explore various vulnerabilities and possible remedies; it also serves to highlight the great cultural differences between nation-states.

Cultural and technological systems/feedback loops such as organized churches and the Web which might well prove critical in the years ahead were weak or nonexistent in the Soviet Union circa 1990. Thus cultural anthropology is as important to any integrated understanding as economic and resource metrics (oil consumption, food production, GDP, etc.).

A comparison of nation-states should remind us that any analysis of interlocking crises must be grounded in a specific land/climate and culture with a unique history, set of values and political/social systems. One set of solutions will most certainly not fit all.

Thus the insolvency of the U.S. Federal and local governments and/or the devaluation of the U.S. dollar which I anticipate as inevitable would, barring a trigger such as pandemic or WMD war, most likely lead to a similar devolution of State control rather than "the end of the world as we know it."

Here is my critique of Orlov's valuable analysis:

1. The collapse of the USSR was a political act. The USA is facing a resource-depletion-financial crisis. Now a financial collapse (K-Wave "winter," or the repudiation of all debts, public and private) certainly could lead to political collapse, but that is by no means inevitable.

The cultural and structural differences between the USSR and the USA are significant, and if Orlov had been an anthropologist his book might have drawn different distinctions. His primary thesis is that the Soviet Union was actually better prepared to weather collapse than the U.S., but I think he missed this critical difference: Russia and the other constituent states of the former USSR were stil resource-rich.

The delivery system for what I call the FEW Essentials (food, energy, water) was decrepit and inefficient, but there was plenty of oil, natural gas, wheat (Ukraine), water and know-how in a relatively well-educated citizenry. The problems were all basically political in nature: a failed totalitarian Nanny State could no longer deliver the goods and services it had controlled.

The U.S. will be dealing with an entirely different set of problems: systemic financial implosion, and shortages in resources that were once abundant: energy and water (in the West). Those limitations in resources present problems beyond mere political corruption and incompetence. In other words, if the U.S. faces a bigger challenge, it's because the problems are far deeper than a failed political structure.

Here in the U.S., the political problem is our system's inability to tackle long-term problems with any sort of foresight and rationality, but that does not necessarily lead to political collapse. The USSR was a totalitarian "Nanny State" (what I term a Savior State) par excellence-- you needed political approval to go to college, to take a job, to buy food, to move to another city--your entire life was governed by the State, which "promised" to take care of you in a fashion captured perfectly by the wry Soviet-era joke, "We pretend to work and they pretend to pay us."

The U.S. has certainly evolved into a Savior State in many ways, but we should be careful not to exaggerate this weakness. Many people in the U.S. are still quite capable of doing things for themselves, including organizing their community around goals the government is either botching or ignoring. As the economy declines and tax revenues dry up, and government at every level spends more and more of its revenues paying interest on old and new debts, then the path of least resistance for government is not collapse but devolution and irrelevance.

Once people realize the Gravy Train has tumbled off the tracks and the government no longer has the money to throw tens of billions at every "problem," then they'll eventually stop trying to get blood from a turnip, i.e. demanding something from the government which the government no longer has--"free" money.

Recall that much of the U.S. government spending depends on borrowing trillions of dollars from willing trading partners. Once they're no longer willing, or no longer have the surplus capital to lend, that source of "free money" dries up. And then so must Federal spending. No more "free" money is made worse by the politically inconvenient reality that we have to pay interest on all the trillions we've already borrowed, and that's running into the hundreds of billions even with interest rates at generational lows.

When the U.S. Savior State becomes financially unviable, as it surely will when we can no longer borrow trillions of dollars from foreign creditors every year, then many people will be distraught that the government can't give them "free" money. But that doesn't necessarily mean the government simply vanishes into thin air; it could still ration gasoline and food, as it did rather successfully in World War II, or fix prices and wages as it did in the Korean War; government can still regulate the economy at a very low cost.

What will go away in the U.S. is the trillions of dollars expended on entitlements like Medicare and boondoggles like Homeland Security. As the speculative profits and transactional churn has dried up, so have tax revenues; the only bills the Federal government really truly has to pay is Defense, its own bloated payroll and interest on the National Debt, which will be growing by leaps and bounds as interest rates rise.

But issuing regulations is very cheap, and so I would expect government to continue doing what is cheap and easy, i.e. regulate, and devolve away from what's expensive, i.e. entitlements and government programs which cost hundreds of billions each year.

Another key difference between the USSR and the USA is that if you stood up and confronted the government there, you were taken away; in the U.S., you're a hero/heroine. That is not to say you can't or won't be dragged off if you challenge the U.S. government on its home ground, but let's not be coy--if you do so, you're widely considered a hero/heroine.

From Daniel Ellsberg on down, people who work around the government or protest its over-reach are admired and encouraged in the U.S., which continues to have an increasingly unmanageable/irrepressible free press (the blogosphere and the Web).

Furthermore, despite being stressed, distracted and brainwashed by the mass media, Americans still retain a vestigial distrust of elites and governmental over-reach. The entire anti-gun-control issue is fundamentally an expression of this skepticism of the State and the Elites who run it.

For every American who will whine when their government check fails to arrive, there will be another American who declares, "good riddance." I am not an expert on the former Soviet Union, but from what I have read (these three volumes are a good start: Gulag Archipelago: 1918-1956, Gulag Archipelago 2 and Gulag Archipelago 3), the cultural traits which enabled people to survive such brutality and repression were endurance and fortitude.

Foreigners have long overestimated the weakness of average Americans; as far back as the Revolutionary era, it was commonly held that Americans were too rich and too lazy to makes sacrifices; and so the bloody footprints left on the snow by Washington's ragtag soldiers were a nasty surprise to the Empire. (The British Empire, that is.)

In World War II, the Japanese Empire expected the U.S. to quickly negotiate a peace advantageous to Japan after Pearl Harbor and the U.S. defeats in the Philippines and elsewhere. But instead, they were treated to U.S. suicide attacks at the pivotal Battle of Midway (40 torpedo planes lost out of 41, a suicidal attack without fighter cover) and the subsequent loss of the cream of their Navy, four aircraft carriers sunk within 10 minutes by the gutless, complacent, lazy, etc. Americans. From that day on, Japan was reduced to a defensive war they were destined to lose.

Hitler famously declared the U.S. a "mongrel nation," and we all know how long his 1000-year Reich lasted and who won the war. So perhaps the people of the former USSR and the seemingly indulgent, soft, lazy Americans have a bit more in common than Mr. Orlov detects.

Which brings us to another key difference:

2. The Soviet Union was not a nation of immigrants; the U.S. is and has been since its inception. Even the Native Americans came from somewhere else, albeit a long time ago (though 12,000 years is merely a blink in geological time). Now on the surface immigration is driven by a number of things: hunger, poverty, desire for religious freedom, etc. But fundamentally it is a form of natural selection. Among any group of people, there will be some who look around at the poverty, corruption, hopelessness and lack of opportunity for non-elite people and decide the best way to change their lives is to leave.

Inevitably, many people don't rouse themselves to that challenge, and they stay put. Who would you bet on when the chips are down, the folks that sweated blood and took huge risks to claw their way into a better place, or those who hung back?

I know many immigrants, from Asia, Europe, Latin America, the Caribbean, etc., and I believe it is fair to say that the average immigrant of any generation did not come here seeking a Nanny State; that was often the motivation for them to leave, along with political and religious repression, poverty, endemic corruption, venal elites, and so on.

As times get tough, then some recent immigrants will pull up stakes and return to their nation of origin. Others will stick it out; still others will have no choice but to stay. In any event, immigrants tend to understand that all government is contingent; if you want to change your circumstances, then you get moving. Sure, as long as the handouts are available, then everyone will line up to get "their fair share" of the freebies. But when the freebies disappear, then life goes on, and those with the drive and perseverance to get here will probably manage to survive.

As a nation populated by recent immigrants (and 100 years is nothing in old cultures like India, China and Russia), the U.S. has certain (along with other immigrant nations) advantages just in terms of brutally non-politically-correct natural selection.

3. Religion plays a unique and powerful role in the U.S. in ways which it did not in the USSR. A quick glance at Russian art suggests the central role of the Church in Russian culture. But if Orlov were African-American, I believe his dismissal of religion might not have been so quick and assured.

Rather than the non-factor Orlov expects, I would reckon religious institutions will play critical roles in organizing people for their own betterment. People didn't come here to ignore their religion, they came here to practice it, and that goes for every religion. It's been said that the black church is the only institution owned lock, stock and barrel by the African-American community, and it will be a central institution of stability, hope and communal reciprocity in that community.

I lived in central Detroit in the summer of 1968 as one of two Caucasian families in about 4 square miles, and I did not see churches reduced to non-factors. I wouldn't underestimate the role of churches, temples, mosques and synagogues in the coming era of turmoil, but would instead expect their influence to grow along with their roles in the community. Churches are populated with imperfect human beings, so they are of course imperfect as well. But when hardship presses, many Americans will turn to their church for more than weddings and occasional spiritual solace.

4. Wandering around as a homeless migrant is not a good survival strategy. Orlov suggests at the end of his book that wandering between two or three sources of food and shelter would be a good strategy. My own view is that freeloading is frowned upon in the U.S. and your best bet to is either stay put (yes, even urban neighborhoods) or move to a place where you have some roots (where you grew up is always a good place to start) or where there is some commonality: a church you belong to, an ecosystem you love and will nurture, etc.

I also think the value of hard work and generosity is still valued in the U.S. If you pitch in and start growing some food, and then share it, you will quickly become a valued member of the community and people will start looking out for you, too.

Wandering around freeloading is a good way to be scorned and loathed. Even in the grittiest neighborhoods, food can be grown in amazing abundance once people put their minds and backs to it.

5. The U.S. is on par with Sadr City, Iraq in terms of firepower in the hands of citizens. As the most heavily armed society in the developed world, the U.S. can easily go the way of well-armed criminal gangs controlling urban zones or well-armed militia sprouting up to take out the criminals. There are historical precedents for either scenario. A third scenario (common in the 3rd World) is for wealthy enclaves to hire private forces to protect the enclave.

While I can't predict which will play out in various circumstances, we should be aware that the U.S. has millions of military veterans and millions of weapons. The USSR had the vets but not the weapons in private hands. People will eventually choose to support an alternative to criminal/gang rule, unless the criminal gang is the only alternative to something worse. Or people will pay extra to maintain a community police force and let go of the other city services, performing them communally via volunteer labor.

My point is simply that a heavily armed culture with tens of millions of firearm-trained vets is not going to follow the route of a society without those two elements.

6. Orlov underestimates the power of the Web/Internet. Orlov is extending his experience in a pre-Internet Russia, in which you had to stand outside in the cold in order to catch a ride. Assuming the Internet backbone will be maintained--and why wouldn't it be placed ahead of every other utility except electricity itself?--then virtually everyone will be able to arrange barters of almost unimaginable range via the Web.

"I need a ride to San Jose and have a bag of fresh lettuce and green beans to trade," etc. It doesn't take much imagination to see how the Web will be leveraged to arrange trade, barter and a vast array of self-organizing groups and alliances.

7. The U.S. has a free press via the Web. As long as Americans turn to the entertainment industry (CNBC, cable "news", etc.) for their "information," then the U.S. faces the enormous disadvantage of a populace in the grip of propaganda-induced fantasy/denial. But the Web (should it be maintained, of course, either officially or unofficially) offers unlimited freedom of expression and exchange of ideas, innovations, practical solutions and communion.

In the brutally totalitarian USSR, free expression was passed literally from hand to hand via Samizdat documents, a form of exchange which was inherently limited. With the Web in private hands, and thus difficult to control even with a vast army of State employees (in China, this army and its vast network of surveillance equipment is called "The Great Firewall of China"), the U.S. has the supreme advantage of free expression and the free flow of information and knowledge.

8. The U.S. value-system still fosters individual initiative. A repressive central State is inherently threatened by self-organizing technologies--thus repressive regimes and kleptocracies restrict or cut off the Web, SMS (texting), cell phones, public gatherings of more than four people, etc., when they sense an aroused citizenry is threatening their power/control.

A repressive central State also seeks to suppress individual initiative (via work and residence permits and other restraints) and any group which has the potential to become a force of resistance--and that boils down to any group but the Party/Elite itself. The State then spends an inordinate percentage of the national income on spying, surveillance and repression--income which could have been spent productively.

Thus State repression acts as a staggeringly large tax on national productivity. As the cost and energy required to support this systemic repression rises, it reaches a point of brittle unsustainability. At that point, the State will devolve, dissolve or collapse.

It seems fair to say the Soviet Union was just such a repressive central State. Despite the domestic spying capabilities of the U.S. government and the mind-numbing ubiquity of the marketing/mass media machinery, it is also fair to say that the U.S. still values individual initiative. This is embodied in the cliche phrase "think globally, act locally."

In other words, a significant number of Americans still recognize that change does not flow from policy tweaks and decrees as much as from individual initiative, self-organizing movements and "meme"/ ideas which spread in "viral" fashion via self-organizing technologies which are largely outside the control of the central State.

As noted earlier: the Remnant leads not by decree or exhortation but by action and example. A society in which any Remnant has been brutally suppressed will be at an extreme disadvantage compared to cultures which have allowed, however grudgingly, individual initiative and self-organizing movements.

Modeling Devolution

The dissolution of the Soviet Union can be understood as the devolution of a large-scale, top-level political institution--the Soviet state/Empire--and its ruling Elite: the Communist Party. Once that structure dissolved, it exposed older political units: the nations of Russia, Ukraine, etc., and nascent nation-states such as Uzbekistan. The demise of the top-level Empire also freed other large-scale structures to emerge from the shadows: the Orthodox Christian Church, for example.

Other large-scale institutions, such as the domestic security and intelligence agencies, essentially retained their identity and role in the State. With the economic controls of the State diminished or dissolved, then an existing underground enterprise--the Russian Mafia--expanded (in a case of windfall exploitation) into the vacuum left by the central planning institutions of the old USSR.

While we cannot generalize much about the process of devolution, we can conclude that any analysis of devolution must tease apart each institution's devolution, evolution or expansion. In other words, the top-level political structure can dissolve but leave a strong network of still-robust institutions in place to knit the economy and society together, even in the absence of a central state.

In other situations, it may be the state religion which devolves, or financial institutions, as in the global investment banking-speculative implosion of 2008. The devolution of major structures, State or non-State, can trigger devolutions in related institutions and eventually in the economy or society at large.

But devolution is not limited to institutions; cultural values can also devolve, with supremely negative consequences.

We should be alive to the subtle but very real devolution in the cultural warp and woof which knits the society and economy together: the work ethic, sense of common purpose, martial spirit, pride in workmanship and business integrity, even the collective sense of optimism. Once these values devolve, as they did in the Roman Empire, then the devolution is reflected in the devolution of institutions which rely on shared purpose, pride in quality and integrity, the willingness to defend the nation-state, etc.

Once the shared values and the large-scale institutions both devolve, then the society and economy as a whole are vulnerable to positive feedback loops (self-reinforcing trends) and thus eventual collapse.

How people react to the devolution of their lifestyles and financial security depends in large part on their belief in the system (if they truly believed the propaganda, then their response will proceed quickly through disbelief and shock to resentful anger) and their spiritual value system. If they considered a middle class life of travel, dining out, numerous electronic toys, full healthcare insurance, a university education and a suburban home as their "right," then the devolution of this lifestyle will strike them particularly hard.

Those with less grandiose expectations will tend to be more adaptive and more amenable to a positive outlook despite the devolution of their wealth and income.

Physical infrastructure can also devolve; as roadways fall into disrepair, then trade declines, reducing the national income and wealth. If aqueducts and canals run dry or become overgrown, then urban centers and productive lands are abandoned for lack of water.

Thus we need to be alert to devolution on three interconnected levels: the political/financial, the physical and the shared-values/spiritual/cultural.

As noted above, devolution can be part of a larger process of evolution, what economist Joseph Schumpeter called *creative destruction*. That is, systems and enterprises that have grown overly complex, costly, inefficient and energy-intensive will topple of their own weight, clearing the way for leaner, more innovative and more sustainable replacements.

But this is by no means certain. If the core shared values of quality, integrity, good governance (which requires transparency and participation), willingness to defend the State and a common purpose have devolved into sycophancy, narcissism, self-aggrandizement, self-deception, fraud, sloth, torpor, addictions to amusements and self-absorption, then the willingness to rework institutions and enterprises has also been lost. Failed institutions and enterprises will not be replaced; citizens will drift into unproductive but stable impoverishment under the protection of local fiefdoms.

In other cases, the will to evolve and rebuild may exist but the resistance offered by the remaining Elites will be so fierce that the only possible outcome is collapse of the structures and institutions they defended from change.

That terrible possibility is the reason I have spent so much of this analysis focusing on the ways that the State and Plutocracy influence and control not just the national income and wealth but the intellectual framework which enables their dominance.

If each citizen dismantles that intellectual framework in his or her own mind, then the physical and financial control wielded by the State and Plutocracy will become exceedingly vulnerable to positive devolution, a devolution caused by opting out (when belief in the system fades), the renunciation of complacency and fatalism and the rejection of the propaganda spewed by the marketing/mass media complex.

As failing institutions and conceptual frameworks devolve, new self-organizing structures and positive values are free to emerge, as are darker forces. That is what life requires: adaptation and evolution. Self-destruction is always an option.

The Special Case of Energy Devolution

The depletion of high energy-density, easily transportable fossil fuels will necessarily cause a pervasive devolution of the global economy.

I am indebted to John Michael Greer, author of The Long Descent: A User's Guide to the End of the Industrial Age and The Ecotechnic Future: Envisioning a Post-Peak World for his clear-eyed explorations of Peak Oil/depletion consequences.

To achieve an integrated understanding of energy devolution we need these key concepts:

- energy density (concentration)
- energy portability
- extraction costs/net energy gain
- Liebig's Law (production is limited by the scarcest resource)
- diminishing output/surplus

Oil is a unique energy source: it is a very concentrated energy source (high energy-density) and it is relatively efficient to transport: stable at room temperature, can be pumped in pipelines or shipped by sea, rail, truck, etc. Until recently, much of the world's oil had a very low cost of extraction: the super-giant fields which provided the bulk of the world's oil were under pressure, meaning little extraction technology was required.

That has changed, heralding Peak Oil. Now super-giant fields require costly extraction technologies (water or gas injection, etc.) and new fields are found in deep water or in harsh Arctic environments which drives extraction costs up.

Shale oil and tar sands provide an example of extraction costs/net energy gain: it requires an equivalent of a barrel of oil (in natural gas, water, post-extraction remediation, etc.) to extract and process 1.5 barrels of oil equivalent from tons of tar sands/shale. The net energy gain is thus quite modest.

In various other settings, hydrocarbon deposits may well require more than a barrel of oil of energy to recover a barrel of new fossil fuel: at that point, the net energy gain is zero.

Many of the alternative energy sources which are presented as "renewable" actually require vast inputs of energy for manufacture, installation and maintenance of the plant. Thus the net energy gain from various biofuels can, depending on the input calculations and the political agenda of the calculators, be marginally net positive or actually negative.

Other schemes such as tidal energy, etc. require permanently high maintenance costs. Nuclear energy has two issues which must be resolved politically: storage of waste and operational safety. Nations such as the U.S. are unable to resolve these issues; centrally controlled economies have been able to impose or manufacture political resolution.

Most alternative energy schemes share one drawback: they essentially gather low-density energy (sun, tides, biofuels, wind, etc.) into easily stored and transported concentrations/ energy densities, and that process is inherently expensive/energy-intensive.

The one "easy" high-density source, hydropower, has largely already been exploited. Geothermal has the potential of tapping high-energy density heat deep in the Earth, but the costs of drilling and maintaining a well 2 miles/3 kilometers deep are very high and possibly prohibitive. In seismically active regions, deep wells apparently have the potential to trigger earthquakes.

As the cheaply extracted oil is depleted, energy costs rise and Liebig's Law becomes a factor in all economic activity: production is limited by the scarcest resource. Thus a mine might have rich deposits of ore but if it is far from energy sources, then the cost of energy will limit production.

As the cost of energy (extracting, concentrating, processing and transporting) rises, so too do virtually all costs throughout the economy. Measured by surplus output, higher energy costs are in essence a heavy tax which lowers surplus/net output of the entire economy.

This devolution of surplus sets up a terrible irony: just as the need arises to invest trillions of dollars to construct an alternative energy complex, the surpluses generated by the economy go into steep decline.

This is what I term *the paradox of energy cost/supply*: once depletion drives energy costs up to the point that alternatives to fossil fuels become financially viable, the economy's surpluses have been reduced to the point the economy can no longer afford to build an alternative energy complex.

To anticipate permanently higher energy costs is to invest funds for low returns; but to wait until costs justify the investment, it's too late to rely on surpluses to fund the investment.

Thus the only alternative to running out of energy (in any form or density) is that other spending must be curtailed to fund the new energy infrastructure. This devolution of the economy is the ontological end-state of oil depletion/rising energy costs/shrinking output surpluses.

Printing $10 trillion to pay for the needed energy infrastructure might be tempting, but such an explosion of fiat money which was not based on actual surplus output would simply destroy the currency being printed, bringing another form of ruin to the economy.

There are no short-cuts: ultimately, only surplus output can be spent or invested. The market will quickly catch "cheating" like creating $10 trillion out of thin air and attempting to pass it off as surplus output; the cheaters will end up with a ruined economy and no new energy production.

The Financial Causes of Devolution

To understand the devolution of the global economy (macro) and our own communities (micro), we need to look up the chain of fallen dominoes to the first one: credit.

The debauchery of credit reached its perfection in the housing bubble. Credit, leverage and speculative fraud came to dominate the global economy: the global housing boom depended entirely on abundant credit at low interest rates, leveraged, securitized debt instruments (mortgage backed securities, CDOs, credit default swaps, etc.) and speculative fraud: housing-backed investment securities fraudulently rated and sold as "low-risk," property appraisals fraudulently jacked higher than market, mortgage applications backed with fraudulently stated income, and high-risk "toxic" exotic mortgages fraudulently presented and sold as "low-risk because the property value is rising."

Household income for all but the top 10% "high-caste" technocracy has been stagnant since the mid-1970s. Consumer spending, which made up 70% of the U.S. economy and a significant share of the global

GDP, was totally dependent on the housing bubble in three ways:

1. Direct equity extraction via re-financing and HELOCs (home equity lines of credit)

2. The "wealth effect": for the 69% of households who owned a home, their home equity was their chief asset and the vast bulk of their wealth. As that rose, it fed the "animal spirits" so beloved by economists: as people feel wealthier, they spend more freely.

3. The housing bubble created vast new wealth for the middle class and the Elite alike due to the huge transactional churn of tens of millions of houses built and sold, then sold again and again, tens of millions of mortgages originated and then refinanced, tens of millions of new insurance policies written for ever larger amounts, tens of millions of new furniture sales, etc.

As for the Elite (the Plutocracy), the transactional churn was in immensely profitable derivatives and mortgage-backed securities, and a stock market rising on this bubbly "prosperity." The top hedge fund managers averaged $600 million a year in compensation each while investment banks distributed tens of billions a year in bonuses.

Now the credit bubble has burst and credit is devolving everywhere. The stock market is encountering a spot of bother this morning as it's been discovered (gasp) that consumers are actually saving rather than spending every dollar (and then some) of their income. The signs of credit devolution are everywhere:

- Credit card and HELOC limits are being dropped
- Credit card issuance has plummeted
- Credit card delinquency has risen to 10%
- The market for mortgage-backed securities (MBS) has imploded to near-zero
- The qualification standards for mortgages have risen

The devolution of global credit and the return of risk aversion means that the transactional churn which created so much of the wealth of the bubble has collapsed.

Even more devastating, the bubble-era asset valuations have also devolved, destroying most of the bubble's illusory rise in home equity. This means the homeowner has no collateral on which to base future borrowing/debt; thus no matter how cheap and abundant credit might be, there is no foundation for additional credit.

The "wealth effect" has devolved as well; people now feel (rightly) much poorer, and their response is to start saving after a decade of euphoric credit0based spending.

The government also debauched credit on a vast scale. The quasi-governmental (and now fully Federally backed) mortgage mills, Freddie Mac and Fannie Mae. churned out over $5 trillion in suspect mortgages. The Treasury borrowed additional trillions, largely from China, Japan and the Gulf oil exporters, to fund the expansion of empire and the distribution of "free money" to vast entitlement programs like Medicare which enriched a vast network of profitably parasitic enterprises.

Now the U.S. is borrowing $2 trillion a year just to maintain the status quo. The notion that every government on the planet can borrow vast sums each and every year, running stupendous deficits to prop up the status quo, and do so indefinitely, will soon be revealed as impossible. Credit cannot rise exponentially while assets, incomes and profits devolve.

At some point the demand for credit (deficit spending) will outstrip the supply of surplus capital and global interest rates will skyrocket. At that point the global game of "quantitative easing" and propping up the status quo with borrowed money will quickly devolve, as will the illusion that any government can repeal the business cycle and inflate additional asset bubbles at will to prop up consumer spending and tax revenues.

As income, profits and assets all devolve, tax revenues devolve, too.

Local and state governments have grown accustomed to ever higher employee counts, ever higher wages and ever richer benefits. The collapse of tax revenues is now causing state and local spending to contract and the services they provided to devolve.

So the devolution of credit led to the devolution of asset valuations/collateral, income, profits and thus tax revenues. All those dominoes are now toppling the one with the greatest impact on households: jobs. Add in the structural causes covered in *Chapter Fourteen: The End of (Paying) Work* and the devolution of household finances and the high-cost, energy-profligate American lifestyle is not just predictable but inevitable.

The Devolution of the U.S. Economy and State

Devolution is both the process of degeneration and the surrender of governmental powers from central authorities to local authorities.

Devolution will take many forms.

The key driver behind devolution is simple: there's no longer enough money to fund the status quo, so something has to be cut, axed, trimmed or devolved. Examples already abound: the number of school days in the year is reduced to shave expenses, two-times-a-week trash pickup is cut to once a week, etc.

The key constraint on devolution is also simple: the status quo power structure must be left intact.

Nobody will willingly surrender their power, so devolution means services and front-end expenses will be cut in order to protect back-end administrative powers.

Thus public union bosses won't be suffering any big cuts in pay or benefits, and neither will their municipal and state administration counterparts. (Of course there will be minor symbolic cuts for PR purposes.) What will be cut is part-time librarians, custodians, county park staff, etc.--the powerless people who actually serve the public.

As the states run out of money, they will surrender some limited powers to local authorities as a mechanism for ridding their budgets of certain costs. As cities and counties go broke, then they will devolve some modest authority to non-profit groups or volunteers.

As laid off workers' unemployment insurance runs out (yes, even the extensions run out as the states' UI funds drain to zero) then their lifestyles devolve/degrade: first, eating out and vacations go, then new clothing, then the second car, then college, then the house, and so on.

Devolution is a painful process, but the State (all government at all levels) and the Plutocracy (owners of capital and productive assets) vastly prefer devolution to revolution because devolution doesn't threaten the status quo.

Devolution depends on humanity's innate ability to habituate to nearly anything. Humans somehow adapt to concentration camps, bitter cold, intolerable heat, mind-numbing work, etc., especially if the new environment is introduced over time in stages.

Thus the middle class household might actually respond with an anger deep and hot enough to become political if their middle-class lifestyle was taken away in one swoop. But devolution insures that the process is akin to the famous analogy of the boiled frog: if the temperature of the water is increased slowly enough, the frog never notices (or so the story goes) that he is being boiled alive.

The formerly middle class household forced to sell everything and move (surreptitiously) into a storage locker or into an RV will feel a shock of recognition that all has been lost, and that perhaps forces beyond their own personal decisions might be at work: forces which benefited from Federal bailouts, for instance, in a way they can never hope to. (That $150 billion transferred through AIG to Goldman Sachs could have funded a very large national unemployment insurance pool.)

But if their middle class life is taken away from them over time, in pieces, they will habituate to each discrete loss without any political enlightenment; they have fully internalized the propaganda (and recall the mass media is owned by less than 10 global corporations) that the "problem" is their own, not "the system's."

A revolution occurs when great numbers of people realize that the system benefits the Powers That Be, not the citizenry, despite the status quo's constant assurances that this is the very best system on Earth.

So the surest way to secure one's lofty privileges and powers is to convince the people who have lost everything that it's all their own fault; if they were just smarter, possessed more degrees, had better judgment, weren't hooked on anti-depressants, etc., then they would be jolly, wealthy, etc.

In a similar fashion, local government will attempt to manage the degeneration of their services in such a way that the public does not realize it's being boiled. If the trains and buses all stopped running, people might be angry enough to turn off their TVs and demand some actual, real political change. But if services are slowly degraded over time, the public will sigh and habituate to it.

Meanwhile, the police chief, mayor, union bigwigs, et al. will be driving by in their chauffeured vehicles, making sure "the little people" are swallowing the devolution whole. The politicos' Masters, the Plutocracy who fund their campaigns, will fill their coffers at election time as long as nothing rocks the boat. If the citizenry gets restive, then the politicos will find their funding drying up (Heaven forbid!).

Many examples of devolution are already visible in both households and local government, and we can expect these trends to strengthen as the Depression deepens. Devolution of credit, leverage, assets and collateral lead to devolution of sales, transactions and profits which lead to devolution of income, jobs and thus of tax revenues. These are positive feedback loops, self-reinforcing and cross-reinforcing: income declines feed asset devaluations which reduces credit and business formation which leaves commercial space empty and essentially worthless, reducing tax revenues even further which triggers public-sector layoffs, and so on.

Household/private sector examples:

1. Devolution of "storage nation": Listings on craigslist announcing the selling/giving away of the entire contents of storage lockers will rise.

2. The number of people living in storage lockers "illegally" will rise.

3. The dumping of abandoned clothing, furniture, old computer equipment, etc. on sidewalks and public parks/byways will increase dramatically.

4. Homeless camps will appear in parks and locales which were previously considered off-limits to such public poverty.

5. Spontaneous protests (over evictions, reductions in service, public union strikes, etc.) will increase both in frequency and in the number of participants.

6. Tourism will devolve to visiting relatives and/or car camping; hotels and restaurants in tourist-dependent locales will start closing in ever increasing numbers. Only the top 10% "high-caste" professional and government-technocrat class will be able to travel overseas.

7. Houses that were snapped up in 2009 for $350,000 on the basis that they once sold for $550,000 will be auctioned for less than $200,000 in late 2010.

8. Major rock/pop concert tours will be cancelled due to low ticket sales; acts which were "guaranteed to mint millions" will cancel their tours.

9. Veterinarians will demand cash to examine pets; people will increasingly be unable to pay for costly procedures for their pets (teeth cleaning, hip replacements, chemotherapy, etc.). Vets will consolidate/close their doors.

Consider the last example as part of the devolution of America's prosperity-fueled spending on pets. As vets consolidate, they will leave commercial space empty, eventually prompting property-owner bankruptcies and reductions in tax revenues. As people move/are evicted/consolidate, pets will increasingly be abandoned, falling into a public animal-care system which will increasingly dependent on volunteers and private donations (authority and control devolving to communities and small organizations).

State/local government examples:

1. Citizens with numerous outstanding traffic tickets will abandon their vehicles when "booted" (locked) by cities as the cars are worth less that the fines due. Cities will start auctioning/scrapping hundreds of abandoned vehicles.

2. The number of citizens cited/arrested for unpaid moving and parking violations will rise; judges will begin dismissing the amounts due as the citizens before them have no means of paying the huge fines.

3. Government at all levels will devote increasing resources to revenue collection; new laws giving the State (all levels of government) new powers to strip-mine private assets will be passed with strong support from government-dependent special-interests.

4. Government at all levels will assign or create domestic intelligence assets to the search for additional tax revenues.

5. Cities which were previously considered immune to the "recession" will declare losses and huge layoffs.

6. Local governments outside of the Rust Belt will start aggressively taking over abandoned houses as banks fail and ownership of the properties becomes ambiguous.

7. Local government fines, fees, permits and other business-related licensing will plummet, decimating what was once considered a "safe" revenue stream.

8. State and local government services will rapidly devolve: twice-a-week trash pickup will devolve to once a week; fire stations, libraries and schools will be consolidated; other services will become sporadic.

9. State and local government hikes in fees to use parks, park downtown, drop junk at the dump, get a building permit, etc. will backfire: people will stop going to parks, stop shopping downtown, start dumping junk at night on quiet streets now that the dump is too expensive and start remodeling without permits. Contrary to government expectations, revenues will actually drop faster after all these fees are raised.

10. State/county attempts to openly raise taxes will increasingly trigger tax rebellions and demonstrations; the trickle of residents leaving high-tax states and counties will grow to a flood.

The political propaganda which infuses every moment of our lives tries to maintain an artificial distinction between our Tweedledum and Tweedledee political parties: The Dees are all for using the power of the

State to "help the little people" while the Dums are all for unleashing the power of "free enterprise," a.k.a. the 1% who control the capital and 2/3 of all productive assets in the nation.

The truth is that the State and the Plutocracy are two sides of one coin; each rules with the support and complicity of the other. The distinction drawn between them is a useful distraction, somewhat like drawing a distinction between professional sports teams who swap players in the off-season. "My team" is an abstraction which serves the goal of enriching its owners; "fan" loyalty draws smirks from everyone in the know even as they proclaim "fan day" and "fan appreciation day." (The cross-town rival team is of course "the hated enemy.")

As we watch devolution in action over the next decade, observe how it is managed so the hapless frog won't jump from the pot. That is what the State and Elites are counting on, of course; a devolution passively accepted by a media-duped, gadget-addicted, self-blaming, depressed, drugged-out populace which leaves the Powers That Be fully intact.

Model 3: The 1960s as Global Model of Social, Economic and Political Innovation, Experimentation and Transformation

In the course of this analysis we've looked at various historical events to deepen our understanding of the present. Each of these eras-- the 13th century, the Great Depression of the 1930s, the end of the Soviet Union and the devolution of the Roman Empire--has features which parallel our own era of interconnected crises.

Even periods of history which seem to have little in common in terms of economic challenges can offer telling parallels in cultural and conceptual devolution.

Thus it seems to me that the period of global cultural and conceptual ferment, the 1960s and early 1970s, may provide us with a largely unappreciated model of devolution: as trusted institutions are revealed as hopelessly corrupt and compromised, as official lies and deceptions which served as foundations of State policy are exposed, then "belief in the system fades."

This institutional betrayal of public trust and the violation of the principles underpinning common interests then triggers anger: betrayal, either personal or social, destroys trust and seeds rage.

Liberated from the social and economic constraints imposed by the

Status Quo, the populace experiences a burst of innovation and experimentation: suddenly, anything is possible.

The history of trust and betrayal in the U.S. began with the stupendous Federal government role as "Savior" during the Great Depression.

Though the programs were largely ad hoc and not as successful as nostalgia now demands, the general sense was that the Central State was acting in the best interests of most of its citizens and was making good-faith efforts to alleviate their suffering and insecurity.

This faith and trust in the Federal government was further enhanced by the gargantuan enterprise of winning a global war (World War II). The government called upon its people to arise to great sacrifice of blood and toil, and in return the government would not only win the war against implacably evil enemies but restore hope and prosperity.

No doubt to the amazement of skeptics and critics, the government did exactly that. Yes, there were mistakes and fumbles and conflicts galore, and even more sacrifices demanded in the Korean War and the Cold War, yet the general sense was the government had earned the trust of its citizenry by serving the broad interests of that citizenry.

Just as the secrecy required during wartime extended seamlessly into the nuclear-armed Cold War era, so too did the Savior State ethos of the Great Depression. Thus vast new powers and social welfare programs were enacted in the 1950s and 60s, and the hundred-year old injustice of segregation was slowly chipped away.

Despite all its inherent flaws, it seemed the Federal government was on "the right side of history" at every major turn, and generally acting on behalf of its citizenry.

But the demands of global conflict--the Cold War against the Soviet Empire and other Communist totalitarian regimes such as China--instilled a fear in the American Elites that perhaps the American people were not capable of the judgment required by the era. Thus secrecy seeped from military and intelligence matters into policy, and the propaganda machine which had worked so well in the 1940s and 50s to whip up patriotic duty and sacrifice was tasked with persuading the public with wartime-like prevarications and deceptions.

The Vietnam War was never a declared war, as dictated by the U.S. Constitution; fearing the public might not support its flawed policies, the Johnson Administration ginned up a propaganda campaign over a minor confrontation in the Tonkin Gulf and rammed a tame-sounding resolution through Congress to enable its vast undeclared war.

As the war failed to meet unrealistic metrics of "success"--the American public had grown accustomed to victory in all circumstances-- then the government turned to lies and deceptions not just at critical points but on a daily basis. The war was "winnable" and being won until the Tet Offensive of 1968 smashed the illusions and broke the fundamental trust in the pronouncements and policies of the Federal government.

On the domestic front, the Savior State social welfare programs did not repeat the easy "Savior" successes of the Depression; rather than ameliorate social problems, the rising expectations and seemingly unfulfilled promises led to urban riots and increasing crime.

The incoming Nixon Administration attempted to perfect the secrecy and deception which had become the favored policy of the Johnson era, a perfection which led to secret expansion of the war in southeast Asia and the Watergate domestic political scandal.

By the end of the War in Vietnam in 1975, in an era burdened by stagflation and economic malaise, public trust in the Savior State had fundamentally eroded. The constraints which had been accepted in trade for the security and prosperity of the 1950s and early 1960s were thrown over, and an explosion of interest in authenticity, world religions, self expression, liberation movements and the environment swept the culture.

The monochromatic, repressed, "phony" nature of the buttoned-down 1950s and early 60s Status Quo was cast aside and a riot of "anything is possible" alternatives sprang to life. Even as some of these trends slipped into self-parody, others led to the personal computer revolution: please read What the Dormouse Said: How the 60s Counterculture Shaped the Personal Computer. for more on the connection between technical and cultural innovation.

In the decades since, these liberations, reactions, experimentations and innovations were absorbed/co-opted by a still vibrant Status Quo. The basic model of American Neoliberal capitalism/hard-and-soft-power global Empire continued unhindered to an unexpected total victory in the Cold War as the Soviet Empire imploded--largely because its repressive regime had fatally suppressed the broad spectrum of cultural freedoms and explorations which resulted in vast technological innovations.

Now we find ourselves in a similar era in which official State policy is based on a carefully constructed web of lies, deceptions, statistical legerdemain and transparent propaganda. Those caught up in the artifice of "partisan politics" each blame the other party for this dependence on lies and deception, but the truth is the entire system is now totally dependent on lies, prevarications, deceptions and shameless propaganda.

As a result, belief in the system is once again fading.

Where the 1960s and early 70s were an era of widespread prosperity--an era which ended in 1973 with the oil embargo and the stagnation of wages and productivity--now we are starting an era of widespread impoverishment.

Nonetheless, the mechanism of liberation from the failed policies of a corrupt, over-reaching State/Plutocracy and the constraints of a "phony" Status Quo dependent on lies, fraud and deception may will be very similar.

In a way, the great promise of the explorations, experiments and innovations of the 1960s and 70s was never fully realized, for the resurgence of a simulacrum "prosperity" built on exponential growth of credit and debt which began in 1981 short-circuited any fundamental transformation of the status quo. The true prosperity of the postwar era which ended in 1973 was replaced by a simulacrum prosperity of rising income disparity and reliance on ever-expanding credit and debt. Now that false "prosperity" has imploded, we are entering a transformation of unprecedented depth and consequence.

Seen in this light, we are finally facing the unfinished business of the postwar era: the construction of a sustainable prosperity measured by completely different metrics: those of *full spectrum prosperity*.

Let the experimentation, exploration, innovation and liberation from failed models begin.

Key concepts in this chapter:
The paradox of energy cost/supply
Full spectrum prosperity

Chapter Eighteen: The Structure of Happiness

Now that the credit/debt-based simulacrum of prosperity has imploded, so too has the consumption-fantasy simulacrum of happiness.

Just as a capitalism founded on production and risk/return has been undermined by a crony-capitalism simulacrum and governance has been replaced by self-aggrandizement, looting and pandering, so too has an experience-based understanding of happiness been reduced to a threadbare simulacrum of shopping, buying, consuming and owning.

If happiness requires a full-employment, credit-dependent, high-cost, fossil-fuel dependent, consumption-based economy that is no longer sustainable, then clearly there will be a corresponding increase in unhappiness as the U.S. economy devolves.

Rather than throw trillions of dollars away in a futile attempt to rekindle a bubble/credit/crony capitalism which has run its course, perhaps it would be wiser (as well as much cheaper) to unburden ourselves of this equally doomed definition of happiness in favor of a sustainable, healthier understanding of well-being: what I term *full spectrum prosperity.*

Full spectrum prosperity is simply the recognition that "real wealth" cannot be measured by the size of one's home or range of possessions but by health (the only irreplaceable wealth), access to the FEW essentials (food, energy and water), meaningful skills deployed in meaningful work and a network of people who care about your well-being. Such mutual concern is founded on reciprocity, i.e. that you actively contribute to the well-being of those who contribute to your well-being.

Lip service is of course paid to such non-quantifiable measures of well-being, but the admiration and respect of the status quo, including many churches, is nonetheless reserved for the financially "successful." Those who aren't wealthy are marginalized in a Darwinian metric derived entirely from financial statistics.

This is not accidental. Water and food in their natural forms simply aren't profitable, and a low-energy intensive lifestyle is equally devoid of profit potential.

If we state that the most valuable possession one can have is personal integrity, this is essentially meaningless in financial terms and therefore it is valueless in the current consumerist frame of reference.

Our integrated understanding is that unprofitable concepts, experiences and objects are derealized in favor of services and goods which can be sold at enormous profit via pervasive mass media marketing.

Thus personal integrity is derealized and tap water is filtered and sold at a stupendous premium in plastic bottles with a brand attached. Real food plucked from the earth is derealized in favor of packaged food loaded with an engineered mix of salt, sugar and fat that is carefully designed to trigger the "reward" centers of the human brain even as it causes chronic disease and deranges the mind.

The goal of the mass marketing/propaganda system is to create what I term an *imaginary causal connection* between an internal state of satiation/satisfaction (in the adolescent framework the system has established as "obvious," this passes for "happiness") and the purchase of profitable goods and services.

The imaginary/fantasy character of advertising/marketing is well-known but less well known is the divergence between the initial causal connection--buying this brand of brandy causes the consumer to experience a sense of coveted elitism sorely lacking in the rest of his/her life--and the quick degradation of this initial reaction into the background insecurity of ennui (boredom)/dissatisfaction/deprivation/pain.

The sad irony is that the marketing/consumerist version of happiness is actually only a simulacrum of true happiness.

The "consumer" experiences happiness only for the fleeting moments of selection and purchase. The inner poverty of this simulacrum remains, gnawing away at whatever fulfillment is left to the incurably insecure "consumer."

This simulacrum of happiness has been distilled down by the marketing/advertising complex to a simplistic, superficial formula:

1. You are a consumer

2. A consumer's worth is measured externally by what is owned, worn, displayed, and by what high-status markers are certified by authority (diploma, elite membership, etc.) or the mass media (desirable avatar, high profile, etc.)

3. Self-worth results from the acquisition of goods and external markers

4. The internal state of consuming/owning scarcity-valued goods and high-status markers is happiness

What is left unspoken is the motivation for this formula:

5. The purpose of this formula is to profitably sell the insecure consumer an unnecessary good or marker which has an entirely imaginary connection to self-worth and happiness.

Being social mammals, humans' reproductive success depends to some degree on the level of status, power and material wealth each individual reaches; thus some 8% of the men in a wide swath of Asia carry genes which trace back to the extraordinarily prolific conqueror Genghis Khan.

But to equate high social status with happiness is to confuse two complex issues: higher status may well provide more access to material sources of well-being, but happiness--a state of mind, an understanding, a practice and a process--cannot be reduced to material ownership.

Indeed, numerous studies of the multi-faceted inner sensation we call happiness (which I would term well-being) conclude that the sources of happiness are largely internal and relationship-based rather than material or status-based. Common sense suggests that the security offered by wealth and income boosts well-being, but studies find additional wealth provides diminishing returns. Beyond a certain relatively low level, additional wealth in any form (cash, goods, travel, etc.) offers little improvement in well-being.

Factors often listed as sources of well-being include: Meaningful work, recreation, love, friendship and worship.

We might ask: since shopping did not make the list, how did the pursuit of happiness shrivel to the pursuit of goods and services?

The answer is self-evident: a secure individual identity does not require status or limitless externalities, and thus it does not offer many opportunities to sell unneeded goods and services at a profit.

The first project of the marketing/advertising system is to break down internally produced self-worth and identity and replace it with a permanent insecurity.

Convince the target audience that their worth is not internally sourced but totally dependent on externalities, and you create a fundamental insecurity: one can never have enough external goods or markers to establish enduring inner security.

A new fad or status marker will soon be introduced, driving down the value of whatever you own and thus your own "value" will plummet. Gratitude is impossible when there is never enough.

In a peculiar dynamic, the derealization/undermining of inner security--that is, of *an independently constructed sense of self*--by relentless marketing has sparked the emergence of a simulacrum of identity and self-worth: the so-called self-esteem industry.

Such is the perfection of the marketing/advertising system's induced insecurity that the connection between relentless marketing and our culture's pervasive sense of inner worthlessness is never made.

Rather than identify the root cause--the marketing/advertising complex--the self-esteem industry focuses on the symptoms, which it attempts to ameliorate with simplistic "feel-good" slogans ("you can be anything you want!", etc.), a counterproductive reduction in standards and a profoundly distorting goal of eliminating all metrics which might introduce a sense of diminished self-worth.

Just as the marketing complex purposefully confuses happiness with consumption (and indeed, citizen with consumer), so too does the self-esteem industry confuse external metrics and slogans with inner security and well-being.

Even some elements of organized religion have accepted the consumerist framework. In a troubling distortion of the Bible's edict that "It is easier for a camel to go through the eye of a needle than for a rich man to enter into the kingdom of God," some churchgoers have come to confuse wealth acquisition with spiritual attainment.

The Declaration of Independence's "pursuit of happiness"--implicitly a structured process, a journey toward a goal--has been replaced with an illusory and ultimately cruelly misleading end-state: happiness has been reduced from a structured journey (with inevitable setbacks) to the fleeting euphoria of a new purchase/acquisition.

An experience-based understanding of happiness is ontologically structured around the experiences of well-being, warmth and satisfaction offered by true friendship, accomplishment, generosity, romantic and spiritual love and the humility of worship. The acquisition of externalities and superficial markers has no place in this understanding.

In a parallel fashion, an *independently constructed sense of self*--what we term an individual's identity--grows from humility, accountability, responsibility, self-knowledge, and the strength of personal integrity, not from an illusory simulacrum of identity conjured by pronouncements ("I am a member of...") and possessions.

Indeed, all that is truly valuable in one's self and identity can never be taken away or even diminished: integrity, experience, self-knowledge and humility.

Rather than accept the derealizing, dehumanizing reduction to passive consumer, the individual seeking internal and external liberation must renounce the impoverishment of "consumer" and embrace the power of a citizen's independently constructed sense of self.

One key feature of the marketing/advertising derealization is the erosion of adulthood in favor of a simulacrum of adulthood: permanent adolescence.

The very traits needed to negotiate adulthood--an awareness of being tricked/manipulated/cheated, an awareness that life is a series of trade-offs in which one desire is sacrificed to support another deemed more important, the ability to put aside short-term impulses to meet long-term goals, the acceptance of responsibility and "no excuses/no blaming others for my own faults" accountability, etc.--are derealized in favor of an easily malleable adolescent worldview of spontaneity (that is, impulse), denial of accountability, malleable (and thus worthless) integrity, immediate satiation of appetites, escape from ever-present boredom and an obsessively insecure monitoring of one's peers for approval.

The adolescent is the perfect marketing target: insecure, focused on gaining approval via external props and cues, easily distracted and bored, powerfully stimulated by "newness" (a key feature of marketing exploitation), drawn to "tribes" of prescribed behavior and identity, fearful of consequences and thus attracted to denial and assigning blame to others, and prone to powerful sensory surges triggered by sexual and physical signals (taste, scent, etc.).

The ideal adolescent can barely restrain his/her impulses and emotions and is ever ready to indulge whims and desires. He/she is intensely insecure and doesn't trust his/her own experience but instead seeks the approval of peers or peer tribes via marketable clothing or other externals, suppressing his/her own inner life and experiences lest they conflict with the security offered by conformity. Regardless of the apparent marginality of the tribe he/she seeks to join/belong to, the conformity is equally intense, marketable and unthreatening to the State and the Plutocracy.

The more the "consumer" internalizes these positive cues for adolescence, the more they experience their own alienation as their own fault; given that the very adulthood skills they would need to break free of the trap have been eroded/derided by marketing, they find their inability to feel what they're supposed to be feeling ("happy") only drives them further into compulsive, self-destructive behaviors (the primordial "eating a quart of ice cream in the bathtub" experience, cutting oneself, sexual/drug excesses, etc.).

The very shallowness of this ubiquitously marketed adolescent worldview insures the participating consumer will feel unfulfilled and insecure after the brief high of consumption wears off. Unable to cross the chasm to their own experience, they turn with increasing desperation to marketed escapes and distractions for relief.

The Debt-Serf Consumerist Connection

Debt is slavery of the free. Publilius Syrus, Rome, First Century B.C.E.

Debt-serfdom--that is, the funneling of the lion's share of household income to debt service--is intimately connected to the false ideology of consumerism. Here is the key concept: **the products purchased all have an end value of zero while the debt lives on.** After the initial thrill of purchase--somewhat like an addict's initial euphoria--the consumer's purchase quickly falls to zero value even as the interest due continues on.

Every purchase other than land, gold, silver, a well-built house and a working system of energy production falls to near-zero value. A well-made and maintained vehicle may last 20 years, but the value will fall precipitously as it ages.

Unfortunately, many consumer goods are simulacrum of former products. Thus a piece of furniture which was once crafted of real wood and thus built to last hundreds of years is now fabricated of wood chips, glue and a paper-thin veneer which offers the facsimile of wood grain. This faux furniture will break apart within a few years (or even months), meaning that the credit card debt will outlast the furniture.

This connection is important, as the financial Elite profits immensely from high-interest consumer credit.

The free are thus enslaved via consumerist debt.

When Consumerist Gods Fail

It is important to recall the context of the current Depression: the U.S. has consumed trillions of dollars of goods and commodities in exchange for rapidly depreciating paper. Once credit/debt cannot be created exponentially, then consumption will fall in line with surplus production.

The marketing/advertising complex will still be flooding every nook and cranny of the nation and its media with messages to consume, but if few have surplus money and credit then it follows that few will have the means to buy, regardless of the persuasiveness of the millions of messages.

Thus it is not that the false god of consumerism will be toppled but that it will be abandoned--in many cases, most sorrowfully--by believers and adherents who no longer possess the surplus cash to offer the consumerist god.

The key factor in a consumerist-based identity is that someone profits by selling you an identity, character and sheen of status.

The idea that what you wear, drive, tattoo yourself with, load on your iPod, etc. has zero bearing on anything meaningful about who you are and what you value is subversive sacrilege of the highest order.

If "my stuff" is no longer "me," then who and what am I? And indeed, what can I sell you if all you really need to be "yourself" and happy is friends, minimal shelter, unprocessed food, homemade music, a library and an Internet connection and spiritual communion/worship? How much profit can I make selling you a used guitar, a DSL connection and a bag of carrots?

It boils down to this: when you run out of money, you switch religions from Consumerism to one of the good old spiritual standbys.

The known sources of happiness require little to no consumption:

1. health
2. friends
3. free time to pursue interests
4. spiritual communion/worship
5. exercise/sports/play
6. gardening
7. meaningful work (unpaid qualifies)

The experience of well-being has been so derealized that the sense of deprivation experienced at the loss of fine dining, Caribbean cruises, season tickets to the games, etc. is itself suspect.

We might even speculate that the experience of genuine happiness and well-being has largely been forgotten, or perhaps is an unknown sensation to media-numbed "consumers."

Since sustaining the simulacrum of consumerist "happiness" will cause much misery as the consumerist economy slides to oblivion, we might profitably ask if the happier choice wouldn't be to jettison the entire artifice of consumerist "happiness." Upon reflection, it was never real happiness after all; it was only a means to reap immense profits.

Dependency, Entitlement, Resentment and the State

There are few conditions more debilitating than dependency. Dependency leaches away self-confidence and leaves insecurity, self-loathing and a self-destructive resentment in its place.

There are two great ironies in Rise of the State (both Marxist/Socialist and Neoliberal Capitalist) in the past century. One is that the State's nurturing of entitlements (and thus dependency) has been "sold" to the citizenry as "providing security" but as noted elsewhere, it has effectively bought the citizenry's silent complicity in the Plutocracy/State's expanding dominance of the nation's assets and income.

The second irony that rather than provide security, this entitlement dependence has actually crippled the citizenry by fostering an amoral "game the system" mentality in which integrity is sacrificed for a perversely rewarding worship of victimhood. Those who sacrifice truth and integrity to file bogus claims are rewarded while those who tell the unadorned truth--such as, yes, I can still work in some capacity--are punished.

Those exaggerating their victim status--a form of outright fraud which has become not just commonplace but acceptable--game the system to the disadvantage of the self-reliant and responsible.

These perverse incentives and feedbacks have created a system in which firefighters claim a heart murmur (a very common and notably benign condition--I have one) as a work-relayed "disability" which then allows their already outsized pensions to flow to them tax-free.

As with finance and politics, the devolution of honesty and integrity has been shunted from public discourse; it would be "rude," insensitive" or "judgmental" to simply state that the firefighters claiming a heart murmur as a work-related injury are misrepresenting the truth. No one dares demand the truth lest their own claim to entitlement be rejected out of spite by those who have sold their personal integrity for State swag.

With integrity rendered not just worthless but a liability and dependency ascendant, then citizens are effectively encouraged by these State dependency incentives to file "stress claims" and "crazy money" (SSI, disability paid out of the Social Security system) and dozens of other frauds.

Indeed, "disability" is now a major drain on the economy at large, though the reality is the vast majority of people claiming disability could still be productive in some fashion. Yes, a small percentage of the populace is truly incapable of being productive--the quadriplegic, the severely psychotic, etc. But there are many "jobs" which even the severely disabled could perform; the simple but highly valuable service of providing "eyes on the street" could be performed by many currently classified as disabled/unable to work.

The key problem with State-encouraged dependency is the internal damage done to what I term *internally derived security*, the confidence of those who have learned to trust their own intuition/judgment, their own ability to learn and adapt and their own inner/spiritual resilience. Come what may, these people have confidence in themselves and their beliefs. They have the experience to back up their confidence--experience built on mistakes, errors and failures.

In the pillowy soft embrace of a perniciously destructive dependence on the State, the concept of *radical self-reliance* sounds harsh and "judgmental," as if dependency has created such a fragility of spirit and intellect that we cannot even bear to hear that we are now crippled by dependency. As with all derealizations and illusions, silence does not make the reality go away; a forbidden topic merely worms deeper into the soul and wreaks ever-greater damage to those seeking to hide it.

It is an irony of human nature that dependency offers the illusion of freedom--freedom from want and freedom of purpose. Yet the exact opposite is true: for in a Devil's Pact, the acceptance of dependency requires the sacrifice of real security--that you can take care of yourself, think for yourself and learn/adapt/pick yourself up on your own.

Ironically, self-reliance is freedom and dependence is a pernicious form of servitude.

Dependency also demands the sacrifice of self-worth and independence. Fearful of his/her own weakness (confirmed by the dependency) and thus fearful of losing the zero-sum game of divvying up the State's tax revenue, the dependent harbors resentment against everyone: other competitors drawing swag from the State, the State for being miserly, critics who question the lies, obfuscation and fraud at the heart of the system and even those who are paying the taxes which fund the entitlements.

The entitlement mindset is equally destructive, feeding multiple resentments and insecurities; the mind of the entitled dependent is filled with justifications, rationalizations, explanations and excuses for why they "deserve" not just the "right" to the State's largesse but the further "right" to their own hostility and resentments.

The resentful dependent (on the State or any other entity) is not a fulfilled person-- ontologically, dependence breeds resentment and crumbles inner strengths and thus it is incapable of fostering fulfillment or happiness.

Self-reliance--what I term radical self-reliance to differentiate it from the simulacrum of "self-reliance" used to mask various levels of dependency--flows from the inner sources of security: experience, belief in oneself and a sturdy belief in the goodness and importance of positive actions, on one's own behalf and just as importantly, on behalf of others.

The voices which rise in strident defense of entitlements are wasting their energy, for the State and its entitlements are doomed to insolvency, and nothing will stop that devolution and collapse.

Thus the only question is what we as a society will do with ourselves once we are thrown back on our own resources by the crumbling of the State's dependency machinery. Just as the servant/serf who feared the bankruptcy of his Master on the principle that the unknown is more unsettling than servitude, the citizenry may awaken in the financial ruins of the State and discover that illusions of security were just that, and that freedom requires self-reliance--and self-reliance requires sustained, well-thought out but flexible action toward limited, carefully selected goals.

Perhaps that sums up life, liberty and the pursuit of happiness.

The Structure of Happiness

Let us revisit a key concept:

This process of bridging the widening gap between what we experience and what we're being told we should be experiencing via the substitution of simulacrum for authentic structures is central to this entire analysis.

In other words: when we have lost the possibility of indulging the marketing system's fantasy of endless consumption of needless goods and services, instead of feeling the loss, deprivation and gnawing sense of insecurity/emptiness we are supposed to experience, we might well feel an unexpected but deeply genuine relief that the burdens of constant consumption have been lifted from our sagging shoulders.

It won't be surprising that an analysis which refers so often to the "politics of experience" seeks to illuminate the darkest corner of the consumerist theology: that the politics of experience deep within an apparently superficial consumerism is a form of servitude, and that the collapse of that theology is liberation.

That is, we do not experience happiness or fulfillment in a vacuum; it is difficult to pursue happiness in a political structure of randomized violence, suppression of free expression, insecure private property rights, theft by other means and centralized, ubiquitous propaganda that is dominated by an over-reaching State and its Plutocratic overlords.

Thus if we consider the Founding Fathers' phrase "pursuit of happiness" closely, we find not only that it implies a personal pathway of goals, progress, setbacks and discipline rather than a static end-state but also a political environment in which the individual pursuit of happiness is not just possible but encouraged rather than suppressed.

Perhaps the first step to such an understanding of an authentic "pursuit of happiness" is to recognize the consumerist theology of insatiable acquisition as a perverse and destructive simulacrum of genuine happiness.

Key concepts in this chapter:
Imaginary causal connection
Internally derived security
Independently constructed sense of self

Section Two:
Structuring Prosperity for Yourself and the Nation

Introduction

Our analysis has finally reached the promised point where we begin assembling solutions to our many interlocking crises.

Before we begin the journey forward, I want to take a moment to offer an assessment of our tangled quandary.

Here is my analysis in narrative form.

The U.S. economy (and the global economy, too) is like a great ship which is running out of fuel. This ship requires vast amounts of oil and credit, both of which have slipped from seemingly endless abundance into terminal decline. As it runs out of fuel, the ship slows to a halt, changing the lives of everyone on board.

Unfortunately, the ship has sprung serious leaks, and the pumps can no longer keep up with the water gushing in. As the ship settles lower in the water, complacency reigns, for the officers have reassured the passengers that everything is under control and the past--easy sailing--is a perfect predictor of the future.

Unfortunately, storm clouds have been scudding across the darkening sky for some time, and just as the ship drifts to a halt and wallows heavily as it takes on water, a "100-year storm" rises up to batter the sinking ship.

That ship is the U.S. economy.

Perhaps I am wrong and the current raft of status quo "solutions" is not simulacra but real. Perhaps borrowing $2 trillion a year in an exponential continuation of borrow-and-spend credit expansion will magically re-set the clock to 1999 or 2005. Perhaps the critical FEW resources (food, energy and water) are actually abundant and shortages are so far in the future that they're equivalent to time travel.

Maybe the consumerist mindset and a State/ Elite partnership which redistributes the nation's wealth to itself is the best of all possible worlds.

As I write this in September 2009, I know the answer as to which is correct--this analysis or the mainstream media/status quo--lies just ahead. If the global economy continues to devolve as this analysis suggests is inevitable, then you will know it by 2011; you won't need anyone to interpret that reality for you.

If on the other hand, abundance in resources, credit, wealth creation, equity, collateral and income suddenly blossom in full flower and continue to do so year after year, then my prediction will be clearly revealed as wrong.

There will be no ambiguity; we will know soon enough if the ship has run out of fuel and sprung leaks just as a typhoon is rising to gale force.

While we await the judgment of reality--devolution or re-set of exponential-credit "prosperity" --I offer *an integrated response* drawn from the preceding *integrated understanding* for your consideration.

The key principles of this response apply to all levels in all time frames.

That is, the principles that form the foundation of solutions apply equally to households, communities, enterprises and nations, and just as equally to all time-frames from short-term to very long-term. They are thus scale-invariant.

I want to be very clear from the start that I will be presenting principles rather than a set menu of solutions for the ontological reason that "one size will not fit all." While the principles are scale-invariant, the specific solutions that arise from those principles must respond to (feed back into) specific situations and contexts.

There are no easy out-of-the-box answers for households, communities or nations in dynamic times. It would be easy if we could state as an investment truth that "gold is the best investment." But while that may be true in certain time-frames, it is not true in all time-frames and all places.

Even as the primary sources of the world's oil slip into depletion, there will undoubtedly be periods of oversupply and low energy prices-- what I term *head-fakes*. We must resist the temptation to extrapolate past trends into the future just as we must resist the siren songs of complacency and fatalism.

As a result, we must remain flexible and alert to feedback. If our solutions aren't working them we will have to modify them. This is the essence of adaptation.

On an individual/household level, what works for some other household may not work for ours. As a result, we must all fashion our own solutions. The Internet provides us with unprecedented opportunities to exchange solutions and adaptations, but the choices and the work fall to each individual and household, each community and each nation.

It is human nature to seek a simple solution and hold it dear, but that is not always a successful strategy. Developing a "Plan B" alternative strategy is thus of paramount importance. Ultimately, *Survival+* is all about constructing a "Plan B" prosperity which is independent of the Savior State and rentier/financial Elite.

As a general rule, the larger the obligations and debt, the more likely default becomes. This too is scale-invariant and true for individuals, households, communities and States alike. As a result, exponential expansion of credit/debt will not be part of any real solution.

At the beginning, I suggested that if this analysis was indeed sound, then solutions should flow naturally from the analysis. While reality is complex, the principles of our response should be straightforward and simple to apply.

Before I lay out the framework, I want to summarize our situation and lay out the pathway which leads to the principles:

Chapter Nineteen: Over-Reach and Inequality

Chapter Twenty: Insurmountable Barriers to Structural Reform

Chapter Twenty-One: Incentives to Opt Out, Disincentives to Protest

Chapter Twenty-Two: The Process of Internal Transformation

Chapter Twenty-Three: The Structure of Change

Chapter Twenty-Four: The Principles of Systemic Response

Chapter Twenty-Five: Applying the Principles

Chapter Twenty-Six: Structuring the New American State

It is tempting to skip ahead and skim the principles, but their power comes with context. Here is the pathway laid out in the above chapters:

1. The ontologically inevitable consequences of over-reach are devolution and insolvency. Without an understanding of this inevitability, few will act on a "Plan B" alternative of prosperity and security.

2. Reforming the status quo is impossible; the only prudent action is to construct an alternative prosperity that does not depend on the Savior State or the financial Elite.

3. An internal process of illumination, acceptance and growth is part of the opting out process.

4. Change has structure. Understanding this will help us anticipate the future though we cannot predict its twists and turns.

With this context in mind, the principles of response, as "obvious" as they may be, emerge from the analysis.

Chapter Nineteen: Over-Reach and Inequality

Our situation can be summarized thusly:

1. All civil societies/cultures develop Elites; this is the nature of social animals. Elites are self-organizing groups which share the same self-interests, that is, a higher-order clique; they are not conspiracies or formal organizations.

2. Under certain conditions, the structural obstacles/negative feedbacks which constrain Elite dominance weaken and the Elites (private and public/State), like any other human group, seek to exploit the resulting windfall.

3. This leads the Elites to over-reach which creates positive feedback: the more wealth and influence the Elites/State control, the easier it becomes to control even more. The net result is the Elites and the State's share of the national income rises to historic extremes.

4. Regardless of the exact nature of over-reach--expansionist warfare or financial leverage and looting are two popular choices--the interests of the Elites and the society as a whole diverge. As this divergence grows, the social contract between the Elites and those whose productivity powers the economy and society begins fraying.

5. Over-reach ontologically (inherently) leads to structural imbalances which then threaten to destabilize the productive middle class which supports the Elites. Due to the overwhelming power of the Elites/State partnership's fiefdoms, structural reform is impossible (see Chapter Twenty below).

6. As the productive middle class's share of national income shrinks, a well-concealed, *opaque parallel system of dominance* with a structure of its own arises to exclusively serve the interests of the Plutocracy/State Elites (apparatchiks). The hidden mechanisms are many: backroom deals, unwritten "understandings," price-fixing and other forms of collusion; cash payments and other "gifts and donations;" political favoritism (special admission to elite public universities for the well-connected); and a cornucopia of financial benefits: access to initial public offerings, special tax laws written to reward a particular enterprise or cartel, and so on.

7. The State, which was intended as a bulwark against the natural dominance of concentrated private capital and Monarchy, has instead become the handmaiden of the rentier-financial Power Elites. The Elites

and the State have thus become partners in the task of diverting ever-larger shares of the national income to their own coffers.

8. As a result, inequality--as measured by shares of the national income and wealth--widens, furthering the divergence of interests between the productive class and the Elites/States' unproductive fiefdoms and dependents.

9. The State/Elites seek to counter these growing imbalances by extracting more from the productive class via taxes and "theft by other means" and masking this rising inequality by manipulating the politics of experience via relentless mass media propaganda.

The goal is four-fold: nurture complacency and fatalism in the citizenry; divert their attention from the concealed parallel system that benefits the Plutocracy and State Elites exclusively; legitimize simulacrum democracy and delegitimize protest.

10. To keep the State dependents passive and unthreatening, the Elites/State placate this class with "bread and circuses," State-funded entitlements paid for by raising taxes on the dwindling productive class. Under the guise of entitlements, the State (and the Elites who control it) has in effect bought the passive complicity of its dependents in the Elites' growing dominance of national income and wealth.

11. Having over-promised entitlements to the unproductive and garnered the majority of national income and wealth for themselves, the Plutocracy/State Elites can only tax the productive class so much lest they kill the horse they ride so majestically. Their only alternative to loss of income and power is to debauch the currency by printing money and debauch credit by borrowing far in excess of what can possibly be paid back.

12. The debauchery of credit and currency and rising inequality/diverting of national income to the Elites continues in a process of devolution until a phase shift/tipping point is reached and the status quo collapses in insolvency.

This process is both post-Marxism (that is, occurring outside the framework of Marxist theory) and post-Neoliberal State Capitalism--in other words, these broad intellectual frameworks failed to predict or account for the coming devolution and collapse of the State/rentier-monopoly capital Power Elite partnership.

The grand experiment of the State controlling the private economy has failed.

Both the Marxist/Socialist model of government control and ownership and the Neoliberal State Capitalist model of the State controlling the economy via monetary and fiscal manipulations have failed, for in each model there is no negative feedback to State over-reach and expansion.

In the Marxist Model, there is no negative feedback to limit *extreme concentrations of power* via State control and ownership of national assets and income. As the State Elites gorge on the national wealth (windfall exploitation), the State's interests radically diverge from those of the citizenry.

In Neoliberal State Capitalism, there is no negative feedback to limit State manipulation of monetary and fiscal inputs (i.e. borrow and/or print money). In theory, the global bond market should act as a counterforce to fiscal over-reach (excessive State debt and spending), but as recent events have shown, the U.S. is effectively unhindered by market forces: the U.S. Treasury sells bonds to primary bond dealers, the Federal Reserve creates money out of thin air, and a few days after the bond auction the Fed buys the Treasury bonds from the dealers.

The circle is complete: when the State creates money to buy its own debt, it establishes a simulacrum of an "open market" which in reality is utterly opaque and manipulated by the financial Elites and State to maintain their wealth and power.

But such perfection in positive feedback (there are no restraints on the State's ability to print, borrow and spend money) leads not to stability but to instability and collapse.

Exacerbating this devolution and eventual collapse are unprecedented external pressures on increasingly vulnerable FEW resources (food, energy and water) and infrastructure: fossil fuel depletion, environmental/soil degradation, fragile supply chains, etc., all of which increase the probabilities of chronic shortages and the geopolitical conflicts which historically arise from those shortages.

At this juncture it is important to recall that any State/government is in essence a luxury that can only exist if an economy generates a substantial surplus.

No surplus, no government. Thus subsistence-level societies do not have stand-alone governments because there is not enough surplus food to feed essentially unproductive members of the society (government). Security and other community needs are provided gratis by the group itself as a form of mutual protection/benefit. The wealthy share their surplus in exchange for status ("potlatch").

As measured by fiscal and trade deficits, the U.S. economy has not produced a sustained surplus for decades.

We have consumed far more than we have produced, and borrowed the difference from nations which have generated surplus capital and goods.

The mass media/think-tank/State propaganda machine produces reams of material claiming to "prove" that this stupendous borrowing is not just sustainable but that it is in everyone's best interests.

But the "surplus" the U.S. is trading for tangible goods and capital is paper money and future promises to pay--both essentially worthless. At some point the fraud at the heart of this exchange of "value" will be revealed and the U.S. State and Elites will be reduced to depending on the actual tangible surplus generated by the U.S. economy.

This sharp reduction of available capital to spend will trigger collapse of the over-leveraged, over-indebted, credit-dependent status quo, which requires trillions of dollars in borrowed capital to support its gargantuan State and Elites.

It is also important to recall that relative inequality in national income and wealth rises and falls in long cycles, and changes are triggered by national crisis.

I previously noted that inequality was rather low in Colonial America and then rose as the U.S. industrialized. One result of the Great Depression was the decline of inequality, which enabled the post-World War II era of rising middle class wealth and income.

Thus it is entirely within historic norms to foresee a national crisis (insolvency) which results in dramatic declines of inequality--that is, the share of national income and wealth currently diverted to the Elites and State will drop precipitously. Since national income is a zero-sum game, this decline in equality means the productive classes' share of national income will rise--put another way, they will keep the income that is being transferred to the rentier/financial and State Elites in the present era of extreme inequality.

This implies the State's role as handmaiden/servant to the rentier-financial Elites will collapse along with State finances. Given the lack of negative feedback on the State's expansion and the positive feedback of printing and spending fiat money, there is no other possible end-state but collapse/insolvency.

Let's examine our era's extreme inequality in more detail.

According to a recent (July 2009) *Wall Street Journal* analysis of Social Security Administration data, the top 6% of wage earners (high-caste) take home 1/3 of the national wage/salary income ($2.1 trillion of the $6.4 trillion in total U.S. pay in 2007); when bonuses, stock options and other non-wage income is included, the percentage rises to approximately 50%. The high-caste share of national income has been rising at approximately double the rate of average workers. Over time, this differential enabled the top 6%'s share to rise from 28% of total income to 33% in just a few years. Thus inequality is rising quickly in the current status quo.

The top 1% of households own 2/3 of the productive wealth of the nation. This number is not static, of course; the gap between the top 1% and the 99% below is widening rapidly. Congressional Budget Office data show that between 1979 and 2006, the before-tax income of the top 1 percent of U.S. households increased by 226 percent, on average (after adjusting for inflation), compared to an increase of just 15 percent for families in the middle fifth of the income spectrum (the middle class).

The after-tax income of the top 1 percent of households increased by 256 percent, after adjusting for inflation, compared to an increase of 21 percent for families in the middle income quintile. The effective federal tax rate for the top 1 percent of households — i.e., the share of their *taxable income* that they owe in taxes — fell substantially, from 37 percent to 31.2 percent As a result, the share of the nation's total after-tax income going to the top 1 percent of households more than doubled, from 7.5 percent in 1979 to 16.3 percent in 2006.

While non-taxable income statistics are hard to come by, we know that the vast majority of tax-free municipal bonds are owned by the top 5% of households, and that the vast majority of Elite wealth is protected from taxes by family and estate trusts, funds and income held overseas and a multitude of other tax avoidance schemes (legal and quasi-legal) unavailable to middle class households. The vast majority of the Elite's income is unearned, that is, not wages but rents, dividends, capital gains, etc., which are either taxed at lower rates or subject to multiple deductions and other tax avoidance strategies.

Thus the top 1%'s share of total national income (nontaxable or protected from taxation as well as taxable) is more on the order of a third. (Approximately 60% of the income-generated wealth of the nation-- rents protected by depreciation, dividends, interest, capital gains, tax-free bond income, non-taxable trust income, etc.-- flows to the top 1%. Thus wages/salaries/taxable income is a poor measure of total wealth and income.)

Historically, this concentration of wealth and income is an extreme for this nation. The State (all government, state, county, city, semi-autonomous public agencies, transit authorities, public universities, etc.) currently absorbs approximately 40% of the nation's GDP, also an extreme. (The Federal government absorbs about 20% of GDP.)

We should also note that the rise of entitlements/dependency has occurred in parallel with rising inequality/ever greater share of national income diverted to the State and Plutocracy; the skyrocketing cost of "pay as you go" entitlements is thus paid with borrowed money and higher taxes on the dwindling productive middle class, leaving the Plutocracy and State fiefdoms' shares of the national income intact.

None of this is of course common knowledge, for the corporate Elite owns the highly concentrated mass media, and it would not serve their interest for this sort of data to be widely disseminated in the mass media.

Given that elites form in all societies with any surplus, the notion of eradicating Elites entirely is impractical.

Clearing away old Elites (liquidating, murdering or imprisoning them on the Soviet, Chinese or Cambodian models) has merely provided opportunities for a new Elite to take the place of the old Elite.

But reducing extreme inequality by restricting the diversion of the productive classes' earnings to the Elite/State partnership is not just entirely possible but it has recent historical precedent (the rapid drop in inequality 1940 - 1970).

It is important to note that eras of relatively low inequality have generally been the most widely prosperous, stable and creative in American history.

As noted elsewhere in this analysis, the U.S. Constitution does not restrict the growth of Elites or the State, nor does it contain any mechanism to limit the concentration of their wealth, power and influence. The Elites and high-caste State elites effectively control all three branches of the U.S. government and so the "balance of powers" is ineffective in limiting the rise of inequality. It is up to the citizenry to limit rising inequality; the structure of government itself only feeds an ever-enlarging State.

Having noted this, we must also note that the U.S. Constitution does not restrict the reduction of inequality, either. The Constitution is itself neutral; if the citizenry allow the Elites and State to dominate the national income, media and the politics of experience, then the Constitution is powerless to obstruct this concentration of power.

Recall that the State and its fiefdoms have no inherent interest in limiting its own reach, income and influence; rather, the State is ontologically constructed to seek a greater share of national income and ever greater influence and control--just like the private-sector Elites which partner with the State.

Put another way: there is no negative feedback to restrict the growth of the State except an engaged, skeptical citizenry who demand and enforces transparency and accountability. This will require new negative feedback loops and strengthening existing regulatory feedbacks that have been reduced to simulacra.

Thus no revolution is necessary; indeed, nothing illegal is required, either. Opting out is perfectly legal, as is constructing an alternative transparent, fully accountable economy and society which will prosper even as the financial Elites and the State collapse in insolvency.

Key concepts in this chapter:
Opaque parallel system of domination
Extreme concentration of power

Chapter Twenty: Insurmountable Barriers to Structural Reform

In a perfect world, both the citizenry and those grasping the reins of power would conclude that serious structural reform would serve their long-term interests better than structural collapse. Yet there are ontological (and therefore insurmountable) barriers to any such reform, obstacles which can perhaps best be understood as forces of nature similar to gravity: to expect any concentration of political and financial power to relinquish its power rather than defend it is akin to expecting gravity to cease its pull on mass.

Elites, by definition, hold concentrations of wealth and control at immensely higher *power densities* than the broad non-elite populace. I term this structural imbalance in power density *asymmetric stakes in the game*, in which the game is the concentration and distribution of national income and wealth, both via State-collected taxes and private capital.

To better understand the concept of *power density*, in which power is financial and political, let's compare a rural, agricultural economy such as the U.S. circa 1783 and a post-industrial urbanized economy such as the U.S. in 2009.

Setting aside the issue of slavery in 1783 America--from one point of view, a forced concentration of labor to serve the plantation model of production--we note the diffusion of power in the non-slave states. Voters--the ultimate source of political compliance and thus power--and private and public financial assets were diffused except for a few (by today's standards modest) urban centers: Philadelphia, Boston and New York. What Marx called "the means of production"--the capital, plant, tools and knowledge required to produce goods and services and thus wealth--were spread over the rural and urban populations alike.

Another way of describing this diffusion of power is to calculate the rate of concentration via the rate of inequality.

Thus a feudal society in which an Elite holds most of the wealth has a high rate of inequality, where a populace of free small landowners and tradespeople has a low level of inequality.

Non-slaveowning Colonial America had a low, stable rate of inequality, a condition which has plentiful academic documentation. According to Frank Ackerman's The Political Economy of Inequality, the top 1% of free adult males held 12% of the wealth in 1774 and 29% in 1860. The share of the top 10% rose from 49% in 1774 to 73% in 1860.

As the North industrialized and the Southern plantation-based economy consolidated, then wealth inequality increased between the Revolution and the Civil War. This concentration of wealth continued unabated through the Gilded Age up to 1929, when the Great Depression wrought vast increases in State powers as wealth was widely destroyed. The net result was a much lower level of inequality from 1940 through the early 1970s--not coincidentally, the era of true prosperity for the middle class and the alleviation of extremes of poverty.

As described above, this true prosperity faded in the stagflation and ennui of the 1970s and was replaced with a credit/debt bubble-based simulacrum of prosperity which masked the diversion of national wealth and income to Elites-- a pseudo-prosperity which is now imploding.

Mass industrial/technical production owned and distributed by global corporations arose from the great efficiencies and profits created by concentrating capital, materials, transport, expertise and labor into monopolies/cartels. Fighting and winning a global war (World War II) greatly expanded the U.S. government's reach and size. These concentrations of capital, expertise, logistics, labor and control created fiefdoms of the State and a private-sector Plutocracy which partnered to extend a mutually beneficial global empire of so-called "soft power" influence and "hard power" military dominance.

Wealth and thus power is now extremely concentrated; at least 2/3 of the productive (income-producing) wealth and 60% of the income-generated wealth of the U.S. is held by 1% of the populace. (According to an analysis by the *New York Times* and Simon Cay Johnson, the top 400 taxpayers' tax rate was 17%--and that, recall, is on taxable income of $250 million each on average, a sum which is only a percentage of their total income, much of which is sheltered.)

From the long view, the cycle of wealth concentration has again reached an apex similar to that of 1929. The primary difference between 1929 and the present some 80 years hence is that the State has greatly concentrated its power and share of the national income.

Perhaps coincidentally but perhaps not, this cycle of extreme inequality aligns extremely well with the 80-year generational cycle mentioned earlier.

The Grand Failure of Government to Limit Concentration of Power

While much is made of the "balance of powers" in the U.S. and other democracies--the power of the executive branch being offset by the legislative and judicial branches--this "balance" completely failed to hinder the credit/housing bubble and the structural fraud and embezzlement at its heart. No branch of the "balanced powers of the State" saw any reason to interfere with the systemic looting and debauchery of credit and currency.

We should also note that in previous periods of extreme concentrations of wealth and high inequality, the "balanced powers" of the U.S. government did not reverse or even seriously challenge these long periods of high inequality. In this sense we should be careful not to overestimate the State's control over wealth concentration and rising inequality.

Despite the supposedly "leveling influence" of income taxes, wealth has become ever more concentrated in the past 40 years, paralleling the high inequality between the Civil War and the Great Depression. Neither the "trust-busting" actions of the Federal government in the early 1900s nor the rise of industrial unions reversed or disrupted the 1860-1930 period of high wealth concentration/high inequality.

This, then, is the *grand failure of government*: due to the concentrations of power accumulated by those with *asymmetric stakes in the game*, any attempt to limit a concentration of power is thwarted by the status quo. All the issues which so worried Madison in *The Federalist Papers* have come to full flower: the power of the State has been legally channeled into Elites which have nothing to fear from any branch of the State because they are the State.

Despite decades of attempted electoral "reform," elections in the U.S. grow ever more prohibitively expensive, and it is still legal to contribute large sums of money to politicians. The cliche has it that "money is the mothers' milk of politics" and as has been noted above, it is far cheaper to buy a legislative loophole than it is to pay taxes, build treatment plants, relinquish monopoly, etc.

These concentrations of financial and thus political power flow ontologically from the concentrations of capital and labor that were necessary to industrial production.

The model of a "factory" mass-producing goods, so successful in manufacture, has been applied, consciously or unconsciously, to fields of endeavor which are structurally quite different from manufacture-- education, for instance, with the mixed results one would expect of misapplied models.

The human mind's power comes from understanding models and applying them to new situations. In the long view, it is understandable that just as Newtonian physics sparked a frenzy of misapplied models (the human being understood as a mechanical device like a clock, etc.), so too would the highly successful model of concentrated mass-production be earnestly and enthusiastically misapplied.

This concentration of materials, machinery, transport, labor and capital--the factory and the industrial corporation--naturally led to a concentration of organized labor, a model which, now that industrial production has faded, has been misapplied to the last outsized concentration of labor: government.

With no real restraints on government largesse, then public-union labor has concentrated its political power and "won" (I use quotation marks because there has never been any real negative feedback to its concentration of power) stupendous benefits and wages which have created the "upper-caste" I have described above: a protected class of technocrats/apparatchiks who are compensated at two or three times (when pension and healthcare benefits are included) the market rates earned by their lower-caste private-sector brethren.

Once financial and political power has become concentrated into monopoly-capital cartels and State fiefdoms, then those Elites hold highly *asymmetric stakes in the game*: they have so much more to gain and lose from the political distribution of taxes and exemptions from regulation than non-Elites that they will fiercely deploy all their power and wealth to preserve and extend their share of the national income.

In contrast, the non-Elite citizenry have vanishingly modest stakes in the regulatory and tax-distribution games; while a narrowly focused tax law will enrich an Elite for decades to come, the consequences to the broad non-Elite citizenry are so diffused as to be akin to the brush of a feather.

Immense State/Elite empires have been constructed from initially modest taxes collected from tens of millions of non-Elites--Medicare, for example--while seemingly minor tax laws have enabled vast empires of private capital to solidify. For example, energy, where fortunes have been built on depletion allowances and other tax schemes far more favorable than those awarded to manufacturers, and real estate, where depreciation hides vast rivers of income behind the perverse idea that a building rising in real value is magically declining in worth.

From its humble tax-funded beginnings, Medicare has grown into a stupendously profitable empire which will soon exceed both the military-intelligence complex (the Pentagon) and the Social Security system in budget. This vast empire is comprised of loosely allied fiefdoms (the AMA, trial lawyers, pharmaceutical, insurance and hospital industries, etc.), each eager to defend its turf from non-Elite interference and the encroachment of the other fiefdoms.

The State's technocrats/apparatchiks have gained income and power along with their private-sector partners, and thus rather than provide a negative feedback counterforce to this concentration of wealth and income, the State is in effect a positive feedback, furthering the concentration of wealth and power into Elite hands.

State Monopolies: Violence, Conscription, Taxation and Inflation

The State itself of course holds monopolies on a handful of powers that are concentrated indeed: the dispensation of "legitimate" violence, the power to conscript citizens to fight wars (legally declared or otherwise), the power to tax the citizenry and lastly, the terrible power to rob the citizenry by means of inflation and/or currency devaluation, what I term *theft by other means*.

Economist John Maynard Keynes quipped, "By a continuing process of inflation, government can confiscate, secretly and unobserved, an important part of the wealth of their citizens." This is theft by other means.

Why does the State seek to steal its citizens' wealth via inflation? The politics of inflation dictate it:

1. Politicians need to distribute swag ("free money") to the electorate every two years. Their perspective is thus necessarily short-term as no politician dares care what transpires a decade or two hence.

As a result, politicians must favor inflation, which enables them to borrow/print money and distribute it as swag to voters and Elites ("special interests") in the present and pay interest on the new debt with "cheaper" future dollars.

2. Voters possess the built-in human bias for present gain over future gain. Thus future insolvency is meaningless to those demanding State largesse in the present.

Indeed, politicians have noted that those who demand sacrifice in the present to address a long-term crisis lose elections while those who distribute swag while ignoring the gathering storm on the horizon win elections.

3. Inflation is thus "good" for politicians and the State as it enables paying off obligations assumed in the present with devalued future currency. But is it "good" for the voters who actually earn income? Is a policy which robs a third of your money every decade a worthy policy? For that is precisely what "low" inflation of 2.5-3% annually does: it reduces your dollars' values by a third every decade.

Will the swag "given" to you (is it "given" when it's your own future earnings?) now in the form of government benefits and tax cuts add up to more than a third of your future earnings over a decade? Unlikely, to say the least.

4. So politicians exploit the human bias for short-term gain even as they rob the taxpayers via inflation over the long term. Inflation is tolerable as long as you're a wage earner and your income rises at the same rate as inflation.

But income from labor (wages/salaries) have been flat since the early 70s for most Americans, and so inflation has only been "good" for those holding assets which have risen more or less in lockstep with inflation.

For those whose earnings rise nominally by 15% a decade while inflation robs 30% of their purchasing power, then "a little inflation" is a long-term disaster.

5. The usual argument in favor of inflation is debt-based. That is, inflation is wonderful because it enable us to pay off our debts with future "cheaper" dollars. But if our incomes are being robbed by inflation, then is that "benefit" of inflation really so valuable? If I lose a third of my purchasing power in a decade does being able to pay down my mortgage with depreciated dollars offset my loss of purchasing power? No--unless my mortgage payment exceeds my income by a fair margin, which is essentially impossible.

6. Deflation is excellent for those with cash and earnings and awful

for kleptocracy governments and those with over-leveraged debt. The entire idea that "inflation is good" masks a perverse incentive: take on as much debt as you possibly can because interest will become "cheaper" to pay in the future (assuming your earnings keep up with inflation).

If your earnings don't keep up with inflation, well, too bad.

7. The government's "earnings" are tax revenues. As profits and incomes have fallen, so have tax revenues. So as the purchasing power of its taxpayers' wages are stolen via inflation--"theft by other means"-- then the State's ability to collect ever-larger sums of money via taxes is crimped. Unless, of course, the government can create asset bubbles via loose credit and unlimited liquidity which then generate huge capital gains which can then be taxed.

8. To enable distribution of swag to voters and Elites, the State kleptocracy offloads the payments into the future. By creating inflation then the State guarantees (or so it reckons) that it will be able to pay the interest on that debt with "cheaper" money collected from taxpayers in the future.

But as taxpayers find the purchasing power of their earnings declining (theft by other means) then they respond to the incentives presented by the government: borrow to the hilt and speculate in asset bubbles as the only way left to maintain purchasing power.

This dependence by both State and citizenry on asset bubbles to maintain purchasing power leads to over-leverage and over-indebtedness which then leads inevitably to a collapse of asset values (which were based on exponential credit expansion) and the tax revenues which were dependent on asset bubbles.

Now the taxpayers find their post-bubble assets decimated and their purchasing power diminished while government finds its tax revenue base has been gutted. Paying interest on all that debt while distributing unlimited swag was predicated on rising tax revenues. That plan has now been revealed as fantasy.

Interestingly, the original Constitution did not explicitly grant powers of conscription or monetary debasement. Yet the vaunted "balance of powers" has not impeded the State from concentrating monetary powers in order to reward Elites and steal not just from its present citizens but even its future citizens.

But even the State cannot control the cycle of over-indebtedness, collapsing asset values and the impoverishment of its people via inflation. The end-state is insolvency, and as the State's monopolies fail to sustain the status quo then its various Elites will battle each other for the remaining spoils: what I term *internecine conflict between protected fiefdoms.*

Internecine Conflict Between Protected Fiefdoms

"Internecine" has an interesting and highly relevant history. The Latin source of the word, a derivative of the verb "to kill," meant "fought to the death, murderous, as in "all the way, to the death." Samuel Johnson defined the word in the 18th century as "endeavoring mutual destruction." The word has now come to mean "relating to internal struggle."

These meanings are the heart of my term *internecine conflict between protected fiefdoms* because they describe how the various fiefdoms, though protected from non-Elite interference by their concentrated political power, must now fight each other to the death for their share of dwindling tax revenues and weakening regulatory perquisites. Rather than accept a reduced share of tax revenues, each fiefdom will endeavor to maintain its own share by cannibalizing the share currently enjoyed by another fiefdom.

This internecine conflict will take precedence over structural transformations which would positively serve the nation as a whole (and even the Elites defending their fiefdoms). As a result, this conflict will demand ever greater resources from each fiefdom and deplete whatever limited resources could have been devoted to structural change. These internecine wars will thus hasten the collapse of the entire status quo.

Each State fiefdom and private-industry cartel which depends on the State for funding or regulatory protection (energy, healthcare, military, etc.) will be fighting a two-front war: one against the taxpaying public (the productive middle class which pays most of the taxes) from which they will be extracting higher taxes and "junk fees" and the other against competing fiefdoms.

An analogy might be a sinking ship on which the officers are fighting each other and the crew. Focused on their internecine struggles for dominance, they pay no attention to the listing deck and other signs of impending catastrophe until the ship is slipping beneath the waves.

When the partnership between the State and Plutocracy unravels, then systemic collapse is at hand.

The partnership was based on a mutually parasitical relationship: the State's elected officials depended on the largesse of the Plutocracy, which depended on the State to protect its share of the national income and wealth.

As the productive middle class opts out (having no other choice), tax revenues continue declining in a positive-feedback death-spiral: the more taxes and junk fees imposed on the remaining productive citizenry, the greater the incentive to opt out by quitting, moving to the underground/barter economy or simply making less money and buying fewer goods and services.

This decline forces the State to borrow and/or print vast sums of money which eventually negatively impact the national economy on which the Plutocracy depends for much of its income. Facing drastically reduced revenues, the State finds its powers to impose regulatory and taxation schemes on the citizenry have weakened. In desperation, the State fiefdoms begin eyeing the vast reserves of Plutocratic wealth and income as untapped sources of tax revenues.

Like the middle class, the Plutocracy will increasingly view the State not as protector or partner but as an unproductive parasite that provides less and less even as it harvests a rising share of the dwindling national income.

Once the State alienates the Plutocracy, the State's days as a solvent enterprise are numbered. The mainstream media will turn against the State (being owned by a handful of global corporations, the mass media will do its masters' bidding) and the Plutocracy will speed the global sheltering of its remaining assets and income, in effect planning to profit from the inevitable collapse of the U.S. sovereign debt and currency.

But without the State to protect it from an aroused citizenry, the Plutocracy may find itself the target of widespread ire and insurrection. Even as it follows the pathway taken by the Roman Elites as their empire crumbled--retreating to well-defended enclaves--the Plutocracy will find its own freedom of movement, capital and monopoly restricted by the State's attack on its assets and the public's awakening to the coming collapse in entitlements and other State services.

The State and Plutocracy share the same hubris: each believes there should be no limits on its own over-reach.

The irony is that once their interests diverge and the partnership crumbles, each is left too weak to control the forces unleashed by their mutual over-reach.

As states around the globe seek to borrow their way out of insolvency, private borrowing is squeezed; this intense competition for dwindling surplus global capital forces interest rates to rise to levels few anticipated. (Readers of oftwominds.com were of course fully aware of both the rising trajectory and its enduring nature.)

The Plutocracy, having engorged itself on profits reaped from the artificially low interest rates engineered by State manipulation of financial markets, will be less than pleased with the sudden disappearance of cheap surplus capital. The direct consequences of much higher rates globally--the destruction of equity, bond holdings and real estate valuations--will also negatively affect the Plutocracy's wealth and income, widening the rift between what the State fiefdoms see as in their best interests and what the Plutocracy views as in its best interests.

Even as what is understood by the State and Plutocracy as "the common good" diverge, the interests of the crumbling partnership (State and Plutocracy) are diverging from those of the general populace.

Facing the erosion or even dissolution of their concentrations of power, capital and labor, the State fiefdoms and the private-capital Elites unite in one last-ditch campaign to preserve their perquisites and shares of the national income via simulacrum reforms marketed as "preserving our institutions" (see chapter Fourteen, "Interlocking Traps").

The State and Plutocracy will never voluntarily reduce their share of the national income when simulacra of reform (funding State largesse with more debt, masking the approaching insolvency with accounting trickery, announcing bogus "grand compromises" which will save the status quo without any visible sacrifice, etc.) can put off the inevitably catastrophic consequences to a future day. When that moment finally arrives, reforms of any type will be as inconsequential as the many edicts issued in the waning days of the Roman Empire.

Asymmetric Stakes in the Game

Government, not just Federal but state, county and city, has two extraordinary powers: it can collect revenues via taxation, permits and fees, by force if necessary, and then distribute those funds however the officials in charge desire.

Theoretically, the voters can express their dissatisfaction with the decisions made every two or four years, but such referendums are inevitably diluted by distracting propaganda paid for by the Elites and high-castes who benefit most from maintaining the status quo.

I say "theoretically" for another reason: those on the receiving end of those stupendous revenues collected by the State have an *asymmetric stake in the game*: the potential losses in their own personal income are not just theoretical, they are very real, and so they mobilize their forces to protect their own fiefdom and perquisites with a frantic, desperate zeal unmatched by the voters, who have a much smaller stake in the division of tax revenues.

Thus the public employee unions, American Medical Association, pharmaceutical companies, trial lawyers, defense contractors and other Elites with asymmetric stakes funnel millions of dollars into the re-election campaigns of politicians. The net result, of course, is that the very expenses which have skyrocketed--public pensions and healthcare, to name but two--are "off the table," sacrosanct, untouchable.

For the politicians, there is an even bigger threat: should they cross the pharmaceutical industry, the AMA, the trial lawyers or any well-funded public employee union, these special interest groups will not just stop funding their campaigns--they will target them for extermination by funding an opponent.

Put yourself in the shoes of an elected official. You collect a small sum in campaign contributions from the general public--the non-Elite "little people" you are pledged to serve. You collect another larger sum from the party organs--political action committees, etc. Then you collect a sum five times greater than those two sources combined from a handful of powerful special interests who hold extremely asymmetric stakes in the game of distributing the tax swag/revenues.

Who are you going to ignore or even double-cross? Not the special interests who have funded your political power. Who you ignore or double-cross is the public, who has a small stake in every decision you make. You can count on that come election time, when an emotional issue can be blown out of proportion via propaganda to make the voters forget the "death by a thousand cuts" taxes and reductions in services they have suffered.

How many taxpayer/voters will write an angry letter to their local politician because parking fines doubled? They may grumble to friends, colleagues, et al. but they'll just pay it, fuming all the while.

How about that 1% increase to sales tax, the surcharge to the municipal water bill, the higher subway fares and the doubled fee to enter a state park? The typical voter is annoyed and frustrated by these additional taxes and fees, but it simply isn't enough money at any one time to trigger their political act of protest.

Added together, these additional taxes and junk fees total a stupendous sum--in the multiple billions of dollars. Yet because we "little people" pay them in small increments and only occasionally, then our stake in the game of distributing the tax swag is asymmetrically trivial compared to the players who are collecting the billions. They are playing for keeps, while we're playing--and losing--small money, again and again and again.

If you rounded up $100 from every neighbor, colleague, family member and other person in your own network, and walked into your local politician's office with $10,000 in a paper bag and a short list of items you wanted addressed, then you'd get a hearing.

Or if you collected 10,000 signatures to recall your local politician over these endless tax increases, then the politician would face a danger other than an desperate-for-swag special interest: an aroused, angry public who was organized to exterminate his/her political power.

But nobody ever collects the $10,000 or the 10,000 signatures of outrage--we all just pay the fines, the junk fees, the extra sales tax, the additional income tax and the higher entrance fees and passively fume. Our stake in each game of revenue enhancement is small, so we do nothing. The special interests' stake is all-or-nothing, gigantic, as important as life itself--and so they will throw their last million at the politicos in charge of the tax revenue (and revenues from the sale of bonds) and demand their fiefdom be protected at all costs.

This is how the states, counties, cities, agencies and eventually the central government become insolvent and unable to pay their increasingly unaffordable obligations.

Asymmetric Stakes in the Game is a key concept in the Survival+ analysis because it plays out in so many fields in which wealth is collected from millions but distributed to an Elite.

The truly Kafkaesque nightmare that is the U.S. "healthcare" (actually sick-care) system is a prime example. The players who gorge themselves on the hundreds of billions of dollars in tax swag will fight to the bitter end to maintain their share of the wealth, even if it eventually causes the collapse of the entire system. That inevitability is what I term *internecine conflict between protected fiefdoms.*

Asymmetric Stakes in the Game impacts every industry which is either funded by the State (tax revenues and State borrowing) or regulated by the State--in other words, virtually every important industry. Those with the most to lose will fight for their share of the national wealth with extreme ferocity, while those paying the endless incrementally higher taxes will never reach the threshold of demanding fundamental transformation.

An asymmetric Stake in the Game also plays out in the stock and financial markets.

Millions of employees and self-employed people contribute to a 401K and/or IRA (individual retirement account), and millions of public employees contribute to pension funds. A relatively small number of money managers decide how to invest/play those billions.

A relative handful of players collect most of the winnings from that game. The tens of millions of players (those with 401Ks, etc.) who have lost 40% of their accumulated wealth in the two years September 2007-September 2009 are either essentially powerless (you get to move your 401K money around any of four funds, all of which lost 40%) or sheep lined up to be sheared by the players with an asymmetric stake in the game.

If you and I can collect $10 million in bonuses each, while our firm can reap $40 billion and then buy political protection for a mere $100 million of that swag, are we motivated to level the playing field? Of course not. We're interested in processing as many sheep as we can, and in keeping the game rigged in our favor.

The swag from the game is so gargantuan that we will move Heaven and Earth to persuade the political/regulatory Powers That Be to solidify/legitimate our advantages. It's literally financial life or death for us, while the "little people" who lost 40% of their stake, well, they will just sigh and passively accept their fate; maybe they'll glance at a headline in a magazine about a new mutual fund or ETF, and that's the end of their discontent.

Though their cumulative losses in the rigged game totaled some $13 trillion between 2007 and 2009, individually each passively accepts their own losses without regard to the nature of the game. Each surrenders political power to the Elites because the losses don't seem to have a political source: **masking the political source of the asymmetry is the key to the power Elites' success in keeping the game rigged in their own favor.**

So the mainstream media dutifully spews the propaganda that the "market is a rational mechanism for price discovery" and all the rest while behind the scenes a handful of players reap $100 million a day by gaming the trading system at its very root.

This account is replayed in every industry at some level, for the concentration of regulatory reach, tax revenues and the power to distribute those revenues is irresistible to those seeking to protect or enlarge their share of the national income. Those enjoying a share of this immense swag will fight to their last breath to defend their share, while the debt-serfs paying the devilishly diffused taxes and fees are too overwhelmed, exhausted and distracted to resist or voice their objections. That is the essence of *Asymmetric Stakes in the Game*.

Illusions of Incremental Change

We introduced the *illusion of incremental change* in Chapter Ten:

The State and Plutocracy respond with incremental changes (simulacrum of fundamental change) which they hope will reverse the decline without affecting their power, wealth and privilege. Alas, merely adjusting the parameters in a failing system is not enough to rescue it from collapse.

The illusion of incremental change is both an appealing self-deception and a crassly conscious attempt to dissipate political discontent.

Various analogies spring to mind: a rotting bridge, to name but one. As boards rot to the threshold of breaking, then patches are made; new boards are tacked over the rotted planks to offer the illusion of repair, even as the beams and posts of the entire bridge weaken by the day. At some critical threshold (the "tipping point" or phase shift), the entire bridge collapses, "repairs" and all.

Superficial "reforms" and repairs made for show are simulacra designed to divert attention from real reforms, and thus minimize the sacrifices required by real change.

We all want to believe that our modest incremental changes will lead to fundamental transformation; but consciously or unconsciously, we select imitations of change rather than real transformation. This provides us with the comforting illusion that all our existing perquisites can continue on untouched by real change.

Believing our own self-deception, we also present these simulacra of reform as authentic in order to win the approval of others and gain a stay from real change. This blatant manipulation never strikes the originator as deceptive or fraudulent. For having convinced themselves that a facsimile of change is equivalent to true transformation, those presenting the illusions are enjoying the best of both worlds: they believe their own deceptions (and thus suffer fewer self-recriminations) and as a result their persuasive powers are enhanced when they "sell" simulacra of reform to others as real transformation.

That the bridge will collapse is not important; what is important is that it will collapse in the future, not now. That is the ultimate power of the illusion of incremental change.

The Decline of Transactional Churn

The credit/debt-dependent financial Plutocracy and the State both prosper off what I call transactional churn--the constant purchasing and sales of new goods and services which can be taxed and which require credit transactions that then generate enormous fees.

As the economy devolves, a new feedback loop forms: as incomes drop, people save more, buy less and speculate less with what remains of their wealth. Transactional and credit-based churn--the lifeblood of both the financial/banking Plutocracy and the State--plummets in a self-reinforcing (positive feedback) decline.

This steady erosion of income is itself a structural obstacle to reform, as it limits the State's ability to service debt and thus to placate all its competing fiefdoms and dependent constituencies with more borrowing.

The High-Cost Structure Economy

Previous chapters have laid out the reasons why the U.S. economy has become a high-cost, high-overhead system: marginal returns, complacency, etc. It is worth noting that together these forces have created a top-heavy economy resistant to cost-cutting. Just trimming budgets triggers internecine warfare, as noted above, but even that process does not address bureaucratic creep, endemic insurance fraud, a legal system which burdens every business with hidden costs, high taxes, an absurdly costly and inefficient healthcare system, etc.

Each layer of this systemic overhead is protected by an Elite or fiefdom with an asymmetric stake in the game, and thus each is impervious to meaningful reform. Since these high overhead costs are systemic in nature--meaning every enterprise pays high costs--then reforming any one layer, as painful as that will be, exerts a trivial reduction in overall systemic costs.

These high systemic costs constitute yet another insurmountable structural barrier to reform as they insure that whatever cost-cutting is accomplished will produce essentially trivial results despite its stupendous political cost.

Key concepts in this chapter:
Power density
The grand failure of government
Internecine conflict between protected fiefdoms
Theft by other means (inflation and devaluation)
Asymmetric Stakes in the Game
Transactional churn

Chapter Twenty-One: Incentives to Opt Out, Disincentives to Protest

When the inevitability of devolution and collapse becomes "obvious," the incentives for the productive to opt out will grow.

If structural reform is essentially impossible due to these mechanisms, then we must conclude the only alternatives are either devolution (erosion/degradation of the status quo into national insolvency) or a positive-feedback (self-reinforcing) collapse into national insolvency.

This conclusion will become increasingly "obvious" in the sense that the simulacrum politics of experience marketed by the mass media will lose credibility as the divergence between the lived experience of devolution and what's being presented as "reality" by the status quo widens to the breaking point.

The non-productive citizenry who are dependent on the State and its Power Elite partners in the entertainment/"news" industry (bread and circuses) will increasingly be channeled into fatalistic resignation, though some stirrings of dissatisfaction may bubble to the surface.

But lacking the organization and the (largely illusory) sense of political importance which the productive middle class enjoys, the unproductive classes are limited to spontaneous bursts of frustration and discontent which are easily suppressed by the still-formidable powers of the State. (Such restive "rebellions" will provide entertaining, titillating dollops of "news" even as they are ruthlessly crushed.)

The productive middle class is currently divided between the dwindling majority basking in a thinly buttressed complacency that the crumbling status quo is still in their best interests and a growing minority who have tasted either the ashes of personal insolvency or experienced the spiritual, ethical and financial bankruptcy of the status quo, including the mass media, the State and whatever cartel of the Plutocracy they have had the misfortune to encounter.

The middle class has been trained by years of "higher education" and other experience to fear the repercussions of political engagement (whistleblowers' careers are always the first fatalities) and to dismiss or discount the larger political forces which trigger crises in households (insolvency, enormous medical bills, etc). That is, they have been trained to internalize all causal factors--"if only I'd done X and Y, this wouldn't have happened"--a politics of experience which gives the State and Plutocracy a free hand to plunder, exploit and manipulate without fear of middle class resistance or insurrection.

Given the legitimate fears of legal and financial recriminations of resistance, the middle class has little appetite for the costs of resistance or protest such as having their heads truncheoned by riot police or garnering arrest records which could dog their career.

Fear of reprisal is a key State control technique even in a so-called free state. The restive nonproductive citizen could find his or her food stamps, disability and other "free" State largesse suddenly cut by opaque administrative measures.

The upstart middle class earner/small business owner could find their contract cancelled, their position eliminated, their bonus axed, their credit cut, trumped up "disciplinary" charges have been filed against them or even their tax records are being audited--all standard repression tactics.

All regimes defend themselves by providing incentives for passive compliance/productive labor and harsh disincentives for resistance, whistleblowing, non-compliance and organized (and thus dangerous to the status quo) protest. Given that visible protest carries the risk of physical beatings and arrest (and subsequent abuse), then the alienated citizen--unproductive and productive alike--will only risk joining "street" resistance if they no longer have a stake in the status quo.

Citizens with nothing to lose and no stake in maintaining the status quo are dangerous to the State (and thus to the Plutocracy), and so the State's first line of defense is to become a Savior State which showers entitlements as a way of providing voters and taxpayers with a stake in the system.

The second line of defense is to become a repressive Police State with an active secret intelligence program against domestic protest (as occurred in the late 1960s-early 1970s with domestic C.I.A. spying and COINTELPRO, the FBI's secret campaign to infiltrate, undermine, marginalize and/or subvert the antiwar movement).

These programs employed illegal entry ("black bag jobs") and surveillance, extralegal force and violence (creating and funding extremist front groups to commit the violence at arms distance from the Federal government), and psychological warfare ("dirty tricks," harassment, misinformation, setting up pseudo-movements run by government agents, threaten activists' parents landlords, employers, etc.)

The 1976 Church Committee formed to investigate the domestic intelligence campaigns concluded:

"Many of the techniques used would be intolerable in a democratic society even if all of the targets had been involved in violent activity, but COINTELPRO went far beyond that...**the Bureau conducted a sophisticated vigilante operation aimed squarely at preventing the exercise of First Amendment rights of speech and association.**"

Anyone who doesn't believe their government is capable of Police State repression and subversion of First Amendment rights should research COINTELPRO more fully. While you might have disagreed with the groups subverted in 1969, the line between "those radicals" in 1969 and "us tax protesters" in 2009 is thin to vanishing.

Nothing will be more threatening to the State and status quo than tax resistance/rebellion and former insiders (those whose belief in the system has faded) turning into whistleblowers on the web.

Here is one source text: War at Home: Covert action against U.S. activists and what we can do about it.

Put simply: the State holds all the hammers, and you know what happens to raised nails.

As German social theorist Max Weber observed, the State claims a "monopoly on the legitimate use of violence." Thus nonviolent, non-antagonistic, non-confrontational, perfectly legal opting out and radical self-reliance is the only viable response to the State's last-ditch attempt to sustain its over-reach by concentrating power, appropriating private wealth and ruthlessly suppressing overt resistance in a "dictatorship of the official."

For more on Weber's thinking, please read Science As a Vocation, Politics As a Vocation.

Unfortunately, the Savior State was only possible via an accident of favorable demographic and economic growth fueled by cheap abundant oil: a huge surge in productive population coupled with an equally massive surge in per capita income. Now that the demographic, resource and economic situation is entirely unfavorable, the Savior State is unsustainable.

The State and Plutocracy would be content to retain the State fiefdoms and eliminate or drastically scale down entitlements, but eliminating entitlements would remove the stake the unproductive class and much of the remaining productive class hold in the status quo. The State's self-destructive "solution" remains the same throughout history-- borrow stupendous sums of money until it can no longer borrow more, at which point it slips into insolvency.

The unproductive (non-tax paying, entitlement-dependent) class has every incentive to avoid risky actions and passively hope the Savior State can continue supporting them, even as the gulf between the State's promises and what it actually delivers widen.

The productive (taxpaying) class has an ever-diminishing incentive to support the status quo: as taxes, junk fees and the cost of the FEW essentials rise (food, energy and water), the Savior State has every incentive to cut entitlements to the middle class and increase taxes to maintain the State and Plutocracy's shares of national income.

In sum: the State can buy the passive complicity of the unproductive class and the active support of the Plutocracy, but the middle class stake in the system is far more problematic: "belief in the system" is the core of middle class compliance. The middle class has to believe that the increasingly obvious inequalities and Savior State/Plutocracy excesses are counterbalanced by the wealth, prestige and "good life" to be earned by laboring for the status quo. But once middle class wealth, income, security and confidence that this is fact "the good life" irrevocably erode, then the middle class "belief in the system" fades.

The only real defense the State can muster against this devolution is propaganda (the system serves your interests, it is the finest system in the world, your sacrifice is necessary, etc.) and punishment for those who question/resist.

The productive middle class can choose a path between complacency and risk-laden resistance: they can opt out.

The spectrum of ways to opt out is appealingly broad; one can work less hours, refuse the overworked/underpaid nightmare of supervisory positions, quit and start a small business in the cash/barter economy, take less demanding work for much less pay, offer services in trade for what services one needs or exit the high-cost urban lifestyle entirely and learn to live on extremely modest sums of cash money.

Having been raised to place a high premium on their own value as cogs in the machine, and perhaps on creativity and self-fulfillment as well, the productive middle class also has the choice to organize a political response to their ever-decreasing share of the national income.

This presents an insoluble double-bind to the State and Plutocracy partnership: they desperately need the middle class to "believe in the system:" to doggedly work as cogs in the increasingly unequal machine and pay enormous taxes and fees to the State while remaining docile and politically compliant.

But to actually increase the middle classes' relative share of the dwindling national income would require choosing between the intolerable--a relative reduction in State/Elite income--and the unpalatable-- arousing the passively dependent underclass by slashing their minimal bread and circuses benefits.

Yet as the gap between the reality of impending insolvency and the strained "happy story" promulgated by the Plutocracy's mass media (supporting the status quo is in your self-interest, etc.) and the not-so-veiled threats of the State (keep silent and pay up or else) widens to an unbridgeable chasm, the middle class is reluctantly roused from its complacent slumber.

The State cannot afford to alienate its middle class worker-bees/taxpayers/voters but neither can it reduce its own share of the national income or take income from the Plutocracy. Their response to middle class discontent will be more of the same but at a higher pitch: more frenzied propaganda, more simulacrum "reforms," more promises that these "reforms" will fix the crumbling system, and beneath the propaganda, more stringent enforcement of rules punishing those worker-bees who step out of line or who avoid their heavy tax burdens.

The game of managing declining national income and an ever more burdened productive class is fraught with risks, and the State's undoing is its over-reach and parasitic partnership with the Plutocracy: in protecting their share of the declining national income as the expense of the middle class, they drive an increasingly alienated middle class to choose between debt-serfdom, insolvency or opting out.

The great irony is that the Savior State cannot save itself.

The reason is the very actions which the State deploys to stave off the threat of insolvency virtually guarantee that insolvency.

The State's reaction to yawning budget deficits is to borrow vast sums of money by issuing debt (bonds) and to expand the money supply by debauching or devaluing the money supply. In the old days, this required issuing new metal coinage which contained less silver and more base metal, and then attempting to pass off the new currency as equal in value to the old. But bad money drives out good money (which disappears via hoarding/saving) and the currency's true value is quickly realized.

As State borrowing crowds out productive private borrowing, then interest rates steadily rise, further raising the costs of servicing the old State debt. This increase in costs must be offset by increased borrowing, and so a positive feedback is established--higher debt pushes up interest rates which then increases the need for even more debt, and so on.

The "solution" of borrowing ever-greater sums is thus self-destructive: that feedback loop alone will bring the State to its fiscally insolvent knees.

But just as destructively, this spiraling-ever-higher cost of interest payments crowds out State spending, and the choices of what to cut are bleak indeed: imposing any additional tax burdens on the Plutocracy is highly dangerous, as the State is doomed once the Plutocracy senses it is now an enemy rather than a partner. Cutting off bread and circuses to the unproductive class raises the possibility of chaotic mass insurrection; as the Bob Marley song noted, "A hungry mob is an angry mob."

Given these dreadful choices, the State finds the least risky option is to lean ever more heavily on the middle class for tax revenue and other sacrifices. But this too is self-destructive, as the State Elites are also doomed once they push the middle class past "the tipping point"/phase shift where opting out becomes visibly less painful than attempting to labor on as a debt-serf, attempting to stay afloat in a sea of rising FEW costs, interest rates and taxes/junk fees.

The State's increasingly desperate plundering of the productive class via taxes and junk fees sets up another positive feedback whose destructive consequences are strangely invisible to the State's Elites/upper-caste: the more they squeeze the middle class, the more reasons they give the middle class to opt out--especially small business owners and entrepreneurs who are the engines of economic vitality and growth.

Those middle class citizenry who still believe the system enables real change will soon be disillusioned of this naive faith, as the State's

Elites and fiefdoms will undermine, suppress, co-opt or otherwise eviscerate all real reforms in order to protect their perquisites. This suppression will be another Pyrrhic victory for the State, as the resulting alienation/divergence will only further erode middle class "belief in the system."

Rising interest rates due to massive State borrowing not only cuts State spending, it also raises the cost of doing business and owning real estate for the middle class. Even as they struggle they will note that behind the propaganda/facsimile reforms, the State upper-caste Elites and the financial Plutocracy continue their unrestrained looting of the system via their well-concealed independent, parallel structure of exclusive enrichment.

The question will eventually arise: why bother working this hard?

At a certain point of pain, *samadhi*/enlightenment will dawn, and middle class households will awaken to their untenable predicament: complacent belief in a failing system is clearly not a guarantee of security and wealth, yet they fear the consequences of protest and have lost faith in the political process as all legitimate efforts at authentic reform are suppressed, compromised or co-opted.

The fatalism of their underclass brethren is also unappealing, as a life sitting in front of the TV/propaganda-delivery-device is not what people accustomed to a productive life find rewarding or even satisfactory.

Opting out is thus the most rewarding solution in an imperfect and limited field of options. I have addressed the context for the decision to opt out in *Chapter Twelve, Squeezing the Middle Class* and in *Chapter Thirteen, When Belief in the System Fades*. At one end of the spectrum of options lies Splendid Isolation, a near-complete withdrawal from the system and from attempts to transform it. At the other end is conscious pursuit of a role in The Remnant, the non-State, non-Elite self-organizing group leading by example rather than by mass media-based exhortation.

Between these lies a wealth of other choices which I term *hybrid work*: one finger in the wage economy (however marginally), one in growing food, another in creative pursuits, another in trading childcare for elderly care, another in hedging/investing to preserve purchasing power, another in helping to develop locally owned distributed energy (as in "owning one's own source of energy") as either a technical innovator, an investor or provider of labor/supervision and yet another in local schooling.

Once taxable incomes fall to a low level (what I term *stable impoverishment*), so too does tax support of the failing State apparatus. Once spending in the status quo economy ($300 handbags, $1,000 electronics, $200 per night hotel rooms, $3,000 per month office rents, $2,000 per month mortgages, re-financing, etc.) falls, then so does support of the debt-serf-dependent financial Plutocracy.

Intuitively, we all understand that money is the source of all power. Reduce their money and you reduce their power. While the middle class has effectively zero chance of diffusing the concentrated power of the State fiefdoms and the Plutocracy cartels by direct electoral politics (for the reasons noted above), it has immense power to "starve the beasts" of tax revenues and transactional churn. And since there are no legal disincentives to these actions, there is no punishment/repression which can be meted out by The Powers That Be.

This is, after all, how all empires collapse: the productive class, crushed by high taxes and "necessary sacrifices," its own interests divergent from the State and Plutocracy, finally acts on its own behalf and opts out, leaving the State and Elites to the unenviable but necessary transformation of insolvency. Life on the ground goes on; it is life in the halls of power and wealth which is utterly changed.

The negative feedback loops which protect the State fiefdoms and private-sector cartels are far more powerful than any political movement the middle class could mount; even heroes and heroines who attempt to work "within the system" get co-opted soon enough by the Powers That Be or ground down by the system's inertia, complexity and resistance.

The State/Plutocracy partnership has no feedback mechanisms to force productivity or consumption once the middle class withdraws its support.

Once the middle class opts out of earning large sums of taxable income and the debt-dependent "American Dream," then the ailing dinosaurs (the State and Plutocracy) will fiscally implode. Their only form of persuasion is the mass media, their 24/7 propaganda machine. But that too has no feedback mechanism to thwart non-compliance. Turning off the broadcasts effectively neuters the entire propaganda machine.

These three opt-out options--turning off the mass media, reducing income to the level where taxes owed are modest and refusing debt-based consumption of superficial goods and services--are within reach of every citizen. Each action is legal and carries no disincentive/ punishment.

There is a great irony is the Plutocracy/State's lack of negative feedback to counter the middle class opting out. The irony is that the middle class has no negative feedback countermeasure to the concentration of wealth and power of the Elites and State, and that lack of influence and options is what will drive the middle class to opt out.

Many middle class households will opt out not by choice but by painful necessity: the loss of any one middle-class job within a household can mean the end of credit, homeownership, savings, college, healthcare and a host of other options which were once taken for granted. This process of loss can be internally shattering, and we must acknowledge the lengthy, difficult process of denial, bargaining, anger and acceptance which characterizes such great loss.

Key concepts in this chapter:

Hybrid work

Chapter Twenty-Two: The Process of Internal Transformation

By definition, internal transformation means our understanding and worldview have changed even as the external world remains unchanged.

By changing our internal expectations, we eliminate one source of misery and internal strife.

Studies have revealed a common-sense correlation between happiness and expectations: those (usually low-income) with low expectations which can actually be met are significantly happier than those with high expectations which cannot be met. Thus part of the process of moving from unhappiness, hostility, grief and loss to acceptance, hope and a positive view of life is to reconcile unrealistic internalized (often manufactured by the mass media) expectations with what life actually offers.

A classic example of the causal nature of expectations originated in Hong Kong a few years ago. Immigrant maids who worked long hours six days a week for wealthy Hong Kong households were found to be much happier than their employers, who often suffered from depression, anxiety and even thoughts of suicide. By the usual material measures of "success and happiness," the outcome should have been reversed.

But while the bourgeois Hong Kong residents internalized expectations for wealth, success and recognition which were impractical or impossible to meet, the maids were buoyed by the meaning of the labor--supporting their families back home in the Philippines--and by their one day of socializing with other immigrant workers.

This essential transformation of expectations is made all the more difficult by the consumerist marketing ethos described earlier which generates insecurity, dissatisfaction and unrealistic externally-dependent expectations as key motivators for buying unneeded goods and services (and thus generating profits).

An entire constellation of complex emotions may be triggered by a devolution in financial wealth and loss of home and livelihood: anger, resentment, grieving, confusion, and even betrayal. The thinking may follow this line: I did what was expected of me, I played by the rules, I worked hard, and now my life is a shambles. This isn't right, it's not fair.

When the credit-dependent path of perversely dissatisfying "material happiness" comes to an end, many who believed in the system may well feel betrayal as well as loss. These emotions may parallel those felt by people who have been intimately betrayed by loved ones or betrayed by business/financial partners. They may feel they "did their part" and as such they don't deserve this harsh fate.

The entitlement mindset that we are each "owed" a pension, healthcare, housing, a livelihood, etc., by the Savior State also feeds a self-defeating resentment and sense of betrayal.

The underlying assumption was that the exponential-credit/bubble economy was supposed to "work" in some enduring fashion: higher debt was supposed to enable a "nicer" lifestyle, rising housing values were supposed to effortlessly fund a permanent increase of material improvements, and so on. The collapse of security and assets/equity may feel like a betrayal, and all those who feel betrayed by their own self-destructive actions will feel a great temptation to blame someone other than themselves.

Ironically, the very forces which rigged the game and manufactured the politics of experience which fostered the delusions of grandeur (wealth without saving or sacrifice, etc.) are rarely identified as responsible by the average middle class citizen, who has been trained to "accept responsibility" rather than probe abstract structural forces.

Thus the person experiencing resentment, betrayal, grief, loss and anger may well blame something other than the two actual causes: their own actions and choices (i.e. embracing the delusion of exponential credit expansion and ephemeral wealth as real) and the marketing/media system which profited from their embrace of delusion.

The process of accepting personal responsibility for one's actions and seeing the system for what it truly is beneath the superficial simulacrum is a painful one for all of us. But placing personal integrity above all else is immensely freeing.

Many who undergo this transformation of understanding describe the feeling as liberating, as if a great burden had been lifted from their shoulders. All that they once thought so important--the private school, the expansive house, the nameplate vehicle, the title, degree or corner office, the seasons tickets to the ball game, and so on--are revealed as unimportant compared to health, family, friends, acting in good faith and with complete individual integrity, true productivity, simple food and simple pleasures.

This transformation eventually extends from accepting responsibility for one's own health, retirement, livelihood and spiritual attainment to a realization that each citizen is also responsible for the larger community tasks of education, governance and security. Once the Savior State collapses into insolvency, this larger responsibility of each citizen will become clear to all.

This transformation is thus not just accepting lower expectations; it also requires consciously chosen positive action. The following quote by Nikola Tesla, submitted by oftwominds.com reader Kenneth R., neatly encapsulates this understanding:

"Every effort under compulsion demands a sacrifice of life energy."

We might also add this quote from Eric Hoffer: *"We lie the loudest when we lie to ourselves."*

Hoffer was one of the first thinkers to grasp how mass movements (religious and political alike) acted as a substitute for self-worth; this is the basis of their tremendous appeal to people who feel lost, adrift, without hope, etc. Hoffer clearly identified the Devil's Pact nature of mass movements: even as they gave the "believers" a newfound, heady sense of purpose and empowerment, they enabled destructive fanaticism and took away the individual's ability to think or judge for himself. This Devil's Pact inevitably leads to fascism, authoritarianism, loss of democracy and national self-destruction.

From one perspective, the entire "religion" of credit-dependent, media-driven consumerism which is the "engine of the U.S. economy" is just such a destructive mass movement; individual critical thinking and engagement in the real world are diverted and diminished in order to maximize the Plutocracy/State's profit and power.

Put another way: the distraction and self-destruction of the citizenry serves the financial-banking Plutocracy and the State quite admirably.

The process of internal transformation is essentially one of illusion, artifice and self-serving denial being replaced by truth, acceptance and integrity.

Chapter Twenty-Three: The Structure of Change

Just as there is an ontological risk in any prediction--for the simple reason the future is unknown--there is an equal ontological risk in prescriptive solutions. Though this is a complex and knotty issue, we can summarize it (slightly tongue-in-cheek) thusly:

Humans only change when they have no other choice.

It is remarkably easy to present prescriptive "solutions" of the idealistic sort which promote working together to save the planet, creating programs to ease human suffering, etc. These "solutions" are readily dismissed because they ignore the reality of human self-interest, greed and self-aggrandizement, all of which reach their perfection in the entirely practical and selectively compelling *windfall exploitation* discussed earlier.

We have also seen how complacency, fatalism, cognitive and structural traps and propaganda all encourage inaction and passivity in the face of gathering crises.

Before presenting solutions, it is thus critical that we first examine the structure and processes of change. In the previous chapter, we looked at the process of internal transformation, what we might characterize as the move from ignorance to knowledge and from complacent acceptance of the status quo's *politics of experience* to a skeptical adherence to authenticity.

This inner transformation leads to changes in behavior and action which then cause changes in the community and eventually the nation. Since the private-sector middle class/entrepreneurial class has no positive choice left but to opt out, that inner decision will speed the State's slide into insolvency.

This will enable the eventual emergence of what I term *The New State* which re-sets the U.S. society to the baseline rights defined by the Constitution--rights summarized in the Declaration of Independence as those to life, liberty and the pursuit of happiness--and offers negative feedback to the current dominance of Elites.

We have already described several models of change.

1. Cycles of price, debt accumulation and renunciation that model long-term periods of stability and instability in economies and societies.

2. Depletion, which triggers technological transformation (development of alternative sources) or social instability as populations

fall or move away.

3. Devolution as systemic challenges are masked but not resolved.

4. Over-reach, vulnerability and collapse--phase shifts, power laws, self-organized criticalities (SOC) and the stick/slip hypothesis.

5. The Pareto Principle: the "vital few" can influence the "trivial many."

6. Feedback loops (adding a new feedback introduces change).

These models share a systems analysis perspective. Societies collapse when energy inputs are no longer sufficient to support their infrastructure, as societies fail complexity decreases, and so on. Though insightful on many levels, this systems approach fails to account for the *experience of change.* To those living through a period of rapid, confusing, even chaotic change, a systems analysis does not illuminate their lived experience nor contribute to their decision-making process as individuals and households.

This is why I approached the structure of change from the experiential *Process of Internal Transformation.* Observations of the real world can trigger changes in our conceptual understanding which manifests in behavioral changes which ultimately lead to fundamental changes in the observable world.

Thus internal changes are structurally integral to any understanding of the process of change.

At a conceptual level, standard economic and political theories have virtually nothing meaningful or predictive to say about the structure of change:

1. Mainstream economists (academics, think-tankers, State functionaries, et al.) almost universally ignore the fact that the economy is dependent on a real world of dirt, rain, oil, trees, bees, seas, etc. and thus all their metrics (GDP, inventory, EBITA, and so on) are essentially superficial and ontologically (that is, inherently) misleading quantitative traps.

Thus the discussion is on "growth" as if that has nothing to do with energy/soil/water depletion, shifting climate trends, bacterial resistance to drugs, demographics, etc.

2. The entire field of modern economics has evolved in the eyeblink of recorded human history in which fossil fuels were cheap and abundant and advances in health and agriculture enabled a stupendous explosion of the human population. It is as if a field of social study was developed

in a brief century or two of Rome's glory years and then held up as universally accurate for all time, even as the Roman Empire imploded.

As the era which seemed permanent to those living in it changes, then their "social science" is suddenly revealed as an absurdly short-sighted and limited byproduct of a unique time. Thus we can anticipate the "death of modern economics" as the underlying assumptions on which the field is grounded change dramatically.

3. In a similar fashion, we can anticipate the bankruptcy of the major ideologies which developed in this same unique era: Neoliberal Capitalism and Marxism/socialism.

As I noted above, an idealized "libertarian" laissez faire society/economy would fully accommodate the worst excesses of exploitation and serfdom. As I discussed in detail in Chapter Fifteen: The Crisis of Neoliberal Capitalism, "unfettered markets" are not self-regulating but rather mechanisms which enable vast exploitation of the gulf between the carefully nurtured ignorance of the exploited masses and the equally carefully protected insider knowledge of the exploiters.

For more on this concept, I recommend Joseph Stiglitz's Globalization and Its Discontents.

What those mired in the dogma of "free markets" (in an analysis of where the knowledge lies, there is never a truly free market) fail to grasp is that capitalism's ontological drive to deploy capital and knowledge in whatever configurations maximize profits will elevate windfall exploitation, monopoly capital/cartels and opacity/secrecy as the most desirable conditions, as each one maximizes profits by reducing risk and concentrating (and thus leveraging) capital, power, production and protected knowledge.

This enables manipulating the market via price-fixing, fraud, collusion, etc. and/or the establishment of an ersatz "crony capitalism" simulacrum and presenting it as "market capitalism" via a mass media propaganda machine.

Just as the selective advantages of concentrating capital, collusion and cloaked knowledge are ontological, so too is the outsized influence such concentrations of power will bring to bear on the State's attempts to regulate over-reach and excessive exploitation. The collusive and mutually rewarding partnership of the State and Plutocracy is thus inevitable, as each gains irreplaceable benefits from the other concentration of power and from looting/exploiting the non-Elite/non-

State productive citizenry.

From one perspective, this (along with globalization) is simply windfall exploitation writ large.

This mechanism explains why socialism and Marxist regimes and structures (such as unions) are prone to the same looting, corruption, collusion and fraud as private capital: the State and unions are also concentrations of power and thus they too have undue influence over non-Elite productive citizenry.

A recent news item noted that the fire chief of a small California community gamed the system to "retire" at 51 years of age at an annual pension of $241,000, while continuing to work for the fire department as a "consultant" at a salary of $176,000 a year. If that is not looting the non-State taxpaying citizenry, then pray tell what does qualify?

Just as is the case with private-sector capital, obfuscation and opacity serve the State and its Elites well; the pension rules in the above case go back to 1931 and run in the hundreds of pages, guaranteeing insiders can game the system while keeping the citizenry safely in the dark.

Since the major print media is also union-dominated, the unions and their State collaborators have had little to fear from media exposure. Indeed, the mass media can only issue shrill appeals to "save our institutions" via ever-higher taxes; investigations of fraud, collusion, looting, gaming the system and other State-authorized mechanisms of exploitation are rare.

Thus both ideological dogmas, capitalism and socialism, share the same fatal flaws of concentrating power and opacity.

Each is a mechanism which exploits the gulf between the carefully nurtured ignorance of the exploited citizenry and the equally carefully protected knowledge of the Power Elite.

Is there any wonder that crony capitalism can thrive under fascism as easily as it thrives under Neoliberal democracy, or that the State and its upper-caste fiefdoms can thrive equally under so-called socialist regimes and so-called free market regimes? Just as the Plutocracy and the State are two sides of one coin, so too are monopoly capital and State fiefdoms two sides of the same concentrated-power coin. Both suppress transparency at every turn.

4. These concentrations are power are ontologically vulnerable to disruption in two ways: any structural concentration heightens

vulnerability (think of a single train station through which all traffic must be routed or a single power station serving an entire state), and any systemic concentration of power leads inevitably to over-reach as every obstacle to their increase of the national income is overcome.

Another way of understanding the momentum of concentrations of power is that the more powerful they become, the more adept they become at sweeping aside institutional negative feedbacks which act to counter their over-reach.

In an structural irony akin to a supernova star, the larger they become the more vulnerable they become to implosion/degradation.

The Pareto Principle, which we invoked to describe the potential leverage of the Remnant, also applies to concentrations of power. Once an Elite controls 20% of the resources of any particular structure, then they wield outsized influence on the remaining 80%. Since State employees (all levels of government and quasi-governmental agencies) exceed 20% of the workforce, they exert outsized influence on the 80% non-State private-sector employees.

Thus at certain thresholds of power--what might be termed phase or quantum shifts--then Elites' power accretion and influence leap to new ever-more dominant heights.

These mechanisms explain how the Power Elites of cartel/crony/monopoly capital (who own or control 2/3 of the productive assets of the nation) and State fiefdoms (which absorb 40% of the GDP) influence the entire economy to enlarge their shares of the national income.

With these two hands firmly squeezing their throats, the declining class of productive non-Elites have no choice but to submit to debt-serfdom, devolve into insolvency/penury or opt out. In this way, their very concentration of power drives the Plutocracy/State to over-reach which then crushes the productive class they depend on for debt servicing and taxes.

Can reducing complex systems and interactions to this level capture the essential structure of large-scale change? Or is such simplicity misleading?

Consider the Plutocracy: calling a complex mix of people, institutions and enterprises a single class is of course simplistic: what are the precise thresholds for membership, and so on. But as I explained earlier, the Plutocracy is not neatly monolithic or neatly conspiratorial, with secret membership lists and the like. It is a self-organizing group drawn together by shared interests: preservation of capital, reduction of risk, expansion of income/return on capital, extending influence within the State, etc.

The same argument can be used on the State: hasn't the social safety net of entitlements eased the suffering of the citizenry? What about all the conflicting political forces within the sprawling vastness of the State?

One way to reach an answer is to turn the question around: is complexity itself a trap of sorts, a black hole into which explanations fall and disintegrate in endless explorations of interactions? In other words, is complexity itself a distraction, or even more troubling, an excuse for passivity?

Complexity creates *information asymmetry*--unequal access to information--and opens up vast opportunities for gaming the system. Thus complexity itself is a tool of domination by Elites and the State. Like its conceptual twin transparency, simplicity is the mortal enemy of Elites key weapons of control: secrecy, obfuscation, disinformation, information asymmetry and complexity itself.

If we cannot divine first principles and fundamental structures beneath the noise and confusion of endless complexities, then there truly is no way forward; we are fated to bob on the choppy sea of complexity without a compass, a navigational system or even a sense of the drifting currents.

Just as identifying the deep underlying forces--resource depletion, over-reach, concentration of power--is the key to an integrated analysis, cutting through complexity to identify key forces of change is the key to selecting responses with high probabilities of positive results.

Primary Processes of Change

Let us now examine the primary processes of change in modern Neoliberal economies (or whatever domestically convenient ideological labels they attach to themselves).

1. Opaque influence of Elites. Since they hold the levers of concentrated power, Elites within the State (especially the Executive branch) and financial Plutocracy can launch profound changes on their own.

Within recent history, the Vietnam War is a prime example: the war was escalated by a mere handful of men in the Executive branch, with fatal consequences for 50,000 Americans and approximately 1.5 million Vietnamese, Cambodians and Laotians.

Neither the public nor the financial power Elites were clamoring for a land war in Asia, though the Elites soon exploited the windfalls the war spending opened.

On occasion a State Elite may instigate a positive change; For example, Theodore Roosevelt enabled the National Park system and limited some of the worst excesses of his class via "trust busting" regulations.

Another recent example is the relaxation of various regulatory structures that were legacies of the Great Depression. Neither the public nor the State's high-caste bureaucrats were clamoring for the evisceration of financial regulations; the rentier-financial Power Elites instigated these changes in order to open more windfall-exploitation opportunities.

This process is the standard methodology Elites deploy to increase their share of the national income.

Examples include: lobbying a campaign-donation-hungry member of Congress to insert a tax break in a voluminous and therefore opaque bill; lobbying the Pentagon to include specifications for a weapons systems which narrow the potential contractors to one; insert language in a pension reform act which vastly increases the opportunities for public retiree looting of the pension system, and so on.

The key is that the lobbying is discrete, opaque and difficult to expose. In general the only way such opaque influence comes to light is via an insider; hence the violent and immediate suppression and punishment of any whistleblowers who dare expose the collusion, cronyism, capture of the regulatory process, looting, embezzlement and fraud at the heart of the State and Plutocracy.

2. Market forces. Despite the best efforts of the State and capital Elites to manage and control market prices, prices based on supply and demand fluctuate as global markets are not within complete control of the Plutocracy or the State. While certain price fluctuations can be extremely profitable to the Plutocracy, the State prefers prices to be stable lest the citizenry rouse themselves from their slumber.

Thus if gasoline doubles in price due to various global

supply/demand/speculative forces, then demand will drop accordingly. If money/credit becomes cheap, then borrowing will increase, and so on. Market forces, especially in energy, can trigger rapid changes in other markets, creating domino effects that ripple through the global economy and trigger negative feedback from the State: price controls, release of strategic reserves, etc.

3. Financial-geopolitical shocks/natural disasters. The world is a collection of uncertainties and instabilities bound by various feedbacks, but all systems are prone to non-linear events which can be characterized as chaotic, fractal, etc. The State responds in some fashion to counteract the instability, and the success or failure of that attempt to restore stability to the system can unleash further change.

Recent examples include 9/11, Hurricane Katrina, oil doubling in price, the Federal bailout of mortgage lenders, etc.

When the State response fails to counter dissolution of stability, when supply/demand lead to chronic shortages and price spikes--in other words, when negative feedbacks fail--then interlocking forces can cascade in falling-dominoes fashion, setting off changes which might at first glance appear unrelated to the initial instability.

As noted earlier, these events and domino-like cascades track the mathematical models of phase shifts, power laws, self-organized criticalities (SOC) and the stick/slip hypothesis.

Similarly, the Pareto Principle models how relatively small forces and effects can wield outsized influence on larger systems: when 20% of the people are unemployed/opt out, then the effect on the employed 80% are outsized; when 20% of a neighborhood's homes are in foreclosure/abandoned, the neighborhood tips into a phase shift in which abandonment gathers momentum, and so on.

4. *Citizen pushback* to Elites over-reach. The Federal government's interest in limiting dumping of toxic materials and other visible environmental dangers was non-existent in the 1960s until rivers caught fire and the public roused itself to demand protection.

In my analysis, this was *citizen pushback* introduced a new negative feedback loop which did not exist before against capital/industrial over-reach (unfettered dumping of toxins because it was the cheapest way to dispose of industrial waste). The State, happily partnered with industrial polluters and other Elites, was forced (over extreme objections of the industrial corporations) to meet the demands of the voters/taxpayers for protection.

In other cases, it is State over-reach which generates citizen pushback in the form of tax rebellions like Prop 13 in California. Until that citizen rebellion, the State was delighted to raise property taxes more or less at will to fund its swelling fiefdoms.

In the case of citizen pushback, ideas which have been percolating in small groups (according to the Pareto principle, groups of around 4% of the populace can have outsized influence on 64% of the populace) suddenly crystallize in the public consciousness as the solution to a problem which suddenly presses on a majority of the citizenry.

It is thus of critical importance that these ideas circulate in advance of crisis.

5. Cultural transformations. The forces of internal and cultural transformation need not have a financial or economic foundation; for instance, consumption of alcoholic beverages rises and falls in cycles which do not correlate that closely to prosperity and depression, but which nonetheless affect legislation, enforcement, sales of alcohol, etc.

In a similar fashion, religious and spiritual movements can arise with profound effects on the body politic and the economy.

In the current era of interlocking crises, I believe it is inevitable that the propaganda, simulacra, ersatz "reforms," looting, collusion, embezzlement and fraud will engender a pervasive loss of institutional legitimacy and fatally erode trust in private and public Elites alike.

Such a movement gathers force not in the streets but in the minds of those whose belief in the system has faded to the point they choose to opt out rather than support a self-serving, over-reaching State and Plutocracy with their labor and taxes. This in a nutshell is how empires collapse: one person at a time changes their mind when they realize the system no longer serves their best interests.

Key concepts in this chapter:
The New State
Experience of change
Process of Internal Transformation
Information asymmetry
Citizen pushback

Chapter Twenty-Four: The Principles of Systemic Response

For those of you who skipped over the tedious analysis to "cut to the chase"--the goal here is what I term full-spectrum prosperity: health, well-being, and a meaningful life.

If this analysis is sound, then the pervasive devolution I have predicted will soon be apparent to us all. If this analysis is wrong, then we shall soon see a return to the debt-based prosperity of the past three decades.

It is an odd trait of both markets and human beings that by the time collapse is unfolding, it is too late to change the momentum or set up alternative plans. The Chinese have a proverb that expresses this very concisely: "When you're thirsty, it's too late to dig a well."

Essentially we face two basic choices: either complacently habituate to devolution and fatalistically accept the dire consequences of collapse, or take goal-directed actions which have a high probability of improving the odds that the Great Transformation will be positive--for us, for our communities and for our nation.

We come now to the heart of our integrated understanding and the responses that are most likely to foster prosperity and security.

Let's establish these contexts:

- The responses are built on principles, not "one size fits all" solutions. There are no "one size fits all" fixes to the many interlocking challenges we face as individuals/households, communities and as a nation. Solutions will be specific to individuals and communities and voluntarily chosen, not imposed.
- The Internet is integral to the transparency and exchange of ideas that will enable positive responses.
- Hybrid models of work, collaboration, capital, production and trade will replace highly centralized, "factory" hierarchical models in many situations.
- Solutions and responses are dynamically evolving in response to changing circumstances and feedbacks. Thus there is no one investment strategy which will maintain purchasing power in all circumstances. Flexibility, adaptability and acceptance of failure as part of the process are key to successfully navigating the

dynamic era ahead. *"Success consists of going from failure to failure without loss of enthusiasm."* (Winston Churchill)

- Since *"There is no security on this earth, there is only opportunity"* (Douglas MacArthur), contingency planning—having a "Plan B"—is essential in every situation.

Let's revisit Chapter Three's "five distinct issues to sort out":

1. The elements of human nature which lend themselves to cycles and manipulation

2. The nature of the energy, financial and environmental trends/crises which are heralding the Great Transformation

3. The nature of the negative and positive feedback loops which determine the system's stability and direction

4. The responses which have a high probability of making the Transformation positive

5. The nature of future work and the skillsets best suited to prospering during the Great Transformation

As for Point One, I think we have adequately addressed the many cognitive traps and the equally unproductive attractions of complacency and fatalism.

As for Point Two, I think we now understand that we face not some isolated, temporary "financial crisis" or even a political crisis, but an interconnected, self-reinforcing series of crises and challenges which span every level of modern life, from the internal politics of experience to depleting resources to degraded environment to financial and political domination by Elites of capital and State and on to demographics and the host of ills triggered by over-reach.

The ultimate context of our integrated understanding is that the world must use the remaining extractable reserves of fossil fuels to construct an alternative energy system that does not rely on cheap, abundant fossil fuels. The cost of such a global system is unknown, but I would start with $100 trillion or roughly three years of global GDP as a starting estimate.

As noted before, wealth is simply stored energy. Without energy, there is no wealth. Virtually all of what we consider wealth is merely a reflection or consequence of cheap, abundant oil.

If humanity foolishly consumes the last of its planetary "gift" of easily extractable oil, coal and natural gas on vacations, suburban lifestyles and other non-productive uses, then when fossil fuels enter the final depletion stage there won't be enough to construct a sustainable energy system.

As for Point Three, we have discussed numerous traps and the nature of positive and negative feedback systems. Most importantly, we discussed how the middle class is being squeezed to extinction and in Section Two how the concentration of power and capital has created institutional and systemic vulnerability. We have also described the insurmountable barriers to standard reforms and thus established that devolution and insolvency (financial collapse) are the inevitable end-state of the current system.

Let us now turn to Point Four: The Principles of Systemic Response that have a high probability of making the Transformation positive.

These principles are scale-invariant, meaning that they apply equally to individuals, households, enterprises, communities and nation-States.

1. Engagement. Democracy is a feedback loop that requires active engagement. Democracy and the liberties it protects cannot be sustained by any "launch and forget" mechanisms. Setting up a regulatory system does not mean no further input is necessary; concentrations of capital and power will eventually capture or co-opt any State structure. That is the nature of concentrated-power Elites and the nature of State bureaucracies.

The majority of citizens are disengaged from participatory democracy. Barely 40% can rouse themselves to vote, never mind serve on committees, lobby local government, contact their representatives, etc. If a people get the government they deserve, then disengagement deserves devolution and collapse.

It is insightful to understand democracy as a series of feedback loops. The Elites will always have access to the State decisionmakers-- this is a feedback loop. As their power becomes more concentrated, then they can purchase ever more influence over the State and thus funnel an ever-larger share of the national income into their accounts. This is a positive feedback loop.

The feedback from the citizens is weak to non-existent and thus it has to date offered little resistance to the positive feedbacks of the Elites and State. Even though introducing (or re-introducing) citizen feedback seems to have no effect, the Pareto Principle suggests that a mere 4% of the citizenry can greatly influence 64%.

As the interests of the Elite and State have diverged from the common interest, a *profound political disunity* has emerged. As we have seen from the example of Rome, the Elites will fight to maintain the status quo even as the Empire collapses around them. No estate, no matter how well-defended, can escape the consequences of devolution and collapse.

This disunity/disharmony is the inevitable result of Elite/State over-reach. The ultimate goal of an engaged citizenry is not to "save" the self-destructive State and Elites from the consequences of their over-reach, but to establish the foundation of what I term *The New State* which can only arise from the ashes of the failed plutocracy/Savior State. This will require transparency and robust feedback loops from the citizenry to the State.

If the citizenry are not already engaged, then there will be no foundation for a New State to emerge.

Advocacy--that is, demanding a larger slice of State spoils--is not engagement, it is lobbying. If we begin by asking *cui bono*, then the difference between engaging in participatory democracy for the common good and for private profit becomes clear.

We can summarize engagement thusly: add a feedback loop or strengthen an existing one which has been allowed to wither or decay.

2. Transparency. As I have described above, transparency is anathema to crony capitalism and the State Elites, for the truly profitable looting, embezzlement, profiteering, price-fixing, State-mandated monopolies, public pension gaming, etc. can only occur in secrecy or purposeful obscurity. I have also noted that it is the nature of capitalism to establish cartels, oligarchy and monopoly as the most profitable alternatives to competition, and to cloak or mask these structures behind facades of free-market capitalism.

The State also has a tropism for secrecy, as all the partnering of the Elites and the State gives the lie to the separation of powers, free-market capitalism, and all the rest of the intellectual framework which supports the status quo.

On a household level, transparency can take the form of an accurate household budget. Without this transparency, then prudent planning is impossible. This holds true for households, enterprises, towns and nations.

The primary goal of an engaged citizenry is thus public transparency in service of this question: *cui bono*--to whose benefit?

Transparency might be called "the three Ts" because it implicitly requires Truth (as opposed to facsimiles of transparency, misrepresentations, deceptive accounting, manipulated data, etc.) and Trust that the feedback from auditors and oversight mechanisms has not been compromised by Elite and/or State interference/influence.

Without truth and trust then transparency degrades into just another simulacrum of authenticity packaged for propaganda purposes.

3. Accountability. A key goal of propaganda, simulacra, facsimiles, misrepresentations, manipulated data, disinformation, secrecy and complexity itself is to misdirect or diffuse accountability from those benefiting from looting, embezzlement, bribes, fraud, sweetheart contracts, gaming the system, monopoly, etc.

There are two ways to eliminate accountability: break the link between action and consequence--that is, incompetence or criminal behavior draw no countering action such as termination, investigation, clawback of embezzled funds, etc.--and confuse/craze the chain of responsibility so that no one individual or group of individuals is held accountable for their actions (or inaction).

For individuals and households, accountability starts at home.

4. An Adult Understanding (Triage and Trade-offs). As we have described above, the marketing/media complex and entitlement/victimhood mindset propagated by the Savior State have both encouraged and incentivized a *permanent adolescence* which is dominated by justifications, excuses, impulsive desires, instant gratification, low competence, irresponsibility, self-destructiveness, profound internal insecurity and a reliance on shrill claims of victimhood and need.

Engagement, transparency and accountability are incompatible with permanent adolescence and require what I term *an adult understanding* of life: that cost-benefit analyses are required on all time scales (short, medium and long-term) and that trade-offs must be made in all situations. An adult understanding grasps the necessity for triage, the always difficult and occasionally ruthless sorting of dead-end strategies from those which may yet be productive. Distinguishing needs from wants is also a form of triage.

As the Savior State implodes in insolvency, permanent adolescence will yield ever more marginal returns (the greater the effort and energy invested, the lower the returns). Recognizing that is the first step to an adult understanding.

A productive second step is seeking to leverage existing assets (financial, skillsets, networks, etc.) and reworking incentives to reward productivity, creation of value and surplus.

5. Redundancy/Distributed Risk/Hedging. One of the key tenets of this entire analysis is the rising vulnerabilities and risks created by long, fragile supply chains and highly concentrated wealth, power and production. Examples abound: if all the electrical power to a region is carried by one set of transmission lines, then that system is far more vulnerable to disruption than one with multiple or redundant lines.

This is yet another case in which markets fail at the least opportune time. It is more profitable to concentrate production and transport than to distribute over a network, and much cheaper to rely on one line or center of production than to invest in redundant systems. Thus when the sole supplier/transport fails or is disrupted, the market spirals into panic because there is no short-term alternative source or supply.

At the household level, hedging, redundancy and distributing risk comes down to actions such as: having a backup skill, trade or alternative source of income; when wheat is cheap, then buy quantities in secure storage against the inevitable time when it become dear; when gasoline is cheap, buy a futures contract which will rise in value if gasoline skyrockets in cost.

Put another way, distributing risk lowers the vulnerability of an entire system. In the present era, the rentier-financial Elites and the State have colluded on a breathtakingly profitable simulacrum of distributing risk.

Ignoring the real world of depleted soil, crumbling aqueducts, aging power lines and extremely vulnerable global supply chains of essential commodities, the State/Elite sought to limit risk by financial legerdemain alone. Thus real-world risks were mitigated by essentially intangible derivatives contracts.

Rather than invest in costly real-world redundancies like power transmission lines, alternative production facilities, etc., the Elite put capital to work in credit-default swaps, futures and other derivative contracts to offset real-world risks.

In terms of profit potential and risk-return--the metrics of free-market capitalism--these State-enabled financial instruments were immensely more profitable investments than investing in actual tangible systems.

In other words: don't grow more grain, simply leverage financial bets such that profits flow from "risk management" rather than production of tangible goods. But if grain is in severely short supply, then a handsome profit in derivatives won't feed the citizenry.

This is the end-state of the Power Elite's financial *windfall exploitation*: intangible wealth and tangible scarcity.

For households, distributing risk means hedging against shortages and high costs of essentials, and developing redundancies and alternative sources of income and essentials. The goal is to preserve purchasing power of current assets, which means tracking the relative value of commodities, precious metals, currencies and tangible goods.

A key tool in maintaining purchasing power and capital is *relative strength* or
relative performance: that is, comparing the shifting values of different assets classes to identify peaks and valleys. By buying during the valleys and selling at the peaks, we can maintain purchasing power and perhaps even grow our capital.

One way to illustrate this is to price a house in loaves of bread: how many loaves of bread does it take to buy a house? Removing the dollar (which is relentlessly depreciated by the State via inflation/devaluation) from the equation offers insight into the real value of both bread and housing.

This is why many investment professionals look at the ratio of gold to oil to identify the valleys and peaks in those two commodities. When gold buys a large number of barrels of oil then they sell gold and buy oil. When oil rises in relative value to historic extremes, then they sell oil and buy gold.

From this perspective, the dollar itself is not a universal measure of value but just another commodity to be compared to other commodities.

We might summarize our focus on minimizing or offsetting risk and seeking opportunities to bolster purchasing power with these two questions:

Where is the opportunity?
What is threatened?

6. Radical Self-Reliance. This is not so much an option as the only strategy with any probability of sustained success, as this analysis has revealed the inevitability of the devolution and collapse of the Savior State and its partnership with the rentier-financial Plutocracy.

This principle follows from the necessity of opting out of the current doomed system and opting into one with a future: distributed/networked/reciprocal self-reliance.

Put another way: radical self-reliance requires constructing a parallel economy and society which is no longer dependent on a financial/banking Plutocracy and Savior State as these intertwined systems devolve into insolvency.

Radical self-reliance requires a distributed/hedged and thus durable system for all forms of power--political, financial and the FEW resources (food, energy, water)--and an engaged, active citizenry to limit state and Elite over-reach/dominance.

Radical self-reliance means accepting the end of the Savior State and taking personal responsibility for one's health, livelihood, education, energy, food, retirement and pursuit of happiness.

Radical self-reliance depends on self-organizing networks of mutual interest, benefit and reciprocity/exchange rather than debt-serfdom or State control.

Radical self-reliance values production over process and recognizes energy is the ultimate form and measure of wealth.

Radical self-reliance plans in depth for contingencies, constantly updating "Plan B" alternatives and "Plan C" emergency measures.

7. Reciprocity. The Savior State rests on two pillars: the demographic accident (a large Baby Boom generation and postwar productivity) which enabled entitlements to appear sustainable for a few decades, and the dependence of both the Elites and the non-productive classes on State largesse. That is, the granting of monopolies and the enabling of looting/gaming the system and the transfer of income from the productive class to the dependent classes.

By fostering the dependence of both the Elites and the unproductive, the State has made both complicit in its dominance; those drawing welfare, corporate or underclass, are in essence colluding with the status quo in return for their share of the State-distributed largesse. The State effectively "bought" their compliance and political silence; the only chatter voiced by the dependents is shrill advocacy for ever-larger slices of State largesse.

Once the State devolves and then implodes in insolvency or an utterly devalued currency (your $2,000 a month pension remains nominally intact but now only buys a loaf of bread) then dependence, collusion, complicity and noisy claims will no longer be rewarding strategies.

In the durable, stable alternative to dependency on the Savior State, the key value and strategy is as old as human nature itself: *reciprocity*. Rather than demand something based on ones' perceived needs, the rewarding strategy will be to offer something of value in exchange for some other store of value. The *offering* comes first, then the establishment of relative value, and then the exchange.

This is a complete reversal of the State/dependency relationship in which the demand came first followed by the transfer from the State. This mirrors the adolescent/parent dynamic in which the spoiled, whining child demands largesse from the parents—an unhealthy, crippling relationship.

In capitalist terms, the investment in productive services or goods comes first, then the establishment of value and then the exchange (sale) can be transacted.

In very practical terms on the household level, you bake a peach pie and share it with your neighbors/network. If it has value, then this "investment" and freely offered value launches a reciprocity of exchanged value: someone will offer to watch your children or elderly parent in exchange for a peach pie, etc.

Yes, some people will take the slice of peach pie and offer nothing tangible in return. But the transaction nonetheless created valuable information: either the recipient placed no value on the offering, or they have nothing of value to exchange, in which case they can be excluded from future offerings of reciprocity.

Those who create no value and who offer nothing freely will soon receive nothing. This too is as old as humanity. The freeloader is shunned and left to his/her own devices. The incentives to reciprocity and creating some value which can be exchanged are high indeed, and the disincentives to permanent adolescence, dependence and fraud/cheating/freeloading are equally high.

Those who are completely helpless and without family (orphans, the completely disabled, the severely mentally ill) will of course depend on the surplus and generosity of the community. Ultimately, the smaller the surplus of real value generated, the less there will be to share. Thus the focus must shift from demands for largesse to generating true surplus rather than the debt-based (and thus bogus) "prosperity" of financial legerdemain.

Once the State collapses in insolvency, the corporate dependents (Power Elites) who had arranged monopolies, collusion and various forms of fraud and embezzlement via the State will be left on their own in a newly competitive world. Those accustomed to an unproductive life subsidized by the Savior State will also discover a new world of incentives and disincentives.

Shrill demands will gain nothing; the entity which vacuumed up surplus from the productive to distribute to others will have devolved or dissolved. The new paradigm will be reciprocity based on freely offered goods and services. The only way to get anything will be to offer something of value first.

8. Diffusion of power and the means of wealth/income creation. Widely distributed ownership of the means of production and power is the foundation of a stable economy and democracy. Recall that inequality is lowest when wealth is widely diffused and highest when income and wealth are highly concentrated.

This diffusion does not require any State-mandated transfer of wealth or income; rather, all that is needed is to end the State's current redistribution of the national income and wealth to the Elites. The State enables and enforces countless cartels and monopolies which concentrate wealth, income and power in positive feedback loops which protect and extend both corporate and State monopolies.

The diffusion model calls for widespread ownership of the means of production (land, tools, innovation, factories, workshops, distribution centers, skills, energy production, etc.) and a flexible, resilient network for exchanging energy, ideas, products and services.

9. Base Decisions on an Integrated Understanding. The mass media/marketing complex (i.e., talk radio, TV "news", etc.) is conceived and manufactured to distract, confuse and misdirect "consumers" into conveniently manipulated narrow passageways: false ideologies, simplistic divisions, life reduced to shopping, integrity sacrificed for financial gain, etc., all of which distract the citizen from an integrated understanding of the State's inevitable insolvency and the collusion of the mass media with the financial Plutocracy which owns it.

An integrated understanding rests on these foundations:

A. Ask "to whose benefit?" at every step of an investigation and digging for a complete, truthful answer.

B. Ask where did this good or service originate, how and where was it manufactured, and what are its full lifecycle costs, that is, the costs not reflected in the price tag as they have been covertly transferred to the community at large. (For example, costly-to-clean sludge is dumped in the Bay for taxpayers to clean up.)

C. Be skeptical of answers provided by self-serving mass media, Power Elites and high-caste State technocrats and elected officials, all of which are beholden to the Power Elite's interests; be alert for propaganda, simulacrum and misinformation aimed at masking self-serving Elites' exploitation and dominance.

D. Subject every transaction/purchase/decision to an adult cost-benefit analysis on all time scales, seeking to reveal marginal returns, hidden costs and comparing the value offered by alternatives--including doing nothing, or saving the surplus to be invested elsewhere at a later date.

E. Investigate the consequences of participating in the transaction, purchase, contract or network; ask what else could have been done with your energy, time, capital and skills.

A practical example would be to reach an integrated understanding of food/diet and its effects on human health. One would quickly ascertain that packaged food and fast food contain unhealthy amounts of fat, sugar and salt and thus must be consumed only occasionally and in small quantities.

An integrated understanding of food and diet requires the growing of actual food to understand the process, the work, the disappointments and the joys, and to taste the difference between a agribusiness product (for instance, a tomato) and a garden-fresh tomato.

It also requires learning how to cook and an acquaintance with nutrition--that is, what the human body is selected to find nutritious and what is inherently unhealthy to humans.

Without an understanding of how food is grown, what is inside packaged and fast foods, how to prepare healthy cuisine and what effects food has on health, then one cannot claim to have an integrated understanding of food, diet and health.

Without an integrated understanding, it is essentially impossible to make responsible decisions or choose productive, positive strategies for full-spectrum prosperity.

10. Leverage capital, assets and skills. In the long view, societies, enterprises, communities and individuals fail when they pour scarce capital and labor into projects with increasingly marginal returns. Examples include constructing large stone monuments on Easter Island while you denude the island of trees and strip the surrounding waters of fish, or drilling for oil in such marginal conditions that the value of the oil extracted barely exceeds the costs of extracting and processing the oil.

In each case, the unasked question is: what else could have been done with this capital and labor? Would other investments have generated higher returns? What perverse artificial incentives are in place which reward misallocation of capital and labor?

Alternatively, societies, enterprises, communities and individuals prosper when they leverage existing capital, assets and skills in ways that multiply positive outputs. In many cases leverage leads not to increased production but radically reduced consumption, which boosts surplus even more effectively than marginally increasing output. In vernacular parlance, this can be summed up as "doing more with less."

Speaking of perverse incentives: the ability to borrow virtually unlimited sums of money encourages grossly inefficient extravagance. That in a nutshell is the crippling context of the U.S.A.

11. ESSA: eliminate, simplify, standardize and automate. Rather remarkably for such common-sense principles, these methods of leveraging capital, assets and skills are widely ignored because the State and Plutocracy have erected various perverse incentives for unrestricted borrowing and money printing, marginal returns, crony capitalism, financial fraud and State collusion with Elites.

Once borrowing is no longer unlimited and surplus must be generated, a new set of incentives takes precedence and ESSA suddenly makes sense.

12. Generate value and surplus (working capital). As noted elsewhere in this analysis, the U.S. has not generated a true surplus for decades. It has instead borrowed trillions of dollars from surplus-generating nations and relied upon an essentially fraudulent trade of paper dollars for tangible goods from abroad.

At the household level, generating surplus (capital, savings, etc.) has been replaced with borrowing and ever-rising debt--the very epitome of unsustainability and inevitable ruin.

13. Secure/produce/innovate the FEW resources (food, energy, water). I have stressed throughout this analysis the supremely misleading artificiality of an economics and economy based on metrics such as "GDP growth," "banking profits," etc. which are fundamentally disconnected from the real world we inhabit, a world in which soil, water, food and energy are of paramount importance. Financial legerdemain and metrics are rendered utterly worthless by severe shortages and degradation of the FEW resources, as no amount of paper currency can be exchanged for tangible goods when the shortage is severe.

If citizens are hungry, with no prospects for relief, then "GDP growth" is revealed as a conceptual artifice if not outright intellectual fraud.

The scale of our dependence on abundant, easily transportable cheap fossil fuels is almost unimaginable. The U.S. consumes some 19 million barrels a day of oil, and it produces about 30,000 barrels of biodiesel. Other alternative sources of energy are equally marginal. An integrated understanding (as opposed to a facile, superficial propaganda-based "understanding") of energy reveals that there are no cheap, easy abundant substitutes. Natural gas and uranium face their own limitations, and alternative energy sources are costly--until such time as the oil supply chain breaks down, at which point it will be too late to fabricate an alternative infrastructure.

Neither the market, a self-serving financial Power Elite nor the current insolvent State are likely to secure the FEW resources for the common good, for all the reasons outlined in the above analysis. The goal will have to be understood and pursued on a much smaller scale-- city, town, community, enterprise, neighborhood and household.

14. Think, plan and act with integrity. Ultimately, our personal integrity is the only value and capital we control entirely. The status quo's intellectual framework which enables and encourages corruption, artifice, misrepresentation, deception, collusion, gaming the system, propaganda, simulacrum, facsimiles and exploitation depends on each of us surrendering our integrity to serve the State/Power Elite's interests, in exchange for a share of the loot.

15. Pare complexity to simplicity. While ESSA (#11) includes "simplify" as a process, the purpose is specifically efficiency and the reduction of wasted energy, labor and capital.

But complexity is not just a wild tangle of inefficiency: **Complexity is a weapon, tool and strategy of control and dominance.** As noted in a previous chapter, the most effective way to game a system (open a windfall to exploit) is to create layer upon layer of obscure complexity: pension guidelines piled up since 1935 into a thick morass only the gamers claim to understand, tax codes which run into the tens of thousands of pages, regulations so complex only a well-funded fiefdom or corporation has the resources to decode the intent and loopholes, and so on.

As noted in the previous chapter:

Complexity creates *information asymmetry*--unequal access to information--and opens up vast opportunities for gaming the system. Thus complexity itself is a tool of domination by Elites and the State. Like its conceptual twin transparency, simplicity is the mortal enemy of Elites key weapons of control: secrecy, obfuscation, disinformation, information asymmetry and complexity itself.

Thus the first step in solidifying and concentrating control (and thus power) is to create a *complexity fortress* of cloaked information guarded by restricted access and specialized knowledge. Once *information asymmetry* has been institutionalized, transparency is impossible and the gaming (and thus the looting) can begin.

The status quo Elites and high-caste technocrats will defend their institutional information asymmetry and complexity fortresses like life itself because these are the ultimate defense of their privileges, power, control and wealth. The wailing, whining and protests will all boil down to this: simplicity is impossible, complexity is necessary, and so on.

This is disingenuous. The tax code of the U.S.A. could be written on one page. Such simplicity would absolutely destroy all the privileges, loopholes and windfalls the State has constructed to benefit and protect the Power Elites. This is why simplicity is the mortal enemy of power concentrations and the Elites who control the power and national income/wealth.

These fifteen principles are scale-invariant, meaning that they apply to small and large-scale enterprises equally, from households to enterprises to cities to nation-states. These principles apply to everyone, regardless of ethnicity, creed, color or class.

In the next chapters, I will sketch out how the principles can be applied to each of the three levels: household, community/enterprise/network and nation.

Key concepts in this chapter:
Complexity fortress

Chapter Twenty-Five: Applying the Principles

Applying the Principles to Individuals/Households
Let's begin by restating this starting point:

The key point here is that dominance flows directly from an intellectual framework which constructs and justifies that dominance as natural and beneficial to all believers. In this sense consumerism is in effect the de facto state religion of the U.S.A., and it directly benefits the Elites who own or control the vast majority of the nation's financial wealth, income, law-making machinery and productive assets.

For individuals and households, what you decide not to do is as important as what you decide to do. Recognizing the status quo's intellectual framework as a con is the essential first step: non-Elites do not share the interests of the State and Power Elites. The con is perpetuated by a specific politics of experience which is "sold" via pervasive mass media/marketing.

It is essential to understand that our actions are not just "self-help," though they most definitely are that--our individual and household actions are feedbacks into the community, enterprise and nation. It is important not to limit the context of our individual action to self-help, as that context is a key control technique of the status quo: in the *politics of experience* promoted by the status quo, the "problem" is not in the system, it's only in you.

The reality is that the "problem" resides on all levels of society that feed back into each other. The mass media attempts to "sell" an agenda and an understanding of the world to each individual "consumer," and the consumer's decision to opt in or out feeds back into the mass media: when marketing/ad campaigns fail to generate the desired consumerist behavior, they are terminated.

There is a well-defined "market" for "self-help" advice, and this market is highly lucrative because people are hungry for ways to improve their full-spectrum prosperity--health, wealth, happiness, etc. This "market" is not just tolerated but encouraged by the status quo's intellectual framework because it is stripped of political content: the "seeker" is isolated, and encouraged to grant his/her loyalty to a safely apolitical "cause" or "spiritual leader," all of whom convey a completely non-threatening, bland *politics of experience* which assigns no accountability to the "State religion" of consumerism or the dominance of the financial Power Elite and State.

Thus the following "advice" is subversive because it places all individual actions in the wider contexts of a politics of experience which justifies and enables Elite dominance.

Within an integrated understanding of mass media, propaganda and the subtle dominance imposed by a specific politics of experience--recall that framing the "problem" predefines the "solution"--then avoiding network/cable TV and "talk radio" and being highly skeptical of mainstream print and Internet "news" media is not just self-help but a revolutionary undermining of the status quo's dominance and control.

Individuals who opt out of consumerism, mass media and debt/tax-serfdom are "starving the beasts" and taking control of their own lives. Refusing to consume propaganda is the first step to living free, and since a handful of global corporations administered by the State own and control virtually all mass media ("talk radio" included), then *cui bono*--to whose benefit?--should always be the first question.

If I believe what's being "sold," who benefits? The answer is never the individual "consumer" citizen, though the simulation of benefit is always the "pitch."

The pursuit of full-spectrum prosperity is not passive, nor does it seek to impose anything on anyone. It is built on the concept of free exchange of ideas and value.

This is not "advice" in the usual sense but an expression of what I consider self-evident principles.

1. Engagement

This could be summed up in one phrase: take control of your life. Since humans are prone to self-defeating thoughts, beliefs and behaviors and manipulation by "leaders" and Elites, engagement starts by deciding to stop self-destructing and by deciding to seek an integrated understanding of oneself and our situation.

The principles of an integrated understanding are ontological and scale-invariant, that is, they work in all times frames and situations.

Engagement means accepting the devolution and demise of the Savior State and recognizing the negative consequences of a debt-serf/dependent/entitlement mindset.

Engagement means understanding that education, security, learning, health, etc.--full spectrum prosperity--is your responsibility. No one can do it for you. We can help each other, but only within networks of reciprocity. If you want me to help you educate your child, you're going to have to help educate mine--directly, not just through the passive payment of taxes to the Savior State.

The Savior State is a compelling fantasy, but it is unsustainable and thus ultimately destructive. Clinging to the hope it will magically become sustainable is one strategy, but it is a strategy with low probabilities of success.

A free community, school, town, group and nation require engagement to remain free (i.e. liberty, not "free" financially). We don't all have to become leaders but we do need to participate. As I write this in September 2009, the citizens of Japan have tossed out a sclerotic, oppressive, exploitative failed status quo at the ballot box. About 70% of the qualified voters participated, compared to the U.S. average of about 40% participation.

Passive debt-serfs will remain debt-serfs. That much is self-evident.

2. Transparency (trust and truth)

Transparency is the public posting of accurate accounts of finances and decisionmaking. As noted above, transparency is anathema to crony capitalism and all Elites, who thrive in secrecy and obscurity.

Transparency is the essential feedback loop of democracy, liberty and free-market capitalism. If transparency is strangled, then liberty, democracy and widespread prosperity expire along with it.

In the household setting, financial transparency starts with an accurate (trustworthy) accounting of the household income, expenses and capital/assets. If a family or individual does not know how much money is being spent and on what, then that lack of transparency cripples cost-benefit analyses and decisionmaking.

As described previously, a key goal of the mass media/marketing system is to transform all consumers into permanent adolescents who act on impulse and instant gratification. Permanent adolescence is the opposite of engagement, accountability and an adult understanding.

The decisionmaking processes within a household should also be transparent. Who decides, and based on what information and cost-benefit analysis? If the process is obscure, then how will children learn to make their own cost-benefit analyses and adult decisions? If transparent household cost-benefit trade-offs aren't being made, then how can the household make prudent decisions which create surplus value?

3. Accountability

If people are not accountable for the consequences of their decisions, behaviors and work, then one of the two essential feedback loops is broken (the first essential is transparency). Permanent adolescence attempts to dodge accountability via excuses and rationalizations; just listen to teenagers for endlessly creative (and ultimately tiresome) examples.

In one sense, the entire American system of "justice" has institutionalized permanent adolescence under the guise of "advocacy." In court, advocacy assumes the all-or-nothing dodging of accountability: the authorities/accusers are evil, repressive, out to get us. If that isn't an adolescent voice, then what is?

This perversion of truth aimed at dodging accountability has poisoned the entire culture. Now the guilty deny the truth until indisputable evidence arises, at which point they blubber out a canned apology which is intended to magically relieve them of their original guilt as well as the additional crimes of perjury, libeling the accusers, false accusations, misrepresenting the truth, etc.

Facing consequences is deemed "unfair," as the superficial apology is, in typical adolescent fashion, supposed to remedy the situation.

Eliminating causal links between performance/behavior and the consequences is ontologically destructive; the spoiled brat, slacker and liar are all rewarded by a system which lacks accountability, while the honest, hardworking and productive are effectively punished.

This was the fundamental reason communes in Communism failed; slackers and cheats drew the same benefits as the productive who had to work harder to compensate for the unproductive.

Thus it is no surprise the U.S. economy is now riddled with protected high-castes, Elites and fiefdoms which operate with little accountability. The status quo creates highly perverse incentives for gaming the system deception, obfuscation, misrepresentation, laziness and a raging sense of entitlement which fuels resentment at any demand for accountability.

The chief technique of avoiding accountability is secrecy, i.e. the avoidance of transparency. Thus transparency, engagement (the demand for transparency and accountability) and accountability are intrinsically bound into one framework.

The status quo is built on the illusion that a lack of accountability is sustainable; reality is not so easily fooled. Whether we like it or not, the Savior State and its Elites are doomed to insolvency, devolution and dissolution. At the household level, every member of the household must participate (engagement) in open cost-benefits analyses and trade-offs (transparency) and be accountable for their contributions and decisions.

We create a society of accountability by first holding ourselves accountable for our own full-spectrum prosperity. We really don't have any other choice; dodging accountability by depending on the Savior State and endless credit expansion is depending on illusions.

4. An Adult Understanding (Triage and Trade-offs)

The key adult understanding is that life requires a never-ending series of trade-offs based on cost-benefit analysis, deliberation and decision. In periods of crisis, then this process becomes triage--making difficult assessments about which aspects of a household must be cut to save the core.

One exercise that may strike many as extraordinary is useful for that very reason. If the household income is $100,000 annually, then plan to live on $50,000. If the household income is $50,000, then plan on living on $25,000. If the household income is $25,000, then plan on living on $12,500.

Put another way: re-design the household budget such that 50% of net income can be saved for surplus/working capital.

Another way to look at trade-offs and triage is to ask: what behaviors, costs and actions cede control of our lives to others, and which ones transfer control from outside forces to our own hands?

Alternatively: what behaviors, costs and actions increase our vulnerability to outside crises, and which ones decrease our vulnerabilities?

Asking these questions is the core of *radical self-reliance* (self-sufficiency), reducing risk/hedging and generating value and capital. I hope it is clear that these 14 principles are interlocking parts of one integrated understanding.

An adult understanding of trade-offs focuses on these three

essentials:

1. What short-term wants must be sacrificed or set aside to secure long-term security, health and control of one's life?

2. What can be done in the present, the short-term and the long-term to secure the FEW essentials--food, energy and water--for the household? If no control can be exerted over supply, then what can be stockpiled? How can more be done with less, which is simply another way of "controlling supply"?

3. What expenditures of money and time are depriving the household of surplus/savings which could be set aside for working capital?

In essence: what long-term investments with potentially enormous payoffs require long-term planning and short-term sacrifice? If supply chains break down due to hurricanes, earthquakes or severe power disruptions, then a 50-pound bag of rice and a propane tank/campstove are "investments" which will provide profound "returns"--having cooked food in times of want.

There are innumerable strategies to cut unnecessary expenditures of time and money and equally innumerable strategies to secure a more secure, less vulnerable future for the household.

Ultimately, making realistic assessments and reaching decisions on trade-offs is all about "Plan B"--preparing the household for "hard times" such as a drastic reduction in income, a natural disaster, a devolution of energy supply or civil order, etc.

"Plan C" is the "last resort" triage scenario if income drops to zero, civil order vanishes, a health crisis disables a key wage earner, etc.

This *assessment, (cost-benefit) analysis, deliberation and decision process (AADD)* is similar to the OODA loop mentioned earlier: Observe, Orient, Decide and Act. The principle is to anticipate risks before they unfold and plan contingencies to counteract the risks--in other words, to establish negative feedback loops which can counter possible runaway feedbacks (fall ill, lose your job, become more ill, etc.) and create a bulwark against the most likely, and most threatening, possibilities.

The process of making trade-offs is implicitly one of setting priorities and goals--what some commentators have described as a *purpose-driven life*. A life without goals or priorities is an aimless, unhappy one; without purpose, humans fall into depression and self-destruction.

The permanent adolescent (the state of mind encouraged by the marketing/mass media complex) seeks distraction and "entertainment;"

he or she has no priorities or goals and thus no purpose other than the next "fun" distraction. This is highly profitable for those selling distractions but destructive for the individual and household.

Trusting the Savior State to provide for oneself heightens one's vulnerability; ultimately, the only elements we "own" that are within our control are our integrity, skills, networks and capital.

5. Redundancy/Distributed Risk/Hedging

I have grouped these three strategies together as the purpose of each is to mitigate or lessen risk. Lessening risk increases security.

I have described in previous chapters the inherent vulnerability of long global supply chains which are dependent on a limited number of nodes, transfer points and sources. On a household level, we can look for the same kinds of vulnerabilities, both within the household and within regional networks we depend on (grocery stores, etc.)

In one sense, a household depending on one job and one skillset is like a supply chain which depends on one source; if anything disrupts that source then the entire supply chain breaks down.

Some years ago a single fire in a Japanese plant which produced a product essential to the fabrication of semiconductors instantly drove up global prices for semiconductors, as only two or three plants made this product worldwide. There were no substitutes or redundant facilities that could be activated.

This is an example of systems in which the apparent stability is illusory; the dependency on a small number of sources and transport networks renders them inherently unstable.

A battery and a solar-powered battery recharger are very small but nonetheless useful redundant systems to the electrical grid. If an earthquake disrupts the grid for days or weeks, I would be very happy to have these modest redundancies. If the supermarkets close for lack of goods (perhaps due to some transport disruption) then the bag of rice in my cupboard is a redundant source of sustenance.

If you have ever observed squirrels, you know that they are genetically programmed to distribute their risks by burying nuts in a scattered pattern. Stashing the entire hoard of nuts in one place heightens the risk of other rodents discovering and plundering the stored food. Thus distributing the food lessens risk and increases security.

Having some food stored at another family member's home as well as one's own is a form of distributing risk. Developing more than one source of income is also distributing risk. As with redundancy, this principle has widespread applications in the real world.

Knowing how to bake and having flour on hand lessens dependency on the supermarket bakery. Creating surplus value and sharing it with your network lessens dependency on the devolving Savior State.

Productive assets, gold and silver are redundant stores of value; owning them lessens dependency on the State's fiat currency, which could eventually be devalued to near-zero. Owning dollars is perfectly fine, but distributing one's assets amongst several asset classes lessens the risks of holding all one's assets in one asset class.

The key to choosing redundancies (backups) and distributing risk is to start with a cost-benefit analysis: how much does the "insurance" provided by redundancy and distributing risk cost, and what are the potential payoffs?

If municipal water supplies are disrupted or polluted by a natural disaster, then a water filter which costs less than $100 will have a value which is difficult to assess because we cannot live without clean fresh water. Filling a few plastic juice or milk containers with fresh water (after rinsing, of course) and storing them is cheap "insurance" indeed.

Creating an independent source of income is time consuming and difficult, but the pay-off-- a security which is not controlled by others--is equally large.

If we perform a cost-benefit analysis and then prioritize the results, we might well conclude that storing some water, grain, canned goods, spare batteries and a camp stove and lantern (items which might be bought used) would be low-cost ways to distribute risk and create household-controlled redundancies for essentials.

Longer term, such an analysis might lead us to distribute some of our assets or add some independent sources of income to the household.

Another key is to understand that reducing consumption is equivalent to increasing supply.

If the household consumes 40 gallons of gasoline a week, then reducing the miles driven or increasing the mileage of the vehicles by 50% is the same as increasing the household supply of gasoline.

If those 40 gallons of fuel enabled vehicles getting 20 miles per gallon to travel 800 miles, (40 X 20 = 800) then increasing the mileage to 30 MPG is the equivalent of getting another 20 gallons of gasoline: 30

MPG X 40 gallons = 1,200 miles, or the equivalent of 60 gallons X 20 MPG.

If a human consumes 3,000 kilocalories a day (we short-hand this to "calories" in everyday speech) then consuming 2,000 calories a day is the equivalent of having 50% more food.

The easiest way to double one's supply of gasoline is to cut consumption in half. Thus conservation is highly cost-beneficial. Reducing expenses by 50% is the easiest way to accumulate savings/surplus capital which can then be put to work for the benefit of the household. It generally costs nothing to reduce consumption, as most consumption is behavioral-based.

In cases where some capital investment is necessary, such as insulating a house to lose less heat in winter, the costs are modest compared to the long-term savings and the overall value of the asset.

Oftwominds.com correspondent Harun Ibrahim has helped me understand the concept of hedging.

From what I understand about hedging it does not matter when one buys or sells. What is needed is an understanding of risk and consciously seeking ways of mitigating the known risks. For example, a farmer must raise and sell his crops. What the market price will be at harvest is unknowable and out of his control. The airline must fly but has no control over fuel prices it must purchase to conduct business. In neither instance is it practical to shut down business until prices become optimal. Since future price is unknowable, what price is optimal? And since crop and flights could not be brought into being instantly, how could we take advantage of the optimal price when it materialized?

The only constant is uncertainty. Learning to manage risk as a producer, consumer or both should be the endeavor.

Since the future is unknown there is no "perfect" time to purchase or sell anything. There is only risk. If one happened to get the highest or lowest price it occurred by chance.

We are immersed in a sea of risk as a function of our existence; however, few give conscious thought to this and therefore take no conscious steps to manage important risks. This failure to live consciously is how government grows and becomes more tyrannical.

In very simple terms, we might observe the risk of wheat rising in price due to droughts in wheat-growing regions, and buy several bulk bags of flour while it is still inexpensive (storing them in secure containers, of course). If wheat rises in price, we can consumer our cheap flour. If wheat does not rise in price, the cost of our hedge-- storing 100 pounds of flour--is relatively modest.

Since the price of wheat can continue declining after we buy, then we might choose to "dollar-average" our purchases--that is, add to our hedge as prices decline rather than buy our hedge at one time.

If gasoline and natural gas are currently inexpensive compared to recent tops, then we might purchase a futures contract on gasoline or natural gas which serves to protect us against future spikes in cost.

The value of the futures contract (which can be purchased at various broker/dealers much like stocks or options, with some restrictions and requirements) varies depending on the current price of the contract month of the commodity being hedged. But just for purposes of illustration let's suppose a futures contract on gasoline costs $1,000 and the household consumes $3,000 of gasoline a year.

The total cost of the gasoline and the hedge is thus $4,000. If gasoline drops in price, then the hedge--essentially a bet that gasoline would rise in price--loses value. So if gasoline drops such that the family only consumes $2,000 a year, then the household budget remains $3,000--the lower cost of $2,000 and the cost of the hedge $1,000.

But if gasoline rises dramatically, then the futures contract may well be worth $4,000. Since fuel prices jumped, the cost of the family's gasoline consumption might rise to $5,000 a year. But since their hedge rose in value as gasoline rose in price, the household can sell the futures contract for a profit of $4,000 (if the trade works the $1,000, which is a performance bond, is returned at liquidation), the net cost of the family's gasoline and hedge is $1,000 ($5,000 gasoline + $0 hedge = $5,000 minus profit from hedge $4,000 = $1,000).

Thus the purchase of the hedge lowered the family's total gasoline expenses to $1,000 for the year (the $1,000 performance bond was returned when the futures contract was sold)--a savings of $4,000.

As Harun explained, large agricultural and transport enterprises must hedge against fluctuations in essential costs and revenues. Global enterprises also hedge against fluctuations in currencies.

While this example might seem complex, the underlying strategy is simple: by investing in a hedge, risks can be offset or reduced.

If a household depends entirely on one income source (one wage earner), then the risk of that wage earner losing their job could be partially offset or reduced by developing an alternate source of income or by buying a "loss of income" insurance policy.

Developing multiple sources of revenue is a form of hedging against the risk of the household losing its sole source of income. This might mean another household member seeks a part-time job, a spare room is rented to a student, a garden is planted in Spring and the produce sold at farmer's markets, a new skill is acquired by someone in the household and marketed through friends, family and other networks, some small-scale Internet-based enterprise is developed, etc.

There is no one answer to how to offset or mitigate risk, but having multiple sources of essentials, rigorous cost controls and carefully planned hedges against potentially catastrophes is a strategy with a much higher probability of success than remaining passively exposed to foreseeable risks.

All of these concepts are simply forms of risk management. We cannot make risk vanish, but we can plan for contingencies.

6. Radical Self-Reliance

While self-reliance certainly implies self-sufficiency, what the term means to me is expressed by this phrase: **To look out for Number One, take care of Numbers Two through Nine.**

In other words, by self-reliance I mean a security and prosperity that is independent of the crumbling Savior State and its rentier-financial Power Elite partners. Since it is extremely difficult to provide all that life demands as an individual, then humans evolved as social animals. Solitary animals are rarely as abundant/successful as social animals; without a network for support, sharing and defense, the risks of a small failure leading to catastrophic failure (death) for a solitary individual are inherently high.

Unfortunately, the entitlement mindset encouraged by the Savior State incentivizes a victim mentality which demands something for nothing even as it directs a perverse resentment at the giver.

This is the exact opposite of radical self-reliance, which works from the basic understanding that to get something, one must first give something, and do so freely. In capitalist terms, capital must be put at risk to earn a return. For individuals and households, "capital" is not just money but social capital (networks) and "time"/labor/skill capital.

Thus the foundation of radical self-reliance is reciprocity, which is mutually self-serving as opposed to selflessly generous. Reciprocity requires freely offered and mutually acceptable exchange which benefits both parties and strengthens the bonds of the group/network/community which facilitates and supports the exchange.

Traditional societies offer many examples of Stateless self-reliance; however, this security comes with a high cost: rigid and oft-times repressive social hierarchies. In the era of devolving Savior States we are now entering, social and commercial networks will be freely chosen.

Nobody owes anyone anything. If you refuse mutually beneficial exchange and the civility, trust and cooperation this requires, then you're on your own. That's the choice each person faces, regardless of his or her conditions, strengths, handicaps and weaknesses.

Groups and communities also have to practice triage: those few who drain an inordinate amount of resources via theft, anti-social behavior or other unproductive demands on limited capital and time are shunned or ejected. Anyone who wants to accept the burdens of dealing with these disruptive souls is free to do so, but they cannot force the group to expend its limited capital and time to benefit a few disruptive people.

I want to be clear here that I am not referring to the incapacitated elderly or mentally ill--those who no longer have the capacity to contribute--but to those who could contribute but who choose to be parasites or disruptive drains on their community.

Since the status quo Savior State still appears robust, this sounds harsh. But once capital, the FEW resources and time become scarce then triage will become necessary. Studies have shown that a relative handful of customers consume much of the customer service provided by a given enterprise. Refusing to serve those customers is an essential step in the survival triage of an enterprise; these customers are simply not worth the time and capital being expended in the fruitless attempt to satisfy their endless demands.

In radical self-reliance, choice recovers ground lost to compulsory obligations. The mindset and expectation that something is "my due" or "my right" will devolve along with the coercive Elitist Savior State. Our rights will re-set to life, liberty and the pursuit of happiness as set forth in the Bill of Rights.

In essence, radical self-reliance is merely the sum of the other 14 principles stated here. Secure (low-risk) prosperity which is independent of the devolving Savior State and the financial Power Elites demands an adult focus on both *process* and *outcome*.

If the process isn't producing the desired results, then it must be modified: engagement, transparency, accountability and management.

If the information is faulty, purposefully obscured or skewed, then it must be made transparent.

If the strategy is failing, then those making the decisions and managing the action must be held accountable. Realistic assessments, cost-benefit analyses and modifying processes and trade-offs requires an adult understanding.

Entitlement mindsets are not secure foundations for survival; freely entered exchange within mutually beneficial networks--reciprocity--is a far more sustainable, robust source of security and prosperity.

For the individual and household, self-reliance starts with a realistic appraisal of risks, vulnerabilities, and assets/capital that can be leveraged to reduce risk and increase production of value and surplus. Networks of reciprocal benefit (families, neighborhoods, guilds, communities, enterprises, etc.) are critical assets: *To look out for Number One, take care of Numbers Two through Nine (or 19 or 99).*

7. Reciprocity

Traditional societies did not have Central State fractional lending or printing presses to create money and credit out of thin air, so they actually had to create surpluses and increase security via sharing, cooperation, pooling of assets and trade.

As described in Item 10 below, there are four basic types of capital: natural capital (fresh water, arable soil, oil. minerals, etc.), built capital (tools, roads, etc.) social capital (networks, guilds, cooperatives, etc.) and Individual capital (skills, experience, health, etc.).

In an ontological (as opposed to financial or legal) understanding, there are only two ways humans can interact with natural capital: either "own/control" it for exploitative purposes (i.e. keeping the gains/benefits for oneself or one's Empire to the exclusion of others), or share it cooperatively. In terms of "profit potential," nothing beats complete ownership of scarce resources that can then be traded/sold for far more than the extraction costs.

This enriches the Elites who own/control the natural capital at the expense of non-owners.

The inherent "profit potential" of this control has powered Elites, Empires and imperialism from the beginnings of formal institutions.

This desire to corral or control scarce resources is of a piece with the natural-selection drives observed within any primate social group: the competition for more food, better reproductive opportunities, etc.

But as the study of sociobiology and animal behavior has revealed, cooperation also offers enormous natural-selection/survival benefits. Hence the social primates (the animals which share much of our genetic code) such as chimpanzees and bonobo combine social hierarchies and stratifications ("alpha" males and females at the top rungs of leadership, ownership of food and reproductive advantages) with complex cooperative networks.

To the degree that Elites are fundamentally parasitic, then once "ownership" becomes too concentrated and/or exploitative, then the rest of the troop either rebels and installs a new Elite leadership or abandons the old Elite to their own devices, depriving them of the population they need to maintain their exploitative extraction of wealth.

This is called "opting out," "walking away" or "voting with your feet."

Thus Elites and the larger social community are also bound in a structural reciprocity: if the leadership is sound and enables stability, security and prosperity for the entire group, their consumption/extraction of an outsized share of the group income/wealth is tolerated as a reasonable trade-off/exchange.

But once the leadership/Elite over-reaches (i.e. grabs most of the food, attractive females, portable wealth, scarce resources, etc.) or fails to secure the common good in a sustainable fashion (what the Chinese term "The Mandate of Heaven"), then the community/city/Empire revolts and replaces the old Elite with a new Elite.

In these basic terms, the Power Elites controlling most of the wealth and income of the U.S. (the State fiefdoms and the rentier-financial Elites) have over-reached and failed to provide for the common good in a sustainable fashion, and hence their days in control of the American Empire are numbered.

Both traditional societies and modern social innovations offer numerous blueprints for reciprocity.

In many traditional cultures, the "common area resources" such as land and water were conceived as community-owned assets. Such assets can also be combined with private property--that is, a "commons" open to all is owned or managed by the community as a whole.

This is basic idea behind the National Park System. But strict management is required lest the human instinct for windfall exploitation destroys the commons--a concept popularized by Garrett Hardin in a classic essay, The Tragedy of the Commons (1968). Hardin concludes that ontologically, there is no technological "solution" to this issue. He proposed instead mutual coercion mutually agreed upon which is in essence the foundation of a democratic State: to protect our mutual interests from private windfall exploitation, we give exclusive control of concentrated, centrally directed coercion to the State.

On a local level, control of the commons can be seen in municipal water districts; windfall exploitation can be seen in private water systems which serve a large community with no other source of water.

Trade is the most ancient form of freely chosen reciprocity.

If there is one single element in financial prosperity--income, wealth and capital accumulation--which is under-appreciated, I think it is trade. Long before a fossil-fuel dependent transport system or the modern State or "Capitalism" with a capital C, humans enriched themselves and their communities by trading over vast distances.

Trade between Rome and China, trade between India, the Mideast and the Mediterranean empires --these trade routes, thousands of miles long, predated the birth of Christ. Trade does not require fossil fuels, the State or even modern finance. Trade springs up on its own as a form of windfall exploitation: the scarce from afar can be sold for an immense profit (especially if competitive sources have been limited) and locally produced surplus goods can be purchased at low cost and sold where they are scarce at an immense profit.

Trade is freely chosen and mutually beneficial. It is only exploitative if Elites control the resources, labor and/or transport.

In the context of the present, then the explosion of small trading enterprises on the Internet (eBay, craigslist, etc.) is a current example of the power of trade to arise spontaneously for mutual benefit/profit.

Another structure which serves common interests is the self-organized cooperative, which can be organized by community, financial or trade/craft interests. In "old Hawaii" (and to some extent, in modern Hawaii), Japanese-American neighborhoods and communities (often small plantation villages) formed voluntary associations known as *kumiai* (pronounced "koo-me-eye").

The kumiai served as a way to pool scarce resources--in a poor plantation economy, money--to aid members in their hour of need. Thus the custom was for all kumiai members to offer a small amount of money whenever a member died, to help the family defray the costs of a funeral service and burial.

Accounts were kept by senior household members to ensure that reciprocity was fulfilled; any household which had given money for a funeral would receive the same sum when someone in that household passed away. In this fashion, expenses such as funerals were shared by the community.

Another function of kumiai's was the pooling of capital. Small sums were collected annually from member households, and the accumulated capital was then "invested" in one member's enterprise. Depending on the group, this could be awarded by bidding (the pot going to the highest bidder), chance (via a drawing or lottery) or by deliberation of the group.

This concept is in essence the basis of Credit Unions.

All of these self-organizing groups/networks are examples of *transparent non-privileged parallel structures*: voluntary, formally organized structures which are independent of State or State-mandated institutions. Where large-scale formal structures are controlled by purposefully opaque Elites--governmental agencies, banks, global corporations, etc.--self-organized groups are transparent (otherwise, who would contribute time and money?) structures based on fulfilling the needs and interests of non-privileged, non-Elite citizens.

As these exist in parallel to formal State and corporate organizations, they are not direct sources of confrontation or competition and are thus not targeted by Elites for destruction.

Indeed, in many cases, the State and Elites enable or at least benignly ignore such community organizations/networks (local gardening clubs, Neighborhood Watch groups, etc.).

The key point is that transparent non-privileged parallel structures exist independently of Elite-controlled formal structures of power. While all such groups are implicitly political in nature--any organization which can wield influence beyond its numbers is potentially political--they are essentially informal (voluntary) parallel structures rather than direct threats to the status quo.

Thus the kumiai operates within a State but its interests lie beyond the State's purview. To the degree the kumiai offers alternative sources of financing to small enterprise, it could be seen as a competitor to the Elite banking/finance cartel, but the cartel would not profit enough from small loans to even bother making them.

Thus transparent non-privileged parallel structures have the great advantage of being non-threatening to Power Elites even as they offer practical alternatives to the dominant State/corporate structures.

To follow up on the kumiai concept of pooling local resources to fund small enterprises: a financial kumiai could become a legally formal (that is, a partnership or non-profit legal entity) but informally structured private mortgage/lending in which a handful of individual investors fund a home purchase or new enterprise completely independent of the financial Elites' banks and venture capital elites.

This concept is also the foundation of "micro-finance" loans that also flourish independent of banking Elites and their State enablers.

Though many traditional cultures around the world have similiar voluntary mutual-aid networks, I will mention another which arose in present-day Japan simply because it is known to me.

In this network, time and labor are traded much like goods. If I watch your children for two hours, I receive two hours of "credit" for that labor which I can "spend" by asking another member of the network to watch my own children for two hours at a time when I need that assistance.

The labor "credit" is entirely voluntary. Thus I might care for an elderly person for four hours and receive four hours of gardening or computer tutoring in exchange. No money is exchanged and thus no taxes are due.

Given the approaching "end of paying work" described in Chapter Fourteen, then this type of cashless, taxless, Stateless network of exchange has tremendous possibilities.

The Internet enables such cooperative, voluntary mutually beneficial networks to operate at a scale and transparency that would not have been possible in a pre-Web, pre-networked world.

The Internet and all its related technologies are thus a critical "commons" asset which must be preserved and kept transparent for the common good, as this technology enables cooperative mutually beneficial exchange of ideas, labor and goods on a nearly scale-invariant level. That is, the Web enables trade within a neighborhood, a town, a city, a State or the entire planet.

For the household, reciprocity begins with existing networks: family, friends, colleagues, churches, neighborhood groups, trade/guild/interest groups, and so on. The possibilities of extending reciprocal networks (transparent non-privileged parallel structures) to operate independent of (or even replace) failing State/Elite structures are essentially unlimited.

8. Diffusion of Power and the Means of Wealth/Income Creation

On a society-wide level, distributing/diffusing the means to create income/wealth makes for a more equitable (less inequality) and more secure economy.

In terms of households, this is just another way of reducing risk and vulnerability. What means does the household own to generate income and accumulate capital? The means might be "soft capital" such as specific skills or it might be a combination of "soft" and built capital (welding skills plus a welding rig). It might be a modest sum of savings (capital) and a willingness to learn.

Dictatorships are ontologically unstable which is why few outlast their founders. Diffusion of power in a household means engaging all members in the AADD and/or OODA loop process of making realistic, transparent appraisals, cost-benefit analyses and then deliberative trade-offs and decisions/action plans.

Capitalism is fundamentally the process of risking capital for a return, and responding to feedback from the market. No one can recommend or predict what enterprises or means of income/wealth creation are available to any particular household; the household itself must become engaged in assessing its assets (skills, interests, capital, tools, etc.) and deciding where best to deploy/invest those assets.

Diffusing income creation means establishing multiple sources of income and enterprise that are not dependent on only one person in the household or one skillset or one market or even one measure of value.

Since our goal is full-spectrum prosperity, then "enterprise" includes not just income as measured in money but improvements in "soft capital" like health, knowledge, skills, working productively with others (networks and management). Working for "free" (that is, generating no cash money) may well generate significant returns when measured in purpose/goals, the joy of productive work, the building of potentially valuable networks and cooperatives, the process of learning, better health due to physical activity and a hundred other increases in value.

9. Base Decisions on an Integrated Understanding

I illustrate this concept with an example which many may find foolish. Since we all have to eat, and we all want health and well-being, then let's start by seeking an integrated understanding of the causal connections between food, nutrition, diet, cooking/cuisine, activity and health.

The key feature of an *integrated understanding* is that it is essentially three-dimensional, not in the spatial sense but in the sense that it combines a structural understanding with a historical and experiential understanding.

Without a knowledge of history, then the present is decontextualized--the precise goal of the status quo's mass-marketing/mass media machine. The person with no awareness of what came before is easily manipulated and exploited by a carefully manufactured politics of experience which supports the status quo.

A structural knowledge means a working knowledge of the moving parts of an entire system. Only those without a working knowledge claim that some task or process is "easy." Partial or shallow knowledge is misleading, and this is the ontological danger of mass media and TV: watching a presentation gives one the illusion of knowledge.

One can watch hundreds of hours of cooking shows but that will not teach one how to actually cook. One can watch hundreds of hours of kung-fu films but that will not teach one a martial art. The "knowledge" gained is illusory because it is not experiential.

An integrated understanding requires two other features: an identification of who controls each link in the causal chain or network, and who benefits from that control (yes, *cui bono*). Since the *politics of experience* presented by the mass media/mass marketing complex shapes our understanding, we must be alert to the subtle ways that we surrender control of our lives, our health and thus our prosperity to enterprises whose only purpose is profit.

Once again, the goal of mass-media/marketing is to encourage *permanent adolescence* and to persuade you that you share the interests of the Power Elites and the State they control. Put another way: the goal is to convince you that they're here to "help" you--to make your life "easier" and "more secure." This is Big Con; their only goal is concentrating and increasing their own income, wealth and power.

Once we understand that our interests are completely divergent from the interests and goals of the State and Power Elites, then we can finally begin to act on our own behalf and in our own interests.

Thus we seek an integrated understanding not for entertainment but to make a realistic assessment of what serves our best interests and what does not serve our best interests, and then act on that awareness.

An *integrated understanding* includes an experiential understanding.

"Old World" skills (both Old World Europe and Old World Asia) were grounded on the absolute mastery of the fundamentals through practice and repetition. Only when this foundation was perfected would the student or apprentice begin adding higher skills and knowledge. This is the structure of scientific knowledge as well.

Thus an integrated understanding of health, well-being, nutrition, cooking/cuisine and life itself requires growing some food oneself. Even if it a single tomato vine in a pot, everyone must gain the experience of nurturing, harvesting, preparing and eating real food. Without this experiential working knowledge, then there can be no truly integrated understanding of health, well-being, nutrition or cooking/cuisine.

It is a simple "obvious" truism that what we put in our bodies for sustenance directly influences our health. No one denies this, yet many stuff themselves with visibly unhealthy foods--mostly packaged by agribusiness/fast-food global corporations for profit, not nutrition.

As a result, the U.S. is a nation plagued by poor health and pandemic chronic illness.

There can be no real understanding of what food is without growing fruits or vegetables or raising livestock/fish and then preparing and eating the results. Even if it a single tomato harvested from a single vine in a single pot on the deck of an apartment, then the experience is necessary to transform one's understanding of food, nutrition and health.

An integrated understanding works back from "the obvious" to the source and then works forward again, grasping each causal link in the entire network.

To understand the epidemic of "diabesity" then we have to trace the causal chain back to our stilted, alienated understanding of food itself.

From there, we can advance through all the other causal links: from the stupor/torpor induced by high-fat, high-sugar, high-salt packaged food to the decline of cooking skills and the saturation of the mass media with messages to consume unhealthy but highly profitable items which are simulacra of actual food, manufactured to stimulate the addiction/reward centers in our brains.

Once a truly integrated understanding is reached, then you stop buying packaged foods entirely and you also lose the desire to consumer fast foods, ice cream and a host of junk-"food" snacks and beverages.

In a similar fashion, there is no way to reach an integrated understanding of well-being without being physically fit along with eating real food prepared at home--even if "home" is a campsite. No gym equipment is necessary to become fit; nothing is needed but two square meters of open space. If one has never experienced well-being, then how can one claim to understand it?

This is a radical departure from the quasi-"scientific" politics of experience which claims a full understanding is possible by quantification alone. This is a politics of experience which leads to *quantification traps* in which simulacrum of understanding are supported by quantifications which are inherently ambiguous or decontextualized of meaning.

Propaganda favors statistics and quantification because manipulated data can always be presented in ways which support a politics of experience under the control of a centralized, concentrated-power Elite. (Does that list of ingredients on packaged food really tell you anything that adds to your understanding? Or is it designed to obfuscate?)

The understanding that Americans are eating their way to death does not support a highly profitable complex of "food" and "sick-care"/pharmaceutical industries. Hence it is suppressed and decontextualized in favor of incentives to continue eating oneself to death so that powerful Elites can increase their profits.

The relentless promotion of "free" media is an integral part of this profitable world; not only does mass media profit from ads for fake-food and medications to counter the diseases created by the fake-food but the media itself acts as a substitute for experience of the real world.

Citizens spending hours watching cooking shows is immensely more profitable for the Power Elites than citizens turning off the TV and engaging the real world of growing and preparing real food. The profit potential of citizens experiencing the real world in these ways is almost zero. There is little profit in seeds, raw vegetables and garden mulch.

Nurturing a single bean plant and preparing the harvest, however small, gives an enlightenment that is unattainable by any other means.

In a way, an analysis of the *politics of experience* leads to this point: lived experience is the key to seeing through the sham politics of experience presented by the Power Elites for their own benefit.

Just as mind and body are one, so too are food, activity and health one. But it is much more profitable to make us ill with "food" manufactured to be unhealthy and then proceed to sell us the pharmaceutical and surgical "cures."

Yes, some diseases are genetic and others are triggered by environmental factors; these will need to be treated by medications or surgery or other treatment. But to ignore the causal connections between food, diet, activity, consumption of mass media/marketing and chronic disease/ill health is to ignore the "obvious." Why surrender control over those elements of health we do influence?

This is why I have said, "A healthy homecooked family meal and a home garden are revolutionary acts." In the context of a State/Elite-shaped politics of experience that profits from unhealthy fake-food and the management of the resulting diseases, then wresting control of one's food is decidedly revolutionary.

A free people will want control of their own lives, sustenance and destiny; an enslaved people will "buy" whatever they are "sold" and accept their Masters' "explanations."

As soon as we buy a packaged "food product" or "fast food," we have ceded control of our nutrition and "cooking" to a corporate entity whose concern is not our health but shelf life, profit margins, and engineering the "taste" of the "product" to trigger the reward centers of our brains in a cocaine-like fashion.

If you think this is exaggeration, please take it up with the former Commissioner of the Food and Drug Administration, David Kessler, M.D. who reached these conclusions after careful study of the available scientific evidence. He published his findings in 2009: <u>The End of Overeating: Taking Control of the Insatiable American Appetite</u>. Among many other points, he found that the nutrition information on packaging is manipulated by the food industry to mask its true composition. Thus the "quantified data" which you are invited to trust is deceptive.

Why should we cede control of our health and well-being to global corporate interests whose sole purpose in marketing their products as "food" is to maximize sales and profits?

It is a reflection of the twisted influence of false ideologies that taking control of one's food, cuisine, nutrition and health can be viewed as either "highly progressive" (down with the corporate parasites and toothless State lapdogs) and "highly conservative" (let's get back to the roots of what made this country great--real homegrown food, real homecooked family meals and hard work) at the same time.

Is there any wonder than an integrated understanding steers clear of ideological entanglements? Ideologies are all about the opposite of understanding: manipulation of public opinion by Power Elites to further their own control and gain.

I would like to emphasize the ontological (inherent) value of control and thus the importance of establishing who holds control in every causal chain or network. We often cede control without even being fully aware of the surrender.

For instance, if I buy a packaged food item which contains more salt than is healthy for me to consume in one day, then I have ceded control of my salt intake to the corporation which manufactured the packaged food and thus control of my own blood pressure and the attendant health risks that high salt intake incurs.

Thus it is critical to distinguish between what we could control if we chose to and what we cannot control. We cannot control our genetic propensities for longevity or disease, but research suggests that our health and longevity are roughly one-third heredity and two-thirds lifestyle (diet and activity).

The classic proof of this is the Pima Indians of the southwest U.S. Genetically identical Pima tribes inhabit the U.S. and Mexico; only the arbitrary national border divides the tribe. Unfortunately, the U.S. inhabitants eat an American diet, and thus they have extremely high rates of diabetes and related illnesses. Diabetes is essentially unknown amongst their Mexican brethren who consume a lower calorie traditional Mexican diet.

The heredity factor is identical in both groups, so the overwhelming influence of lifestyle is evident.

According to Dr. James Marks, a former Assistant Surgeon General and now senior vice president at the Robert Wood Johnson Foundation, no more than 15 percent of preventable mortality is linked to health care. Ultimately, No one can save us from ourselves except ourselves.

In reaching an integrated understanding of food, diet, activity and health, we become aware of how we cede control over our own lives and full-spectrum prosperity in the simple acts of buying unhealthy products and absorbing mass-media propaganda and marketing.

No one can save us from ourselves except ourselves; self-defeating and self-destructive behavior is only within our control and no one else's. Ultimately, no one can make us do anything; we make our own decisions. An integrated understanding includes an adult understanding and accountability.

If I watch hours of network/cable TV every day then I have ceded a considerable amount of my attention and productive time to what a handful of global mass-media corporations deem "newsworthy" or "entertaining," along with the advertisements which enriches them at the expense of my productive time. I have thus surrendered control of my productive time to these corporations.

The goal of an integrated understanding is to make a realistic assessment of what serves your best interests and what does not serve your best interests, and then act on that awareness.

Health is perhaps the most important aspect of what I term full-spectrum prosperity because if we lose or degrade our health then we can no longer work as long and effectively, nor can we enjoy the pursuit of happiness as vigorously.

Thus the integrated understanding of food/diet/cooking/activity/health is integral to *full-spectrum prosperity*. No amount of money or technology can restore health once it has been squandered, and "prosperity" loses meaning when health has been lost.

The causal chain connecting growing food, diet, nutrition, cooking, activity and health is just one example of an integrated understanding.

At a minimum, we should each seek an understanding of the FEW essentials (food, energy, water) in our home region and the nation's interlocking political and financial power structure--the goal of this book.

In seeking to understand energy, it means having some grasp of the inherent ambiguity of "proven reserves" (i.e. knowing this number is manipulated for political purposes); knowing what open-pit coal mines and tar-sands mining operations look like; understanding the concept of energy density and "equivalent barrels of oil" so apples-to-apples comparisons can be made, the total energy consumed by the nation and the world at large, etc.

Such a working knowledge is readily available from the Web or books. Without this basic grasp of the physical realities of energy, then a citizen is easily misled by propaganda which exploits their ignorance. For instance: "We have enough shale oil to last 400 years."

Really? How much energy does it take to produce a barrel of light crude oil from tons of shale? How much does it cost to return the landscape to something other than a moonscape? How many barrels of oil can be produced per day by gigantic shale-oil operations? We know the vast tar sands of Canada are producing 1.4 million barrels a day--a mere 7% of current U.S. consumption of oil. Given the vast scale of these operations, is it plausible to expect shale oil producing even half of the 19 million barrels of oil the U.S. consumes every day?

The deeper our working knowledge of energy, the easier it to say, "No, it is not" with the confidence of knowledge.

Let us return to the concept of control. Control is an asset in its own category. Let's take energy production as an example.

I cannot control the future production of 100 million gallons of bacteria-derived fuel a day. I can however seek a modestly informed integrated understanding of exactly what is required for algae or bacteria to assemble hydrocarbons biologically, and the inherent difficulties of scaling up such production.

Despite all the glowing hype about hydrocarbon biofuels derived from genetically engineered algae or bacteria, production by these means is currently zero. The deeper one's working knowledge of the exact processes involved, the more daunting the project becomes. Even producing 50,000 gallons of fuel by these means is science fiction at this point, never mind a significant percentage of the 378 million gallons of gasoline the U.S. consumes every day. In 2008, the U.S. consumed 137.80 billion gallons (or 3.28 billion barrels) of gasoline. To breezily declare that a significant percentage of this stupendous quantity can be replaced by biofuels is willful ignorance or propaganda.

It's easy to make claims when working knowledge is essentially zero.

Since we cannot control global production of oil or the magical introduction of substitutes, then what can we control? We certainly control our consumption. An experiential baseline on energy use is to visit a developing country and observe how little energy the average citizen consumes.

Backpacking or car-camping to walk-in campgrounds also offers an experiential baseline. Very modest amounts of energy can make a big difference in "quality of life."

Economists place no financial value on control. Thus if electricity is currently "cheap" then "it makes no sense" to install photovoltaic solar panels because the electricity you buy from the utility is "cheaper."

But since you don't control the price or availability of the utility's electricity, then it might quickly become "expensive" or sporadic or simply unavailable at any price.

Control has great value, but it is difficult to "price."

If the utility crashes or power is rationed or sporadic, then what is the "value" of being able to generate your own power supply, however modest?

Regardless of price or cost, the geothermal system (geo-exchange system) you install to help heat and cool your house is within your control, as is a solar water heating system, photovoltaic cells and a windmill on the lower 40.

As noted earlier in this analysis, the market is ineffective in responding to depletion or permanent disruption. Oil will be "cheap" until it isn't, but due to the fact that markets are always priced on the margins then the price rise will be sudden.

In theory, a substitute will arise or be created, but this is deceptive. There are no substitutes for wild tuna or salmon once these reserves are depleted; farmed fish are not truly equivalent in genetic "wealth" or in "adding value" to a complex ecosystem. They are simulacrum substitutes which markets can falsely label "equivalents."

Oil is uniquely energy-dense and transportable. There is no equivalent, and substitutes are costly half-measures. Liquefying natural gas for transport is inherently costly, transforming shale into liquid fuel is inherently costly, and so on. Drilling 1,000 wells to capture pockets of natural gas is inherently more costly than drilling 10 wells into a supergiant under-pressure oil field.

Thus the vaunted faith that "the market will find or create substitutes" should be viewed with skepticism. Is a barrel of oil (or equivalent energy) that costs $300 per barrel "equivalent" to $30 per barrel oil? Clearly, the answer is no.

It's important to recall that markets price on the margins. If the U.S. consumes 20 million barrels of oil a day and the supply drops to 15 million barrels, then no more than 2 MBD can be conserved without dramatic changes to transport and industry. That means there is a shortage of 3 MBD. Though that is only 15% of demand, that shortage could double or even triple prices as those with money or credit frantically raise the bid.

In other words, the supply does not have to drop in half for the price to double; modest drops in supply can cause explosive rises in prices. That is the way the market works: prices are set by marginal supply and demand.

Unfortunately, it takes many years or even decades to increase the supply of energy on a large scale. Biodiesel production is currently about 50,000 gallons a day--a relative drop in the bucket of demand. No amount of magical thinking can ramp up biodiesel production from 50,000 gallons a day to 50 million gallons a day. Due to the shortage of feedstock for biodiesel, that level of production is simply not possible, regardless of what technology or government spending is thrown at it.

So when electricity suddenly becomes "expensive" and solar panels "make sense," you won't be able to buy any at any price or the cost will have leaped to absurd levels due to spiking demand. *"When you're thirsty, it's too late to dig a well."*

Thus the standard analysis of "price" and "value" is fundamentally flawed. The point at which it "makes sense" to buy and control your own energy production is when "it makes no sense because oil/natural gas/electricity are so cheap." Once they're no longer cheap then you may not be able to afford your own energy production assets--assets which were cheap when they "made no sense" to the conventional financial/consumerist analysts.

The goal of an integrated understanding is to make a realistic assessment of what serves your best interests and what does not serve your best interests, and then act on that awareness. Conventional wisdom should be viewed with extreme skepticism. Do your own research and make your own analysis of costs and benefits, including the value of control.

10. Leverage capital, assets and skills

The word "capital" might evoke large sums of money or large-scale enterprises, but I use it to describe two assets: the means of production, which include tools, manufacturing equipment, software, etc., and surplus money or tradable assets (gold, bartered time and goods, etc.) which can be invested in productive assets.

The scale of capital can be very small. All you need to cultivate a garden is a shovel. Thus the capital required to start growing food is one shovel, some seeds and some compost, much of which can be assembled via labor (time).

With the aid of one 100-pound helper, I built a 12-foot by 16-foot shed in 1978 with a handsaw, a level, a square, a few hammers and nail aprons, a measuring tape, a screwdriver, and a few other hand tools (snapline, etc.) This structure served as living quarters and storage; it is still in use today, some 30 years later. The total capital required--the tools, not the lumber and other building materials--were modest. No power tools were necessary.

The tools required to repair furniture, sagging doors, torn screens, leaky faucets and dozens of other common household projects are also minimal. Even woodworking requires few tools. I have built an entire set of kitchen cabinets with a Skilsaw and some simple jigs--no table saw, cut-off saw, etc. Clamps, a square and a straightedge are all that is necessary to fabricate effective jigs.

Of course some capital equipment is more expensive: welding rigs, log splitters, cranes, etc., all the way up to semiconductor manufacturing plants which cost $2 billion each. Nonetheless, many means of production are modest in cost. Software coding requires little more than a computer and an Internet connection.

By any measure Chinese cuisine is incredibly diverse; its wealth of regional styles, range of ingredients and combinations of taste, texture, nutritional value and aesthetics are arguably unmatched. All you need to prepare the majority of Chinese dishes is a wok, a cutting board, a spoon/spatula and a good knife or cleaver. A stockpot and a colander are helpful as well. Any other tool or cooking implement is superfluous.

The rest of the "capital" required to prepare Chinese cuisine is skill and experience. Skill requires both knowledge and experience. One could watch cooking shows for hours and learn something about preparing Chinese cuisine, but without experience then the knowledge cannot be leveraged into edible/tradable dishes.

Just because an asset has marketable value does not make it capital. A house which generates no income is not a productive asset in the same sense as tools, equipment or an enterprise. Only when rooms are rented to create a source of income does a house become productive. Land may have value on the open market, but if it is devoted to lawn then it is not productive. Only when the lawn is replaced with a garden or orchard producing edible/tradable produce is it productive.

This distinction is important because it explains why a household may appear to be worth a lot of money in the sense of assets owned, but when measured in productive capital (means of production and skills) it might well be impoverished.

There are only two end-states when the State debauches its currency: the devaluation of that currency or the default of State debt. Thus counting on a State which is borrowing profligately to maintain the value of its currency is inherently risky. If defaults rise and credit becomes scarce--a common enough occurrence in eras of heightened risk and caution--then assets which had great value in times of easy credit (such as houses) could languish unsold, effectively reduced to capital traps.

This is why I emphasize capital over assets. Many things listed as assets may end up being unsellable or greatly reduced in value. In contrast, surplus capital in the form of productive assets will always have value because they are the means to producing value and income and thus security and wealth.

In sum: unproductive assets are not capital. Their value can fall precipitously because they are neither the means of production nor necessarily tradable for the means of production.

Thus the goal is to acquire, and then leverage, productive capital: the means to produce value and the skills required to do so.

We might also make a distinction based on scarcity and substitution. Some useful assets can be substituted rather freely. If you don't own a shovel, a hoe will do. A cart can be substituted for a wagon. But when you need to weld two pieces of steel, then you need a welding rig. Substitutes (drilling holes and assembling through-bolts, etc.) are cumbersome at best.

At the highest levels, there is no substitute for semiconductor manufacturing equipment. If you want to fabricate solar cells, you need very costly capital equipment and the infrastructure and skills to operate and maintain it.

On the other hand, if you want to assemble a household solar water heater, then a length of black hose and a few other basic materials will do.

Thus we should all be aware of what productive assets cannot be substituted and what is intrinsically scarce or limited.

One useful way to organize capital into a taxonomy of scarcity and value is to recognize four basic categories of capital:

1. Natural capital: fresh water, arable soil, coal, oil, minerals, fisheries, sunlight, geothermal hot springs, etc.

2. Built capital: buildings, infrastructure, equipment, machine, etc.

3. Social capital: education, skills, family, community, networks, government

4. Individual capital: skills, experience, health, ability to learn, ability to work with others, etc.

At the most basic level, arable land and fresh water are essentials which are intrinsically limited. Sunlight and geothermal are virtually unlimited but each requires intensive capital and technology to tap or gather. Nonetheless, as noted above, very simple equipment can be deployed to gather the sun's energy to heat water or an enclosed space.

Leverage, like productive capital, is a key concept.

Why acquire additional capital if you haven't first leveraged what you already own? Why dream of a farm when your backyard lies fallow? Why assemble a shop full of tools when you haven't learned how to productively use the few you already own?

The two fundamental individual skills are the ability to learn and the ability to work with others. If someone wants to start acquiring capital even when they have no money, then these two assets are the place to start.

It is impossible to predict which skillsets will become more valuable than others in any time frame; certainly being able to cook, grow food, care for others and maintain infrastructure will always have intrinsic value. More important than any one skill is the ability to learn additional skills, and the ability to work within groups for reciprocal benefit.

Working with other people is an acquired skill; it is not inherent, it must be learned just like any other skill or body of knowledge. Since the foundation of radical self-reliance is working with others for reciprocal benefit, then the "internal capital" of knowing how to work with others is, along with the ability to learn, the most important capital.

If a person possesses these two "internal" assets (capital), then they can leverage them into developing social capital and individual capital (additional skills). Once a person is creating value within a network, then he/she can begin generating surplus capital which can be exchanged for built and/or natural capital.

The key point cannot be over-emphasized: everyone who has the ability and willingness to learn, and to learn how to work with others, has a source of capital to leverage. No physical capital is required to start creating value and generating surplus capital which can be traded or exchanged.

In terms of full-spectrum prosperity, possessing some of each type of capital lowers vulnerability and increases security.

Land and equipment are potentially productive assets, but skills are needed to leverage the asset into productivity. That requires individual capital. An isolated point of production has little value if its surplus cannot be exchanged for reciprocal benefit (profit, access to scarce goods or additional means of production, etc.) so social capital--a market, a network, a neighborhood, a guild, a town, a family--are also necessary. And if there is no infrastructure of transport, roadways, electricity and social order, then exchange and security will both be limited.

Though I have devoted much space to the inherent dangers of an over-reaching State, a well-managed, competent State with transparent governance is an essential asset of social capital. Regions with weak, incompetent states riddled with opaque governance (corruption, collusion, etc.) are inevitably lacking in the infrastructure which enables commerce, trade and thus income and wealth creation.

Most of us have latent skills and networks which we do not leverage. Most of us have internal assets we do not fully leverage. The acquisition of skills and networks requires time and effort; tools can be borrowed or acquired via trade. On the individual and household level, capital need not be large-scale or costly; the goal is to leverage existing capital and start generating value and surplus which can be exchanged.

Risk-return: to earn a return, we have to put capital at risk. In the vernacular: try something, risk something, check the results; do more of what works and less of what doesn't.

11. ESSA: eliminate, simplify, standardize and automate

These powerful tools are self-explanatory. Eliminate wasted motion, wasted time, wasted expenses. Simplify processes and procedures. Standardize, a.k.a. don't reinvent the wheel every time. Automate: on the household level, that could mean auto-pay utility bills.

These concepts leverage triage. When push comes to shove, what can be eliminated with no real loss to the core? How about an auto payment, a mortgage, stuff nobody has used in years? How about "prestige" items and prestige itself? How about substituting the internal value of personal integrity for "prestige"?

Those unused to triage might find the goal of cutting household expenses in half daunting. ESSA provided the conceptual tools to do so.

Humans tend to complicate matters for a variety of reasons, mostly accretion: we add layers and objects without removing previous layers. We grow attached to the status quo conventions for the reason that we habituate easily and relinquish habits with difficulty. This "conservation trait" offers some selective advantages; in the vernacular, "if it ain't broke, don't fix it."

Unfortunately devolution doesn't "break" anything until a phase shift occurs, at which point it's too late to introduce feedback loops or modify inputs.

Many middle-aged people look fondly on their youth not just for its easy health and invincibility but for the simplicity of goals and daily life. Just as the body reinvents itself constantly (if given the right inputs: healthy food, vigorous activity and a purposeful life) then the goals and processes of our daily lives can also be reinvented constantly.

Some complexity cannot be eliminated. Calculating taxes remains complex. Running an enterprise remains complex. Learning a difficult new skill cannot be simplified; achieving mastery is messy and filled with errors and repetition. But taxes can be somewhat automated with inexpensive software and an enterprise can be constantly scanned for ways to simplify.

For households, it can be as "simple" as combining errands rather than leaving the house in a car three times a day. People are smart; once they decide to implement ESSA, solutions abound.

12. Generate value and surplus (working capital)

Stop diverting surplus to the State and rentier-financial Elites. Deprive the investment/money-center banks of your capital and fees; use debit cards, cancel credit cards, close accounts, keep money in credit unions, transfer IRAs and 401K accounts to non-money-center banks.

Pay the taxes that are legally due--render unto Caesar that which is Caesar's-- but reduce surplus paid to the State by earning less money and starting self-employed businesses which enable deduction of more expenses. Substitute barter and exchange of labor/solutions for wages/money. Ideally, reduce cash income to the point that legally no taxes are due.

Minimize purchases to limit sales taxes and superfluous spending/ expenditures which reduce surplus capital.

Move out of high property tax states or sell high-property tax properties unless they are able to generate operating profits in a decades-long Depression.

If the household or enterprise is insolvent, then accept reality and declare bankruptcy.

13. Secure/produce/innovate the FEW resources (food, energy, water)

I have touched on the importance of redundancy and decreasing vulnerability; a slightly different way of approaching the subject is to focus very simply on what I term the FEW resources: food, energy and water. (I will add the Internet later but it remains in a different taxonomy of scarcity and need.) If we "cut to the chase," i.e. triage goals to the absolute necessities, then we come to the FEW resources. Yes, it is possible to die of exposure without clothing and shelter, but death is assured without food and water. Energy is a special resource, as it stores and enables all that we call wealth.

We've covered the importance of growing/raising some food, no matter how modest the harvest, and the concept of hedging/distributing risk via storing some dried/canned food and water. Energy is a difficult and costly resource, as it is not available to the household without large capital investments. However, households can reduce their dependence on utilities and Elite sources of energy by simply using less.

I have described the importance of networks and voluntary community/Internet associations (self-organizing, transparent non-privileged parallel structures). While it maybe difficult or impossible for a single household to raise the capital to produce energy, a "kumiai" or neighborhood/village/city cooperative could raise the capital via contributions from many households.

We've also noted how locally controlled energy "makes no financial sense" until the devolution of cheap abundant oil/coal natural gas reaches a phase shift and suddenly "it makes excellent sense" but the means of production are suddenly unavailable or exorbitantly prohibitive.

Once again I stress the "value" of control which cannot be measured by financial metrics.

Non-fossil fuel transport is arduous in locales with long winters. But there are bicycles in summer and cross-country skis in winter. People traded goods over thousands of miles long before coal or other fossil fuels were extracted. The human landscape has sprawled out in response to the windfall exploitation of cheap, abundant oil. As oil becomes ever more costly, then households can move closer to places they frequent: schools, farmers markets, town centers, concentrations of commerce.

There is a source of latent energy within a few hundred feet of every square meter of dry land on the planet: the Earth. Though it is claimed that the soil is frozen to the depth of 700 feet in eastern Siberia, in less extreme climes then the ground temperature below 100-200 feet remains fairly constant (with the usual variations): around 50-60 degrees F (10-15 C). While it is costly to drill holes and install a geo-exchange loop, the source is renewable. As noted above, heat pulled from the earth has the distinct advantage of being within our own control. Yes, I understand the heat pumps require electricity, and that is another set of vulnerabilities and solutions. And once again, a community has the scale to raise capital and at least heat/cool one building at modest cost to the entire community.

Households which have to relocate for other reasons might survey potential locales for their proximity to fresh water, agriculture and energy sources. Not depending entirely on global corporations and distant nation-states for our essentials seems like prudent risk management.

14. Think, Plan and Act with Integrity

As I noted in the introduction, what we might term morality and ethics have no "value" in the status quo, which incentivizes looting, lying, embezzlement, misrepresentation, manipulation of statistics, propaganda, gaming the system and a vast host of other behaviors which are the opposite of integrity and honesty.

Ultimately, we cannot totally control any assets other than our personal integrity, experience and skills. If we act with integrity, we have a capital asset no one can take from us, depreciate or debauch.

It isn't complicated or difficult to think, plan and act with integrity; it is easy unless one is mired in an entitlement/something-for-nothing mindset seething with greed and trumped-up resentments.

As the risks of phase shifts and dissolution increase, those with integrity will gain the trust of others with integrity; those without integrity will not, and they will consequently be left with their own kind.

The Remnant which thinks, plans and acts with integrity has a source of capital which is beyond financial valuation.

15. Pare complexity to simplicity

On an institutional level, complexity is a tool of control and concentrating power. In households, it is a source of confusion. Decisionmaking and planning are inherently difficult because no one can know the future consequences of action or inaction.

There is a vernacular term: KISS--"keep it simple, stupid." But major decisions like moving to another state are complex because the ramifications tumble like dominoes once the decision is made.

Ironically, there is no simple method for paring complexity. Reducing possibilities to "if-then" statements, and working through the assessment, (cost-benefit) analysis, deliberation and decision process (AADD) or the OODA loop (Observe, Orient, Decide and Act) are helpful processes.

Natural selection plays complexity and simplicity as it does conservative and bold. In general, bold action (which typically arises from the reduction of complex situations to a simple "grasp the nettle" understanding) increases the risk of failure, so organisms and organizations tend to make changes only when forced to do so. With the risk bias favoring conservative action or no action, they make changes to lessen the risk of a false step.

So complexity piles up as new adjustments and layers are added to existing systems. Over time the entire system may become energy-inefficient and unwieldy, at which point it collapses under its own weight or is forced to make radical adaptations to survive.

Households can be viewed as an ecological system. When they become overly complex and inefficient, consuming more than they create, then they are vulnerable to collapse.

The process of paring complexity can be summarized as "getting rid of what no longer works to our benefit and keeping what does." Humans habituate to circumstances very quickly, and so just as we stop noticing the clutter in the garage we also stop noticing behaviors and processes which are no longer in our best interests.

Do more of what's in the household's best interests and pare away what isn't. That is a starting point.

If I was asked to draw up an "action list" derived from the above principles, it would include these items.

A stupendous number of people are smarter and more experienced than I am; they will figure out solutions which work for them in their situation. I don't claim to have solutions for anyone--recall that the way the "problem" is posed sets the "solution."

Regardless of the situation, these principles are at least a good place to start.

An integrated understanding is not dictatorial or coercive. It focuses our attention on what's in our best interests and attempts to avoid/limit what is self-defeating or self-destructive and thus not in our best interests.

1. Add a feedback loop. On the household level, if there is no accurate, transparent budget of true income and expenses, then assembling such information is adding a feedback loop which did not exist before. If you write an email to your city council representative, you are creating a feedback loop which did not exist before.

As we have carefully described, the market is not invincible or even very prescient. Its power rests in being a feedback loop; central planning fiefdoms (such as the Federal Reserve) which attempt to bypass or over-ride the market by creating perverse incentives have limited feedback from reality and hence they fail on an ontological (inherent) level. They are systemically doomed from the start.

Magical thinking and wishful thinking have no feedback from reality, hence they too are doomed.

Making realistic assessments means obtaining feedback from reality. Engagement via AADD and/or OODA is adding feedback loops which do not exist when we sit passively by.

2. Stop watching network/cable TV except as a rare guilty pleasure. A responsible parent limits his/her children/teens' time absorbing the destructive propaganda of network/cable TV/videogames; what works for kids works for adults, too: everyone in the household should be restricted to an hour or two of "guilt-free TV" a week. (Now that the TV propaganda has migrated to the computer via the Internet, then that also means limiting exposure to MSM propaganda on the computer.)

Setting limits forces a healthy triage: having to pick your favorite two or three shows and letting go of all the rest is a good exercise.

The way to stop being poisoned is to stop taking the poison.

As I hope I have made abundantly clear, the primary means of controlling our experience and thus manufacturing our passive acceptance of a debt-serf/financial "Plantation" economy ruled by a partnership of a corrupt, over-reaching State and rentier-financial Power Elite is the mass media/marketing complex owned and operated by a handful of global media corporations.

To stop the poisoning of our souls, spirits, minds and lives, the solution is simple: stop watching.

The "news" is not "news"--it's carefully filtered propaganda. "Talk radio" is entertainment, not engagement; it too is another form of propaganda. (Who owns the radio station networks and how much money do they reap off "talk radio"? *Cui bono*--to whose benefit?)

The only hope of avoiding pure propaganda is to read a variety of sourced materials. If you get your "news" from one source, then the editor has shaped your experience. The only way to avoid that is to become your own editor: browse a variety of sources on the Web, including independent blogs and reputable global sources of mainstream reporting such as *The Economist, Wall Street Journal, New York Times, The Atlantic, National Review*, etc. as well as smaller publications and local sources.

Yes, these sources have been carefully edited to support a status quo *politics of experience* but with a wide enough "harvest" of sources then it's possible to see through much of the blatant propaganda or at least become skeptical of received conclusions (always ask *cui bono*).

Reading reportage from overseas (for instance, the *Financial Times*) is a good way to avoid confirmation bias which is the tendency to read only what supports your current views.

An hour of TV "news" (if it bleeds, it leads) provides the "nutrition" of a small package of potato chips: not just zero, but a destructive serving of fat. The same hour spent on the Web simply browsing a half-dozen sources can be an actual "meal."

As noted above, TV programming offers the attractive illusion of value: the cooking show, the travel show, the history program, etc. have some content beyond entertainment (which remains their primary goal). But the "content" is a simulacrum of real knowledge; a hundred hours of watching cooking programs teaches less than fifteen minutes of actually cooking/baking.

Yes, there is some value in PBS programming (*Nature, NOVA, American Masters, Frontline*, etc.) and some BBC programming, but we should never confuse passive watching with the pursuit of mastery or the acquisition of experiential capital.

In that sense, every hour of passive watching takes away an hour which could have been spent acquiring some individual capital (skills, knowledge, etc.).

The goal is simple: limit the consumption of mass media propaganda/marketing, as it is designed to encourage a passive consumerist politics of experience.

Many of my blog readers report that the solution which works for their household is to cancel cable TV entirely or even get rid of the household TVs.

What works for me is to avoid watching any "news" other than the occasional PBS *Frontline* which takes one issue and devotes an hour to that one topic. Like any other "news," it is edited to present a specific point of view, and thus skepticism is in order. The point is that a few minutes of network "news" is not enough to provide anything more than a superficial and thus misleading jolt of packaged "news."

I have a few favorite shows and when there is new programming then I watch a few hours of TV a week. As noted above, an integrated understanding is not dictatorial; it simply focuses our attention on what's in our best interests and what is not in our best interests. If we need some entertainment, maybe a film or documentary is a better choice than network/Cable TV.

There are so many wonderful documentaries and films, why waste a minute on completely worthless network/cable TV programming? This is why I maintain lists of movies and documentaries (as well as books) on my website. I don't keep exact count but the lists include over 600 books and films--many suggested to me by readers.

Personally, I find network "sports" to be unfulfilling in terms of what I enjoy about sports. I would rather watch a local high school game in the real world than some corporate simulacrum of the "local team"--a program which is essentially advertising packaged with a bit of mostly boring "sports." I'd rather play than watch, and if I'm going to watch, then I want to know someone on the team.

3. Remove your money from money-center/investment banks; "starve the beast" of fees, interest and the use of your money. Place your money in credit unions or small local banks which actually recycle the money into your own community. Transfer your 401K accounts out of money-center broker/dealer accounts, and place your IRA funds in your own control.

Stop paying interest to the rentier-financial Elites; pay off credit cards, auto loans and even mortgages if at all possible. Make exiting debt-serfdom a goal. Pay cash or pay off your credit cards each month. Stop generating huge fees via "churning" debt (refinancing, etc.) unless you eliminate debt in the process.

4. Grow some food yourself, no matter how modest the amount. The mass media/marketing complex would have you believe this is trivial and thus "it makes no sense in dollars and cents." It also "makes no sense in dollars and sense" to have a local dairy when a corporate agribusiness dairy hundreds of miles away can supply hormone-laden milk for a "cheaper price." As I noted above, control and experiential capital have a value that cannot be measured by financial metrics.

It is not "trivial" to grow a single bean plant in a single pot on the balcony of an urban apartment or rooftop; it is vitally important because it is within your control and the experiential knowledge gained cannot be replaced by any commodity.

5. Only buy food with real ingredients and little added salt, sugar or fat. Corn flakes and shredded wheat are examples of corporate food products which contain grain and almost no added salt or fat. Better yet, buy bulk rolled oats and stop paying global corporations to package bulk grain in their brand. Avoid packaged food with copious amounts of salt, fat and sugar. The easiest way to take control of your diet, cuisine and health is to stop buying packaged food and fast food entirely and only eat real food except for an occasional guilty pleasure. One fast food meal a month--how does that sound? You will certainly enjoy every bite if it is limited.

6. Consume less of everything. The marketing politics of experience is that more is always better. The exact opposite is true; less is always better. The big house is just more work to clean, more costly to heat, etc. Bigger portions means more weight added to the consumer and thus lower health/higher risks of chronic illness, etc.

7. Start valuing control. As I have described above, control is an under-appreciated asset. The reason to own something is that you then take control of it. If it is not productive then get rid of it, otherwise it ends up controlling you. Nobody makes us buy or eat specific things; taking control means breaking free of the mass-media/marketing mindset of impulsive, distracted, stimulation-driven, excuse-dependent permanent adolescence.

This is why it is critical to own your own means of production: your own tools, knowledge and network of exchange.

8. Start valuing experiential capital. The most bizarre aspect of the consumerist *politics of experience* is the way it replaces experience of real life with the act of shopping and buying. Want to express your love for someone? Buy them a gift. Want to become more fit? Buy an exercise machine or shop for a gym membership. This bizarre substitution of highly profitable simulacrum for reality is so pervasive that it has become difficult to experience anything beyond this shallow consumerist imprisonment.

This is why I invested so much of your time earlier in this book on understanding the *politics of experience* and how it is shaped and manufactured to benefit the State and Plutocracy at our expense.

9. Seek an experiential understanding of well-being. Once again--how can we claim to understand well-being when we haven't experienced it? The simulacrum of well-being is "sold" at stupendous profits: magic pills of one sort or another, bogus "prestige" items--the list is endless.

Ask any experienced physician for the "magic formula" and the answer will be simple:

A. Lower stress (in my analysis, re-align expectations with realistic assessments of what's in your best interests: less "prestige" and more purpose)

B. Eat a healthy diet (a diverse variety of real food cooked at home, and some home-grown)

C. Be active (there is no substitute for being fit; all that's needed is six square feet of open space)

D. Realize the mind, body, emotions and spirit are one (emotional health and physical health are one; know your own limits, strengths and challenges; be a friend to yourself and others; express yourself honestly; seek a humble understanding of Spirit, etc.)

E. Be grateful rather than resentfully entitled (the baseline is always zero; no food, no electricity, no clean water, no income, no power, no friends, no family, no social order, no Internet, no citizenship, no entertainment, no health, no shelter, and so on)

All of the above become much easier once you turn off the TV, radio, videogame and computer.

10. Become an engaged citizen. If you do nothing else, vote out the incumbents. If they were doing such a great job, why is everything corrupted and falling apart?

Beyond the few minutes it takes to vote every two years, choose one issue to engage: local schools, bikeways, the local flea market/farmers market, neighborhood watch, poorly maintained public parks, community recycling, etc. An engaged citizenry is the only feedback which can counter the pervasive influence of the monied Elites, which includes public unions, government fiefdoms and the usual well-funded special interests.

If "fighting city hall" is not your cup of tea, then join a *transparent non-privileged parallel network or organization* that has self-organized to fulfill some purpose or interest which you share.

One example would be a neighborhood group which cleans up and cares for the local park. As cities lose tax revenues and get squeezed by unsustainable pension obligations, they will not have enough money to pay $100,000 in wages and benefits to have a city employee adequately care for the park. Those neighbors who want a clean, safe park for their kids, parents, families and friends will have to self-organize to get the job done.

The cash-strapped city will probably be willing to work with the group or at least not hinder its progress. Once again, I stress that such networks exist independent of State/corporate structures and thus they operate as *parallel informal power structures*.

Avoid confrontation and unlawful activity--The State seeks "enemies" it can violently repress.

11. Focus on the FEW resources in your household and community and build your own household's capital. That includes cash, tools, the FEW resources, knowledge/skills and networks.

12. Opt out of consumerist passivity and construct a self-reliant alternative which is independent of the devolving State and financial Plutocracy. The Plutocracy rules via persuasion through the mass media/marketing complex which establishes a politics of experience that then dictates how we experience events. This manufactured "experience" directs our thought processes, decisions and serfdom.

The rentier-financial Power Elite controls the State and thus the State's monopoly on coercion and violence. Opting out is legal and non-confrontational: turn off the media and "starve the Beasts" by reducing consumption, debt and income. Own/control your own means of production.

13. Encourage local enterprise. This ranges from putting your voice behind cutting red-tape restrictions on new enterprises in your city/region to buying real wood furniture from a local supplier/craftsperson rather than purchasing a foreign-made particle-board facsimile of furniture which will soon break apart and be hauled to the landfill. Only a sliver of your money spent on facsimile furniture stays in your own community while all the money spent on a real wood item constructed nearby stays in your community.

Furthermore, the real wood item will last decades rather than a few months.

14. Be open to the opportunities of hybrid work. One of my "jobs" is to pick up litter in the block around our home. Nobody pays me for it but it produces value: the neighborhood is tidy. Another "job" is watering the flowers in the city right of way which we and our neighbors planted. Many people have similar "jobs" which create value and for which they receive no money. Yes, we all need some paying work as well, but hybrid work recognizes value in many kinds of labor.

The core ideas of *hybrid work* are simple.

Hybrid work is fun. A variety of work is more fun and more rewarding than repeating one task.

Work projects and collaborative tasks you choose are more satisfying than those you are coerced into doing.

Hybrid work is inherently flexible. If you don't like a task or collaboration, seek another.

Hybrid work responds to your interests and talents and to the needs of your community.

Hybrid work celebrates creating value. If you're creating music, art, theater, food, joy or a hundred other creative enterprises then the line between "fun" and "work" fades.

Creating value—be it maintaining an overgrown trail, collecting compost, working out a "good governance" set of transparent rules for a committee, mentoring someone else, organizing a multi-event street fair, tinkering with a new practical software application or a thousand other tasks both mundane and creative—gives your life purpose.

Service to others or a community gives your life meaning.

Hybrid work is a choice in today's economy for those with low-debt, low-cost lifestyles. As formal jobs become scarce, then many will have few opportunities for fulltime employment and thus embracing the endless possibilities of hybrid work will be the healthy, fulfilling choice.

Hybrid work honors and values the mundane necessary tasks of culture: collecting the garbage, sorting out the compost, weeding the garden, keeping an eye on the kids, helping the elderly get some exercise, caring for pets, providing security, and so on. The mundane and the creative and the paid and unpaid share the same places of honor in hybrid work.

15. Join or construct networks (*transparent non-privileged parallel structures*) that diffuse concentrations of power. In today's global economy, capital is rarely concentrated and locally controlled. Thus union organizing is difficult because global capital simply moves elsewhere when employees demand a larger share of the corporate income.

Nonetheless, the concept of diffusing or counteracting concentrations of power (resisting financial and political dominance by an Elite or cartel) is still valid because local government remains accessible to citizen influence and pressure, and even multinational corporate/financial institutions must obey local laws.

At the community level, an Elite might dominate the school board or other institution which controls concentrations of authority or assets: planning department, transportation council, police oversight committee, and so on. Once the Elite becomes self-serving and no longer serves the public good, then it is our duty to unseat that Elite or attempt to diffuse its power (add a feedback loop which did not exist before).

Naturally, every Elite, no matter how small or localized, will resist any dilution of its power. Thus the strategy is to form self-organizing groups and networks which are large enough and robust enough to match the concentrated power of Elites.

Alternatively, citizens can bypass the entire established Power Elite and form alternative/parallel structures: charter schools, farmers market co-ops, and other types of *parallel informal power structures* which operate independently of status quo structures dominated by Elites.

One example of this is to simply pay off and then close credit cards and other loans owed to the banking cartel and establish local merchant credit as needed. Small contractors have accounts at the local lumberyard which they pay off monthly. This is a form of local credit that requires no global banking cartel's involvement.

A web-based self-organized local group could share local credit availability (local credit union, informally organized private lenders, etc.) which exist independent of the global banking cartel. "Starving the Beast" (that is, no longer paying the banking cartel fees and interest) is a boon to the local economy as that money circulates locally rather than being shipped to New York, Zurich or Hong Kong.

As noted before: the possibilities for self-organizing, transparent non-privileged parallel networks are virtually unlimited.

16. Work from core principles. (Add more principles as you see fit):

1. Engagement
2. Transparency (trust and truth)
3. Accountability
4. An Adult Understanding (Triage and Trade-offs)
5. Redundancy/Distributed Risk/Hedging
6. Radical Self-Reliance
7. Reciprocity
8. Diffusion of power and the means of wealth/income creation

9. Base Decisions on an Integrated Understanding
10. Leverage Existing Capital, Assets and Skills
11. ESSA: Eliminate, Simplify, Standardize and Automate
12. Generate Value and Surplus (working capital)
13. Secure/Produce/Innovate the FEW Resources (food, energy, water)
14. Think, Plan and Act with integrity
15. Pare complexity to simplicity

The Nature of Work and Skillsets

In discussing the responses that have a high probability of making the Transformation positive, we have also addressed Point Five: The nature of future work and the skillsets best suited to prospering during the Great Transformation.

In other words, in discussing full-spectrum prosperity, lowering risk, creating value/capital, leveraging assets and skills, and all the other topics we've covered, we've already addressed work and skillsets. Just to review previous sections:

Capitalism is fundamentally the process of risking capital for a return, and responding to feedback from the market. No one can recommend or predict what enterprises or means of income/wealth creation are available to any particular household; the household itself must become engaged in assessing its assets (skills, interests, capital, tools, etc.) and deciding where best to deploy/invest those assets.

Diffusing wealth/income creation means establishing multiple sources of income and enterprise which are not dependent on only one person in the household or one skillset or one market or even one measure of value.

Since our goal is full-spectrum prosperity, then "enterprise" includes not just income as measured in money but improvements in "soft capital" like health, knowledge, skills and working productively with others (voluntary networks).

Working for "free" (that is, generating no cash money) may well generate significant returns when measured in purpose/goals, the joy of productive work, the building of potentially valuable networks and cooperatives, the process of learning, better health due to physical activity and a hundred other increases in value.

And this:

The two fundamental individual skills are the ability to learn and the ability to work with others. If someone wants to start acquiring capital even when they have no money, then these two assets are the place to start.

It is impossible to predict which skillsets will become more valuable than others in any time frame; certainly being able to cook, grow food, care for others and maintain infrastructure will always have intrinsic value. More important than any one skill is the ability to learn additional skills, and the ability to work within groups for reciprocal benefit.

Working with other people is an acquired skill; it is not inherent, it must be learned just like any other skill or body of knowledge. Since the foundation of radical self-reliance is working with others for reciprocal benefit, then the "internal capital" of knowing how to work with others is, along with the ability to learn, the most important capital.

If a person possesses these two "internal" assets (capital), then they can leverage them into developing social capital and individual capital (additional skills). Once a person is creating value within a network, then he/she can begin generating surplus capital which can be exchanged for built and/or natural capital.

The key point cannot be over-emphasized: everyone who has the ability and willingness to learn, and to learn how to work with others, has a source of capital to leverage. No physical capital is required to start creating value and generating surplus capital which can be traded or exchanged.

In terms of full-spectrum prosperity, possessing some of each type of capital lowers vulnerability and increases security. *Land and equipment are potentially productive assets, but skills are needed to leverage the asset into productivity. That requires individual capital. An isolated point of production has little value if its surplus cannot be exchanged for reciprocal benefit (profit, access to scarce goods, additional means of production, etc.) so social capital--a market, a network, a neighborhood, a guild, a town, a family--are also necessary. And if there is no infrastructure of transport, roadways, electricity and social order, then exchange and security will both be limited.*

It's important to note once again that my analysis could be completely wrong. Perhaps the status quo will manage to create yet another credit-asset bubble which re-energizes the debt-dependent consumerist economy, and perhaps the global energy complex will magically drill 10,000 new wells at almost no cost and deliver "100 years of (coal, natural gas, shale oil, take your pick)" in super-abundance at low cost for generations to come.

Maybe the U.S. can print or borrow a $100 trillion to fill the gap between its income and the future expenses of Empire and entitlements without any consequent ruination of its currency or credit.

If that's the future, then the status quo understanding of careers and work will go on untouched.

We should know by 2010, or 2012 at the latest, which future is unfolding.

If the above analysis is wrong, then much of the paid work which holds the center of the U.S. economy will remain in place, and the "hybrid work/capital" I foresee will remain on the margins.

The ultimate key is the abundance of cheap energy. The entire structure of modern civilization, dating back to the Industrial Revolution, depends entirely on abundant, cheap energy. If that resource become expensive or scarce, then all the "guarantees" we take for granted slip away at once: retirement, travel, entitlements, cheap abundant food, and so on.

If my analysis is correct--that the exponential growth in credit, State over-reach/obligations and energy consumption are unsustainable and about to crack--then (status quo) salaried careers will slip to the margins and hybrid work/capital will occupy the center of the U.S. economy.

At the top layers of the economy, there will always be paid positions for very highly trained research and development staff. If you earn a graduate degree in materials science or immunology, then you will very likely enjoy a long career within that field--though you may not work for one enterprise for your entire career.

But the pipeline for high-level R&D and scholarship is small: if 10 million of us get PhDs in molecular biology, electrical engineering, chemistry, geology, network security and so on, it does not automatically follow that there are 10 million paid positions awaiting us. The pipeline of useful research in all fields is theoretically limitless, but in practical terms it is quite limited. Yes, we can print a trillion dollars and pay 10 million people to pursue all manner of research, but history suggests that this leads to the currency losing most of its value.

So research has to generate marketable value at some point. Very little research does so, hence the intrinsic limits on the R&D pipeline.

The same is true of the professions such as physician, attorney and engineering. The Third World is filled with professionals working in mundane jobs because there are not enough paying slots in their professions.

In the U.S., there are shortages of doctors and nurses in some areas and an oversupply in others. The entire healthcare ("sick-care") system is currently so distorted that the market "need" for physicians and nurses is impossible to ascertain.

Western Pennsylvania has more MRI machines than all of Canada. So how many MRI machines and technicians are "needed" once Medicare/Medicaid collapses under its own weight?

As much of the money is drained out of the lucrative FIRE economy (finance, insurance and real estate), then the "need" for lawyers will greatly diminish. Once the State is undeniably insolvent, then the number of paid positions for attorneys will drop.

If the State's mismanagement results in the destruction of the dollar's purchasing power--a distinct possibility--then the entire notion of "paid work" becomes meaningless.

Thus the "guarantees" which we currently expect may vanish: that a professional degree will "guarantee" high earnings and wealth, that "paid work" will result in purchasing power, and so on.

We can distill the following work/skill points from the "application of principles":

1. Entitlements are doomed, so focus on enterprise.

2. You can invest capital or labor (time) or both, but you must invest something if you want a return. Enterprise requires putting capital/labor at risk for potential return. This is called "putting capital to work."

3. There are no guarantees in life, only opportunities.

4. To get something, first you have to give something. This is reciprocity.

5. Gaining control of all four types of capital (natural, built, social and internal) diversifies your income/value streams and lowers risk.

6. The key skills are: the ability to learn ("learning how to learn") and

the ability to foster reciprocity/social capital--the ability to work productively with others.

7. Own/control your own means of production: your own tools, knowledge and networks of reciprocity/exchange.

8. The market for skills will fluctuate just like the market for anything else. The "answer" to "what's the most valuable skill?" will change. Flexibility and "owning" multiple skills are key assets.

9. The FEW resources (food, energy, water) will always be in demand, though they can be in oversupply in specific times and places.

10. Feedback is your friend. If there's no local market for your skill or product, then either move to a new market or adapt by learning new skills/making other products.

11. The mundane task of human life will always need to be done: childcare, caring for the elderly, "eyes on the street" security, cleaning up/disposing of rubbish, etc. Trade "up" by performing these tasks and bartering/trading for tools or higher-level skills.

12. Scarce skills and tool/skill combinations (welding kit and knowing how to weld, biotechnical lab skills, etc.) will always be in demand, though they can be in oversupply in specific times and places.

13. Use ESSA, AADD and OODA to assess your skills, assets, interests and the market/need for your capital/labor, and then act in your own behalf.

14. Plan your actions and complete your plans. If the plan doesn't work, adjust, adapt, modify. If you reach a dead-end, move to a new enterprise. Seek advice and mentors to help make your assessments and plans. Do more of what's working and less of what's not working.

15. Unpaid work can yield enormous benefits: new skills, new networks/social capital, better health, new purpose/meaning.

16. The new model is *hybrid work*: a flexible, adaptive mix of paid and unpaid work, menial labor, mentoring, "fun" work (playing music, habitat restoration, fishing, putting on plays, etc.), learning, teaching, trading/reciprocating, contributing, finding new purpose and meaning in a variety of skills and work.

17. Working productively with others is a skill. Being able to organize work to the benefit of all involved (management, leadership) is a high-level skill even in democratized, self-organizing groups. Somebody still needs to organize the clean-up, etc.

18. Focus on creating value (some activity, service or good which

can be exchanged for other services/good you need/want) and creating surplus capital (saving money, trading labor for tools, etc.) which can be "invested" in new enterprises.

19. Personal integrity is an asset no one can ever take away from you; it will never depreciate, it only grows in value.

20. Control, integrity and purpose do not lend themselves to financial metrics, yet their value is beyond measure.

21. New localized or web-based models for funding scientific research and development, software development, local enterprise networks, etc. are arising, along with independent, self-organized networks for sharing revenues, ideas and resources. If the status quo is no longer providing you with employment, then pursue these new models of research, development and hybrid work.

There are other work/skill points embedded in the principles: seek them out.

Investing, Speculation, Relative Value and Purchasing Power

Oftwominds.com readers often ask me for investment or real estate advice. I understand the motivation behind the question: we all want a straightforward answer as to how to protect our capital or make it grow.

I don't offer investment advice for a number of reasons, chiefly that I am not qualified but also for this reason: if I was any good at speculation, I'd be rich, and I'm not. I am not even average in this respect, so why add poor investment advice to the already long list of my faults and mistakes?

Nonetheless, I think I can offer a context—a step toward an integrated understanding--for protecting capital, investing and speculation.

When we speak of capital, assets, value, wealth and investing, we do not speak only of money.

In some respects, money is a very poor metric of value or wealth.

For instance, health is essentially invaluable, because once you've lost it then no amount of money can restore it. Yes, certain infectious diseases can be cured, certain illnesses fended off and certain cancerous growths removed or eradicated; but health is more than just the absence of disease: it is well-being, strength, alertness, endurance. Once these are lost (or squandered), then no amount of money can restore them. There is no "miracle pill" or surgery or treatment for the generalized loss of health, for the mind-body-spirit is too complex to be reduced to one causal chain.

If you look at a chart of the immune system--one of many complex systems--you will see a staggeringly complicated network of interactions, cascades and signals. As I have noted elsewhere, the entire "magic pill" concept is basically the model of fighting infectious diseases being misapplied to complex interactions. Yes, if a bacteria is the cause of a disease, then eradicating that bacteria will cure the disease.

But most illnesses are not caused by a single agent, and the interactions, influences, feedbacks and cascades which led to the illness are nuanced and difficult to understand. After all, many studies have shown belief in a specific treatment (the placebo effect) is as real as any medication. How do we quantify the placebo effect, or call it forth? It's not that simple.

Thus we can say that any "investment" you make in your own health will pay enormous "dividends."

The proper "investments" are well-known: reduce stress, eat a variety of real (unprocessed) foods and stay active/fit.

Given that health is essentially priceless, then the investment of time (activity) and care (growing and preparing real food) is perhaps the "best investment" we can make. Just as there is no wealth without energy, there is no wealth without health, either.

Once again we benefit from the Chinese proverb: *When you're thirsty, it's too late to dig a well.* Once health has been compromised, it's often too late to "fix" it. If you want to drink from the well of health, you have to dig it while you're healthy.

From this perspective, the obsession we have with our financial "wealth" is somewhat misplaced; we should start by "investing" in our health, skills and social capital.

I have addressed hedging and risk management, but there is more to say in terms of investment and speculation. Some investments are inherently riskier than others. That "obvious" statement is actually quite profound.

We might start by considering intrinsic (inherent) value.

Can the value of gold and silver drop to near-zero? It has never happened, as these precious metals have utility as jewelry and industrial metals and a long history as "money"--a near-universal means of exchange and a predictable store of transportable value. We can say they possess intrinsic value.

The relative value of gold and silver rises and falls according to supply and demand. In the Yukon Gold Rush, eggs were relatively scarce and gold relatively plentiful. So the owner of a dozen eggs was able to trade them for (let's say) one ounce of gold.

With gold at $1,000 an ounce as I write this in September 2009, then the relative value of eggs and gold is quite different due to supply and demand: one ounce of gold buys around 500 dozen eggs.

Thus scarcity and high demand and plentiful supply and low demand set the relative value of all stores of value and assets. **The value of any money or asset can only be measured in terms of some other store of value or asset.**

This concept can be confusing, for as consumers we naturally measure everything in our "home" currency. For example, as I write the S&P 500 (SPX) stock market index is around 1,000, and gold is around $1,000 per ounce. Thus we can say one ounce of gold can "buy" one "share" of the S&P 500. This is pricing the relative value of both the SPX and gold in dollars.

But if we price the S&P 500 in gold, then we reach a completely different valuation. At the top of 1999-2000 stock market, gold was about $300 an ounce and the SPX was above 1,000. Thus it took three ounces of gold to "buy" one share of the SPX.

Now that gold and the SPX are both 1,000, then it only takes one ounce of gold to buy a share of the SPX. **Measured in gold, the SPX has fallen in value by two-thirds.**

This fact draws instant violent protest from those holding a belief in the nominal value of the SPX: the only thing that matters is the nominal value (that is, whether it's 1,000, 900 or 1,100 today, yesterday, or ten years ago).

But this is obviously not an accurate measure of value or wealth. If the SPX priced in dollars is 1,000, and the dollar loses 90% of its value against all other measures of value (commodities, other currencies, gold, etc.), then the SPX at 1,000 represents a 90% loss of value.

One way to express value is purchasing power--what you can buy with a specific store of value. This is just another way of establishing relative value.

Put another way: how many loaves of bread does it take to buy a house? The answer gives us insight into the relative value of wheat and housing.

To sum up: we can measure value by intrinsic value and relative value.

Let's take another example: stocks and bonds. Can the value of stocks and bonds fall to near-zero? Yes--they have done so repeatedly in history. Ultimately, stocks and bonds are both valued on their income streams. If the income stream stops, and the promise of renewing the income is no longer credible, the value drops to near-zero.

While we can hope that these "claims on future income" still reflect the intrinsic value of the underlying assets--mortgages, factories, etc.-- the intrinsic value of these underlying assets depends on the income being generated by those assets. If no income can be derived, then the value of those assets drops to scrap value (near-zero).

Thus we can conclude that investing in "claims on future income" is inherently risky and speculative in nature.

Does shelter/housing have intrinsic value? Yes, but in low-demand, abundant-supply situations, the value can still drop to zero. Abandoned farmhouses in the middle of nowhere illustrate this characteristic, as do empty condominium towers and decaying exurb developments.

Thus we have to careful to recognize that possessing some intrinsic value (shelter, lumber, arable soil, and so on) does not guarantee that the asset will have any market value in all places and times.

In credit booms, sellers of marginal raw land like to say, "they're not making any more of it." Later, when the credit bubble bursts, the value of that "scarce" land drops to near-zero as the demand drops as the supply of land available on the market expands.

The reason why investing and speculating is inherently difficult is the relative value of all tradable assets is constantly shifting in relation to all other assets. I am indebted to oftwominds.com correspondent Harun Ibrahim for helping me grasp this key concept.

The only way to maintain the purchasing power of whatever asset you own (money, gold, beads, bushels of wheat, acres of forest, etc.) is to be alert to the shifts in relative value. There is no one measure of value; many use gold as a measure of "real money," but gold also fluctuates in relative value. Priced in dollars, it has risen from $450 to $1,000, dropped to $700 and then risen to $1,000 in a few short years.

Priced in some other currency, its fluctuations would be measured somewhat differently.

Many analysts compare the relative value of gold, currencies and oil: how many barrels of oil will one ounce of gold buy? Compare that to the relative value of a currency--for instance, the dollar--and one can discern historical patterns. Over time is oil near the bottom of its value range when an ounce of gold buys 10 barrels?

This analysis of relative value and purchasing power leads us to conclude that the only way to maintain (much less increase) the purchasing power of our assets is to buy an asset when it's cheap and sell/trade it for another asset when it's dear. To do that, we have to become aware of each asset's value in relation to other key assets such as gold, oil, wheat and various currencies.

Once again I return to the concept that control has intrinsic value. If I own a piece of arable land, the relative value will fluctuate against other assets. But unlike gold, I do not need to sell the land to realize an income. I can plant some crops and create an income stream--or, if the relative value of the crops is low, then I can decide not to plant, or rotate to another crop which is in demand/scarcity. Owning oil which has yet to be pumped shares this same feature: I don't control the market value of the oil, but I do control when and how much I will pump out and sell.

The same can be said of stocks which pay dividends, with the important caveat that I do not control whether the dividend will continue to be paid or not. My control is limited to holding or selling. If the dividend vanishes, much of the value of the stock will vanish before I can sell it.

If I own photovoltaic solar panels, the "income stream" is measured in kilowatts. The relative value of those kilowatts will fluctuate, but regardless of the relative value, the income stream is within my control. Energy has intrinsic value; it can drop in value but not to zero.

If a virus from space kills 50% of humanity then demand for energy would drop, and the price would plummet. But the surviving owners of energy would quickly cut production until supply aligned with demand, forcing prices up to the point a profit could be earned.

Supply and demand are not static, which is why measuring purchasing power is inherently challenging.

One last point needs to be made about relative value and intrinsic value. All fiat currency (paper money) is in essence a promise of future value. It has no intrinsic value. Thus it is vulnerable to rapid fluctuations in relative value and even a collapse to near-zero valuation. Thus we need to be especially sensitive to the difference between assets with inherent/tangible/ intrinsic and their relative value to currencies which have no intrinsic value.

If a currency is being devalued by the State which produces it, then owning some tangible income-producing asset is a much better hedge against a loss of purchasing power than holding the paper currency.

Modern States have freed themselves from the burdens of maintaining a currency with intrinsic value--that is, one backed by some tangible assets such as gold and silver. The promise of future value is cheap to reproduce, hence the slow but steady loss of relative value of all paper money over time.

There may come a time--perhaps after the default, insolvency and ruination of all these fiat currencies and the States which manufactured them--when the citizenry of a State will demand a currency which has intrinsic value--that is, one backed by assets owned by the State which issues the currency.

Tangible assets have some intrinsic value, intangible assets do not.

While all assets can be traded on some market somewhere, a medium of exchange--money-- simplifies the transactions for everyone. Paper money is a means of exchange, and gold is widely recognized as a time-tested means of exchange as well.

I bring this up to draw one more distinction: that between assets and means of exchange which earn interest or create income and those which do not.

Though fiat currencies tend to lose relative value over time (when measured in tangible assets like oil) in periods of high interest rates and deflation (that is, when money and credit are contracting and the value of tangible goods is falling when measured in currency), then paper money earning interest may outperform all other assets.

I note this to illustrate that there are no hard-and-fast rules in relative value and thus there are no hard-and-fast "answers" on how to invest/speculate to maintain or increase the purchasing power of your existing assets.

We can only be alert to relative value, flexible in our observations, expectations and plans, and keen to buy cheap and sell/trade dear. We can seek to "own"/control some of all four types of capital, and seek income streams from assets which are in our control--which generally means tangible assets such as orchards, arable land, tools/equipment and other means of production, income-producing housing/shelter and some "liquid" capital which can be shifted between assets to maintain our purchasing power.

In terms of risk management, we can remain aware that some assets have intrinsic value which is unlikely to fall to zero, while paper money and paper assets (stocks and bonds) all have long histories of falling to near-zero in periods of financial crisis. As they can also outperform all other assets for long periods of time, we should perhaps conclude not that they should be avoided but only that they are inherently speculative in nature.

I will have provided some lasting value in this section if readers in 2019, ten years hence, can still profit from the ideas presented here.

Applying the Principles to Communities/Enterprises

The key feature of communities and enterprises is that membership is voluntary. One can quit, move away or otherwise opt out of membership.

By "community" I mean any self-organizing group of people. That includes school districts, transportation districts, farmers markets, building co-ops, organized swap-meets, churches, local sports leagues, local small-business associations, bicycle clubs, and hundreds of other organizations which self-organize around a specific purpose or interest (*transparent non-privileged parallel structures*).

Enterprises are organized to enter and profit from a specific market. These can be sole proprietorships, corporations, community co-ops, non-profit educational centers, performing arts councils, city-owned utilities, and so on. The key feature of an enterprise (by my definition) is that it does not depend on grants from a government--grants which are essentially non-market redistributions of tax revenues directed from concentrations of power.

Thus the arts council must charge customers money for a service rendered in a market (be self-supporting) to be an enterprise.

The distinction is not arbitrary. Since the devolution and eventual insolvency of the Central State is inevitable, then any organization depending on State redistribution of tax revenues for its livelihood is doomed. A community may be called upon to support such organizations with donations of money and goods, but that requires an entirely different understanding. In essence, the group is serving a market which generates no financial activity (for instance, a homeless shelter). If the community values the service, then it will support it. If not, then the organization must seek another market or go out of business.

There is potential overlap of community and enterprise. Municipal-owned utilities are both community-based and enterprises.

Applying the Principles of Systemic Response to communities and enterprises is largely self-evident: public business should be conducted publicly (transparency), and so on. Participation and thus payments are essentially voluntary and thus there is a "market" even if there are no "customers" in a retail sense.

Feedback from users, customers and those paying the bills (such as property owners paying property taxes to support a school district) is the essential feedback loop.

Monopoly and cartel are the enemies of efficiency, opportunity, transparency and liberty. The solution is all cases is competition from new sources. If a utility is mismanaged, then customers need to opt out and be able to choose a new source. Since the State enforces the vast majority of monopolies, then the State's devolution will open up the possibility of ridding ourselves of monopolies and cartels.

If the municipal trash service is overpriced and provides poor service, then the public should have the opportunity to choose a private trash service. If the State has granted a private trash service a monopoly contract, then the monopoly must be broken.

It is important to understand the feedbacks in both local government and non-local enterprises.

A brief story will help illustrate the key role of local government in countering the concentrated power of Power Elite Capital.

A small community/town has abundant fresh-water resources. A large multinational corporation approaches the town council to purchase the rights to the water. The multi-billion dollar corporation sees the water as a windfall inviting exploitation, and so they present what appears to be a windfall to the small city leadership: new jobs, a new park, stable tax revenues, and so on.

But the small-city government is no match for a global corporation which possesses the great advantage of *information asymmetry*: the corporate leadership knows their own long-range plans while the city leaders know only what the corporate public-relations team decides to tell them.

Given the legal thickets of water rights and contractual laws, the global corporation can easily construct a *complexity fortress* that is essentially impenetrable to the inquiries of the small-town leadership.

Presented with what appears to be a windfall, the town leaders agree to the corporation's contract.

Very quickly, information asymmetry flashes its polished teeth: the company decides to renege on various employment and public improvement promises, citing "market conditions" or other excuses. The town residents soon discover that the ceding of their water rights is legally unbreakable but the promised dividends from the global corporation are all rescindable without recourse.

The corporation, of course, has a veritable army of attorneys and consultants to defend its rights, while the township has none.

While I have endlessly pointed out the inevitable implosion of State finances, this does not mean local or even national government is superfluous.

It simply means that the Savior State which has over-reached and sold itself to Power Elites will collapse.

At a fundamental level, the citizenry has feedback into the government/State. Even in despotic dictatorships, the people can arise and overwhelm the dictatorship's army or secret police. Where votes are held, depending on the level of corruption, then citizens may actually be able to eject their political leadership via the ballot box.

As poor and limited as this may be, it is still a powerful feedback loop.

With enterprises, then people have the feedback of opting in (buying the good or service) or opting out (not buying). Their decisions as "consumers" is their feedback.

But concentrated global capital can ignore local consumer feedback.

Thus the townspeople who were essentially swindled out of their town's water rights can boycott the global beverage corporation but their votes as "consumers" weigh less than a mosquito to the global multi-billion dollar corporation. In other words, despite the propaganda about "the power of consumers," consumers have essentially no feedback into global corporations unless they are organized on a vast scale.

And since self-interest discounts most small purchases (just as it discounts the innumerable small fees and taxes imposed by the State) then no large-scale body of consumers can be motivated to expend energy on behalf of a small town which ceded its water rights to a global corporation.

The global company holds all the power and all the advantages. The only entity with sufficient power to counter that of concentrated global capital is the State. But since global capital can easily purchase the cooperation of the State, then what recourse do citizens possess?

Local government is still marginally in the hands of the citizenry--if they demand it.

At least there is a feedback mechanism: votes, boycotts, protests and the like still influence elections at the local level. Demands for transparency in city council deliberations and decisions might actually be met because the local Power Elites still depend on local citizens for their power base.

Unlike the Central State and global capital, the local power Elites cannot afford to ignore the feedback from their citizenry. (Recall that the citizenry of the U.S. flooded their national elected officials with pleas to vote against the bank bailout TARP legislation 300-to-1 in 2008. The pleas were ignored, TARP was passed into law, and undoubtedly 99% of the incumbents who voted for TARP will be re-elected as usual in the next election. That illustrates the futility of citizen feedback on a national level.)

Local government can raise capital via special assessments and taxes. This means it can raise enough money to counter the worst excesses of information asymmetry when dealing with concentrated capital. It also means it can construct its own complexity fortresses to mask the insiders' looting and sweetheart contracts with Power Elites from its citizenry.

Whether that locally raised capital is spent wisely or squandered depends on an engaged citizenry.

In other words: no local community can field the resources needed to fend off global capital without an engaged citizenry who can disempower local Elites should they sell out to concentrated capital (rentier-financial Elites). The blandishments of global capital will win the day unless the local Power Elites are effectively guaranteed of losing their own power.

The same can be said of school board members, church officers, and indeed any power Elite in any organization. Protected fiefdoms generate monopolies, cartels and other forms of looting and exploitation. An active, engaged citizenry is the only feedback which can counter the forces of windfall exploitation and concentrations of power.

As all levels of government become insolvent, then local government must be forced to leverage what remains after the insolvency.

Here are two examples of leveraging existing assets, solutions and skills.

If devolution of fossil fuels proceeds as expected, then providing safe avenues for non-auto transport might prove beneficial to a community. In the current paradigm, then costly plans will be designed by costly consultants for new bikeways, cross-country skiing trails, elevated bridged and so on. All are good ideas but once money vanishes, then as per Principle 10, the alternative is to leverage what assets and solutions already exist.

Thus a city could "create" a bikeway (and a cross-country ski-way in winter) by simply closing off an existing central street with a few concrete bollards and a few signs. The cost of this leveraged solution is extremely low, well within the means of a small community. The bollards and the signs could even be produced locally.

Yes, the closing of a street is a politically fractious issue. The benefits must outweigh the disadvantages in the eyes of the community and an open, transparent debate may or may not resolve the issue. But the point is that solutions that leverage existing capital, assets, skills and solutions need not be costly.

In the current paradigm, a town or city seeking low-cost housing faces borrowing stupendous sums of money and a raft of complex restrictions to build new "affordable housing" which ironically ends up costing a fortune.

In the model of leveraging existing capital, assets, skills and solutions, then the city inventories abandoned properties, checks which are delinquent in taxes and notifies the owners (or the last known owner) to pay up/fix up their "public nuisance" property.

If the owners do not respond within 30 days (or if ownership has been so muddied by mortgage-backed securities, foreclosures and other financial complexities that ownership is no longer claimed unambiguously) then the city acquires the properties via eminent domain and auctions the properties off to anyone who contractually agrees to restore the property to habitability. (If they fail to do so, they forfeit the property.)

The total cost of increasing the available housing in this manner is a mere fraction of the costly "build and maintain housing" model. This approach leverages the existing assets and solutions at low cost to the community government's taxpayers.

Indeed, many cities with shrinking populations and far-flung housing are acquiring and then dismantling housing in just this fashion, as a means of shrinking their boundaries to manageable urban cores.

When money was essentially free--redistributed and/or printed by a Central State--then solutions could be costly because insiders had a windfall to exploit. Once the State largesse is gone, low-cost leveraged solutions will be seen as "idea windfalls" which can be exploited at very low cash costs.

Placing alternative solutions in the public domain via the Web before the implosion of the status quo is of paramount importance.

As detailed above, reforming the status quo is fundamentally impossible, just as its devolution and implosion are inevitable. But the process of reaching a new understanding is not instantaneous; new perspectives the solutions need to be presented and discussed long before the devolution spins into insolvency. Like seeds, they must be distributed into fertile ground before any harvest is possible.

The key understanding here is that the process of transformation requires a certain length of time--the process of anger, denial, bargaining, acceptance and hope--and the last step, hope, needs practical solutions grounded on an integrated understanding of the problems.

Since structural reform at the national level is essentially impossible for the reasons outlined earlier, then the fundamental alternative solution is to bypass or diffuse concentrations of capital and power via *transparent non-privileged parallel structures* and *parallel informal power structures*--what might be called *small-scale counter-government.*

One goal of every community should be to offer purpose to those willing to work.

As described in previous chapters, paying work will be in short supply, but unpaid work will be plentiful. People need purpose and meaningful work. The loss of purpose and meaning is as devastating as the loss of a livelihood, and the over-arching goal of every community, however small, should be to provide purpose and the opportunity to participate by leveraging existing organizations: citizens watch committees, farmers markets, building co-ops, churches and church-based groups, city parks foundations, volunteer-based animal shelters, etc., and encourage the establishment of new transparent, non-privileged organizations formed around specific interests and purposes.

Such civic groups already have an organization set up to manage volunteers; there is no need for a costly (and thus unsustainable) new bureaucracy.

The Internet is an essential "utility" for self-organizing networks and communities, transparency, reciprocity, trade and citizen engagement.

Cities and towns would be well-served by making the Internet available (via a tax or fee which explicitly and solely funds Internet access for the entire area) to all their citizens via "free" broadband wireless service and library computers. The goal should be to enfranchise every resident, even those without computers.

Compared to other services, Web access is modest in cost given its tremendous leverage. "Free" (paid for and controlled by the local community/city) is not just another example of low-cost leverage but also of the guiding goal of community: create equal opportunities for engagement and enterprise.

As a large entity, towns (or groups of nearby towns) and cities may be able to bypass the existing monopolies which control the Internet in many locales.

Internet access is one "utility" (along with the FEW resources) which cannot be ceded to distant global corporations. Local control of Internet access and FEW resources is essential.

(The benefit of local control of local resources, assets and community is that those without Internet access--hopefully few if the community provides it--can just walk into meetings and participate via the real world.)

The usual arguments in favor of the status quo--that is, State and global Power Elites' control of all key utilities, assets and sources of financial capital-- rest on variations of this financial case: "costs are lower for global corporations due to their large scale, and we will all benefit from lower costs."

True, until they're no longer low--monopolies and cartels sole reason for existence is to raise prices without losing customers--or available at any price.

As noted above, control has a value which cannot be completely reduced to financial metrics. Global capital could care less if the people in your community have Internet, food, water or energy; this is the fundamental reason why control of these resources and assets must be developed locally--even if it "costs more."

Once again the Chinese proverb encapsulates this truth exactly: *When you're thirsty, it's too late to dig a well.*

Local communities have the same Elites as everywhere else, Elites which will fight to protect their monopoly (on trash service, cable TV, education, etc.) or fiefdom, and the only way to avoid the exploitation of monopoly and fiefdom is competition in a transparent market.

This is true of all markets. Recall that profits are highest when the risks of competing have been removed via monopoly, cartels and State fiefdoms, and insider/Elite fraud, looting, gaming the system, embezzlement, price-fixing, etc., are cloaked, obscured and hidden. Thus the two key demands of engaged citizenry should be transparency and competition in transparent markets. These are the only mechanisms which counteract Capital and Elite's tendency to gather ever greater concentrations of power.

The goal of community action--county, city, town, neighborhood--should be to create equal opportunities for engagement and enterprise.

As the State devolves and implodes financially, then the unsustainable "rights" to healthcare, housing and other entitlements will vanish. The local government will be better served by focusing on leveraging opportunities for engagement and enterprise rather than attempting to redistribute dwindling tax revenues.

One example is providing limited Internet access (via wireless hotspots, computers in the library, etc.) to residents. Compared to healthcare, housing, etc. the cost of Internet access is modest, and could be paid for with a small local fee collected for that express purpose.

This goal can also be expressed by the old saying, *The Lord helps those who help themselves.* The goal is creating equal opportunities for engagement and enterprise, not equal entitlements. Thus a community could regain control of abandoned properties as outlined above and then lease the open parcels to residents for gardens. Unused plots would revert to the community, but those willing to work the land could build a small source of income from these community-owned, individually worked parcels.

The same mechanism could be used to lease out reclaimed commercial space for nominal fees. If the cost is low and the opportunity open to any resident (via a lottery system, an auction, first-come, first-served, or other reasonably fair and transparent system) then the community benefits as residents start enterprises.

Conventional wisdom states that wealth flows from a concentration of capital: that is, the factory in town generates the wealth that supports the residents. While large-scale enterprises should certainly be welcomed (manufacturing, biotech, research and development, etc.) as long as control of resources remains in the hands of the community, it is misleading to discount small enterprise as an engine of diffused income and wealth. To assert that a community without a large-scale enterprise is doomed to poverty is to blindly put one's faith in the "factory model" of wealth production.

As noted in previous chapters, the Scalability Trap quickly reduces the workforce of any scalable manufacturing to low levels. Thus the communities which pin all their hopes on a factory coming to town find that the factory closes a few years later and the global capital moves elsewhere to exploit some new windfall.

The wealth of the community flows from low-cost opportunities for enterprise and the widely distributed ownership of the means of production.

Rather than counting on the absurdly hopeless prospect of mythical entrepreneurs renting empty storefronts for thousands of dollars a month, cities and towns should acquire abandoned/tax delinquent commercial properties, open up a few walls and rent out small stalls within larger spaces for a nominal fee such as $10 a month, just enough to pay the utilities.

Once the opportunity cost is low enough, people will take a chance on starting enterprises. If all it costs is $120 a year to rent a space, then the "owner" won't have to make much to turn a profit.

If energy is the ultimate source of wealth, as I assert, then local communities might decide to raise capital incrementally and build a community-owned source of electricity. Using the "kumiai" model discussed above, a community could buy a drilling rig as community property and hire local crews to drill and install geo-exchange systems to provide heating/cooling. Those who put up capital could then have a system installed on their property for a deep discount.

Community and enterprise are not mutually exclusive; they are different aspects of the same system of local, distributed ownership of resources and the means of production and the encouragement of enterprise.

The more FEW resources and enterprises which are locally owned and controlled, the more wealth and income remains in the community.

Communities would be well served by organizing a non-monetary structure of purposeful work and enterprise.

The system of formal salaried/permanent paying job will, for all the reasons stated earlier, decline. As noted earlier, people need meaningful work not just to create value and surplus capital (be it money, tradable hours of labor, energy credits, or any other store of value) but to have the meaningful life which is part of full-spectrum prosperity.

Everyone has something to contribute; even a person who is no longer mobile can be "eyes on the street." What is fading is not work that needs to be done but the notion tat someone somewhere will pay large sums of money for that work to be performed.

Given the realities outlined in previous chapters, it seems future work is very likely to be flexible in nature: that is, a person might perform a mix of paid and unpaid/bartered labor in a variety of fields rather than one "career" which is supposed to be their "life's work." Some may choose this but few will be paid formally to do the same work for 30 or 40 years.

Thus the entire formal "factory" model of production and wealth creation and paid labor is shrinking (the Scalability Trap mentioned earlier) and a new much more flexible, less autocratic structure of work and enterprise must be constructed. Such concepts can also applied in large-scale enterprises; see Maverick: The Success Story Behind the World's Most Unusual Workplace.

Thus a critical role for the community is to facilitate the growth of a parallel system of work being freely chosen and "invested" in meaningful tasks.

Preparing for this alternative to the "factory/lifelong career" paradigm of work requires a revolution in our understanding of not just work but education and training--topics I cover in the next section.

Here is one last example of how communities can create paid work and value without relying on a factory to generate jobs: consider a high-tech manufactured product like a solar panel. Those who assert only factories create wealth do not have an integrated understanding of the entire supply chain.

In terms of labor, the factory is the least part of the entire system, especially as scalability drives the costs ever lower. If we examine the costs and labor of the entire system, the manufacture of the panels is a relatively modest part. From the factory, we add shipping through various hands, delivery to a wholesaler who adds a slice of overhead, and then delivery to a resaler which assembles other components (inverters, rooftop frames, etc.) into a system which is then installed onsite.

Of the total paid labor, very little is at the factory.

Thus local communities actually have considerable leeway in capturing much of the paid labor in the entire system. Every kilowatt of power generated or saved by sustainable locally controlled productive energy assets (geothermal, solar, wind, hydroelectric, etc.) means the significant income which used to stream out of the community now stays in the community.

Recall my previous description of the "plantation economy" in which a handful of monopolies/cartels extract the wealth of the "plantation" debt-serfs. Please count the number of global owners of mass media. There are perhaps six. Global oil/natural gas distributors: perhaps six. Global manufacturers of large commercial aircraft: two. Global banks which own/control the vast majority of bank branches and consumer debt in the U.s.: perhaps six. The number of major retailers in the U.S.: once again, a mere handful accrue the vast majority of sales. Phone service: a handful. The number of global pharmaceutical companies: perhaps six.

If you add up how much of your monthly income flows to global cartels of concentrated capital, you may find that the overwhelming majority of your income flows to cartels (mortgage, credit card, auto loan, Wal-Mart/Safeway/Target, mass media/cable TV, pharmaceuticals, gasoline, etc.) and taxes paid to the over-reaching State.

This is the very definition of debt-serfdom, which is sold as a "consumer paradise." Given the stupendous rivers of money which flow out of every community in the land to concentrations of capital and control, is there any wonder why communities are impoverished? Just imagine how different it would be if all those trillions of dollars went to locally owned banks, local farmers markets, local energy sources, and so on, and if citizens were no longer debt-serfs paying most of their income to service debt of one kind or another.

A tremendous sum of money which was previously diverted to global cartels would circulate in the local community.

This is the power of looking at systems not just in the limited perspective of "consumerism" (the lowest cost must always be the "best" choice) but in terms of control, production of income and wealth and what serves the best interests of the community in the longer run.

Once again I return to the idea that global supply chains are inherently fragile and total dependence on global capital and long global supply chains for FEW resources is simply imprudent when measured in risk management terms.

Everything is "cheap" until it isn't, and then it's no longer available at any price. As for the global cartels: it's not their concern, it's ours.

Once again, here are the principles for community action:

1. Engagement
2. Transparency (trust and truth)
3. Accountability
4. An Adult Understanding (Triage and Trade-offs)
5. Redundancy/Distributed Risk/Hedging
6. Radical Self-Reliance
7. Reciprocity
8. Diffusion of power and the means of wealth/income creation
9. Base Decisions on an Integrated Understanding
10. Leverage Existing Capital, Assets and Skills
11. ESSA: Eliminate, Simplify, Standardize and Automate
12. Generate Value and Surplus (working capital)
13. Secure/Produce/Innovate the FEW Resources (food, energy, water)
14. Think, Plan and Act with integrity
15. Pare complexity to simplicity

Tailoring Education to Future Practicalities

Our concept of education will have to revamped to meet future practicalities, not just conceptually but at the community level. Since the State, municipalities and school districts alike will be sliding into insolvency, then the hope that there will be "free" money to "throw at the problem" will likely meet with disappointment.

"The problem" will not be the Federal government's, or the "educators" but the community's and the parents' problem: how to educate our children for the emerging world on a limited budget.

In the "industrial fantasy" world, factories are staffed by thousands of well-paid union employees. In the real world, factories are "staffed" by robots and machines with a few dozen human "handlers" on hand to keep watch. Each largely automated factory can produce enough for an entire small nation. **All scalable production will be scaled up and automated (the scalability trap).**

The entire industrial paradigm of factories filled with thousands of people had its last incarnation in China. As wages rise and production costs drop, then even factories in China are automating to lower costs and minimize defects.

In the post-industrial fantasy world, "knowledge workers" scurry about cubicle-segmented office buildings performing FIRE economy paper-shuffling (finance, insurance and real estate) or back-office functions (integrated data bases and "business intelligence" data mining, tracking RFID tags and inventory, etc.) for a vast consumer economy based on endlessly rising credit and debt and a keenly insatiable "demand" for cheap goods and "prestige" services.

In the real world, demand was not organic, it was spurred by "free money" disguised as low-cost, abundant consumer credit. As debt levels rose, "consumers" were transformed into "debt-serfs." Now that interest rates are rising, incomes are dropping and prices are deflating, the relative burdens of servicing all that debt are rising, further crimping "consumer" spending.

As for the FIRE economy, it was all a bubble created by the fantasy of "financial innovation" which was simply an exponential increase in credit and debt instruments. There is no need for millions more new homes, condos and commercial buildings, and no need for millions of "service sector" jobs based on credit bubbles in construction, real estate, financing and insurance.

As for back-office work: the low-hanging fruit of office automation is gone and gains from here are increasingly marginal. As revenues and profits fall, enterprises are realizing huge expenditures in new software, computer/Internet equipment and "knowledge workers" are yielding fewer returns.

A few laggards such as healthcare may yet benefit from software automation, but since the healthcare "industry" is heading for insolvency then back-office "productivity" will take a back burner to reinventing overstaffed organizations to function in a "cash-only" healthcare model.

National, state and local government is also heading for massive reductions in staffing, so "expansion" of any sort is not possible. There will be less of everything as every enterprise has to re-size to fit its revenues.

In essence, the entire system of inefficiencies and spending built upon cheap, abundant credit and endlessly expanding money supply will shrink to match the nation's net income and surplus capital. That means less of everything: paid positions, software sold, etc.

In the high-tech R&D (research and development) fantasy world, millions of jobs will be created in high-tech fields like bioengineering, nanotechnology, life extension and new energy technologies.

In the real world, the "pipeline" of jobs into this very high-knowledge level of R&D is tiny--only a few thousand new people a year are needed for research, and only a few thousand positions can be supported. To perform research at this level of technology, PhDs are required, and few of us are capable of reaching this level of academic accomplishment.

In the real world, sudden shifts in technology can render thousands of highly paid people redundant. When drug research was largely chemical in nature, then thousands of chemists worked for global pharmaceutical companies. With the advent of monoclonal antibodies and other biotechnologies, the chemists were fired.

As for nanotechnology, we already have a nano-technology industry: it's called the semiconductor industry. Yes, a small group of highly trained researchers are needed, but refinements and new "inventions" within this technology only serve to lower costs and move further away from the factory paradigm of "job growth."

When the healthcare system seizes up in insolvency, then who will be paying $1,000 per dose or handful of pills? If the pharmaceutical companies' revenues are slashed by 80%, then how many researchers will they be hiring?

Much of the research is ultimately funded by the Federal government. As the central government totters toward insolvency (or its currency is debased to near-zero, which is ultimately the same end-point), then the "free" money machine grinds to a halt and the funding for costly research dries up.

The same can be said for the military-industrial complex: the era of $300 million fighter aircraft is over, and the era of $3 million pilotless drones is here.

If we subtract what the U.S. has borrowed publicly and privately from its net output, we are faced with the jarring reality that the U.S. as a nation has been living beyond its means for decades. That profligacy is about to end, one way or another. We can only spend what we create in surplus.

Education, like every other "industry," will have to do more with less. What principles should guide the reinvention?

1. The responsibility for educating our young does not fall on some distant amorphous bureaucracy, but on parents and the community. The notion that it's the "school and teachers' job to educate my kid" is false. Teachers are hired to teach a curriculum chosen by a community; the mis-education or education of the young people is still the responsibility of the parents and community at large.

Parents will have to collaborate closely with teachers and schools. The role of parents in home-schooling may be far closer to a practical model for education than the "professionalization" of education which follows the "factory model" (see below).

As borrowed money drains out of the system, the idea that schools should feed kids, manage their life crises, etc. will fade along with the funding. Parents and the remaining paid staff at the school will have to actively recruit community collaboration and participation.

Note that collaboration implies a free exchange within a non-autocratic structure. Telling people what to do is not collaboration. Autocratic bureaucracies depend on endless sums of "free money" spent with little accountability. Once money is not longer "free" and accountability increases on how it is spent (i.e. education spending is slashed along with all other government spending), then autocratic authority structures will be bypassed or wither as collaborators (and taxpayers) opt out of participating in variations of the "this is our fiefdom and you are our serfs" game.

2. Full-spectrum prosperity is the template. This can be summarized thusly: your health, knowledge, skills and purpose are your responsibility. We can give you the basic tools but the rest is up to you.

Since the citizenry will be responsible for their own health, and since knowledge of food, nutrition, diet, and health are so poor, then perhaps the biology curriculum should be organized around an integrated understanding of the food/nutrition/health chain. Plants use photosynthesis to turn the sun's energy, water and chemicals in the air and soil into fibers, sugars, etc., which we eat and metabolize via oxidation, and so on. Other curricula could be organized around an integrated understanding of the other FEW resources (water and energy) and the Internet.

The key task of students is to "learn how to learn." The current educational paradigm is a variation on the "factory" model of production: thousands of "units" (students) are assembled and "processed" (injected with "information") in a large central facility, tested and graded for quality, and then wrapped and "shipped" for use in other factories.

Rather than this essentially passive model of "information injection" and "quality testing" of the injection process's success, a collaborative, project-based model is much more aligned with both the actual work-worlds of high-skill R&D, enterprise, innovation and creation of value, all of which are essentially collaborative projects which a specific purpose that require constant learning.

The goal should not be to prepare students to fill static jobs which no longer exist but to create their own hybrid job--probably not a steady-state "career" of performing the same tasks for 30 years but a hybrid assembly of projects, collaborations, grunt work, learning, volunteering, trading, "fun" work, etc.

3. Teach reciprocity and creation of value/surplus capital. Collaboration requires not just the social skills of working with others but an understanding of reciprocity and exchange. This is ultimately on the opposite end of the spectrum from authority structures. For how this works on the large-scale enterprise level, please read <u>Maverick: The Success Story Behind the World's Most Unusual Workplace</u>.

Since schools are enterprises, too, then the collaboration, shared responsibility and focus on innovation and cost control described in this book will be worth studying.

4. Windfall exploitation can be a positive attribute. Students who learn that opportunities for exploiting a "windfall"--an unfilled need or undervalued resource--abound will be much better prepared for full-spectrum prosperity than those indoctrinated with a static "just give me a

job" perspective.

Windfall exploitation, after all, is built into our genetic heritage as a trait with large selective advantages. It behooves us to teach the difference between looting (exploitation at the expense of others) and the filling of unmet needs/opportunities for gain/surplus.

We can either invest capital or labor or some of both, but some investment must be made to generate value and earn a surplus. The necessity of enterprise can be taught.

5. Provide students with opportunities for *experiential capital*. By that I mean the inner capital which is built from experience as opposed to formal learning. In essence this means creating a rich network of apprenticeship and internship options which span all productive fields from lab research to stone masonry to preparing cuisine to childcare.

Much of what we now consider formal education can be moved to the Web and Web-based collaborations and projects.

Universities could open up more informal (unpaid) internships for high school and intermediate school students who have shown an aptitude for scholarship or research. Small businesses and even sole proprietors could offer more short apprenticeships. Without work experience in a range of fields, how can students assess their own aptitudes and interests?

If work is to become more hybrid in nature, then a variety of collaborative learning experiences in a variety of fields may be the best training possible for those who do not have the aptitude or interest to pursue highly technical graduate-level careers.

To help illustrate more practical, future-oriented models of education, I offer the following summary from educator/teacher Zeus Yiamouyiannis, Ph.D.:

The first thing to understand is that the Greek and Latin roots of education mean literally "to lead out." This notion of education has a long and noble history quite compatible with what we would legitimately call "learning": preparing someone to engage the world and contribute their unique genius and talent to a growing body of human knowledge.

This notion was traumatically abused, subverted, and interrupted by a late 19th century ideological push that the institution of education could use formal schools to "cram in" rather than lead out.

"Learning" became identified with "training," especially for the profit and use of a small minority of extremely wealthy and influential industrialists and "administrative elites."

Efficiency experts and other clerks to power in the late 19th century and early 20th century advocated for a formalized system of training to advance industrial development and expansion. Education became identified almost solely (and soullessly) with job and professional preparation. Life-long learning and learning for character, learning for its own sake, and learning as an act of creativity were not only ignored but militated against as dangerous and counter to a factory-like "quality" control. We are now being forced by global circumstance and personal and social opportunity to return to the original meaning of education, but one brought forward in a very new context.

The second thing to understand is that learning (and thinking) have always been viewed (until the Industrial Era) as social, public intellectual acts and not simply as individual, cognitive acts or as institutional cogs in an efficiently running social engineering scheme. We are entering into a return to learning as a social act and not simply a cognitive act.

The late 18th century marked the rise of not only industrialism but specialized professions in the social sciences like psychology, sociology, and education, often patterned after the quantitatively-tilted natural sciences, economics, and mathematics. These professions took the metaphors of industrialism-- that everything was a complex machine that could be broken down by Reason into principles, natural laws, and tiny parts, that could be examined, and reassembled in wondrous and Utopian ways.

[This had a double-edged effect. Eugenics sprang out of this mentality as did some truly amazing inventions-- like radios and airplanes.] Intelligence, as a result, became understood as an output of a complex, but knowable, cognitive machinery located in the brain of an individual. Learning and education because a way of modulating the doors of perception "swinging inward" to the individual mind.

If you look at the development of artificial intelligence and research, even to this day, they almost all rely on this largely outdated individual, cognitive model.

The emerging interconnected, global and technological world has produced a new and fast accelerating form of practical and theoretical intelligence, what I call the "social mind." The social mind is a distributed intelligence accessed, and added to by individuals, but possessed by no "one." In this understanding of intelligence and the learning that must spring from it, the doors of the individual mind "swing outward" in communication with others almost as neurons within neural networks. Our social neural networks are communities of neighbors, shared interest, profession, and so forth. These linked together form the global "brain" much like computers can be arrayed to hyper-charge computing power.

The world wide web, search engines, and filtering, referencing, and organizing devices like Wikipedia are a perfect demonstration of this kind of distributed accessible, powerful, intelligence and information system. It is highly democratic by NATURE not by conviction. In other words, it is in the very design and being of this emerging form of intelligence to be necessarily democratic to operate at all. It is not an ideological commitment (though it certainly could be helped by the democratic liberalization of rigid social systems).

There is much research and work that needs to be done to understand this emerging new way of understanding and developing intelligence, but in the interim it might be helpful to observe some of its attributes and contrast these with the still useful but fading assumptions about intelligence and learning we have grown so accustomed to:

New Learning:
1) Founded on a kind of "cool" anti-establishment value system (pro-autonomy, choice, freedom)
2) Democratic (structure of the Internet, open access, advocacy)
3) Responsive to community (charter schools)
4) Creative, fluid in nature
5) Fast-moving, highly adaptive by necessity
6) Integrated
7) Horizontal in structure and proliferation
8) Small working groups
9) Project-oriented
10) Productive capacities emphasized

11) Design-mind, engineering approach to specific and general problems

12) Holistic, joining school and social system

Old Learning:

1) Pro-establishment, static [monopoly that eschews choice, openly attacks "non-expert" non-sanctioned learning]

2) Bureaucratic, industrial in structure (teacher unions vs. management "Who would we have to collectively bargain with?")

3) Reductive and rigid in nature (lecture, certification, accreditation; quality = accurate replication of professional norms and forms)

4) Unresponsive to community; they are recipients not participants

5) Slow-moving to the point of intransigence (highly resistant to change; same basic structure as late nineteenth century)

6) Compartmentalized

7) Vertical in authority structure and proliferation

8) Large classes

9) Working on abstracted problems

10) Receptive capacities emphasized

11) Unreflective, uncritical approach to internal problems, learning and teaching

12) Isolated understanding of "my" classroom, student learning disabilities, etc.

Education systems which attempt to "prepare" students for static jobs which no longer exist will clearly fail to create full-spectrum prosperity. The educational choices will be up to communities, but what works will be assessed by feedback from reality.

Key concepts in this chapter:

Assessment, (cost-benefit) analysis, deliberation and decision process (AADD)

Transparent non-privileged parallel structures

Small-scale counter-government

Parallel informal power structures

Chapter Twenty-Six: Structuring the New American State

The idea that the mighty Ming Empire was vulnerable to collapse did not exist in Imperial Beijing in 1634, yet ten years later the Dynasty fell in a sudden paroxysm of disorder, conflict and shifting loyalties.

As noted in Chapter Four, even as the financial and moral infrastructure of the Empire crumbled around them, complacent Roman commentators were still trumpeting a line of magical thinking that somehow Rome was too great to fail. A few years later, their magical thinking failed and the Western Empire collapsed in a heap.

We stand now at a similar point. The greatness and reach of the American Empire seems undiminished and incapable of collapse. Yet beneath the superficial solidity projected by the mass media and the State, the financial and moral infrastructure of the U.S. is crumbling rapidly.

The adolescent fantasy of the Savior State--that paying $100 in taxes would yield $1,000 in benefits--is being propped up by the mad, frantic borrowing of trillions of dollars each year: a "solution" doomed to insolvency.

In essence, the feedbacks which resisted State and Plutocracy over-reach have been overwhelmed or withered, enabling a vast extension of the State/Plutocracy partnership's share of the national income and wealth.

The mass media--a corporate cartel within the State/financial-rentier Elites--has masked this fundamental dynamic with an unprecedented campaign of mutually reinforcing propaganda and marketing.

Those trapped in the various ideological boxes cannot escape their self-made prisons. "Progressives" are abjectly terrified by the prospect that a central Savior State might implode, as they are unable to see that the Savior State's vast programs only serve to enrich the Elites while indenturing the productive and buying the complicity of the unproductive.

In another iron box, "conservatives" are incapable of understanding that the entire project of financial-rentier Elites is to subvert free markets with the State's connivance, and to establish carefully obscured "shadow" branches of governance and banking hidden behind a willful confusion of free-market capitalism and the Elites' crony-capitalist monopolies and State-protected cartels.

Shrill cries to "defend free market capitalism" by weakening the

State's already fatally weakened regulatory structures are tailor-made to support the Elite's unopposed concentration of capital and power. Thus the "conservatives" are the most blindly vociferous supporters of the Elites' strip-mining of the American citizenry and economy.

In a third locked box are Libertarians who place a naive faith that a passive, weak State is the "solution" to the Elite/State partnership's dominance. But they fail to understand that concentrations of global capital and power are delighted to find passive weak States, as they offer no resistance to exploitation of a multitude of windfalls. Weak, passive States are ontologically kleptocracies, as the citizenry have no feedback into either the State or the "shadow" government and financial systems of the Power Elites.

As I noted before, all the ideologies are catastrophically wrong in their understanding of the dynamic between State, markets and Power Elites. "Progressives" are convinced that free markets are rapacious and a vast central State must dominate and control the market lest it devour the citizenry.

The real dynamic is precisely the opposite: the Elites' primary drive is to subvert competition and establish the lowest risk, highest return situation which is monopoly or cartel protected by the State. Rather than protect the citizenry by throttling transparent markets, the State hands dominance to the Power Elites who have eliminated the threat of competition by partnering with the State.

For their part, "conservatives" are blind to capitalism's intrinsic drive to eliminate competition and exploit all windfalls without regard to the social and environmental consequences. Thus weakening paltry State oversight--the exact goal of the Power Elites' monopolies and cartels-- does not "strengthen" competition but speeds its destruction.

All of this can be illustrated with the insanity of the food-disease-sickcare complex which I have described previously.

As it stands now, a handful of agribusiness, fast-food and packaged food cartels manufacture blatantly unhealthy simulacra of real foods and relentlessly market them as "good tasting" and "trendy" via the mass media cartel.

A toothless set of State agencies, totally dominated by Power Elites via a "shadow" system of governance-- elected officials who demand loopholes and favors, "fox hired to guard the chicken coop" revolving-door high-caste technocrats, and cartel lobbyists writing regulations and laws--enables simulacrum "consumer protection" which is predictably ineffective.

Having addicted a media-enthralled, distracted citizenry to sugar, salt and fat-laced fake-foods (please read The End of Overeating: Taking Control of the Insatiable American Appetite by the former head of the FDA for a detailed, scientific elaboration of this dynamic), then the resulting chronic diseases and ill-health are managed by another set of Power Elites under the guise of "healthcare."

Once again, the State partners with the Power Elites to funnel a rapidly increasing share of the national income and wealth to these Elites via State-managed "free money" programs like Medicare and Medicaid which are falsely packaged as "healthcare for the citizenry" even as the actual causes of the citizenry's worsening health is essentially ignored.

Regulations which once protected citizens from direct advertising of medications are dismantled as the pharmaceutical industry (and the mass media which profits so immensely from the adverts) institutionalizes the idea that there are "magic pills" for every condition-- and when no condition exists, then the industry creates new ones out of whole cloth.

An unholy alliance of concentrations of power and influence--the AMA, insurance cartels, trial lawyers, pharmaceuticals, manufacturers of MRI and other medical machinery, etc.--have seized on this windfall of "free, limitless" State funding in the same manner as the military-industrial complex has exploited essentially limitless funding of "national defense."

The net result is that "healthcare "(a.k.a. sickcare) spending has leaped to some 16% of the entire U.S. economy, even as the citizenry's health by most measures declines and the inequalities of healthcare in the nation rise.

It's a staggeringly profitable confluence of windfalls, State-enabled cartels, State redistribution of income to Elites and "shadow" governance by concentrated centers of power and influence.

First, sicken the citizenry with facsimile foods expressly designed for "mouth-feel" and the triggering of narcotic-like brain centers that are sold at immense profits via a mass media/marketing cartel.

Next, mount a propaganda campaign to mask the causal connection from corporate agribusiness/fast-food/manufactured food to ill health behind a screen of "the U.S. has the finest healthcare system in the world."

Third, enable direct marketing of largely ineffective medications and treatments directly to the public, even as the true cost of the treatments are obscured behind a "free money, free treatment" facade which collects trillions of dollars from citizens and enterprises (via "insurance" or taxes for Medicare/Medicaid) and distributes it to various cartels--the very opposite of the "competitive market" touted in media/State propaganda.

Fourth, misdirect public attention from the known causes of their ill-health--their consumption of unhealthy food, their lack of activity and their ignorance of nutrition, chronic disease and the system they are ensnared in--to magical-thinking "magic pills" and the ever-increasing consumption of drugs and treatments for lifestyle diseases.

Fifth, create a complexity fortress of State bureaucracy and industrial obfuscation (side effects small print, ginned-up Phase III trials, absence of testing interactivity with other common drugs, and so on) which collects vast sums of money and distributes it without regard for efficacy or efficiency into the various "healthcare" cartels.

Sixth, manage the multitude of diseases created by poor diet and inactive lifestyle with increasingly complex treatments of multiple medications and costly surgical interventions, both of which are found to be ineffective or dangerous years later--but only after even more costly "treatments" are devised.

Seventh, fund the ballooning cost of this highly profitable system by borrowing trillions of dollars from overseas creditors, effectively shoving the costs onto future generations.

Eighth, never admit the system creates the illnesses it then manages so profitably, or that it is not a competitive open market system at all but a State/Elite partnership operated for the benefit of the State fiefdoms and the Power Elites which control them.

This same "shadow governance," propaganda and State/Power Elite partnership can be found in "national defense" (defense of the Empire, and who benefits from that?), banking/finance, and every other market which is controlled by a State/Elite partnership to the benefit of State fiefdoms and Power Elites.

No enterprise--be it a sole proprietorship, a global corporation or a national government--can spend more than it creates in surplus.

In vernacular terms, we call this "going in the hole every month." The U.S. economy has not generated a surplus in decades; the difference between what we have earned as surplus capital and what we have spent has been borrowed or paid for with fiat dollars created out of thin air.

This con is unsustainable over the long term. Just because we as a nation have continued the con for decades does not mean the con will not catch up to us at some point. Rather, the con is unraveling right now as the world grows nervous about the instabilities being created by one nation passing off trillions of dollars in worthless paper and in funding its profligate spending by borrowing ever larger sums. Every level of the U.S. has embarked on an unprecedented explosion of borrowing and debt: the central State, local government, corporations, banks and consumers.

This edifice of exponentially rising credit is fundamentally a fraud. Regardless of whether you applaud or decry the Federal government's skyrocketing obligations and promises of future value, it is guaranteed to collapse in insolvency.

History suggests there are two paths to this end-point, and obsessing over which path we will ultimately take is less important than the end-state. Either a profligate nation's currency falls to near-zero value (also called hyperinflation) or the State runs out of the ability to borrow enough money to fulfill its expanding obligations. It then defaults on its debts and other obligations.

We in the U.S. have lived like every day is Christmas for years; whatever excesses are desired, we have purchased them by creating money/credit out of thin air. More MRI machines in Western Pennsylvania than in the entire nation of Canada? Yes, it's our "right" to have as many MRI tests as we desire.

$300 million for each fighter aircraft? Yes, it's our "right" to "the best." Granite counters, snowmobiles, luxury cruises--all of these have also been our "right." Cheap, abundant oil is also our "right," even if it costs thousands of American lives and trillions of dollars in (borrowed) money to enforce that "right" on distant shores.

The ability to create and spend "free money" has distorted reality for so long that we as nation now consider this magical ability to save little and create no surplus and yet spend as freely as we desire as our "right."

We have repealed reality with a gigantic con--the exponential rise of credit and debt--but reality cannot be completely replaced by magical thinking forever. Thus we can foresee the financial collapse of the Federal government within the next decade (by 2021). The mighty engines of credit creation, market manipulation and propaganda are straining at maximum RPM, and they may yet create one more asset bubble which will extend the con for one more cycle.

Or they may fail to inflate yet another asset bubble, in which case the devolution will begin sooner rather than later.

It is important to note once again the ad hoc nature of the Power Elites' and the State's response to the unprecedented challenge of maintaining exponential credit expansion.

Perhaps some of the players actually believe that infantile incantations and magical thinking will enable infinite credit bubbles into the future, but it is more likely that they are reacting in ad hoc fashion, hoping that their propaganda, credit expansion and massive State giveaways of "free money" via deficit spending will stave off disaster long enough for them to contrive a sustainable Plan B.

Alas, that hope is pure fantasy. Exponential credit and deficit expansion is not sustainable.

Many observers look ahead and see a future in which the U.S. Federal government has dissolved, and the 50 states of the Union break into small city-states or natural units of governance. Some see this as inevitable, others as preferable.

I have tried to explain that there is no "either-or" choice to the State, Elites and markets. The citizenry have no feedback into global capital except to opt out wherever possible from feeding the Beasts (cartels and oligopolies). But the citizenry do have feedback into the State--even if it has withered, it can be strengthened, or a new citizen feedback loop can be added to the governance system.

Global capital has no concern for the well-being of the citizenry of any landscape, town, city, state or nation; their concern is simple: dominate markets and States sufficiently to eliminate or bypass competition, and exploit all available windfalls to the fullest. Thus slavery and its modern equivalent, serfdom in the developing world and debt-serfdom in the developed world, are the ideal (lowest-risk, highest profit) ecologies for concentrated global capital.

But global capital has its own crises: as I described in Chapter Sixteen, Neoliberal global capitalism is suffering from a terminal crisis of over-capacity and over-accumulation. Having exploited the low-labor costs windfall created by the opening of Communist China, global capital had to create new "debt plantations" in its home markets via asset bubbles which could be leveraged into new consumer spending.

This "financialization" of the global economy has triggered unintended consequences; the end-point of all these machinations and manipulations is global financial implosion.

Now that consumers have maximized their debt and the last global asset bubble in housing has burst, global capital has no new windfalls to exploit except rising tax revenues diverted by the State and funneled to Power Elites via government "programs." But as credit expansion fails to create new spending, then tax revenues are collapsing; global capital and State Elites are both reduced to creating money/credit out of thin air and funneling these new trillions into the State/financial-rentier Elites' coffers.

But this fraud, this giant con game, cannot long endure. Thus the citizenry will face a choice: slip into fatalistic acceptance of ruin, or form a new government from the ashes of systemic financial ruin.

The State is the only concentration of power strong enough to counter over-reach by global capital Power Elites.

Yes, the State can be co-opted and captured by Power Elites; that is the current status of the U.S., where the citizenry are passive, fractured, besotted by consumerism and distracted by ideological propaganda and theater. But an *engaged, active, well-informed citizenry* can wrest control of their State, or reconstruct it once it has imploded into financial insolvency.

The role of the State is simple: to limit the over-reach of Power Elites and deny them the non-competitive monopolies and State-enabled cartels they ceaselessly seek to impose.

The role of the citizenry is to be engaged in governance to limit the over-reach of the State and to fend off the very partnership of the State and Power Elites which we have described in this analysis.

If the citizenry slip into passive complacency, the Power Elites (which exist in all eras and all civilizations) will gladly exploit the open windfall/power vacuum and grasp the reins of the State.

I have already described how the "balance of powers" in the U.S. Constitution has failed to limit the emergence of a "shadow" system of governance and banking/finance which flourishes within the Federal

State/Elite partnership. Once again: no regulatory system, even one as thoughtful as the U.S. Constitution, can operate without citizen feedback and engagement. There is no system on Earth which can be set up to counter Elite influence and then left to run on automatic.

We in the U.S. have become complacent and disengaged, and as a result our government has been co-opted and captured by the financial-rentier Power Elites, whose mass media have obscured this reality behind a "we live in a consumerist paradise" politics of experience.

As devolution takes hold, technocratic "solutions" will be presented by all the engines of Elite control: the think-tanks (conceptual lobbyists), the "liberal media" which represents the high-caste, well-educated technocrats who serve the Power Elites, and various theocratic schemers hoping to exploit the vacuum left as the intellectual framework which supported the State/Elites partnership for the past 60 years is discredited.

The Power Elites' media and technocrat/high-caste intellectual flag-bearers will ceaselessly tout essentially worthless "reforms" (as if tweaking the parameters of an imploding system will fix its structural flaws) to extend the dominance of the Elite/State partnership. Rather than succumb to these wily blandishments, the citizenry must make the key economic decisions in their own best interests; the market and the State regulatory agencies are the two primary mechanisms of implementing democratic decision-making.

Thus the citizenry must focus on insuring the transparency and power of these two mechanisms: transparent, competitive markets and regulations which limit monopoly, cartels, price-fixing, crony-capitalism, embezzlement, fraud and the pernicious panoply of "shadow" institutions, inventory, banking and governance.

We might summarize the three sources of feedback in U.S. governance thusly:

1. Rentier-Financial Power Elite (Plutocracy): These concentrations of power are roughly comparable to feudal fiefdoms that wield great authority over the State and enforce the loyalty of their technocrat minions.

2. Aristocracy: high-caste technocrats, policy mandarins, think-tank/State apparatchiks (the revolving door) and corporate/State cartel contractors/managers.

3. Citizenry, divided into two populations: those with the time, interest

and will to become engaged in constructing a new intellectual framework of governance and those who do not. Both could be transformed by The Remnant, as the ideas of a New State percolate and eventually influence the unengaged and powerless.

We might also consider these historical conditions of revolution:

1. A profound crisis in the status quo leadership (the Elites no longer control events)

2. Rising hardships suffered by the productive class--often a collapse of purchasing power or the equivalent, an unbearable spike in the cost of living

3. A rise in social unrest and political engagement by previously disenfranchised and unengaged citizenry.

As noted before: *No one can save us from ourselves except ourselves.* We have enabled the capture of the government by Power Elites and passively allowed the Elites and the State to over-reach to the point of terminal instability.

When the central State defaults or otherwise implodes financially, we can devolve into hundreds of fiefdoms or establish a new American State.

It can be argued that small local governments are the ideal form of governance, but I would caution that global capital and other predatory forces would look upon the dissolution of a central State as a wonderful windfall to exploit. No small local government would be able to mount a defense of territory or financial integrity against highly concentrated capital and power.

Thus we can anticipate that while global capital will mourn the loss of its Federal fiefdoms, which enabled "one-stop shopping" for crony capitalism and profiteering banking, the emergence of small centers of governance will provide little barrier to the re-establishment of their dominance.

The advantages of a small, limited but active New American State accountable to its citizenry outweigh the risks of central governance. The Founding Fathers decided as much and we would be foolish to dismiss the wisdom of their choice.

Our goal, then, is to establish a new model of governance to replace the failed Savior State/Plutocracy partnership when it collapses into insolvency.

The New State requires no changes in the Constitution but rather a *radical re-set* to the Constitution. Though the Constitution does not limit concentrations of power or Elite/financial domination, it also does not limit the citizen's control of Elites, should they choose to do so.

The fundamental premise of the U.S. Constitution is simple:

It is not the government which gives limited rights to the citizenry, but the citizenry which gives limited rights to the government to protect the public trust and the citizenry's rights to life, liberty, and the pursuit of happiness.

The principles guiding the establishment of the New American State are the same which guide households and communities/local government; as noted before, the principles are scale-invariant and can be applied to organizations of any size, in any era.

We might summarize the goals thusly:

1. Transparent, limited in scope and mandate; eschew global Empire.

2. Protective of its citizenry (and the public trust) rather than its Elites.

3. Cost-benefit based, i.e. only deploys its resources in extremely high-leverage (leveraging existing assets, solutions and skills) situations.

4. Regulatory goals: limit concentrations of financial and political power, enforce transparent markets, limit "shadow" restrictions on equal opportunity rather than attempting to enforce equality, and expose "shadow" political and financial structures that benefit the privileged few to the detriment of the public trust and citizenry.

5. Issue a tangible-asset based currency, forbid leveraged fractional lending and State expansion of credit (i.e. institute and maintain sound money).

6. Foster/defend/secure the FEW resources (food, energy, water) for its citizenry.

7. Limit transfer of wealth to Elites via the State and perverse incentives to misallocation of capital and the transfer of private risk to the taxpayers.

8. Encourage and enable diffused-ownership enterprise. Eliminate taxes on earned income, i.e. enterprise; the primary source of tax revenue is a simple low-percentage tax on all financial transactions (loans, mortgages, sales/trading of stocks, bonds, derivatives, sales of

real property, goods and services, etc.).

Items 2, 4, 6 and 7 are the regulatory heart of the State mandated to protect the public trust. Oftwominds.com correspondent Steven Rodriguez describes the ontological challenges of limiting concentrated-wealth Elites' constant attempts to bypass or dilute State protection of the public trust for their private profit:

Think of regulation as a firehose trying to put out a fire. One interest puts its hand over the hose in order to preserve a profitable "fire"--some exclusive use of the public trust. The force emerges anew in two more locations. Two more special interests step forward to divert the stream away from their "HOT" projects and enforcement divides again into four streams. Reiterate ad infinitum and you are fighting the fire with a sprinkler instead of a fire hose.

Imagine being tasked to do some really great things but finding that you are blocked at every turn from doing what is needed to accomplish your charge. The size of state bureaucracy is directly proportional to special interest opposition to its mandates. The environmental consulting business dwarfs state resource agencies. It is an enormous misallocation of resources. Its only function is to permit resource destruction one parcel, one project at a time.

There is a better way. It is called collaborative planning. Collaborative planning cannot happen without an enormous public participation component. But the issue is far more complex than that. Everything about global industrial corporate capitalism is designed to conquer public spirit, and to conceal and subvert the right of the public to participate in all public trust resource planning and development decision making.

The public trust means any resource the access to which is essential for developing healthy, thoughtful, fully enfranchised citizens with all the rights thereto. Cooperation with full participation of the community is the only development strategy that provides high quality habitat for humanity.

Weak, corrupt central states are soon taken over by Elites and devolve into kleptocracies. Loose confederations of small city-states devolve into fiefdoms in perpetual conflict weakened by shifting alliances and betrayals; they lose the economies of scale and the potential for widespread good governance.

The goal should be a re-set to a small central State with strong institutions capable of leveraging its powers to accomplish limited goals with limited funds.

The goals should be narrowly mandated, as per the Constitution: defense of the borders and national interests (which is not the same as global Empire), regulation of commerce and banking, issuing a sound-money currency, and the establishment of common-sense, transparent, accountable good governance.

The basic rules are simple: demand transparency, accountability and enable citizen oversight and engagement. At the risk of boring you, here are the principles of good governance:

1. An engaged citizenry
2. Transparency (trust and truth)
3. Accountability
4. Govern with an Adult Understanding (Triage and Trade-offs)
5. Enable redundancy/Distributed Risk/Hedging
6. Enable radical Self-Reliance
7. Enable reciprocity
8. Diffuse power and the means of wealth/income creation
9. Base Decisions on an Integrated Understanding
10. Leverage Existing Capital, Assets and Skills
11. ESSA: Eliminate, Simplify, Standardize and Automate
12. Generate Value and Surplus Capital
13. Secure/Produce/Innovate the FEW Resources (food, energy, water)
14. Think, Plan and Act with integrity
15. Pare complexity to simplicity

We as a nation need to construct a new understanding of government and governance, one which has not been poisoned by the current politics of experience.

Thus the tax code should be one page long: "A 2% fee will be levied and paid to the U.S. Treasury on all financial exchanges, sales and trades of real estate, financial instruments, real goods and services, without exception. No other taxes will be levied, though government agencies may levy modest fees for services provided."

This sort of radical simplicity is impossible in the current mindset and system, yet it not inherently impossible or even difficult. In proposing it and discussing it, we sow the intellectual seeds for an eventual integrated understanding of the perverse incentives of the current system and its corruption by Elites (special interests) and fiefdoms (in the case of taxes: corporations, the super-wealthy, accountants, tax attorneys, etc.)

Here are a few examples of common-sense good governance.

1. Restrict political donations to the residents and enterprises within a district; post every donation (the donor, their address, the board of directors of every group or enterprise and the size of the donation) prominently on the Web.

2. Limit districts to contiguous simple geometric boundaries which cannot be gerrymandered to protect the powers of incumbents or incumbent political parties.

3. Rescind all Federal drug laws. The Savior State is gone; it is no longer the mandate of the State to attempt to protect its citizens from themselves. The spectacularly ineffective "war on drugs" is no longer affordable. Drug laws, if any, are left to local jurisdictions.

The same can be said of all existing Federal laws pertaining to anything beyond the limited mandates of the Constitution: defense of the nation, regulate commerce, enforce the Bill of Rights, etc.

4. The government must live within the means provided by its limited tax on all financial transactions. It is no longer the State mandate to manipulate financial markets or the currency; the State's sole mandate is to insure transparent and open markets and eradicate "shadow" financial structures.

It is beyond the scope of this book to address every possible avenue of common-sense good governance; I have laid out the principles which I believe guide and underpin good governance, and have stated the first and foremost requirement: an engaged citizenry. Without that, then governance will soon slip back under the influence of various Power Elites.

Though I believe there is common ground for the citizenry not on the payroll of various self-interested Elites, there is also room for disagreement. It is not the agreement which is important at this point, but the dissemination of radically common-sense proposals which follow from the 15 principles outlined above, and a civil discussion/discourse on those good governance proposals which arise from them.

Just as further food for thought, I would like to share a few more examples of what I consider common-sense good governance of finance, provided by correspondent Zeus Yiamouyiannis.

Proposition one: It is high time we rigorously re-visit the notion of public charters for corporations. If corporations are chartered by the public, then they need to be both answerable to and regulated by that public. There should be no unregulated, quasi-regulated, or self-regulated publicly chartered companies. I don't have a problem with unchartered privately chartered companies. If a hedge fund or private equity firm wants to take private funds (and that means only personal private funds, no public pension fund money, for instance), then they should be allowed to do so with no guarantee from the public or for their investors. They gain, they gain; they lose, they lose. If fraud happens, the investors can sue and/or press criminal charges. Any public business done by an unchartered company must be audited to ensure real assets back that business and guarantee primary standing for repayment in any downturn.

Proposition two: We should revisit the public/private dynamic regarding distribution of risk. Current laws and practices seem to favor a system that privatizes benefits and publicizes liability. Presently any person can set up an unregulated, dummy company (i.e. a mortgage or brokerage firm), use it to essentially fence financial goods (i.e. bad loans or CDS's) and then sell them off. This "any person" can also skim off huge fees and salaries, and just walking away when the company goes bankrupt without any consequence—no injury to personal credit score, no requirement to give back ill-gotten wealth, etc. If there were a tax on these free-wheeling deals, and if one's private credit score and net worth could be at least somewhat affected by one's financial decisions as leader or manager in decisions that have public consequence and from which there was private benefit, then one could conceive that some of these excesses might be mitigated.

Proposition three: Corporations should not be considered persons and should not have the attendant rights of citizens. This was based on court decision at a time in the country's history when corporate robber barons basically ran the government. It was a nonsensical decision, allowing for a raft of abuses, and should be vacated.

Proposition four: Bankruptcy laws should be restructured so that citizens who legitimately fail on the private level can get back on their feet. Two-thirds of personal bankruptcies result from divorce, job loss, or failure of health. Well-considered attempts to start a business, for instance, aided by scrupulously examined lending, and personal investment should be encouraged and supported toward success, through training tax incentives, etc. If the business goes under, the hit one takes should not swallow one's ability to simply live and provide for family.

Proposition five: The "good life" should not be about retiring early with wealth gained from speculative investing, but rather investing time, talent, treasure, and trust in communities of care and exchange with "returns" in higher quality living and respected, honored retirement as an elder within the community. "Get rich quick" mentalities should be called out as simply an effort to elope with other people's money and leave them holding the bag.

Proposition six: Quality should be emphasized and rewarded over quantity/volume. Currently the "maximum profit" meme that drives big business incentives to cut corners and think short term. It contributes to the practice of creating phantom assets, so one can appear to be increasing market share. It contributes to corporate heads pulling gimmicks like buying back their own stock to inflate prices. It reinforces the generation of transactions, just for the sake of transaction so one can deduct fees. Quantity without any regard to quality or long-term impact is another way to say "mindless business, heedless of consequence."

Proposition seven: Use microfinance as a model for good business. After the tsunami hit Southeast Asia in 2004, it was microfinance institutions that continued to get steady repayments and which remained viable and even profitable.

Microfinance, small loans to the working poor largely in developing countries, demonstrates not only the opening of the world market to a new class of entrepreneurs and a way to lift many millions of people out of poverty, it also serves as a template for good financial practice to so-called developed countries: diversification (many loans are given to many different people), low default (2% or less, usually), high stakeholdership (lendees need the credit to run their lives and business; it is not expendable), cooperation (group lending allows lendees can to cover each other and lower default rates), pro-social lending practices (focus not just on absentee exploiters trying to ring every penny out of a business, but on clients and owners themselves providing real services and goods to maintain a modest income which is invested in family and community).

Once again, I list these proposals not as "the answer" per se but to forward the idea that the only "answer" is an informed dialog and exchange of ideas among the citizenry, a discourse and debate which must be undertaken long before the Savior State devolves and collapses in insolvency.

We must be ready to establish the New American State, not with a set of canned "answers" (which smacks of the usual technocrat reliance on ideology rather than practicality) but an engagement of ideas which will form the intellectual framework for a new integrated understanding of limited yet strong governance which protects the citizenry and public trust from exploitation by Elites.

It is not difficult to start with the common ground of the U.S. Constitution and the fundamental rights set down by the Declaration of Independence: life, liberty and the pursuit of happiness.

I cannot predict nor would I dare try to predict the outcome of the coming insolvency of the Savior State. But it is my hope that the citizens of the United States of America do not retreat into fatalism or wallow in complacency, but instead grasp the nettle of self-governance and liberty as laid down by the nation's Founding Fathers.

Charles Hugh Smith, citizen and taxpayer
September, 2009

Further Reading: Books mentioned in the text (and a few other relevant titles)

The Long Emergency: Surviving the End of Oil, Climate Change, and Other Converging Catastrophes of the Twenty-First Century   James Howard Kunstler

Financial Armageddon: Protecting Your Future from Four Impending Catastrophes
and
When Giants Fall: An Economic Roadmap for the End of the American Era   Michael Panzner

The Future of Life   E.O. Wilson

Beyond Oil: The View from Hubbert's Peak   Kenneth Deffeyes

Fewer: How the New Demography of Depopulation Will Shape Our Future   Ben Wattenberg

The Coming Generational Storm: What You Need to Know about America's Economic Future   Laurence Kotlikoff and Scott Burns

The Rhythm of War   Terence Parker

The Fourth Turning   William Strauss and Neil Howe

The Great Wave: Price Revolutions and the Rhythm of History
David Hackett Fischer

Collapse: How Societies Choose to Fail or Succeed   Jared Diamond

The Collapse of Complex Societies   Joseph Tainter

The Upside of Down: Catastrophe, Creativity, and the Renewal of Civilization   Thomas Homer-Dixon

How The World Really Works Alan Jones

The Rich and the Super-Rich, A Study in the Power of Money Today
Ferdinand Lundberg (out of print, but used copies are available)

Tragedy & Hope: A History of the World in Our Time Carroll Quigley

Wealth and Democracy: A Political History of the American Rich
Kevin Phillips

The Power Elite C. Wright Mills

Who Rules America? Challenges to Corporate and Class Dominance
G. William Domhoff

This Land Is Their Land: Reports from a Divided Nation
Barbara Ehrenreich

Planet of Slums Mike Davis

Weblogs & New Media: Marketing in Crisis Charles Hugh Smith

The Long Descent: A User's Guide to the End of the Industrial Age
and
The Ecotechnic Future: Envisioning a Post-Peak World
John Michael Greer

The Third Chimpanzee: The Evolution and Future of the Human Animal
Jared Diamond

Sociobiology: The New Synthesis E.O. Wilson

Who am I? The 16 Basic Desires that Motivate Our Actions and Define
Our Personalities Steven Reiss

The Fall of the Roman Empire Michael Grant

The Art Of War Sun Tzu

The Tipping Point: How Little Things Can Make a Big Difference
Malcolm Gladwell

The Decline of the West (Abridged version) Oswald Spengler

Politics of Experience R.D. Laing

Fiasco: The Inside Story of a Wall Street Trader Frank Partnoy

Confessions of a Subprime Lender: An Insider's Tale of Greed, Fraud,
and Ignorance Richard Bitner

Manufacturing Consent: The Political Economy of the Mass Media
Edward Herman and Noam Chomsky

Propaganda: The Formation of Men's Attitudes Jacques Ellul

Age of Propaganda: The Everyday Use and Abuse of Persuasion
Anthony R. Pratkanis and Elliot Aronson

Propaganda Edward Bernays

The Hydrogen Economy
And
The End of Work Jeremy Rifkin

The Dollar Crisis: Causes, Consequences, Cures Richard Duncan

The (Mis)behavior of Markets: A Fractal View of Risk, Ruin, and Reward
Benoit Mandelbrot

Reinventing Collapse: The Soviet Example and American Prospects
Dmitry Orlov

What the Dormouse Said: How the 60s Counterculture Shaped the Personal Computer John Markoff

The Political Economy of Inequality
Frank Ackerman, Neva R. Goodwin, Laurie Dougherty and Kevin Gallagher

War at Home: Covert action against U.S. activists and what we can do about it Brian Glick

Science As a Vocation, Politics As a Vocation
and
Economy and Society: An Outline of Interpretive Sociology Max Weber

Globalization and Its Discontents Joseph E. Stiglitz

The Gulag Archipelago, Part 1, Part 2, Part 3 Aleksandr Solzhenitsyn

Capitalism, Socialism, and Democracy Joseph A. Schumpeter

The Road to Serfdom F. A. Hayek

The End of Overeating: Taking Control of the Insatiable American Appetite David Kessler

Maverick: The Success Story Behind the World's Most Unusual Workplace Ricardo Semle

Distinction: A Social Critique of the Judgement of Taste
Firing Back: Against the Tyranny of the Market
Acts of Resistance: Against the Tyranny of the Market
Pierre Bourdieu

The Sovereign Individual: Mastering the Transition to the Information Age James Dale Davidson and William Rees-Mogg

Unequal Protection: The Rise of Corporate Dominance and the Theft of Human Rights Thom Hartmann

It Takes a Pillage: Behind the Bailouts, Bonuses, and Backroom Deals from Washington to Wall Street Nomi Prins

The Good Life Scott and Helen Nearing

When Technology Fails: A Manual for Self-Reliance, Sustainability, and Surviving the Long Emergency Matthew Stein

Made in the USA
Lexington, KY
25 April 2010